THE LAST LANGUAGE ON EARTH

# THE LAST LANGUAGE ON EARTH

## Linguistic Utopianism in the Philippines

OXFORD
UNIVERSITY PRESS

# OXFORD
UNIVERSITY PRESS

Library of Congress Control Number: 2021027802
ISBN 978–0–19–750992–0 (pbk.)
ISBN 978–0–19–750991–3 (hbk.)

DOI: 10.1093/oso/9780197509913.001.0001

# DISCLAIMER

This book brings together a diversity of views and interpretations. For this reason, it cannot, by itself, serve as evidence in support or opposition to applications for rights or recognition under Philippine law. I defer to the authority and expert testimony of Eskaya people and their chosen representatives in all legal matters.

It is nonetheless my sincere desire that this book serve to demonstrate the significance, longevity, and continuity of Eskayan cultural expressions. I hope, especially, that it will be of practical benefit to the Eskaya community and to all who are interested in understanding more about this important aspect of Bohol's heritage.

# CONTENTS

*Maps*                                                                      xi

*Acknowledgments*                                                          xvii

*Abbreviations*                                                             xix

*A Note on Terminology*                                                     xxi

*Prologue*                                                                 xxiii

1.  Introduction                                                             1
    What This Book Is About    2
    What Pinay Understood About Language    6
    A Language Forgotten, a Language Foretold    10


PART I:  *Locating the Eskaya*

2.  Language, Literacy, and Revolt in the Southern Philippines              15
    Pre-contact Visayan Literacy    16
    The "Problem" of Language Diversity in the Colonial and Early
        Commonwealth Periods (1593–1937)    19
    Shamanic Rebellion and Indigenous Outlaws in Bohol (1621–1829)    29
    Enter the Eskaya (1902–1937)    31

3.  Contact and Controversy                                                 38
    First Contact    39
    Media    41
    Institutional Tribehood    48
    A Formal Alliance and a Lost Report    51
    Eskaya Responses and a New Research Agenda    54

PART II: *Language, Letters, Literature*

4. How Eskayan Is Used Today                                         63
   Bohol in the Visayas   64
   Language Use in Bohol   66
   A Picture of the Field Site   72
   The Spoken and Sung Domains of Eskayan   75
   The Written Domains of Eskayan and Ideologies of Writing   83

5. The Writing System                                                87
   Writing Eskayan Sounds   89
   Numbers   98
   Script   101
   The Past and Future of Eskayan Writing   103

6. Words and Their Origins                                           107
   Eskayan Grammar   108
   The Lexicon   111
   Sources of Inspiration   114
   Pinay's Lexical Agenda   129

7. Eskaya Literature and Traditional Historiography                  134
   The Origins and Scope of Eskaya Literature   137
   Language History in Eskaya Literature: A Summary and Analysis   146
   Discussion   165


PART III: *Insurrection and Resurrection*

8. From Pinay to Mariano Datahan (and Back Again)                    175
   Datahan and the Origins of the Biabas Encampment   176
   The Return of Militant Cults, 1902–1922   189
   Accommodation with the U.S. Regime, Circa 1914–1937   197
   Datahan's Final War and Posthumous Legacy   199

9. Eskayan Revealed: A Scenario                                      211
   The Rise of English in Bohol as a Catalyst for Eskayan   212
   How Pinay's Language Was Revealed   214
   Prophecy, Prolepsis, and Time Depth in the Revelation of Eskayan
       Literature   226
   Summary   229

10. Conclusion: The First Language and the Last Word                231
    Imagining Indigeneity from Above: The View from the Helicopter   231
    The Form of Eskayan and the Identity of Pinay   234
    Imagining Indigeneity from Below: The View from the Village   238
    Regional Parallels   241
    The (Re)invention of Linguistic Tradition   245
    The Future of Eskayan   248

*References*                                                        251
*Glossary of Eskayan Terms Used in This Volume*                     269
*Index*                                                             277

# MAPS

Map 1.   Regions where Visayan is spoken as a home language
(dark gray) and as a second language (pale gray)          xii
Map 2.   The dialects of Visayan                                          xiii
Map 3.   Map of Bohol indicating places mentioned in this book          xiv
Map 4.   Borders of the Ancestral Domain Claim area                      xv
Map 5.   The Dagohoy rebellion                                          xvi
Map 6.   The origins and relative scale of migrations into Biabas
from the great-grandparent generation and earlier.        184

**MAP 1.** Regions where Visayan is spoken as a home language (dark gray) and as a second language (pale gray)

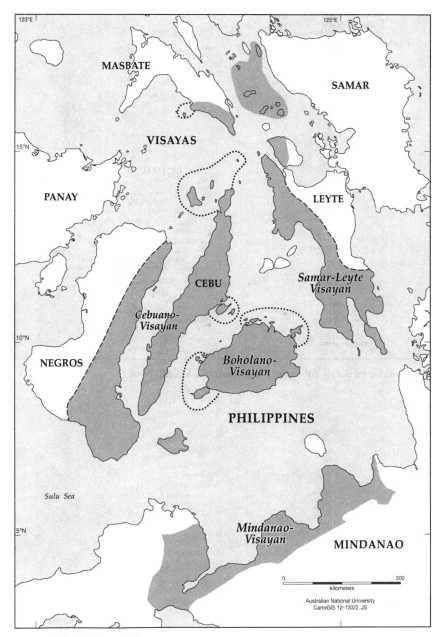

**MAP 2.** The dialects of Visayan

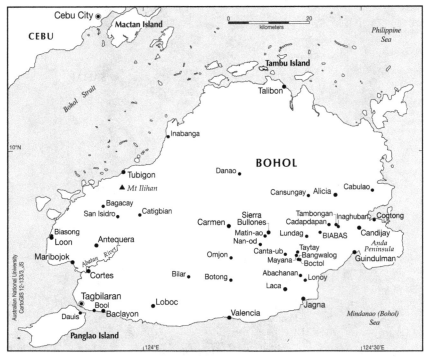

MAP 3. Map of Bohol indicating places mentioned in this book

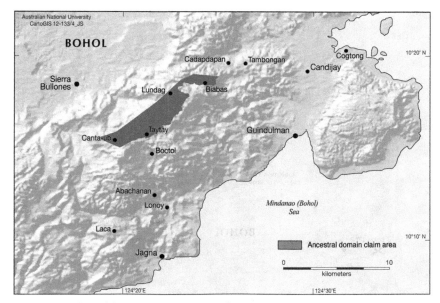

MAP 4. Borders of the Ancestral Domain Claim area

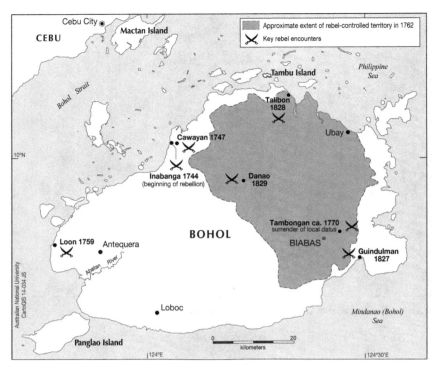

**MAP 5.** The Dagohoy rebellion

# ACKNOWLEDGMENTS

My interest in Eskayan began long before I knew anything substantial about either linguistics or the history of Bohol. From that time numerous people have enlarged my understanding of both.

I am sincerely grateful to my partner Sally Dixon for helping me make sense of endless linguistic problems, to Lawrence A. Reid whose early encouragement was crucial to my decision to pursue the question, and to the erudite Fr. Ted Torralba, who was the first to frame Eskayan as a historical as much as a linguistic conundrum and who gave me access to his field notes.

My teachers of Eskayan were numerous, but I am particularly indebted to Decena Nida Palma Salingay of Cadapdapan, who patiently collaborated in the translation and analysis of many thousands of words of literary texts that have formed the basis of my understanding of the language, and to Gaudencia Pizaña, who was the final authority on linguistic matters that arose during this work. I am thankful to Juan Datahan, late chieftain of Biabas, for generously giving his time to recall the history of his community, sketch out genealogies, and track down rare photographs and manuscripts. The late chieftain of Taytay, Fabian Baja, agreed to meet and be interviewed despite his illness at the time. I am thankful to Federated Chieftain Datu Roberto "Berting" Datahan for having faith in me and facilitating this work at every stage, and to Tribal Bishop Elpidio Palaca.

In Cadapdapan I was also assisted by Martina Buses, Panfilo Datahan, Peliculo Datahan, Macuala Licayan, Gemina Palma, Guillermo Palma, Luz Palma, Panfila Palma, Romualda Palma, and Ruel Palma. In Biabas I had extra support from Vicenta Besinga, Quinciano Buntug, Susan Carmona, Esteban Codilla, Jovino Datahan, Tolomeo Datahan, Cayo Lusica, Cleofas Pabon, Rustica Palma, Sisinia Peligro, Julieta Viscayda, and Toni Viscayda. In Taytay I was assisted by Anacleto Acerda, Pedro Bag-o, Rominador Bag-o, Rufino Bag-o, Adricula Bagotsay, Estanislao Deloso, Alberta Galambao, Hilario Galambao, Maura Galambao Jamawan, Marciana Galambao, Naning Galambao, and Lina Ipanag. (Eskaya consultants have decided not to be anonymized in this book, but note that all research enquiries are managed and assessed through the National Commission on Indigenous Peoples, Bohol.)

I owe a tremendous debt to historian Marianito Luspo, whose wit and encyclopedic intellect were a constant inspiration. Marianito identified significant historical leads I would not otherwise have followed. Other scholars including Rose Sarabosing, Jes Tirol, Jes Peralta, and Regalado Jose were sources of advice and encouragement. Alma E. Aparece worked on an early free translation of "The Itch-mite Tumaw" and occasionally assisted in the field. Raymond Datahan, Leonela Dika, Sisinio "Boy" Amplayo, and Emilou Gonzaga of the National Commission on Indigenous Peoples in Bohol kept me under their wing and put essential materials at my fingertips, as did Saidali Dika and Andy Dika. Zoë Bedford, Regina Estorba Macalandag, and Stella Consul gave me access to their important research. Fellow travelers Lyndon Patterson and Mark Little contributed their perspectives and helped contextualize the Eskaya phenomenon.

Beyond the Philippines I am thankful to Jean Mulder, who got me started; Alan Rumsey, who offered excellent advice from the beginning; and Nick Evans, who reminded me that to write a history of a language without linguistic analysis would be like writing a history of the platypus without mentioning biology. I relied on further guidance from Hannah Bulloch, Roger Casas, Tom Cliff, Noelyn Dano, Mark Donohue, J. Joseph Errington, Courtney Handman, Tom Honeyman, Paul Hutchcroft, Siva Kalyan, Sébastien Lacrampe, Alan Libert, Kate Matthews, James McElvenny, Christopher Miller, Meladel Mistica, Resil Mojares, Alexandra Roginski, Rupert Stasch, Nicholas Tapp, Ray Wood, Tony Woodbury, and Ghil'ad Zuckermann. The Eskaya glyphs reproduced in this book were developed with assistance from Lloyd Alden, Mark Eastwood, Marsiana Galambao, Michelle Gamboa, Cleobie Impang, Siva Kalyan, Mikka Lagrimas, Wap Martinez-Mercader, and Joe Elvis de los Reyes.

All translations of Spanish and Visayan sources are mine, unless otherwise indicated. With few modifications, almost all glosses and definitions of Visayan words have come from John U. Wolff's monumental dictionary of 1972. Wherever Eskayan lexemes clearly occupy the same semantic space as their Visayan counterparts, the definitions are modeled on Wolff's.

In the course of writing this book, earlier and less complete versions of my research were published elsewhere. This work is cited in the text and reused with permission. I am thankful to all those who have given feedback on this material in the intervening years. Lastly, I want to thank Alessandro Duranti for his brilliant guidance, and Meredith Keffer for maintaining a steady editorial hand through some of the darkest days of the COVID-19 pandemic.

# ABBREVIATIONS

| | |
|---|---|
| AV | actor voice |
| DEM | demonstrative |
| DENR | Department of Environment and Natural Resources |
| DMN | demonymic |
| EXCL | exclusive |
| F | feminine |
| GEN | genitive |
| INCL | inclusive |
| lit. | literal |
| LK | linker |
| LOC | locative |
| M | masculine |
| MED | medial |
| NEG | negative |
| NSPC | nonspecific marker |
| OSCC | Office for Southern Cultural Communities |
| PFV | perfective |
| PL | plural |
| POSS | possessive |
| PV | patient voice |
| Q | question particle/marker |
| RE | realis |
| *RPC* | *Report of the Philippine Commission* |
| SBJ | subject |
| SG | singular |
| Sp. | Spanish |
| SPEC | specific marker |
| syn. | synonym |
| Tag. | Tagalog |
| Vis. | Visayan |

# A NOTE ON TERMINOLOGY

## Visayan or Bisaya' or Cebuano

The term 'Visayan' is used as a generic label to denote the totality of mutually intelligible dialects of the central Visayan region (Map 2), of which Cebuano is the prestige variety. This is a conventional English counterpart to the word *Bisaya'*, which carries the same meaning. 'Boholano-Visayan' denotes the varieties spoken on Bohol, while 'East Boholano-Visayan' specifies the eastern dialect spoken in the field site. Differences among all Visayan varieties are slight, to the extent that linguists do not typically distinguish them at all and tend to use 'Cebuano' as the generic term for the language as a whole. However, speakers (particularly those outside Cebu) readily identify certain marked differences in lexicon and accent as representative of geographically circumscribed lects.

## Eskaya or Eskayan

Throughout this book I have used the terms 'Eskaya,' for the people, and 'Eskayan' for the language. An appropriate comparison would be the conventional use of 'Maya' for people, and 'Mayan' for language in Mesoamerican studies. Occasionally I employ both words as a modifiers: e.g., 'Eskayan classes' or 'Eskaya fiestas.'

These terms are not intended to be prescriptive. In reference to Eskayan, I often use the word 'language' to mean 'language and script,' as Eskaya people make no categorical distinction between the two.

## Bisaya', Bisayan Diklaradu, or Bisaya'-Eskaya

In Biabas, the original settlement of the Eskaya, the people once referred to themselves and to their language as *Bisaya'* or *Bisayan Diklaradu* ('declared Visayan'). Recently, this term has begun to fall into disuse in favor of *Eskaya* or the compromise term *Bisaya'-Eskaya*. At the time of my research, the Eskaya community of Cadapdapan, made up of migrants from Biabas and their descendants, had not accepted the labels *Eskaya* or *Bisaya'-Eskaya* and continued to refer to themselves as either *Bisayan Diklaradu* or just *Bisaya'*. In Cadapdapan, the Eskayan language was simply called *Bisaya'*, a term that most Boholanos apply exclusively to the Visayan language spoken throughout Bohol and its adjacent islands. This can be a source of confusion to outsiders, but by convention the Bisayan Diklaradu of Cadapdapan differentiate Visayan as 'Cebuano.'

## Other conventions

For clarity, all romanized Eskayan words in this book are rendered in bold, while Visayan and Spanish glosses are in italics and English glosses are in quotation marks. In Part II I adopt a convention of using 'Pinay' to specify the creator of the Eskayan language and 'Anoy' to designate the putative author of Eskayan traditional literature. Pinay is the name Eskaya people give to the ancestral originator of their language, and Anoy is the affectionate name for the Eskaya patriarch Mariano Datahan, derived from the last two syllables of his first name. Both 'Pinay' and 'Anoy' are here applied as narrative constructs to avoid imposing concrete claims of origin and authorship. Lastly, even though the primary medium of Eskayan communication is writing, I refer to those who use the language as 'speakers' who form a 'speech community.'

When the isolated Eskaya people of the Philippines first entered into the media spotlight, their sudden presence on the national stage provoked wonder and debate. As observers came up with conflicting accounts of the hitherto unidentified group, the precise details of the earliest encounters with the public were lost. This is what I heard.

In 1980 a team from the Ministry of Agriculture and Food made a visit to the province of Bohol, a large and impoverished island in the south of the archipelago. Over the previous decade the conjugal dictators Ferdinand and Imelda Marcos had presided over increasing year-on-year surpluses in rice production, and now a burgeoning population, and a restive rural poor, made continual growth a matter of urgency. The agricultural advisors had an ambitious mission: to discourage slash-and-burn swidden agriculture in the highlands, open up wild areas to cultivation, and convince local farmers of the benefits of the so-named Green Revolution. When used correctly, they explained, pesticides, fertilizers, and new high-yield rice cultivars would increase their harvests significantly.

Moving from village to village, the officials delivered lectures, handed out freebies, and inspected equipment. Ascending at last to the southeast uplands, they enjoyed views across the sea to neighboring islands, and inland to a surreal interior of enormous conical mounds known as the Chocolate Hills. The majestic view belied a violent history. It was in this part of the island that the anti-colonial rebel Francisco Dagohoy and his descendants had maintained an eighty-five-year rebellion, taking advantage of the sheer hillsides, jungle canopy, and deep limestone caves to oppose Spanish rule until their defeat in 1829. The same strategic landscape protected Filipino guerrillas opposing the Japanese military in World War II, and by the 1970s it became a favored redoubt for communist insurgents. This was a landscape of resistance.

The men from Manila eventually scaled a steep and slippery mountain track that led to one of the highest, and coldest, locations on the island. With the mountain mist now mostly beneath them, they arrived at the crown of a broad ridge and looked down into a large depression that resembled the crater of an overgrown volcano. Perched around its circumference were dozens of bamboo and cinder block dwellings that were barely visible amid the greenery but whose presence was betrayed by the smoke from cooking fires. As they descended into the village, the impression of untamed wilderness resolved itself into order and cultivation. Well-swept paths traversed neat vegetable gardens that were interspersed with patches of pink anthurium flowers. There was a granary with a galvanized iron roof, and a large bore drew water into a brick reservoir. Unaccustomed to visitors, the villagers regarded the men with cautious curiosity. But the newcomers were just as intrigued by the strange appearance of the mountain people. Their raffia shirts and blouses were cut in an archaic style, and some wore unusual headdresses: the women's were similar to the habits of Catholic nuns, while the men wore pleated cloth caps that bulged to one side like berets. More surprises were in store. When the advisors began to introduce themselves and explain the purpose of their visit they were puzzled to discover that their hosts also spoke another language that was utterly unrecognizable. Yet these were not the illiterate highland natives they had learned about in their high school primers. A well-constructed two-story building stood in the center of the village where tribal scribes, men and women alike, maintained a vast library of native literature written in a florid and indecipherable writing system. Here, apparently, were epic narratives, long predating the arrival of Spanish colonizers, carefully preserved and recopied into hand-bound and beautifully illustrated codices.

The specific circumstances of this interaction are not recorded, but this is more or less the account that reached people living in the main township of Bohol, and that was passed on to me many years later. In another version, reported by a local journalist at around the time of this encounter, it was the mountain people themselves who decided to venture out of the wilderness. Under previous regimes, he claimed, they had lived as virtual outlaws, rejecting any integration with lowland Filipinos. It was only when they heard reports of the utopian "New Society" promoted by President Marcos that they were emboldened to make formal contact.

Whatever the case, news of a "lost tribe" who called themselves the "Eskaya" spread rapidly. In the short term, contact with the lowlands precipitated a flurry of speculation, fueled by tabloid stories that exoticized the group as the living ancestors of a surviving precolonial Philippine civilization. Their language was puzzled over, resulting in conflicting hypotheses: it was an ancient indigenous tongue; it was the result of a distant migration from long ago; it was a recent innovation. Eskaya voices were either ventriloquized in support of local agendas, or they were erased from the discussion altogether.

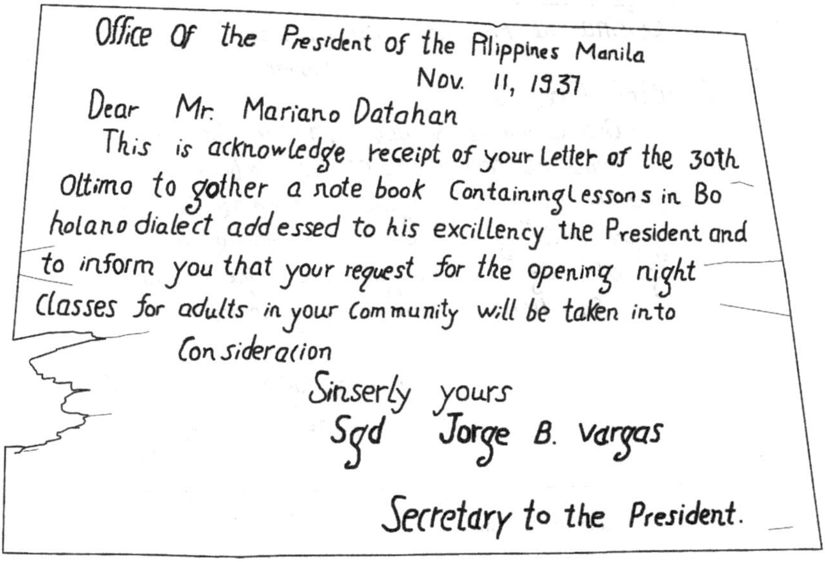

Office Of the President of the Filippines Manila
Nov. 11, 1937
Dear Mr. Mariano Datahan
This is acknowledge receipt of your Letter of the 30th Oltimo to gother a note book Containing lessons in Boholano dialect addessed to his excillency the President and to inform you that your request for the opening night Classes for adults in your community will be taken into Consideracion
Sinserly yours
Sgd Jorge B. Vargas
Secretary to the President.

**FIGURE P.1.** Carved text in English with transliteration.

Known as Taytay, the picturesque settlement that was "discovered" by the agricultural advisors was not quite as isolated or timeless as it first seemed. In fact, its inhabitants were to point out that it had existed for a mere thirty years, having been established as a satellite colony of an older village called Biabas that stood further downhill on the same ridgeline, below the mist. Later visitors noticed that the tribal lifestyle on full display in Taytay persisted in a more muted form in Biabas even if many of its inhabitants could still speak, read, and write in the Eskayan language. A small team from the National Museum of the Philippines made a whistle-stop tour to Biabas, but their recorded observations were never disseminated. Yet in both villages there was written evidence that the Eskaya people had not, in fact, cloistered themselves from the outside world but had made an effort to be recognized at the highest level of government. In the center of each settlement a series of inscribed boards gave testimony of a 1937 correspondence with the president of the Philippines. Etched on rare molave timber, the first of these large tablets (Fig. P.1) was a transcription of a formal response from Manila, acknowledging receipt of "a notebook containing lessons in Boholano dialect addressed to his Excellency the President." It remains on display to this day. By its side are a series of carved translations into both the regional Visayan language (Fig. P.2) and the mysterious "Boholano dialect," (Figs. P.3–4) a language that is now known as Eskayan (𝓅₈₈ℓ𝒜·) and that is the subject of this book.

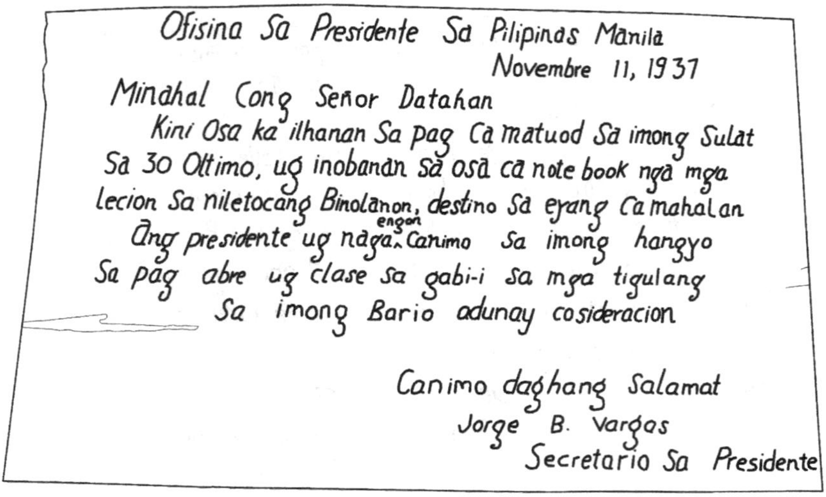

Ofisina Sa Presidente Sa Pilipinas Manila
Novembre 11, 1937
Minahal Cong Señor Datahan
    Kini Osa ka ilhanan Sa pag Ca matuod Sa imong Sulat
Sa 30 Oltimo, ug inobanan sa osa ca note book nga mga
lecion Sa niletocang Binolanon, destino Sa eyang Ca mahalan
    Ang presidente ug naga Canimo   Sa   imong   hangyo
Sa pag  abre  ug clase  sa  gabi-i  sa  mga  tigulang
            Sa  imong  Bario  adunay  cosideracion

                        Canimo  daghang  Salamat
                        Jorge   B.  Vargas
                            Secretario  Sa   Presidente

**FIGURE P.2.** Carved text in Visayan.

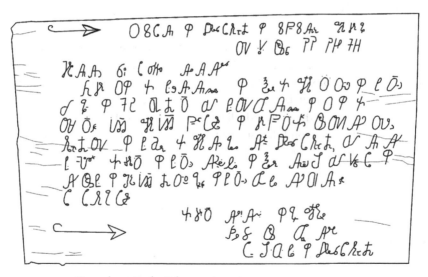

**FIGURE P.3.** Carved text in the Eskaya script.

Where might this Eskayan writing have originated? Although Spanish chroniclers described and often reproduced scripts from many parts of the Philippines,
there is nothing that points to the prior existence of an indigenous writing system
on Bohol. Curiously too, the form of the Eskayan script, with its elegant loops

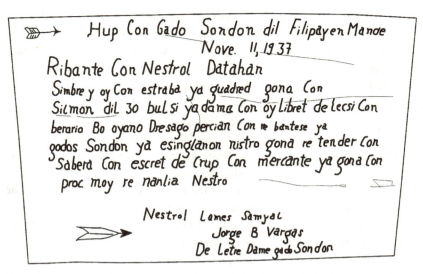

Hup Con Gado Sondon dil Filipayen Mande
Nove. 11, 1937
Ribante Con Nestrol Datahan
Simbre y oy Con estraba ya quadred gona Con
Silmon dil 30 bulsi ya dama Con oy Libret de lecsi Con
berario Bo oyano Dresago percian Con re bantese ya
godos Sondon ya esinglanon nistro gona re tender Con
Sabera Con escret de Crup Con mercante ya gona Con
proc moy re nanlia Nestro

Nestrol Lames Samyat
Jorge B Vargas
De Letre Dame gach Sondon

**FIGURE P.4.** Carved text in romanized Eskayan ('Boholano dialect').

and ornamentations, bears a closer resemblance to Roman copperplate handwriting than it does to the compact Indic scripts of island Southeast Asia.

Beyond questions of the script and its genealogy, the Eskayan *language* is deeply puzzling in its own right. Of the varieties of Visayan spoken today on Bohol, none can be said to show even the remotest relationship with "Boholano dialect" as romanized in the translation above (Fig P.4). A closer inspection raises troubling questions. There appears to be a virtual word-for-word relationship between the Visayan and Eskayan texts while many of the Eskayan lexemes are highly atypical for the region. Words like *proc* and *crup*, for example, display consonant sequences that are rare in languages of the Philippines, while others such as *con*, *nestrol*, and *berario* are strongly reminiscent of Spanish. That the English word 'office' has been translated as *hup* rather than an expected loan such as *ufisina* or *ufis* is intriguing, but the fact that the long-established place name 'Manila' is rendered as *Mande* is entirely remarkable.

\*\*\*

Eskayan is still used for limited purposes by around 550 people in Biabas and a cluster of small villages that radiate from it in southeast Bohol. For four decades, discussion of Eskayan has reeled between characterizations of the language as a hoax or crude fabrication of marginal sociological interest, to equally reductive accounts that romanticize it as a lost sacred tongue of exotic origin. While these commentaries have brought to the fore folk-linguistic assumptions about the essential nature of language, and its intrinsic power to constitute and circumscribe communities and histories, they have tended to overlook the Eskayan language itself, not to mention those who speak it, as a valid source of historical knowledge.

I was first introduced to Eskaya people in late 2005 when I began a ten-month internship at a service center of the National Commission on Indigenous Peoples (NCIP) in Bohol, sponsored by the Australian government. Two earlier studies (Bedford 2004; Orcullo 2004) had underscored the indigeneity of the Eskaya through ethnographic descriptions of distinctive cultural practices, including the intergenerational transmission of native literature, but had dealt with the Eskayan language and script in only a cursory way, a fact readily admitted by their authors. My task, therefore, would be to evaluate Eskayan as a language, and to locate its speakers within the broader ethnolinguistic context of the Philippines.

Before I accepted the position several linguists advised me to be skeptical of the outlandish claims that Eskaya people were said to be making about themselves and that due to the avowed secrecy of the community I should make contingency plans if fieldwork were to prove impossible. I was also to learn that the National Museum of the Philippines had raised serious questions about an ongoing Eskaya petition for legal recognition under the Indigenous Peoples Rights Act (IPRA) and had brought its concerns to the attention of the national government. In fact, not long after I had settled into the NCIP office in Tagbilaran, rival interest groups claimed exclusive stewardship of the project, each presenting me with contrary demands on my role as a linguistic adjudicator. This state of affairs, I would learn, was merely the backwash from a low-intensity conflict that had been seething for some time. When I consulted archived newspaper and magazine reports I learned that the controversies I was now confronting could be traced all the way back to those earliest encounters when local commentators first presented divergent accounts of the language and its speakers.

After acclimatizing at the NCIP office in Tagbilaran I began regular fieldwork in the two principle Eskaya villages of Biabas and Taytay. The Eskaya, it transpired, were neither hostile to my presence nor particularly concerned with my opinion of them. Far from the clandestine agendas and rash claims I'd been led to expect, I witnessed from Eskaya people a modesty about their culture and history, and a genuine intellectual pleasure in their language, a pleasure that I would soon experience for myself.

Wedged between competing interests in the lowlands and benign indifference in the highlands, I felt the need to emphasize my neutrality and focus as much as possible on quantifiable data. Thus, my internship resulted in two deliberately dry government reports comprising a review of existing commentaries on Eskayan and a test of prior claims about the language's origin and type through a basic lexicostatistical analysis.

This work did little to assuage my curiosity, and a few years later I had the opportunity to make more in-depth investigations, returning to southeast Bohol over the dry months of 2009 to 2011. I attended the Eskayan language schools, first as an observer and later as a student, where I was instructed by teachers in rough shirts of pineapple leaf fiber and embroidered berets. On some days, village life bewildered me with its serene strangeness. At other times I was struck by its globalized homogeneity as the one-hour morning ration of electricity brought every dormant television and karaoke machine to life at once.

Released from the constraints of government report writing, I resolved to produce a thick linguistic description of the Eskayan language and its script. Decoding the Eskaya puzzle became a real obsession, and I have no doubt that there would have been more forgiving languages on which to cut my teeth as a linguist. I was doubtful that such a complete set of social and linguistic facts could be so audaciously manufactured yet also thrilled by that same possibility. Over my several visits to the field site, which now extended further downhill into the village of Cadapdapan, I began to believe that the single most interesting aspect of the language was not so much its material and analyzable form but its extraordinary history, a history that nevertheless resounded throughout its grammar, lexicon, and literature.

I soon realized that, whatever its origins, Eskayan could hardly be dismissed as a naive fabrication. In Eskaya manuscripts meanings are doubly encrypted under layers of opaque script and rare combinations of sounds. A single syllable might have multiple symbols to represent it, while other symbols stand for sounds that are never used in the language at all. Eskayan vocabulary is riddled with false friends, or words that seem to mean one thing but stand for something else entirely. And after mapping the maze of diversions and blind trails the would-be interpreter of traditional texts is sometimes left with phrases that are fragmentary and often nonsensical even to the most competent Eskayan speakers and teachers. Adding to the mystery, the lexicon encodes glosses for archaic Visayan words whose meanings cannot be recalled by any in living memory, or that were last recorded in nineteenth-century Spanish wordlists.

In the course of my field research I was frequently asked by people in Bohol's capital if I considered the Eskayan language to be "real." Understood literally, the question can have no satisfying answer: Eskayan is self-evidently spoken and written by a community of people who live in the southeast interior of the island, even though I continue to encounter Boholanos who still doubt this. But I came to understand that, like minoritized languages elsewhere, it is not so much the existence of the language that is questioned but its *right* to exist, a right that is almost always contested in historical terms. In response, Eskaya people regularly invoked history as a means of defending and authenticating their linguistic subjecthood. It is hardly an exaggeration to say that the Eskaya are themselves self-confident local historians, producing and reproducing a lively body of hand-written historiography. Language and writing surface throughout these texts as palpable historical entities, capable of transforming reality but also subject to inexorable forces of change. In short it is history, as much as language, that has come to delineate the primary site of cultural validation and contestation.

Contrary to the three origin stories offered by outsiders—that the language is indigenous, displaced, or recently invented—Eskaya people told me that their language was the inspired creation of the heroic ancestor Pinay in the year 600 CE. Taking the human body for inspiration, Pinay fashioned a unique and distinctly Boholano tongue for his people. At first known simply as *Bisaya'*, Pinay's creation is believed to antedate the imposter language of the same name that would later come to dominate the island, all but destroying Bohol's true linguistic legacy. Pinay's authentic *Bisaya'*, sometimes differentiated as *Bisayan Declarado* (meaning 'declared' or 'stated' Visayan), was encapsulated in a script, allowing it to be carved onto tablets and stored for posterity. Thus it was that a veteran rebel soldier by the name of Mariano 'Anoy' Datahan (ca. 1875–1949) was able to retrieve Pinay's suppressed language and breathe new life into it among his followers in Biabas.

It is clear, then, that all these contemporary narratives of the origins of Eskayan are not categorically distinct but turn on competing beliefs about the nature of indigeneity, of creation versus fabrication, of what 'language' means, and of the degree of agency that a community is permitted to exert within and over its cultural heritage. Yet if Eskayan really was, as certain media pundits were later to claim, evidence of a fossilized indigenous community that had withstood the ravages of successive colonial occupations, this hypothesis deserves serious scrutiny. After all, an ancient or precolonial origin for Eskayan is still compatible with positions taken by its speakers, even if the language was, in the traditional account, artificially created by an ancestral individual. In this scenario, Eskayan might sit in the same category as Damin, an engineered Australian register once used by initiated men on Mornington Island and attributed to an ingenious ancestor. Alternatively, Pinay's supposed creativity might serve as a vivid just-so story accounting for the presence of a distinctive minority language in an area of relative linguistic homogeneity. Consider too that natural languages with well-established lineages have also been associated with creative ancestors. The Yuki language of California was said to have been devised by a wandering creator, while Shiva and his son taught Tamil language and writing to the sage Agastya.

In Abrahamic traditions, God left it up Adam, the first man, to coin words for all living things. Evidently then, origin myths that credit ancestral individuals with original linguistic knowledge cannot, by themselves, corroborate the true ancestry of a language.

This book is the result of my search for the identity of Pinay, however conceived, and of the rich linguistic legacy that he or she brought to an unmapped corner of the southern Philippines. It is a complicated account, marked by controversy and lingering uncertainty. But in an age when it has become a journalistic cliché that a language is lost every two weeks, and with it a unique understanding of the world, the birth and continued survival of Eskayan is a life-affirming event, dramatizing raw human ingenuity amid relentless linguistic decline.

# 1 INTRODUCTION

"Serious history," wrote the Philippine historian David Sturtevant, "is not a form of suspense literature" (1976, 13). In the same spirit I want to sketch the outlines of my own conclusions about the history of Eskayan, while remaining conscious that my position is simply one among many. As a foreigner to the Eskaya villages, trained to look at language in a systematic and skeptical way, I have found it very difficult to accept that the Eskayan language is "ancient," at least in the sense that paleographers and historical linguists might construe the term. Nor is it easy for me to inhabit a worldview in which words are created out of a body on the basis of divine instruction even if I accept the *experience* of this history as truthful. My own perspective on Eskayan, however, is perhaps less interesting than the relationship it has with its speakers, and the unlikely fact that it ever came to exist in the first place. By necessity, then, the writing of this book has been an act of translation on more than one level. Just as I have tried to translate Eskayan texts as faithfully as possible, I have also done my best to convey a sense of the contexts that make these textual artifacts meaningful to their owners without disguising my own location on the map, so to speak.

In this volume I dodge the banal question "Is Eskayan real?" by recasting it in more productive terms: "What story does the language tell us?" and "What does this story mean?" I argue from several lines of evidence that the present form of the language and script is the result of intentional creative effort that took place within a single generation. A product of systematic engineering, the new language was a radical and deliberate departure from Boholano-Visayan, the principal language spoken on the island of Bohol.

If this scenario is accurate, it would indicate that the Eskayan phenomenon is exceptional: only a handful of cases of simultaneous language-script creation are known elsewhere in the world. The earliest to have survived in the documentary record is Lingua Ignota, developed as a mystical tongue by the Benedictine Abbess Hildegard

*The Last Language on Earth*. Kelly, Piers, Oxford University Press. © Oxford University Press 2022.
DOI: 10.1093/oso/9780197509913.003.0001

of Bingen in circa 1200 in what is now Germany. A partial relexification of Latin, Hildegard's language was written with a constructed alphabet of twenty-three letters that she termed *litterae ignotae*. Little is known about the role of Lingua Ignota, or whether it even had a community of practitioners, but its use did not continue beyond the death of its inventor. More successful was the creation of Ibrahim Mbouombouo Njoya, a nonliterate sultan who ruled over the kingdom of Bamum in Cameroon from the late nineteenth century. With help from his court Njoya invented a special language represented in an elaborate script that proceeded through six revisions, each version becoming simpler and more systematic. Not long after Njoya's death in 1933, another language-script was to be invented in the village of Ikpa, Nigeria, not far from Njoya's kingdom. Known as Medefaidrin, its originators were two prophets of a new syncretic faith who had received the system in a series of visions. Medefaidrin was to be used in the production of several canonical books of prayers, prophecies, and catechisms (Hau 1961).

Just like Lingua Ignota these two engineered language-scripts of West Africa were unable to sustain their early momentum and are barely known outside of their places of origin. Today, most popular discussions of utopian or artificial languages will center instead on higher-profile inventions such as Esperanto and Volapük with their ambitions for universality. More recently, blockbuster productions like *Star Trek*, *Avatar*, and *Game of Thrones* have introduced the public to the exuberant world of intentionally constructed languages in the form of Klingon, Na'vi, and Dothraki among many others. Yet all these constructed languages, or 'conlangs,' were developed from the outset as bounded intellectual products within highly literate industrialized societies. Unlike Eskayan, they have never been regarded by their fans or creators as being especially indigenous to anywhere, nor have they become integrated into the everyday routines of community life and transmitted from teacher to student over successive generations. As this book will show, Eskayan is something more than an intellectual exercise, an artistic product, or a utilitarian project. I will argue that the language was the result of a coordinated effort to reimagine a community's place in the world by resetting the very foundations of linguistic representation.

## What this book is about

This book is about the history of an unusual language and of the patterned ideas that its creators brought to the task of building it. As a consequence of these dual themes, it pivots between historical narrative, linguistic description, and theoretical reflection. Just as I began my own journey with no expertise on the history and languages of the Philippines, I do not assume any such prior knowledge on the part of the reader. Instead, the book follows a somewhat unconventional structure that replicates the same faltering process of discovery that I experienced in the course of researching it. Above all, I have aimed to give primacy to the language itself as an authorative source of knowledge about its own past. Traditional oral and literary narratives concerning the origin of Eskayan are also taken seriously and not merely as post hoc corroborations for what is already "known." For this reason, it is only in the final chapters that I begin to introduce more detailed contextualizing information about the Eskaya community derived from non-Eskaya sources, information that may be considered rather more "primary" for readers whose main concern is with twentieth-century Visayan history. However, I will consider that the book has been successful if I have managed to give central prominence to the Eskayan language, producing a work that is recognizable and meaningful to its speakers while remaining open to criticism from them, as well as from other specialists.

Part I presents a wide-angled view that takes in the broader historical and linguistic terrain. I describe how Spanish and American colonial regimes in the Philippines adopted a paint-by-numbers approach to documenting cultural and linguistic difference, and that their projections glossed over the composite social realities of highland communities. The fact that linguistic minorities were most often cast in the role of heathens or outlaws contributed to an environment in which both rural unrest and linguistic diversity were misrecognized. The influential work of James C. Scott (1985, 2009) on the political dynamics of upland and non-state societies is of special relevance to my attempts to make sense of the turbulence that has smoldered for centuries in the highlands of Bohol, where authorities tried, and ultimately failed, to come to terms with recurring rebellions. Here I take stock of the long line of folk heroes, guerrillas, and charismatic shamans who animated the landscape, right up until 1980 when the Eskaya people made their dramatic entry onto the national stage.

The ensuing representations of Bohol's "lost tribe" in local media would generate a parallel discourse with its own independent mythos, but one that for better or worse continues to be entangled with the Eskaya narrative today. Speculative local newspaper commentaries that romanticized the Eskaya in mystical terms fed directly into government reports that went on to racialize and even stigmatize them. It may appear curious that the Eskaya community so readily acceded to rigid administrative definitions of "tribehood" that neither coincided with their experience nor seemed to serve their interests. However, the history of the Biabas settlement, as glimpsed through sparse records, oral histories, and genealogies, tells the story of a resilient community adept at strategic imitation. Just like the American administrators who began to dominate the lowlands following their conquest of the islands in the early twentieth century, the residents of Biabas originated a counter-regime on very similar terms. My reconstruction will show how a large group of people fled a ravaged fishing village on Bohol's west coast and made their way uphill to colonize a remote corner of Bohol's southeast highlands. Here they cleared space for a new town grid, where they mirrored the policies of their lowland antagonists by codifying an original set of laws, introducing a new flag, constructing their own schools, and developing textbooks for teaching a prestige language that was then foreign to its students. This language, Eskayan, was soon used in precisely the same domains that English had lately come to occupy elsewhere on the island, namely, for schooling, prayer, songs, official texts, and formal speech-making.

In Part II, I begin to make sense of the history of the language and script from the inside out. Peering over the shoulder of Pinay I describe and evaluate the formal features of Eskayan in terms of its writing system, phonology, morphosyntax, and vocabulary, before approaching the rich literature written in this system. I show that the primary Eskayan alphabet presents as a direct cypher for the Roman alphabet, while its spoken form incorporates markedly local sounds that are subsequently built into syllable structures more typical of Spanish and English. The same cypher-like substitution operates at the level of sentence structure that is shown to replicate the patterns of Boholano-Visayan, as if Eskayan vocabulary had been slotted into a ready-made matrix. Even so, the new words devised by the ancestral creator were by no means arbitrary formulations. I will show that Eskayan verb forms show "naturalistic" patterns of irregularity that are drawn from Spanish and English models, and just like better-known Philippine languages, the lexicon has distinguishable sets of "native" versus "loaned" vocabulary. Colonial languages have nonetheless influenced Eskayan in unexpected and paradoxical ways. For example, contrary to expectation Pinay refused to default to Spanish or English sources for lexifying the novel technologies that had been introduced by colonial occupiers. At the same time, he exploited foreign loanwords for concepts that were much closer to home including features of the natural environment and body parts.

From its script and phonology through to its syntax and lexicon, Pinay's language was contrived through a dynamic of replication and occasional overdetermination. As I show, this process reached an apex in the Eskaya manuscript tradition and its oral intertexts. Here, Pinay's policy of substitution was projected outward and upward into a detailed canon of foundation myths, religious precepts, and utopian visions of past and future social arrangements. In these narratives, the parallel society established in Biabas is shown to be the thwarted successor to a former Boholano civilization that had once enjoyed all the same spiritual, technological, and administrative accoutrements latterly *re*introduced by foreign occupiers. In this impressive literature we learn that Pinay's precolonial linguistic creation was inspired by the human form, but that due to centuries of Spanish suppression a second resurrection was needed through the medium of his modern spokesman, Mariano Datahan, a prophet who restored and reconstituted the original linguistic body.

Primed by key insights from the Eskayan language and its literature, in Part III I reexamine Eskayan from the outside looking in by turning to more conventional historical archives, including government reports and village genealogies. Though the archival evidence is thin, these sources reveal that Datahan was a veteran soldier of Bohol's short-lived republican government, defeated by the U.S. army in 1901. Having subsequently become a staunch pioneer of the breakaway Iglesia Filipina Independiente (Philippine Independent Church; PIC), Datahan's hybrid spirituality exceeded the bold new catechism, drawing liberally on aspects of local Boholano folklore and from the millenarianist movements that were menacing U.S. authorities throughout the Visayas. Datahan was soon to make peace with the new regime, and even benefit from its rule. In World War II he allied himself with the U.S. army against the Japanese, and by the time of his death in 1949 he was a prosperous landowner in the southeast highlands with numerous wives and countless children and grandchildren.

Eskaya people have long maintained that Datahan accessed their lost language, by accident or inspiration, through the intercession of the ancestral creator Pinay. However this may have transpired, my analysis proposes that the recuperation occurred in stages, and that it likely took place in the decades of relative stability and nationalist optimism prior to the Japanese invasion and occupation. Earliest to be revealed were the first letters of the Eskaya writing system, followed by texts that Datahan dictated for transcription in Visayan to a group of trusted scribes. Within these works a small number of Eskayan words began to be revealed, piecemeal, but their idiosyncratic forms encouraged the further development of the writing system. In time, Pinay revealed entire wordlists to Datahan, and this permitted the full back-translation of Datahan's Visayan tales into Eskayan. The process was collaborative but not systematic, and the resulting language was replete with redundancies in both the lexicon and the ever-expanding syllabic script. Along with Eskayan's irregular verb forms, this complexity and non-systematicity is evaluated in different ways by Eskaya people today. For example, some Eskaya people do not even notice, let alone acknowledge, the existence of redundancy in the syllable signs (Chapter 5). Others attribute linguistic irregularity to inefficiencies in the early transcription method (Chapter 7), or to distortions that have arisen through the natural passage of time (Chapter 6).

## What Pinay understood about language

What was it that first drove a lowland refugee community to plant new linguistic roots in old soil, and what do such events tell us about our human relationship to language? In other words, what does this story *mean*? I make the case that the resurrection of Eskayan was part of an intellectual and spiritual reaction to waves of conflict and crisis in the early twentieth century, with powerful antecedents in prior utopian uprisings on Bohol. Spearheaded by Mariano Datahan, the Eskayan project was born of a contest between humanized native words and the impersonal mechanics of the colonial printing press. A consistent political agenda emerges in the stories Datahan dictated to his scribes. Appealing to a glorious Philippine past he elaborated an ideology that fused indigenous tradition with hyper-nationalist ambitions. Colonial occupiers, whether Spanish, American, or Japanese, had no place in his defiant republic. His teachings and historical ruminations embraced an epistemology of the miraculous, as did his numerous prophecies of future calamities and utopian social orders.

I argue that Datahan's project was radical in both senses of the term. It was politically revolutionary, and it was enacted at the presumptive *roots* of social formations. His enduring goal was to affirm a pristine and foundational indigenous identity with which to counter the territorial, cultural, and religious claims of foreign empires. He did this by mobilizing an idea about language that has long been globally hegemonic despite its origins in European intellectual traditions: the notion that a people is defined by a common tongue, which in turn confers natural political rights to independent nationhood. Yet his project began, not with language, but writing (Chapter 5). The native script that he recuperated was used for representing the traditional stories that he first dictated, in Visayan, to an elite cohort of literate assistants. In time, the script would pave the way for the revelation of "forgotten" Eskayan words when Datahan and his scribes set about compiling new wordlists by first identifying lexemes in Visayan and Spanish and then discovering their indigenous Eskayan equivalents (Chapter 6). From this lexical grid the written Visayan literature could now be reproduced in Pinay's primordial tongue (Chapter 7). Together, the restored Eskayan script, its language, and its literature became the authenticating basis for a radical counter-state that—like a mirror—replicated yet inverted the attitudes of cultural and linguistic supremacy projected by Bohol's colonial aggressors.

I maintain that Pinay's creative enterprise is a powerful illustration of the ways in which language is manipulated to perform all kinds of extracurricular work. In so doing I continue an important tradition within linguistic anthropology of examining what are conventionally termed "language ideologies," or the "self-evident ideas and objectives a group holds concerning roles of language in the social experiences of members as they contribute to the expression of the group" (Heath 1977, 53). Meaningful description, in this light, involves attention to the ideas that people hold about language, its relationship to society, and all of its moral and political loadings (Irvine 1989, 255). The work of Brian Street (1984, 1993) and others has shown that *literacy* practices, as much as language, are saturated with comparable ideologies and thus cannot be analyzed independently of the contexts in which they are embedded and reproduced (for a review see Bartlett et al. 2016). The goal of analyzing language-and-literacy ideologies in this frame is to make the underlying values visible without, however, presupposing the existence of a non-ideological position from which neutral evaluations are made (Gal 1998, 319–320; Irvine and Gal 2000, 36).

I suggest that Datahan's politico-linguistic maneuver was propelled by four interrelated language-and-literacy ideologies that I will return to throughout this book: the notion that writing precedes and is superordinate to speech; that authentic language is both biologically grounded and a product of the human intellect; that language confers natural political rights; and finally, that language is a discretely bounded, ownable, and contestable object. These four ideas were unified in a strategy of anticolonial resistance that was effective, I argue, not because it challenged the prevailing colonial discourses about language and dominance but precisely because it met them on common ideological ground.

Pinay, as Datahan's folkloric originator of the Eskayan language, enacted language and literacy myths that were attractive to the residents of Biabas, even if their tenets were contradictory in revealing ways. At its root Pinay's creative agenda challenged the doctrine of "sociolinguistic naturalism," namely, the assumption that a given linguistic form is "rightfully authoritative because it is the natural, unmediated expression of a state of social life in the world, rather than the outcome of human will, effort, intervention, and artifice" (Woolard 2016, 30). Authentic cultural identities, its proponents imagine, grow from organic linguistic roots that can never be contrived, falsified, or misidentified.

By contrast, true authenticity for Pinay was a synthesis of this opposition. In Eskayan origin myths (Chapter 7), artificial acts of creative agency are represented as natural, even biological, channels of divine will, exemplified in the inspired derivation of letter shapes from the form of the human body, and recalling the linguist August Schleicher's famous assertion that "languages are organisms of nature" (Schleicher 1869, 20–21). Those who wish to gain proficiency in Eskayan must submit to an effortful intervention in the form of direct schooling and private study. That the language thereby lacks any "native" speakers is by no means a threat to the identity claims of Eskaya people today for whom active engagement in the language-learning process is a marker of cultural commitment.

Pinay's bold reclamation of artifice and human intervention nonetheless left intact two ideological accessories to sociolinguistic naturalism, already mentioned: the view that writing is the most genuine embodiment of language, and that languages are isomorphic with cultural or political identities. As I will show, speakers of Eskayan regard their script to be inseparable from speech, a position emphasized in the anthropomorphism of Eskaya letter shapes. In local tradition, written Eskayan words must never be crossed out, as if to do so would not only be an act of physical violence against a body but a negation of naturalized truth. On this reading, Eskayan literacy ideology might be viewed as an unusually literal exemplar of what Irvine and Gal refer to as "iconization", or the impression that linguistic forms depict or display their speaking subjects (Irvine and Gal 2000, 37–38). Reinforcing such iconization, key texts within the Eskaya literary corpus promote the conservative notion that languages are constitutive of discrete cultures and of territorially bounded societies.

As if to substantiate this ideology Pinay ensured that Eskayan competed on the same footing as colonial languages by rendering it visible in a unique writing system and by enregistering it in authoritative and standardizing texts. Objectified in this way, his language was shown to be as much a tangible artifact as the paper and ink that captured it. And yet, contrary to the naturalist model, this very property of materiality did not render the Eskayan language inert or sterile. Rather, the forms of Eskayan letters indexed their dynamic origins in an animate body, a body that was capable of acting on the world with its own agency. Of special interest to the present study is the ways in which the animacy of Eskayan would allow it to reshape the social and political regimes that language was presumed to order.

In the course of writing this book I became struck by the ways that Datahan's fugitive community recapitulated, in miniature, James C. Scott's conception of Zomian landscapes. Having noticed curious cultural consistencies between otherwise isolated highland communities across mainland Southeast Asia, a non-contiguous area projected as 'Zomia,' Scott suggested that their forms of social organization, political dynamics, and even their subsistence systems were merely convergent strategies of state evasion (Scott 2009). Resistance to state enclosure, Scott argued, also accounted for why highlanders were so attracted to millenarian religions since they produced temporary state-like formations that inoculated their communities against domination from without, while preventing power concentrations from within. Even more contentiously, he hypothesized that the ancestors of today's Zomians had once been members of lowland populations that fled uphill to escape wars, epidemics, taxation, or conscription, and that they might even have gone so far as to abandon their prior literacy to better resist becoming fixed in an official written narrative.

While Scott's model does not account for the deep timescales of linguistic diversity in Southeast Asia's upland regions, it does elucidate the dynamics of lowland–highland interactions in more recent eras. In particular, it sheds light on the mercurial ways that isolated upland communities are seen to elude government domination while at the same time appropriating and reinventing symbols of lowland state power. Contrary to the stronger versions of Scott's model in which Zomians are seen to reject literacy outright, the historical record shows no less than *nine* unique new scripts and associated textual traditions that have been invented wholesale by notionally "nonliterate" societies of mainland Southeast Asia in the period of European colonial occupation and its aftermath (Kelly 2018a). In the Philippines too, groups other than the Eskaya have gone so far as to invent scripts and linguistic registers in a range of contexts; these are summarized in Chapter 10.

In this book I develop and problematize Scott's Zomian model by building on recent extensions to Gregory Bateson's notion of "symmetrical schismogenesis" (Bateson 1936), whereby a given imported category—such as nationhood, writing, or a scriptural religion—is countered with an equivalent, yet superior, indigenous one. This concept has been refined by Anna Tsing via her proposed dialectic of "accommodation and resistance" (Tsing 1993) and repopularized by Marshall Sahlins in his historical ethnography of the Tikopians (Sahlins 2012). I reformulate Bateson's model in terms more familiar to postcolonial theory, drawing on Rahul Rao's observed tension between "mimicry and rejection" in anti- and postcolonial movements (Rao 2010). For Rao, mimesis does not entail a deferential replication of state power but a strategic elaboration and replacement of it. Throughout this book I will show that mimicry-and-rejection is very much a productive process across all Eskaya cultural forms, from the foundational phonology of the Eskayan language, to the miraculous history and cosmology envisioned in Eskaya literature.

Rao's dynamic is an uncomfortable one for those who might otherwise be inclined to view the Eskaya phenomenon in terms of a radical rupture with the state, or even as an inspirational precedent for contemporary decolonizing efforts. Pinay's creativity was constrained, after all, by the linguistic and ideological models that were most accessible to him. To generate the Eskayan lexicon he resorted to the calquing of Spanish and Visayan words: that is, he copied their meaning space in a very literal way. This act foreshadowed the wholesale calquing of cultural categories in Eskaya literature. It is hard to avoid characterizing such grid-like replication as an expression of the "colonial mentality," a vernacular term that Filipinos today use to denote their personal experiences of internalized oppression and to account for behaviors that are presumed to be motivated by a subservience to colonial cultural models (David 2014). There is no doubt that Datahan accepted the terms of the colonial predicament and even managed to benefit from it, but he did so while keeping the lowlanders at arm's length. That Eskayan speakers today recognize and even rejoice in the pervasive Spanish influence on their language might be read as evidence of a certain cultural self-confidence as opposed to double consciousness. Much of Eskaya literature, I will show, is centered on conflict with the Spanish, but whether the native actors triumph or are soundly defeated in these narratives, their actions are seen to confer an equal amount of glory. Spain, in other words, has added weight to Bohol's past without obliterating it.

Languages, like nations and histories, are themselves imaginative projects, ever subject to strategic interventions and revisions. In their creation of Eskayan, Datahan and his ancestral muse announced a linguistic Year Zero, forging a utopian language from new and salvaged parts. Eskayan did not, however, remain captive to its sources of inspiration, nor did it arrive fully formed and frozen. Even today, Eskaya people continue to cultivate and expand their language, a process that will continue so long as it is still spoken, written, and transmitted.

## A language forgotten, a language foretold

Stories abound in Bohol of powerful treasures, deliberately concealed to prevent plunder by colonial oppressors, but which are now lost. I have earlier argued that these narratives offer a means to reassert a sense of agency in the face of the devastating cultural losses brought about by colonialism (Kelly 2016a). Understood in this way, a cultural possession is never wholly destroyed but merely suspended, awaiting some future reconstitution. Such stories are almost always accompanied by a prophecy that the lost object will be salvaged by a future champion. Mariano Datahan, in his retrieval of Eskayan, was the incarnation of just such a hero.

Adventurers from Tagbilaran who "discovered" Eskayan in the 1980s would cast themselves as pivotal actors in similar recuperation narratives. In fact, in 1985 Eskayan writing was once again discovered inside a cave by a local amateur historian (Chapter 3), just as Mariano Datahan was said to have done so in the early twentieth century. No doubt, more discoveries and rediscoveries lie in wait. From its humble reawakening Eskayan has not yet fulfilled the grand destiny that has been predicted for it. One ambitious prophecy holds that Eskayan will flatten our polyglot world in order to take its place as the last language on earth, spoken by people of all nations. In spite of such lofty visions, Eskaya people are content to carry their prophecies lightly, revising them, replacing them, or disagreeing with each other about their meaning and import. In the same gentle spirit this book represents one more narrative jostling for attention and one more attempt to recuperate knowledge that has remained buried in memories, manuscripts, words, and letters.

# LOCATING THE ESKAYA

*. . . and the drama of it all, yes, there*
*the characters of a lost alphabet abound:*
*from the ages leap the dialogues*
*of history, only we can't dare speak these ourselves,*
*for we too are lost—*
*artfully we try just an alphabetic remembering,*
*then wonder if our tongue is genuine or fake*
*since the language of the Eskaya is real, real*

—CLOVIS L. NAZARENO,
*from "Transcribing the Lost Language of the Eskaya" (1999)*

# 2 LANGUAGE, LITERACY, AND REVOLT IN THE SOUTHERN PHILIPPINES

Before I was permitted to meet with members of the Eskaya community for the first time, my colleagues at the National Commission on Indigenous Peoples took me to see the elderly mayor of a small town in the vicinity of Biabas. The mayor told me solemnly that, unlike himself, the Eskaya could lay claim to being *true* Filipinos. Just about everyone else on the island, and in the Philippines at large, was the descendant of migrants who had arrived from Borneo, Sumatra, and China and had pushed the original inhabitants into the highlands. It was a story that I would hear again in various forms from Eskaya and non-Eskaya alike. With its echoes of the Zomian hypothesis, the theory is invoked to account for the cultural diversity found in the country's less-accessible upland regions as well as a perception that highland minorities are less civilized or less technologically sophisticated than the second wave of occupants that continue to enjoy political dominance. It also explains how many lowland Filipinos today have come to regard themselves, to a greater or lesser extent, as colonists of the islands with an obligation to either protect or to assimilate the "indigenous" minority populations they sometimes regard as more vulnerable, more dangerous, but also more authentic than themselves. This retrospective de-indigenization of lowland Filipinos, I will argue, offered a way for them to rationalize, if not justify, the subsequent waves of occupation on the part of Spain, the United States, and Japan. Further, it set the stage for the emergence of an indigenous/non-indigenous binary that has now become well naturalized in local development discourses.

The terms by which speakers of Eskayan were represented as indigenous will be discussed in Chapter 3. In the present chapter I will examine how distinctive Filipino communities first came to be circumscribed, in colonial discourses, on the basis of the languages they spoke, the religious beliefs they espoused, or the places they came to occupy within political hierarchies. I explore the ways in which colonial administrations deployed language-and-literacy ideologies that

*The Last Language on Earth*. Kelly, Piers, Oxford University Press. © Oxford University Press 2022.
DOI: 10.1093/oso/9780197509913.003.0002

overlapped with concerns about religious orthodoxy and submission to low-land authorities. As I will show, the formalization of ethnolinguistic categories as a technique of governance resulted in the reification of certain cultural identities and the subordination or outright erasure of others. This goes some way to explaining how a language as unusual as Eskayan might have languished in obscurity for so long, and how its "reality" continued to be questioned even after its speakers entered into the public eye. By briefly summarizing the history of anti-state rebellions in the Visayas, I contextualize the re-emergence of southeast Bohol as a site of sustained opposition to colonial rule of which the Eskayan language was to remain an enduring manifestation.

## Pre-contact Visayan literacy

The scarcity of documentary materials on Eskayan may be considered revealing in and of itself, but this absence is by no means conspicuous. To appreciate just how easily Eskayan escaped the notice of the outside world it is worth reviewing the historical status of minority languages in the Philippines and the terms by which they have been acknowledged and documented. The celebrated Filipino linguist Ernesto Constantino remarked as late as 1971 that the quantification of Philippine languages was "incomplete" and "largely done by guesswork" (1971, 114) and that "the history of Philippine linguistics is largely the history of the study of the major Philippine languages, especially Tag [Tagalog]" (118). A cursory glance at Philippine colonial history shows that defense, evangelism, trade, and nationalist objectives have to a large extent dictated linguistic research, resulting in a patchwork documentary picture wherein languages from strategically more important regions are far better represented in the public record.

This kind of documentary erasure is clearly in evidence in the Visayan archipelago, to which Bohol belongs (Map 2), even if the region represents an important historical site of early linguistic description. It was here that the Portuguese navigator Ferdinand Magellan mistakenly landed after a grueling voyage across the Pacific, arriving in the trading center of Cebu, on the April 7, 1521 (Map 3). Magellan's ill-fated sojourn, ending with his death at the hands of Lapu-Lapu of Mactan, lasted a mere three weeks, but it was in this brief period that his Venetian crewman Antonio Pigafetta recorded a list of 166 words, making Cebuano-Visayan the very first Austronesian language ever to be documented by Europeans (Pigafetta [1525] 1903).[1]

Whether Cebuano-Visayan had its own written form at the time of Magellan's visit is doubtful to say the least, but few twentieth-century Filipino historians could resist citing the Jesuit chronicler Pedro Chirino, who in 1604 observed,

"So given are all these islanders to writing and reading that there is barely a man and much less a woman who does not read and write" ([1604] 1969). This is a remarkable claim indeed, especially in consideration of the fact that an equivalent statement could hardly have been made of the citizens of Spain at the time it was written. Certainly, the Tagalog script was in such wide use in Manila that in 1593 the church authorities invested considerable resources in the production of a bilingual catechism in Spanish and Tagalog, using the local writing system.[2] But if Visayans were also employing a writing system in the period of initial European contact, the earliest surviving documentation of Visayan languages would surely be embodied in the extant native literature, however fragmentary, and not in Pigafetta's brief wordlist. That paleographers have not uncovered any examples of pre-Hispanic Visayan writing might be attributable to the fact that Filipinos did not write on durable materials. The few examples of Visayan syllabaries that have been handed down to us, as recorded, for example, in the Cuadro Paleografico (Fig. 2.1), do not represent instances of actual use but are instead transcriptions and re-transcriptions made by Spanish scribes for the purposes of reference or comparison.

It is clear, at least from these texts, that the Visayan script is a close relative of the other known Philippine scripts, of which Mangyan is the only variety

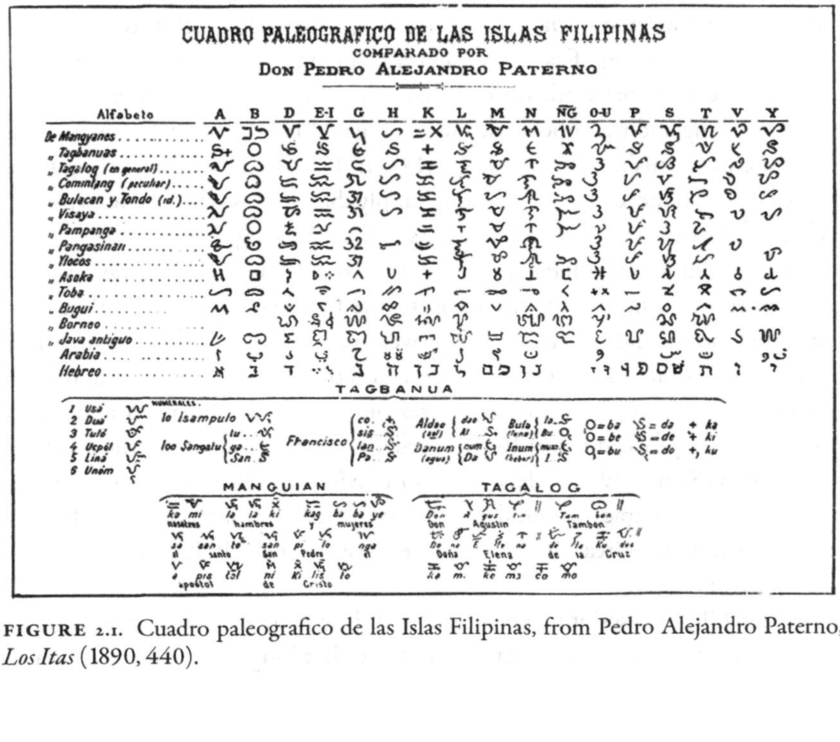

CUADRO PALEOGRAFICO DE LAS ISLAS FILIPINAS
COMPARADO POR
DON PEDRO ALEJANDRO PATERNO

FIGURE 2.1. Cuadro paleografico de las Islas Filipinas, from Pedro Alejandro Paterno, *Los Itas* (1890, 440).

still in active traditional use. The outward differences between Philippine writing systems—now collectively known as the Philippine Script—are largely the result of a regional "typographic" variation rather than a matter of any genuine systemic difference (see de Tavera 1884, 12). Indeed, Ignacio Villamor went so far as to assert that the reification of script varieties in the Spanish era resulted from a misinterpretation of individual handwriting styles as characteristic of distinct linguistic areas (Villamor 1922, 5). Despite this, writers seized on superficial differences in order to project an impression of "multiple cultural complexes in the Philippines" (Francisco 1973, 21), an attitude still in evidence to this day in nativist script revival movements.

Prior to the late nineteenth century script enthusiasts occasionally speculated that scripts and languages of the Philippines had a Semitic origin, which may explain why Hebrew and Arabic scripts are included in Paterno's comparison (Fig. 2.1). Scholars have long recognized the Philippine scripts as members of the Brahmic (or Indic) family of writing systems, although consensus on a precise lineage has not been reached.[3] Like other Brahmic systems, the Philippine script is an alphasyllabary, meaning that each letter is realized as a syllable with a consonant-vowel (CV) shape; the quality of the inherent vowel alters depending on its context in a word or with the use of diacritics.

The apparent absence of paleographic texts in Visayan languages does not prove an associated lack of literacy in the region, but it does elevate the first-hand accounts written in the early phase of Spanish colonization to a position of greater scrutiny. Significantly, Pigafetta made no mention of a native script. In fact, he reports that while on Limasawa, "I wrote down the names of things. When the king and the others saw me writing and I told them their own words they were all astonished" ([1525] 1903, 118).[4] In 1582 the conquistador Miguel de Loarca was even more explicit, asserting simply that the Visayans had no writing,[5] a claim that would be reiterated by others in the following century.

More recently, William Henry Scott argued that Visayan writing was a *post*hispanic phenomenon, drawing attention to the fact that in 1565 the Boholano chieftain Katuna and others on Bohol were unable to write their own names for the royal notary of Miguel de Legazpi, and that the only extant examples of Visayan "penmanship" are the signatures on Bernadino Dimabasa and Maria Mutia's divorce proceedings of 1647, recorded on Bantayan island at the northern tip of Cebu (Scott 1992). Indeed, the most vivid "documentary" record of pre-contact Visayan literacy is found in the so-named Pavón manuscripts, a literary hoax perpetrated in circa 1912 but taken seriously by many Philippinists until the 1960s (Pavón 1957).

If the Philippine script had managed to diffuse more successfully throughout the Visayas *after* colonial contact, it was not to last long. By the late eighteenth century indigenous literacy was virtually unheard of anywhere in the Philippines, at least to Spanish authorities (Totanes 1745).[6] Many Filipinos today offer a folkloric explanation for the worrying absence of prehispanic textual artifacts. In a widely circulated story, the pre-contact Filipinos were in possession of a rich store of documents representing an ancient record of indigenous cultural knowledge. The loss of these hypothetical texts is blamed on early Spanish clergymen, who burned them in a conscious act of cultural genocide (Pajo 1954; Zaide 1959; Tirol 1975; Ileto 1979b; Aguilar 1994; Ongsotto and Ongsotto 2002). Given the policies of Bishop Diego Landa de Calderon, who was notorious for having ordered the destruction of Maya codices in Mexico in the early sixteenth century, the suppression of native literature is certainly plausible. In the Philippines, however, no evidence favors the view that such conflagrations ever took place.[7]

## The "problem" of language diversity in the colonial and early Commonwealth periods (1593–1937)

Whatever may be supposed about the nature or extent of prehispanic language records in the Philippines, it is clear that linguistic documentation in the form of reference materials about local languages took place only after the Spanish established a sustained presence in the islands in the sixteenth century. The first books to be published were the *Doctrina Christiana en lengua española y tagala* (1593) and the *Doctrina Christiana en letra y lengua china* (ca. 1593), making use of the Philippine and Chinese scripts, respectively. In 1604, after at least two more ecclesiastic texts had been successfully printed in Tagalog, Chirino made the succinct observation that "there is no single language that is spoken throughout the islands" (Chirino [1604] 1969). This was a serious understatement that reflected a generally poor understanding of the true extent of language diversity in the Philippines in the period of early contact. The absence of an obvious overarching lingua franca or dominant ethnicity in the Philippines meant that Spanish clergy had to be strategic in their acquisition of local languages. At the time of conquest, Cebu and Manila were both relatively prosperous hubs of local inter-island traffic, attracting trading vessels from Maluku, Siam, China, and Japan. The respective languages of these two trading centers—Visayan and Tagalog—were quickly elevated to positions of local prestige and set in opposition to those spoken by the unevangelized populations living beyond the reach of the missions. The formulation of a language hierarchy on the part of the colonizers was not only a political expediency but was also consistent with Christian interpretations of linguistic diversity. Spanish explorations of the New World had already presented a challenge to the biblical paradigm of human population dispersals; if the *indios* of the Americas and the Philippines were truly the descendants of Eve, their existence had to be accounted for using evidence from scripture. Thus, the biblical twelve sons of Jacob provided a ready explanation for ethnic differences, and the observation that the *indios* spoke a cacophony of different languages was likewise explicable with reference to the Tower of Babel. Indeed, in the sixteenth and seventeenth centuries, European investigations into the origins of specific languages were not necessarily distinct from efforts to discover the origins of Language itself. As ancient Hebrew was believed to have been the sacred *Ursprache*, a primordial linguistic unity that had shattered into multiple languages as a consequence of divine punishment, it was assumed that all languages contained traces of Hebrew and that linguistic prestige could be then measured by appraising the distance from the originary immaculate tongue. Right up until the nineteenth century, a dominant assumption among European scholars was that Biblical Hebrew, Latin, and Greek epitomized languages in their most ideal form.[8]

Naturally, Spanish scholars admitted Castilian into this exalted company, and it was from this linguistic worldview that missionary writers in the Philippines assessed the relative superiority of the two languages they were most exposed to, namely, Tagalog and Visayan. By extension the qualities exhibited by these languages were seen to reflect the moral temperaments of those who spoke them, in a sharp illustration of the ideological process of iconization, as introduced in the previous chapter.

Chirino was such a firm proponent of Tagalog that he gave orders for Manila's church of Saint Anne to be decorated with Tagalog tapestries and scrolls hanging alongside others in Hebrew, Greek, Latin, and Castilian (Chirino [1604] 1969, 284). He informed the Jesuit General Claudius Acquaviva that:

> Of all these languages the one that I have found most satisfying and admirable is Tagalog, for [ ... ] I have found in it four qualities from the four finest languages in the world, namely Hebrew, Greek, Latin and Spanish. From Hebrew, the intricacies and subtleties; from Greek, the articles, and the distinctions applied not only to common but also to proper nouns; from Latin, the fullness and elegance; and from Spanish, the good breeding and courtesy. (Chirino [1604] 1969, 275)

By contrast, the "other two languages of the Visayans have none of these refinements, or at least very little, being as they are coarser and less polished"[9] (276). Notably the inferiority of the Visayans, for Chirino, was further reflected in the fact that they had no writing system of their own.

Ignacio Alcina ([1668] 2005), alternatively, was so impressed by what he perceived as the superior expressiveness of *Visayan* that he was moved to evaluate it with the same criteria, writing that "scarcely will there be found any other language among the most universal ones, which may have an advantage over it like Latin or Greek" (17). The wealth of the Visayan vocabulary, in Alcina's judgment, outshone even Spanish, or more specifically the degenerate vernacular Spanish spoken in the colonies, whose purity was contaminated by loan words. Visayan vocabulary was not only lexically richer but also semantically more precise, making "clearer the meanings of the things and causes than other languages" (21). On the other hand, this same expressiveness had a morally dangerous side as witnessed in a plurality of Visayan words for genitalia "as befits a people much addicted to immoral things" (23), while vocabulary for abstract and rational concepts was, in his view, impoverished. Similar criticisms were later leveled at Tagalog by Sebastian de Totanes, who complained, in the preface to his own grammar of the language, that it was full of needless superfluities while remaining bereft of the basic and necessary terms (Totanes 1745). Although such statements about Tagalog or Visayan now appear ludicrously quaint, they were trotted out ad nauseum in the twentieth century by nationalist pundits who favored one or other to be crowned as the national language.

While Tagalog and Visayan were set in a contest for preeminence, minority languages were scarcely acknowledged, let alone formally documented. Francisco Colin, in 1660, complained that Philippine languages were "numerous," counting six on Luzon (Ethnologue now lists 69) while in less densely populated zones such as Mindoro they were "more numerous as almost every river has a different one" ([1660] 1904, 58). For Colin, linguistic diversity was tantamount to barbarism:

> The lack of police and communication is the cause for the multiplication of their languages. For, as learned men observe, just like the early multiplication of languages that took place in the tower of Babel, which were as numerous as the families of Noah's descendants, so too amongst the barbaric nations in which each man lives for himself with neither recognition nor respect for public laws, all is brawling and internal dissent. And lacking communication, the common language is lost, and each is left with his own language that is so corrupted that it is not understood by the others. (Colin [1660] 1904, 58)[10]

The characterization of highlander diversity as an almost deliberate act of insubordination and anarchy was consistently entertained by Spanish authorities and Filipino elites. Two centuries after Colin's complaint, the Spanish compilers of a popular encyclopedia of the Philippines explained ethnolinguistic diversity as the natural consequence of savagery, ignorance, and isolation (Buzeta and

Bravo 1851, 64), while the Filipino writer and activist Isabelo de los Reyes wrote, in Spanish, that his indigenous countrymen were natural corruptors of language and "inventors of a thousand and one new terms" (1889) with homophones between major languages only stirring up further confusion.[11]

Those who had no clear affiliation with the major groupings were sometimes referred to as *remontados* ('mountain fugitives') or *rebeldes* ('rebels'). With the change of regimes in the early twentieth century, the new American administrators imported a frontier vocabulary into their emergent narrative of colonial progress, referring to the cultural minorities that they encountered as 'Indians' belonging to 'tribes' presided over by 'chiefs.' It was at this time that the anthropologist H. Otley Beyer rebooted the theory, mentioned at the beginning of this chapter, that coastal Filipinos were descended from technologically more advanced Malays who arrived from the south and pushed the original inhabitants into the mountains. While the theory had been proposed earlier by Spanish thinkers such as Fr. Francisco Baranera (1884), Beyer's formulation of it fell on more receptive ears, perhaps because the United States was by now recapitulating the same narrative. Colonial land reforms in the early twentieth century encouraged agricultural expansion into highland interiors where lowlanders were more likely to confront non-Christian communities who maintained different subsistence systems and spoke undocumented languages.

William Henry Scott has unraveled the incremental historical process by which successive administrations constructed and reinforced a highlander–lowlander dualism in the Philippines (see, for example, the discussion in Scott 1974, 1992). Later, James C. Scott (2009) attempted to explain how the cultural systems of highland Southeast Asia did not so much represent a retention of pre-contact lifeways as they did a *strategic adaptation* to the relentless incursions of lowland regimes. Swidden agriculture and the cultivation of root crops, for example, allowed highlanders to avoid taxation and to stay on the move, while acephalous forms of social organization prevented co-option and subordination. However, I believe the later Scott errs by defaulting to the perspective of lowland administrators and regarding the hills solely as sites of political disobedience, rather than as places of long human habitation and cultural continuity, with or without states to evade. This leads him to the unfortunate position of agreeing with the likes of Francisco Colin, who iconized linguistic diversity as a defensive political choice like any other.[12] In reality, the diversification of languages is a slow, non-directed, and multidimensional process, and a few centuries of lowland rule would certainly not suffice to stimulate the multiplicity of languages in upland regions of Southeast Asia. To revise James C. Scott's position, it would be more reasonable to say of the Philippine highlands that a *pre*existing linguistic diversity was already in place to obstruct the homogenizing agendas of lowland colonial administrations. Further, these ready-made and state-resistant communities provided ideal refuge for lowlanders who later chose to flee colonial enclosure and to assimilate with the highland "rebels," as I will outline later and in Chapter 8.

## Spanish for the people

Throughout the period of Spanish rule, instruction in Castilian was advanced as a solution to the pressing "problem" of linguistic diversity. Indeed, two decades prior to the conquest of Manila, Carlos I issued a decree that natives of all the colonies receive their religious education in Castilian and not the indigenous languages (Hau and Tinto 2003, 338–339). Despite the issuing of similar decrees by subsequent rulers, the policy was never successfully or consistently implemented in the Philippines.

Various reasons are cited for the failure of the Spanish to diffuse their language to the islands. The most charitable accounts point to a lack of support by the rulers in Madrid in terms of resources. Others cite evidence that friars actively disobeyed or obstructed the decrees since proficiency in Spanish among the natives threatened the power of the friar class, whose knowledge of local languages made them indispensable as intermediaries.[13] Certainly, the task was not always approached in a spirit of generosity.[14] Whether through disobedience, resource scarcity, or bad faith, the school system did not achieve its ends, and by the time of the American administration's census of 1903, only 10 percent of the population had any proficiency in Spanish.

Access to linguistic privileges had a powerful class dimension. In the late nineteenth century, wealthy schools in Manila for the emerging Filipino elite were teaching not only Spanish, but also Latin and Greek (*RPC* 1900, vol. 2, 279, 459). The so-called *ilustrados*, members of an educated Hispanicized class that formed the backbone of the nationalist movement against Spain, tended to graduate from private Spanish schools, and many of them continued their education in Europe.

José Rizal, the preeminent *ilustrado* and the most iconic figure of Filipino nationalism, was a polymath with a deep interest language, and his 1887 publication of a Tagalog grammar and orthography marks him as the first Filipino linguist, emerging as he did from the tradition of nineteenth-century European philology. Although he famously advocated reform over revolution, he was accused of fomenting and encouraging the Katipunan, an armed anti-Spanish movement lead by Andres Bonifacio.[15] He was executed by the Spanish authorities in 1896, an event that did nothing to quell growing revolutionary unrest. By 1898, Katipunan soldiers were enacting a full-scale revolt against colonial rule. Under the leadership of Emilio Aguinaldo, who wrested control of the movement from Bonifacio, the Katipunan formed a military alliance with the United States, which was then engaged in the Spanish–American War. By June, Katipunan and American troops had succeeded in taking control of most of the country except for the walled city of Intramuros in Manila. The independence of the Philippines was proclaimed by Aguinaldo on June 12, 1898. American forces captured Manila two months later, although the Katipunan were not permitted to enter the city. The United States refused to recognize the declaration of Filipino sovereignty and annexed the Philippines in December of that year. In turn, the nationalists ignored U.S. claims of sovereignty, and the fledgling government declared war against its former allies. Even the names given to the ensuing conflict reflect different understandings of the terms of the confrontation. For the U.S. government, the devastating military events of 1899–1902 would be known simply as the Philippine Insurrection; for Filipino historians it has since become known as the Philippine–American war.

The "Constitución Provisional de la República Filipinas" drafted by the Katipunan leadership at Biak-na-Bato in 1897 declared Tagalog to be the official language of the Republic, although Spanish was to stay on temporarily as an official language (Frei 1959, 27–28). The First Republic, which ended with the capture and surrender of Emilio Aguinaldo in 1901, did not last long enough for its bold language policy to be implemented.

## The American era, the birth of a native church, and a national linguistic consciousness

As a missionary outpost of the Spanish empire, local governance in the Philippines devolved to five monastic orders. Civil government, which concerned itself mainly with taxation and trade, had little in the way of direct contact with ordinary Filipinos. It is small wonder, then, that in the years leading up to the Philippine Revolution (1896–1898), criticism of the Spanish administration found its earliest expression in opposition to the rule of the 'friar class,' or *frailocracia*, rather than in outright rejection of Spanish sovereignty. Even within the Spanish Empire such an indissoluble marriage of church and state was considered unusual, leading Juan Ruiz de Apodaca, viceroy of Mexico, to remark that "in every friar of the Philippines was a king, a general and an entire army" (Villacorte 1833, 204).

The failure of the friar–state complex to implement an education system that would provide literacy in Spanish to ordinary Filipinos was a frequent complaint. Moreover, the loudest protests on the matter were from Spanish-speaking *ilustrados* who had had access to Spanish education and the opportunities it entailed. The activist Marcelo H. del Pilar even framed the failure to diffuse Spanish as a deliberate countermove of the *frailocracia* against efforts to install Spanish as the national lingua franca and thus overcome the supposed barriers created by linguistic diversity (del Pilar [1898] 1987, 136). In this way, the intransigence of the friar class on the issue of language policy became a potent symbol of Spanish obstructionism and opposition to nationalist goals.

Leading a mostly Roman Catholic populace, the revolutionary Malolos Congress found itself in a difficult political relationship with the Catholic Church. Without a meaningful division of church and state, Filipino Catholics faced a potential crisis of allegiance. The task of reconciling this dilemma was left to Fr. Gregorio Aglipay, appointed by General Aguinaldo as Military Vicar General toward the end of 1898. In light of the proclaimed dissolution of Spanish sovereignty over the islands, Aglipay issued a manifesto urging all Spanish clergy to relinquish their positions in order to be replaced by a newly ordained Filipino priesthood. His maneuver was not received favorably by the Spanish clergy, and Aglipay was duly excommunicated in May the following year.

After the surrender of the Katipunan, the reformist Isabelo de los Reyes urged Aglipay to found a national Philippine church, independent of Rome. Aglipay was at first hesitant to accept the proposal, but by September 1902 he assumed the role of Obispo Maximo in the newly promulgated Iglesia Filipina Independiente (Mojares 2006a). Later known colloquially as the Aglipayan church or simply 'Aglipay,' it soon achieved widespread popularity through its nationalist, revolutionary, and anticolonial proselytizing. The Iglesia Filipina Independiente, or IFI, maintained the core of the Catholic liturgy, but its doctrine was vigorously secular, embracing science over religious mysticism, and rejecting Latin in favor of Spanish (Aglípay y Labáyan 1912). Within the space of a few years the IFI had attracted millions of followers, especially in Luzon and Mindanao (de Achútegui and Bernad 1961), where it was reported that Aglipayans outnumbered Catholics (Dauncey 1906, 209).

From its beginnings Governor Taft expressed anxiety about the new movement, reporting to Congress in November 1902 that Aglipay's church, "may, perhaps, add much to the labor of maintaining peace and order in the archipelago" (*RPC* 1904, 319). The fact that many of the church's staunchest adherents were former rebel leaders, not least Aglipay himself, exacerbated the unease felt by the new colonists toward the emergent church.[16] But the threat posed by Aglipay to the American establishment proved to be overstated. By 1906, the IFI was already in steady decline. Taft's negotiations with the Vatican, together with successful court actions, brought by the Roman Catholic Church resulted in the expulsion of Aglipayan congregations from the buildings they had come to occupy.[17] The 1905 *Annual Report of the Philippine Commission* conceded that "It was claimed at one time that [the IFI] was not a religious organization but the groundwork for a revolution. I believe that the theory has been entirely exploded" (*RPC* 1905, 61).[18]

Early American efforts at understanding the cultural and linguistic heterogeneity of the Philippines were to mirror those of the Spanish three centuries prior. As the first Philippine Commission, appointed in January of 1899, advocated a limited form of local rule, the general level of education in the country was of central concern on the stated grounds that "the fitness of any people to maintain a popular form of government must be closely dependent upon the prevalence of knowledge and enlightenment among the masses" (*RPC* 1900, vol. 1, 17). To this end, the Commission undertook a study of literacy and numeracy in all the administrative regions. In so doing they encountered an overwhelming linguistic diversity, a fact that was soon implicated in a perceived disunity of the Filipino population and presented as grounds for delaying the demands of nationalist agitators. The Commission concluded that:

> In spite of the general use of the Spanish language by the educated classes and the considerable similarity of economic and social conditions prevalent in Luzon and the Visayan Islands, the masses of the people are without a common speech and they lack the sentiment of nationality. The Filipinos are not a nation, but a variegated assemblage of different tribes and peoples, and their loyalty is still of the tribal type. (*RPC* 1900, vol. 1, 182)

American scientific interest in Philippine languages soon followed the end of hostilities, but accurate mapping of their number and distribution continued to prove difficult. The administration's interest in language was part of a much broader drive to map and quantify resources in America's latest colonial acquisition. This enterprise, supervised and summarized in indexed reports by the Philippine Commission, encompassed everything from inventories of plants, minerals, and arable land to brief ethnographic descriptions of Filipino communities and their associated languages and cultural practices. As quickly as this information was collected it was put to the task of reconstructing the Philippines in the image of American nationhood.

Significantly, this period of colonial nation-building coincided with the development of a new national consciousness among the Filipino elite. Urban-based artists and intellectuals of the early twentieth century began to articulate an indigenous aesthetic for an emerging and distinctly Filipino identity, an identity that paradoxically relied on U.S. categories to sustain it. In art, music, theater, dance, literature, and historiography, the nation was, to a large extent, imagined through imported symbols, from the canonization of national heroes, to flag-raising ceremonies, and new traditions of "national dress." As Resil Mojares put it, "Philippine civic nationalism [of the early twentieth century] was constrained by the conditions of its production, complicit in the realities of profound political, economic, and cultural dependence that U.S. rule created. It was a colonial school-house nationalism that affirmed colonialism at the same time that it sought to negate it" (Mojares 2006b, 25).

And yet, even as cultural elites were anointing themselves as state iconographers, a parallel narrative of national awakening was unfolding in the margins. Driven by the same anxieties and yearnings for a collective identity, vernacular movements were disrupting the bourgeois narrative of an orderly progress to independent nationhood. Militant cults inspired by José Rizal or the Katipunan reinterpreted the nation in terms of spiritual reawakening while outsider historians like Pedro Paterno, José Marco, and Pedro Monteclaro developed radical counter-narratives of prehispanic statehood in the Philippines—the latter two going so far as to manufacture influential "indigenous" manuscripts to elaborate their visions.

## The announcement of Eskayan amid a contest of national languages

For the underground movements, as much as for the Filipino elite, language and literacy became sites of imaginative possibilities for a future Filipino unity. After the Commonwealth of the Philippines was established in 1935, ushering in the first popularly elected government in the nation's history, the new constitution granted official status to English and Spanish but mandated the development of a national tongue based on one unspecified Philippine language (Hau and Tinto 2003, 342).

Nonetheless, the question of how to choose a single language to embody the emerging state ranged well beyond the constitutional mandate. Some pundits lobbied in favor of retaining English, which was already firmly established as the language of administration. Others preferred Visayan, the lingua franca of the south, which had the most speakers and the greatest geographic range. By far the most popular option was the Tagalog language as spoken in Manila since it was the mother tongue of many indigenous elites including the martyred novelist and linguist José Rizal. Yet many still worried that Tagalog would fail to take root because it presented a cultural and political barrier to those living outside the capital. Others, alternatively, warned that Tagalog as a national language would be *too* successful and result in the obliteration of minority languages. Then there were the idealists who suggested that a brave new language should be forged from a fusion of Philippine vernaculars. The diversity of ideas points to the increasing inclusivity of the debate. Formerly the preserve of an intellectual minority, the so-named National Language Problem was seized on by an optimistic public to be thrashed out in broadsheets, popular magazines, and radio broadcasts across the country (Frei 1959).

In 1937, as these debates were at their height, the president of the Commonwealth of the Philippines, Manuel L. Quezon, received a notebook inscribed with curious symbols (see Prologue). An accompanying letter, signed by one Mariano Datahan, explained that the notebook contained lessons in his native tongue and went on to invite the president to observe "night classes" in his tiny upland village of Biabas, a place so out of the way that state cartographers had not yet plotted its location in southeast Bohol.

The precise content of Datahan's letter may only be guessed at since all that has survived is an imperfect transcript of the reply from Quezon's secretary:[19]

Office of the President of the Philippines

Nov 11, 1937

Dear Mr Mariano Datahan,

This is to acknowledge receipt of your letter the 30th ultimo, together a notebook containing lessons in Boholano dialect addressed to his Excellency the President, and to inform you that your request for the opening night classes for adults in your community will be taken into consideration.

Sincerely Yours,
Sec Jorge B. Vargas

On the very day after this reply was sent from Quezon's office, the Institute of National Language formally recommended to the president that Tagalog should be chosen as the basis of a revised national tongue. Spoken at this time by only a quarter of the population, Tagalog would soon require urgent reform with new native-like words engineered to fill important lexical gaps, among them: *bansa* 'nation,' *pamahalaan* 'government,' and *pangulo* 'president.'

Whether Datahan was attempting to influence this debate, or was simply moved by the linguistic and nationalist zeitgeist to draw attention to his language, is a matter of speculation. But to this day, Eskaya people living in Cadapdapan recall a prophecy issued by Mariano Datahan that Eskayan will one day become the national language of the Philippines. Needless to say, however,

President Quezon never did make an official visit to Biabas, and Datahan's high-level attempt at raising the profile of Eskayan cannot, on these terms, be considered a success.

## Shamanic rebellion and indigenous outlaws in Bohol (1621–1829)

Emanating from Manila, the various policy declarations, language-planning exercises, and political reformations had only a limited resonance in the southern Philippines. It is remarkable that at the time of Datahan's submission to the president, no language documentation had ever been carried out on Bohol, and indeed, almost none has taken place since.[20] Granted, Boholanos are known to speak a variety of Visayan that is closely related to the well-described prestige dialect spoken on neighboring Cebu (Map 2), and against the objections of some Boholanos, the dialect of Bohol continues to be termed 'Cebuano" by outsiders (see "A Note on Terminology" at the beginning of this book). But perhaps more significantly, the province has always been of marginal interest to colonial governments. Its rocky and less fertile interior made it an undesirable source of tribute, while all of the most essential regional trade was diverted through the port of Cebu City. Until the mid-nineteenth century, Bohol was governed from Cebu, before which time only a handful missionaries were stationed on the island in any given year (Luspo 2005, 12).

Furthermore, Spanish occupiers never wholly succeeded in bringing Bohol to heel. This is despite the fact that the process of Christianization, which began as early as 1595, was seen to have been miraculously swift. Within a mere five years, the entire island had reportedly submitted to the spiritual authority of Fr. Gabriel Sanchez and Fr. Juan de Torres, who established the first colonial outpost at Baclayon (Map 3). The missions had some cause to expect harmonious relations with the locals. After all, it was in Bohol that a celebrated ceremony of alliance was performed when the conquistador Miguel Lopez de Legaspi and the Boholano *datu* ('headman') Katuna ritually drank a cup of each other's blood thirty years earlier.

In 1609, an indigenous shaman by the name of Kariyapa sang a stark prophecy to the headmen of Dauis that foreigners would soon come to possess Bohol and that surrounding islands would also soon be subjugated (Brewer 2004, 87). It is said that her song was met with ridicule; however, events took an unexpected turn in 1621 when a local shaman by the name of Tamblot rose up in defiance of the intruders. Under his leadership, indigenous shamans encouraged the people of Bohol to abandon Christianity, and recruits to the cause were promised invulnerability from Spanish muskets. The rebels set about desecrating religious imagery, and as more communities joined the movement, a steady migration began into the wild upland interior (Sturtevant 1976, 79–80; Romanillos 1997, 3). Soon after, troops arrived from Cebu and forcibly quelled the rebellion (Luspo 2005, 9).

In 1673, a similar uprising took place in Bohol, led by a *babaylan*, or indigenous shaman, whose followers addressed him first as "Bishop" and then "Pope" (de los Reyes y Florentino 1889, 43–44). Later in the century a more significant uprising took place on the island of Panay to Bohol's northwest (Map 1). The instigator was a *babaylan* by the name of Tapar who called for the revival of traditional rites but who incorporated Christian iconography into his movement. In what was later described by the authorities as a "diabolical farce," Tapar named himself "God Almighty," two of his assistants were "Jesus Christ" and "the Holy Ghost," and a female comrade was consecrated as "the Most Holy Mary." The higher echelons of his troops were ordained as "popes" or "bishops" (Sturtevant 1976, 81). Though tolerated for a brief period, Tapar and his followers were brutally executed for their heresies.

Tumult in Bohol continued throughout the Spanish period, during which the eighty-five-year-long Dagohoy Rebellion (1744–1829) would come to represent the longest and most successful anti-colonial project in Philippine history. The Boholano rebel leader Francisco "Dagohoy" Sendrijas was a larger-than-life Robin Hood figure whose long struggle resulted in a virtual republic in the interior of the island. Sparked by the refusal of a Spanish priest to grant a Christian burial to his brother, Dagohoy's insurgency soon swept through the entire province: in the life of the rebellion only the towns of Baclayon and Loboc (Map 3) refused to participate (Luspo 2005, 10). Finally, in 1829 the last of the Dagohoy rebels were routed at Danao (see Map 3), and the Spanish initiated a massive resettlement program. Although by the 1820s the rebels had ceased to be a formidable military force, their numbers remained large. Captain Manuel Sanz reported that 19,420 surviving rebels surrendered and approximately 3,000 fled to other islands (cited in Misa 1970); the combined numbers represent over one-quarter of Bohol's population at the time (Romanillos 1997, 49).

For these rebels and their families, who had lived as outlaws for generations, the defeat necessarily involved the foundation of new towns in the interior, such as Batuanan (now Alicia), Cabulao, Catigbian, and Bilar (see Map 3). To this day, the Dagohoy Rebellion looms large in the Visayan imagination and is a source of pride and identity to Boholanos. The Visayan phrase *kaliwat ni Dagohoy* is an old cliché designating 'the people of Bohol'; literally it means 'descendants of Dagohoy.'

Little is recorded of the social organization of the Dagohoy insurgents, though Spanish authorities conjured a vision of sacrilegious depravity from circulating rumors or from the accounts of penitent insurgents. One witness, in 1765, expressed horror that Dagohoy's followers were replicating religious roles and rites of the Spanish clergy, with spurious ministers solemnizing weddings and performing baptisms.[21] Another claimed in 1792 that the rebels had abandoned belief in hell and the efficacy of Christian sacraments, professing an unmediated relationship to God while using "oils and roots" to make pacts with the devil.[22]

Less speculative Spanish reports of successful raids on rebel settlements do suggest that prehispanic traditions were widely maintained, revived, or integrated with Christian doctrine; even today Bohol's traditional *babaylans* take inspiration from Dagohoy, with some claiming to be his reincarnation (Aparece 2003). According to a Spanish curate, the rebels at Agbonan (now San Isidro; see Map 3) engaged in customary burial practices and a limited form of polygamy prevailed. Here bamboo chapels were erected, in the words of one cleric, to celebrate a "the most repugnant amalgam of Christianity and idolatry" (Hilario Sánchez, curate of Catigbian, cited in Romanillos 1997, 21). These chapels were sited alongside purpose-built schools with their own teaching staff. Whether schooling and literacy were widespread in Dagohoy's territory is unknown, but it is more certain that in areas under Spanish control, institutionalized education was virtually unheard of in Bohol until the 1860s. According to Sotero Nuñez Misa (1970), who relied primarily on oral history for his account of the Dagohoy rebellion, the insurgents formed a government that mirrored colonial institutions with a division of civil and military affairs. Christian rites were performed by an informal laity, while the *babaylanes* were permitted to continue practicing a pre-contact spirituality (Misa 1970, 76, 82, 126). As much as Spanish chroniclers literally demonized the Dagohoy insurgents, Misa may also be guilty of romanticizing the rebel community. Nonetheless, his oral reconstructions are reflective of how many Boholanos today choose to lay claim to a past beyond the gaze of colonial administrators.

## Enter the Eskaya (1902–1937)

The actual degree to which the Dagohoy rebellion may have served to safeguard precolonial culture into the nineteenth and twentieth centuries, or the extent to which this culture was simply reconstituted or reimagined, is a subject worthy of serious consideration. Perched in the upland region of southeast Bohol, Mariano Datahan's village of Biabas was well within the territory inhabited for so long by the followers of Dagohoy (see Map 5). Indeed, the single most extensive contemporary chronicle of the rebellion makes explicit mention of rebel *datus* occupying the "hill of Tambongan" situated in the immediate foothills of Biabas.[23] If a language as idiosyncratic as Eskayan was spoken and written within this difficult terrain, there is little reason to expect that it would have been encountered by outsiders and made known to the rest of the world. As I have shown, neither the Spanish nor the American colonial authorities ever came to grips with the true extent of the ethnolinguistic diversity in the Philippines, and various linguistic minorities of the highlands were acknowledged only to the extent that they occupied the roles of "savage" foils to the "civilized" lowlanders. As elsewhere in the Philippines, linguistic difference, distance from governing institutions, or a simple refusal to assimilate to orthodox Christianity were conflated and recast as barbarism and rebelliousness. One American visitor to the Visayas remarked as late as 1900 that the "heathen" of Bohol would have died out had they not been "reinforced continually by *remontados*, or fugitives of justice" (Sawyer 1900, 296).

American administrators could be forgiven for associating religious "heathenism" with banditry and sedition. Throughout the Philippines, cult guerrilla movements proliferated amid the instability engendered by the Philippine–American War. These groups adopted a variety of mystical names, but generically they became known as *colorums*, *dios-dios*, or *pulahanes*; the U.S. authorities also referred to them as *ladrones fanaticos* ('fanatical bandits'). Some devised red uniforms in continuity with the red-garbed warriors of prehispanic times. Others, like Tamblot and Tapar centuries before them, appropriated Catholic clerical hierarchies and addressed their leaders as "Pope" (see Chapter 8).

In this tumultuous period many Boholanos emigrated to Mindanao and Cebu to join guerrilla sects, but there is little in the way of detailed documentary evidence pointing to the existence of homegrown movements on Bohol itself. One nameless Boholano agitator was, however, sufficiently threatening to the authorities that he was mentioned in passing in the *Fourth Annual Report of the Philippine Commission: 1903*. Described as a "lieutenant of the barrio of Biaba [sic]," the report warned that he had "made some fanatical speeches that gained him considerable followers on the island of Bohol" (*RPC* 1903, vol. 3, 116). There is little doubt that the report was describing the charismatic Mariano Datahan, who, in this year, began converting the people of Biabas to the Iglesia Filipina Independiente and spreading its radical message to surrounding villages, even reaching as far as the coast. As it transpired, Datahan was an Aglipayan in name only, and his religious practice was far more nativist and syncretic than the official dogma allowed (see Chapter 8). Moreover, while Gregorio Aglipay had negotiated a peace with the U.S. regime, the residents of Biabas were in ongoing rebellion against the new order such that four years after the official cessation of hostilities in Bohol a contingent of Biabas militia attempted a full-scale guerrilla attack on the town of Carmen and its officials (Map 3).

The fact that a militant religious movement was identified as emanating from Biabas, the homeland of Mariano Datahan's "Boholano dialect" and the epicenter of an eighty-five-year resistance, is worth investigating further. Did this incidental report of Biabas fanaticism really point to the existence of a new insurgent movement on Bohol? Or was it simply the reinvigoration of a long-suppressed group from Bohol's highlands, speakers of a minority tongue who were reflexively dismissed as outlaws? Either way, the 'people of Dagohoy' were once again raising hell in the hills.

Some thirty years after the incident in Carmen, and with the nation on the brink of independence, the aging speechmaker appealed directly to the president, inviting him to see with his own eyes the language and education system that had flourished under his leadership in southeast Bohol (see Figure P.1). The opportunity for a face-to-face encounter between these two men—both committed veterans of anti-colonial wars whose lives took very different paths—was missed, and with it went the last chance for an official engagement with Eskayan in the lifetime of its chief advocate. Sporadic mentions of Datahan and his isolated community surface in a few World War II memoirs of Boholano resistance movements, and in a compendium of Boholano folklore (see Chapter 8). Nowhere in these accounts, however, is there any mention of a special language and script, nor of a grassroots school system in the highlands.

Eskayan was not destined to come to public attention until long after both Datahan and Quezon had passed away. When outsiders finally took notice, they approached Eskaya people as docile objects waiting to be discovered and brought into history, rather than as active participants in the national project. In this chapter, I have aimed to adjust for this view by foregrounding the broader historical and political context that preceded their "discovery." The complicated Eskaya story becomes easier to unravel when we examine the political terms of engagement between highland linguistic minorities, lowland Filipinos, and colonial administrators. The contested narrative that Spanish missionaries had destroyed the once-abundant native records was made all the more credible by the activities of early colonists who enacted forceful policies of governance and cultural assimilation that resulted in artificial linguistic hierarchies. Later American administrators reinforced the ideological program of their predecessors by continuing to characterize linguistic diversity as a destabilizing threat to governance. Yet these same highland linguistic minorities would eventually come to be exoticized as the living remnants of primordial societies that had valiantly resisted the incursions of lowland newcomers and thus deserved recognition and protection.

An island notorious for its near perpetual state of rebellion against colonial authority, Bohol appeared to a certain extent as a dark space on the map, a site of anxiety, mystery, and possibility. In the chapter that follows I look more closely at the events surrounding the "first contact" with the Eskaya and their language in the 1980s. I then consider how the Eskaya were integrated into evolving narratives of Filipino indigeneity and how members of the group creatively adapted to these representations.

## Notes

1. Robert Blust has emphasized the historical significance of this wordlist, as it represents the beginning of Western interest in what scholars would later recognize as the largest and furthest-reaching language family in the world (Blust 2013).
2. There is some suggestion that the script was used by Tagalogs for writing in Spanish. Purportedly drawing from primary sources, the compilers of an early Philippine Commission report claimed that "In place of F [the Filipinos] used a P and thus they wrote fuego instead of puego [sic]. Y took the place of LL, and they said Yuvia instead of Lluvia. They used a similar method in writing other words, supplying the sounds for which they had no characters with similar sounds, a defect which they retain until to-day, for a similar misuse of consonants is to be heard amongst the Indians" (*RPC* 1900, vol. 3, 403). Following the accepted convention, the Reports of the Philippine Commission (Philippine Commission 1900–1907) are here abbreviated as *RPC* followed by the date, volume number, and page numbers. Note that the date refers to the year covered by the report rather than the date of publication. Thus, for example, the *RPC* for 1903 was actually published in 1904.
3. An Indic origin was suggested for the Philippine script at least as early as Jacquet (1831); for an excellent contemporary analysis of script ancestry see Miller (2014).
4. "scrisse asai cosse como le ciamanão Quanto Lo re et le alti me vistenno scriuere et li diceua qelle sue parolle tutti restorono atoniti" (117). All translations of primary sources are mine unless otherwise indicated.
5. "and for lack of letters these natives [Visayans] preserve their ancient lore in song" [y por careçer de letras guardan estos naturales sus antiguedades en los cantares] (De Loarca 1903 [1582], 120).
6. Pardo de Tavera (1884, 23) believed that by the end of the seventeenth century, the Philippine script was known to only a few educated men. Meanwhile, a German account relates that priests were still using the 'old Malay letters' on the east coast of Mindanao up until the beginning of the nineteenth century (Semper 1869, 81). Outside of the Mangyan-speaking region of Mindoro, this is the latest dating for literacy in the Philippine script that I am aware of.
7. To the best of my knowledge, H. Otley Beyer is alone in providing any concrete example of Spanish-led book burning, writing that "One Spanish priest in southern

Luzon boasted of having destroyed more than three hundred scrolls written in the native character" (1979, 9), though no reference is given for this claim.

8. On the history of European beliefs about language origins see especially Padley (1976, 1988) and Seuren (1998).

9. Presumably these 'other two languages' were Cebuano-Visayan and Hiligaynon, the first varieties to be documented.

10. "La falta de policia, y comunicacion, es causa de multiplicarse las lenguas. Porque como en la primitiua multiplicacion de ellas, que fue en la torre de Babel, obseruanlos Doctores, que fueron tantas quantas eran las familias de los descendientes de Noe; assi entre las naciones barbaras, que cada vno viue de por si sin reconocimiento, ni sujecion a leyes publicas; todo es guerrillas, y dissensiones entre si; y faltando la comunicacion, se oluida la lengua comun, y cada vno queda con la suya tan corrompida, que ya no entienden los otros" (Colin [1660] 1904, 58).

11. "Los indígenas son naturalmente corruptores de lenguas é inventores de mil y mil términos nuevos: el tranvia, por ejemplo, cuando aun no contaba un año en el Archepiélago, ya estaba filipinizado, dando este nombre los de Manila á la muger pública. [ . . . ] por ejemplo *gamút*, en tagalo significa *medicamento* y en ilocano *veneno; kayo*, en tagalo es *tela*, y en ilocano *madera*; etc." (de los Reyes y Florentino 1889, 99).

12. Of Zomia Scott writes that "[i]t is as if the difficulties of terrain and relative isolation have, over many centuries, encouraged a kind of 'speciation' of languages, dialects, dress, and cultural practices" (Scott 2009, 18).

13. This strategy was known outside the Spanish Empire. Beverley A. Blaskett writes that in Western Australia Catholic missionaries learned local languages but prevented Aboriginal people from acquiring English. This was done to enhance dependency on the mission and to lessen the influence from 'evil' whites (Blaskett 1983, cited in Thieberger 1988).

14. An 1887 textbook for teaching Spanish to Waray-speaking children includes a comprehension exercise in which students would have had to recite, perhaps in unison, the following wincing statement in Spanish: "A heroic Spain consecrated to itself the duty of magnifying human dignity by introducing into its conquered and now-civilised overseas territories the saving light of evangelical truth [ . . . ] strengthening those relations that united it with inferior races in their degradation and ignorance of eternal truths, its gentility imposing upon them the respect and consideration that they were due and the obligation to help raise them up from the lamentable state in which they languished in an existence unworthy of rational beings" (Sanchez de la Rosa 1887, 2–3)

15. Megan C. Thomas suggests that Spanish class prejudice set the stage for the misidentification of Rizal and other elites as active revolutionaries: "Neither Jesuits nor Dominicans," she writes, "could imagine that the revolutionary Katipunan, the secret plebeian organization [ . . . ] could possibly have acted without the instigation of more educated elite leaders" (Thomas 2012, 3).

16. Certainly, the emergence of pulahanism coincided with the rise of the IFI, and both pulahanes and Aglipayans alike shared a forceful rhetoric of nationalism coupled with spiritual renewal. Indeed, after the defeat of the pulahan-colorum group known as the Guardia de Honor, former adherents were absorbed into the ranks of the IFI (Sturtevant 1976).

17. Taft originally ruled that the party in peaceful occupation of a church building was the rightful owner, a policy that was largely accepted by the Aglipayans and that coincided with an important land reform: the public subdivision and sale of the vast friar-owned hacienda estates. The Roman Catholic Church conceded the sale of estates after Taft's negotiations in Rome, but it successfully challenged the ownership of churches themselves via the courts that were more likely to rule in their favor (Laubach 1925, 149; Willis 1905, 214–215).

18. This was a view supported by Helen Taft in her memoirs (Taft 1914, 260). In fact, from the outset, Gregorio Aglipay himself was public in his acceptance of U.S. sovereignty and in his admiration for Governor Taft, whom he appointed president of the church in 1903; Taft graciously declined the appointment (Blunt 1912, 312). American Protestant missions were also favorably disposed to Aglipay on strategic grounds. One Protestant missionary wrote, "These people would never have left the Roman Catholic church to become Protestants, feeble as was the hold of the old Church upon them; but once outside and hungry for spiritual food they hear and are saved. Aglipay loosens this fruit from the tree, and we gather it. God is thus overruling the shortcomings of the leaders of this revolt against the Romish Church to the spiritual good of many souls" (Stuntz 1904, 494–495).

19. The text is adapted from the molave tablet itself, as sketched in Fig. P.1. Datahan's original letter and notebook have not survived in any Philippine archives.

20. Frank Blake (1920) noted that remarks on the Bohol dialect could be found in Domingo Esguerra's *Arte de la lengua bisaya de la Provincia de Leyte* (1747) and Zueco de San Joaquin's *Gramatica bisayo-española adaptada al sistema de Ollendorf* (1890). According to Ward (1971) some lexemes of Boholano provenance are given in Encarnacion's revised *Diccionario Bisaya-Español* (1885). Although I have not had access to San Joaquin, I have been unable to identify any of these comments or lexemes in the other documents. In the introduction to his corpus-driven two-volume dictionary of Visayan, John U. Wolff (1972a, 1972b) notes that oral and written materials were sourced from all over the Visayan-speaking area but that due to a lack of reliable informants Bohol-specific terms are mostly absent. To date, the only published research that looks, in brief, at Boholano-Visayan is that of Tinampay (1977) and Endriga (2010).

21. "The revolted Indians in the island of Bohol solemnize weddings among themselves, confer baptism, and perform other functions of the Catholics, for which purpose they have some persons who perform the duties of the father ministers in the villages" (de Viana [1765] 1907, 202).

22. "Subsistiendo en su infidelidad decian, que Dios tambien estaba en los montes se podian salvar en ellos sin necesidad de Sacramentos y de Ministros: no creían los mas, que huviese Infierno; por que ninguno de ellos (decian) no le habia visto: que los Padres y Españoles, que dicen le hay, sería para ellos: se ocupaban mucho en la supersticion, é idolatria; y usaban con frecuencia de azeites, y raizes pactando con el Demonio; y á lo que se experimentaban de su partido, como se veia en los que se habian empadronado en los pueblos, que estaban como insulsos, espantadizos, y con los ojos sobresaltados, atarantados, y casi inservibles" (de la Concepcion 1792, 105–106).

23. These datus were compelled to give themselves up to lowland authorities in exchange for amnesty as the tide of the insurrection began to turn toward the end of the eighteenth century. As Juan de Concepcion reports in 1792, "Bernardo Sanóte decia que él y demas datos de el monte de Tambungan, en que residian por el gran miedo que tenian á sus Padres antiguos, ya que no habia tal inconveniente, querian volver la servicio de Dios y de su Magestad, siendo de el agrado de el Señor Governador perdonarlos, y tener compasion de ellos, y concederles el formar pueblo en el recodo, ó ensenada de Guindulman, para cumplir con las obligaciones de christianos [ . . . ]' (de la Concepcion 1792, 95–96).

# 3 CONTACT AND CONTROVERSY

During my research visits to Bohol, locals asked me what I was doing on the island, and I always replied that I was working with the Eskaya people and their language. This elicited a range of reactions. Many had never heard of the Eskaya; others were skeptical about their existence but were prepared to take my word for it. For the rest, attitudes ranged from romantic fixation to mild resentment. Lowlanders often asked me whether the Eskaya were "civilized" or whether, on the other hand, they went barefoot and wore loincloths. Some described them as the true Boholanos, investing them with attributes of innocence and technological primitiveness.

The opinion that the Eskaya were one of the lost twelve tribes of Israel was widespread. A woman I once met at a cafe in Tagbilaran believed the Eskaya were holy people and asked me to confirm that their language was Hebrew. When I said that I couldn't find evidence for this she was not discouraged, asserting that the Bible corroborated her intuition. Another common opinion in Tagbilaran was that the Eskaya were a hoax, perpetrated or at least intensified by members of the local press. Others believed they were a cult. A few remained undecided and were keen to know my own opinions.

Many of these popular positions can be traced to the unusual circumstances in which the Eskaya entered into public discussion. In this chapter I will present a narrativized account of how the Eskaya community came into sustained contact with Bohol's lowlanders, and how the group was subsequently enregistered in the emerging discourse of indigenous development. I will show how key lowlander advocates relied on well-established ideologies of linguistic prestige to fix the Eskaya in a biblical image of tribehood in a way that was consistent with the theological traditions described in the previous chapter. By contrast, those who rejected the ethnicization of the Eskaya gave authority to their arguments by appealing to ideologies of sociolinguistic naturalism. Lastly, I will consider how Eskaya people themselves absorbed and resynthesized these positions, paving the

*The Last Language on Earth*. Kelly, Piers, Oxford University Press. © Oxford University Press 2022.
DOI: 10.1093/oso/9780197509913.003.0003

way for a new research agenda that gave greater prominence to Eskaya voices and experiences.

## First contact

What was it that finally brought Bohol's restless and unassimilated highlanders out into the open? According to the version of events outlined in the Prologue, the "discovery" of the Eskaya was first made by government advisers who, in 1980, were touring Bohol to implement Green Revolution policies (Abregana 1984). In a mountainous and densely forested corner of the island they had encountered an isolated community speaking a peculiar language, altogether unlike Visayan, and writing in an unrecognized script. Soon after, news of the "lost tribe" reached the National Museum of the Philippines, which was preparing to send an archeological team to Bohol to excavate prehistoric sites on the Anda peninsula (Map 3). As the planned excavation sites were not far from where the isolated group was said to be living, the National Museum scheduled a side trip to investigate further. The "Eksaya" (sic) of Bohol were described by the archeologists as a "cultural community" that inhabited the village of Biabas in upland Guindulman and maintained an agricultural economy based on rice, corn, and *kamúti* (a variety of sweet potato). Most belonged to a single clan descended from a legendary ancestor. Through a series of interviews the museum team was able to copy out a reference syllabary of the group's complex script, record a basic wordlist, and describe the number system. The final document included photographs, a comparison of the script with known Philippine writing systems, and some conclusions about where the group belonged within the ethnolinguistic picture of the Philippines (Jesus Peralta, personal communication). The report was never made public. Of the five copies produced, all have been lost: only six non-contiguous and barely illuminating pages have survived.[1]

Quite independently, the circulating stories of a lost tribe in Bohol piqued the curiosity of Brenda Abregana, a local librarian who in August of 1980 embarked on a personal expedition to the area in question. Her aim was to examine a collection of old manuscripts rumored to be in the possession of the tribe. Both Abregana and the National Museum team were mutually ignorant of each other's missions, and even their field sites were different. Abregana's investigation took place in Taytay (Map 3), some 13 km to the southwest of Biabas, and the first impressions of what she observed there were aired, months later, in the form of a grant application to the Fund for Assistance to Private Education in Manila (FAPE). The funding proposal explained that the lost "Bisayan Eskaya" people of Bohol were the indigenous custodians of ancient texts written in a forgotten language and script (Ramos 1980). Their native records, she explained, were of

**FIGURE 3.1.** Photograph of Eskaya tablet in the Bohol Provincial Museum, presumed to have been taken by Brenda Abregana.

incalculable value and had been hidden away for almost 450 years for protection against the destructive impulses of Spanish missionaries. In her assessment, the five "Old Books" of the Eskaya, alleged to have been large and leather-bound with thick, shiny material for paper, had not been seen since 1932, but faithful copies of their contents were still extant (Fig. 3.1). It was imperative, Abregana wrote, for a properly resourced expedition to be launched in order to make formal contact with the long-estranged Eskaya people, and to document their records. Further, her proposed project would attempt to determine the origin of the Eskayan alphabet with a view to discovering whether it was, in fact, the earliest alphabet in human history. "Since archeological evidence points to Southeast Asia as the first home of man," she mused, "there is enough reason that the alphabet must originate also in a Southeast Asian country" (6).

While Abregana explained that the community had its own writing system, literary tradition, and school institutions, from her perspective the Eskaya way of life was hopelessly primitive. Remarkably, no actual details of the tribal lifestyle were mentioned, but an important additional benefit of the proposed project was the improvement of general living standards toward a "new progressive condition" (6). The research team would be tasked with introducing the Eskaya to modern tools and know-how: the ancient library of manuscripts was to be "updated" with the latest information technology and the community given instruction in painting, sculpture, and the culinary arts. Agriculture was also on the agenda, with suggestions that included education in cotton-growing techniques and a system of producing a petrol substitute from cassava oil. Within her draft budget were provisions for trained interpreters to facilitate communication.

Abregana's application was submitted on Monday, November 10, 1980, and by Friday of the same week the governor of Bohol, Rolando Butalid, issued a letter to the Director of the Institute of Philippine Culture at Ateneo de Manila requesting further financial and technical assistance for the expedition. According to the governor, the lost library of the Eskaya "yielded fragments of significant historical accounts of the founding of the islands of the Bisayas some 2,000 (?) years ago" (question mark in original). A copy of the FAPE project proposal was appended to the letter.

## Media

Despite backing from Bohol's governor, no support was forthcoming from universities or government departments. In the meantime, public interest in the Eskaya was served by the local tabloid press. Journalists invariably took a supernatural angle, a theme encouraged by Abregana herself. Some writers amplified earlier reports, weaving in sensational theories of the group's ancient and biblical connections. Those who actually visited the Eskaya villages returned with equally sensational stories of dire native prophecies on the cusp of fulfillment and of chieftains with paranormal talents. These implausible reports, mostly written in Visayan for a Visayan audience, failed to attract any attention beyond Bohol and its neighboring islands.[2]

In one account the celebrated Boholano rebel leader Francisco Dagohoy was said to be an Eskayan native, and the Visayan sentence *Mabuhi ang pinulungan ni Dagohoy ug ang mga Bisaya* ('Long live the language of Dagohoy and the Visayan people') was duly translated into Eskayan, on behalf of the eager reporter, as **Liberwi esto bedaryo kon Dagohoy chedas esto may Bisaya**. The author concluded with yet another appeal to send qualified researchers from Manila, specifically experts from the Philippine National Library and the Ministry of Education and Culture, on the grounds that "the ancient materials here are related to our former culture and these should be made known to the present generation."[3] Shortly after, another article appeared, maintaining that the residents of Taytay and Biabas spoke a language related to Latin, Greek, and Etruscan, while using a script that had the appearance of Glagolitic (a ninth-century Slavic writing system whose invention is attributed to Saint Cyril and Saint Methodius). The

**FIGURE 3.2.** Eskaya girls in traditional headwear reciting a lesson in Taytay, 1981 (photograph: Tito Gomez).

people remained secretive in their use of it, preferring to speak Visayan in public (Payot 1981). According to its author they were also afraid that the government would pursue the schools for operating without a license but that recently, under the New Society of President Ferdinand Marcos, they had become emboldened to reveal their schools to the public.

When the Eskaya community did eventually find itself in the national spotlight, it was as the subject of a feature in *Who*, a Manila-based English-language magazine (Logarta 1981). After a brief sojourn in Taytay and consultation with a high-profile linguist at the University of the Philippines, investigative reporter Margarita Logarta concluded that the Eskaya were little more than a curious rural cult. Striking pictures accompanied the article (Figs. 3.2 and 3.3), showing Eskaya women in long, elegant dresses with matching headscarves that resembled nun's habits while Eskaya men stood barefoot in smart *barung* ('formal shirts').

Logarta's first-hand description of an Eskayan class in Taytay was equally vivid: students were crammed into the top floor of a two-story community hall where segregation of the sexes was rigidly observed. Younger students studied Eskayan grammar and lettering, while the more advanced were taught origin stories and psychology. These classes were patrolled by the Tres Marias, three women of authority who answered students' queries. In the room below them, librarians worked tirelessly to copy out Eskaya books that would later be bound by hand. She noted with wonder that the Taytay headman Fabian Baja could read and write only in Eskayan.

FIGURE 3.3. Eskaya men standing for the national anthem, Taytay, 1981 (photograph: Tito Gomez).

Impressed by the lively spectacle, Logarta was nonetheless dismissive of the esoteric claims of previous journalists as well as the testimony of the Eskaya themselves regarding the antiquity of their culture. The piece itself was not a wholesale vilification of the community, nor did it paint the Eskaya as the perpetrators of an elaborate hoax. Indeed, Logarta openly admired the tenacity of the Taytay community whose members subsisted in a virtually inaccessible part of the island, and she commended their commitment to maintaining their own cultural education without any government support.

But most astonishing were her own conclusions about the language. When she presented the linguist Ernesto Constantino with samples of Eskayan text, he commented, "It might be an artificial language invented by one person or a group of persons. Like disguised speech when you don't want people to know what you're saying. Actually, you are using your own native language with some distortions and additions." Her concluding explanation of the Eskaya phenomenon was permeated with an odd mixture of condescension, mockery, and sympathy:

[ . . . ] Baja and his followers continue to dream in their mountain aerie. That one day the government . . . the Ministry of Education . . . whoever will take heed and give them the roads they need to reach the flourishing lowland towns, repair their flimsy social hall so they can expand classes, shoulder the printing of Eskaya textbooks so no one will have to share, listen and encourage them for their puny efforts forging a language which they earnestly believe is 'sariling atin' [Tagalog: 'our very own']. If not, well they are content to wait again as they have for over 30 years. For people like them, accustomed to deprivation and neglect, there seems to be no other choice. (Logarta 1981)

Clearly Logarta was imputing a hidden motive for the community's promotion of its language. Poverty stricken and isolated in the mountains, the people of the village were desperate for any form of institutional development. Thus, the so-called Eskaya had developed a unique culture and exotic language with the sole aim of attracting government patronage.

Brenda Abregana, whose earlier foray into Taytay had drawn attention to the group, was greatly dismayed by Logarta's feature. Now curator of the recently opened Bohol Provincial Museum, Abregana responded to Logarta's feature in an outraged letter to the editor of *Who* (Brenda Abregana to Cielo B. Buenaventura, September 7, 1981). According to Abregana, questions over the authenticity of the Eskayan language had already been resolved by "older persons of authority like priests," who had confirmed that the language was still used in the forested interior of Bohol prior to World War II. While describing Logarta as a "gifted young writer with a touch of greatness even at the start of her career," Abregana obliquely criticized her apparent lack of academic qualifications and offered broad methodological advice. Calling once more for a formal and sponsored study of the Eskaya, she specified that the ideal researcher "does not tarry with his voluminous text references" and should instead be "possessed with a creatively active mind" (Abregna 1981).

For the next three years, there would be no more commentary on the Eskaya communities of Taytay and Biabas. This was likely due to the fact that the New People's Army (NPA), a communist guerrilla organization, had recently secured influence across the island's upland regions. Abregana's creatively active mind eventually resurfaced in the middle of 1984 when she drafted a detailed press release introducing the Eskaya as a mystical, secretive society descended from "Semitic" Etruscans. In March of the following year, she made another field trip to Taytay on her own initiative and reported her findings to the governor. She claimed to have passed through a restricted area controlled by communist insurgents to acquire three important Eskaya documents. The first of these was a notebook dated 1908 and written in English, Spanish, and Eskayan (Fig. 3.4). It is still in the possession of the museum. The others comprised a blue notebook containing the Eskaya alphabet, and a photocopy of prayers in Eskayan. These last texts have

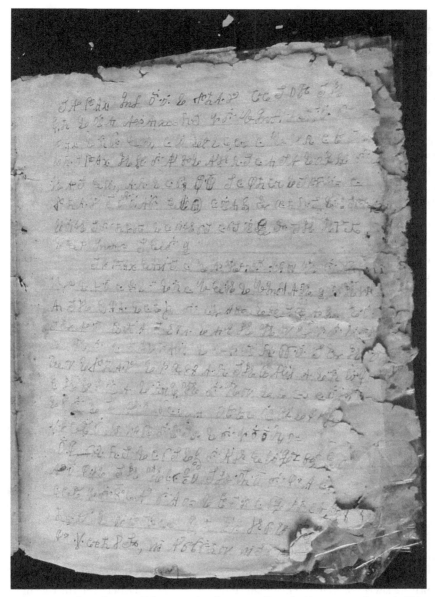

FIGURE 3.4. Page from an Eskaya notebook given to Brenda Abregana and now held by the Bohol Museum.

not been seen since 1993, but it was reported to me that they were retrieved by Fabian Baja and returned to Taytay (Alberta Galambao, personal communication). In any event, the documents bequeathed to the museum were relatively trivial artifacts in Abregana's view. The Eskaya, she maintained, were the likely guardians of the lost Book of Enoch, and another text that spoke of the past and future entitled *Ang Sagbut ni Marilen Kinadak-an ug Kinagamyan sa yuta* ("Grass of Marilen, the Biggest and the Smallest in the Land"). In her presence the Eskaya revealed ancient carvings that proved that unicorns existed and had once been used by humans for finding water. Another artifact depicted a creature known as a *salimao*, "smaller than a lion with a snout like a pig which possessed wings like the bat." She went on to reveal a deep secret intimated to her by the head Eskaya teacher, which she had promised to conceal under solemn oath, an oath she would now "have to violate for the sake of Science." Somewhere in the mountains of Bohol was the lost City of the Sun where the world's destiny was controlled by three judges, and goods could be obtained cheaply by all. The site of the city could not yet be disclosed since the world was about to be renewed. Far from merely reporting ethnographic details from local folklore, Abregana presented this information as a series of stand-alone facts for the urgent attention of the governor.

Talk of unicorns and winged pigs may not have been beyond the pale for the fantastical realm of Visayan tabloids, but some of those who knew her recall that in this period Abregana's grasp of reality was increasingly tenuous. An introvert who sometimes failed to recognize her children, Abregana rarely discussed her research openly (Fe Corazon C. Licong, personal communication). A visitor to the provincial museum recalled her as a "shaggy, uncombed woman, oblivious of the world's cares" (Deguit 1991), and under her curatorship she began to display mystical exhibits of doubtful historical worth.[4] Her report to Governor Butalid was to represent the last of her musings on the Eskaya before she suffered a stroke and passed away.

In the documentation of her visits to Taytay, Abregana had made mention of Mariano Datahan, but her only identified source of biographical information was a prominent lawyer by the name of Victoriano D. Tirol who was among those who founded the University of Bohol in 1946. Tirol, who died in 1992, was the private lawyer of Mariano Datahan, and a correspondence between the two men was preserved for some time in the university's museum. Tragically this was lost in 1999 when a fire destroyed most of the campus. Tirol's intellectual inclinations and passion for local history and culture were shared by several of his children. Victoriano Tirol Jr. wrote his Ph.D. on Boholano literature (1968), and his youngest daughter, Lumin Tirol, wrote hers on the history of Bohol (1975). His eighth child, Jes, was an engineer by training who had a great enthusiasm for language and history. This latter interest resulted in his publication of a detailed work of local history, *Bohol: From Spanish Yoke to American Harness*, in 1998.

However, Jes was best known as the oddball columnist for *The Bohol Chronicle*, sometimes under the rubric of 'Jestory,' where he still enjoys a large local following. From the late 1980s he regularly made the Eskaya the subject of historical essays, in which scholarly interest was interspersed with spiritual ruminations. As a child Jes had visited Biabas with his father and recalled hearing the language spoken spontaneously but was dismayed at its rapid decline (J.B. Tirol, personal communication).

A key event in Tirol's many columns on the Eskaya concerned the discovery of undeciphered writings in 1985. In April of that year two American biologists, led by Peace Corps volunteer Dennis Drake, explored the Inambacan cave near the town of Antequera (Map 3), where they found the writings carved on a mud bank. Intrigued by their reports, Tirol returned to the cave with Drake later in the month to see for himself. The short inscription, which could only be reached after a difficult three-hour crawl along a tunnel, was partially covered in stalagmites, suggesting great antiquity. Four years later, Tirol was to argue that the cave inscription was in Eskayan, and he offered his own multivalent decipherment of it (J.B. Tirol 1989).

In a brief interview with me in 2005, Dennis Drake, now director of Bohol's International Deaf Education Association (IDEA), gave more details about the second trip joined by Stephen Williams, a Vietnam veteran with a wooden leg, and Jes Tirol. Far from looking for ancient inscriptions, Drake recalls that Tirol was hoping to find a lost bell. Across the Philippines, storytellers recount tales of precious bells that were hidden by locals to prevent pirates from seizing them. The stories have many folkloric variations and additions, but the existence of such a lost artifact in Bohol is assumed by many locals to be a historical fact, and least one attempt was made to retrieve a bell from a river in the 1930s. As I will describe in Chapter 7, Eskaya scribes have even recorded a version of their own lost bell story with strong moral and anti-colonial resonances.

In Drake's recollection of the exploration, Tirol was forced to abandon a bulky rope he had taken with him, and as the team entered the narrowing tunnel they wound inner tubing around their knees to prevent injury from the jagged rocks protruding from the floor. After about an hour of crawling through the water the tunnel was completely submerged. In turn, each member of the party dived underwater to resurface in a small cavern where Drake recalled seeing the writings. Tirol, who had taken the precaution of wrapping his camera in a waterproof bag, took photos. Drake remembered that the cavern walls were lined with a soft, sticky clay that had the texture of wet soap; it was his view that the grooves photographed by Tirol could not have held their shape over a long time. This was an opinion independently expressed by local historian Marianito Luspo, who told me that he once whimsically carved out his family name on the muddy wall of the tunnel's entrance with his finger, remarking that if his imprint survived, its meaning would be a problem for future paleographers to puzzle over. Toward the end of 1990, Tirol referenced the expedition in a series of short articles in which he proposed that the Eskaya were a literate Semitic population who landed in Bohol in the seventh century, and that their language and script might be used as a crib for deciphering the Butuan silver strip, a paleographic artifact excavated by Jesus Peralta in Mindanao in 1976.

Later in the following year, the Eskaya attained minor celebrity status as the subjects of a feature in the inflight magazine of Philippine Airlines (Policarpio 1991). Illustrated with stunning photos of Taytay residents in full regalia, the article described the village as a rural idyll of cool mountain breezes and social harmony. Drawing largely on earlier press commentaries, the article informed readers that the group came from west Sumatra and that their language had survived thanks to the legendary Mariano Datahan, a man credited with superhuman talents.

## Institutional tribehood

The Eskaya were not to be recognized by any agencies of the national government until the Office for Southern Cultural Communities (OSCC) was formed in 1987. In this year, the University of Bohol presented the new body with 'write ups' about the Eskaya that became the basis of approved development projects for the group when an OSCC service center was established in Tagbilaran the following year.[5] The OSCC later compiled a seven-page report, much of which was derived from Abregana's writings, but there were also a number of new ethnographic particulars presumably recorded from visits to Taytay by OSCC staff in circa 1991 (Fig. 3.5).[6] The population of Taytay was given as 344, with a long series of age brackets broken down into percentages. Houses were described as being made of wood with either galvanized iron or *kugun* ('wild grass') roofing. The traditional dress of the Eskaya was, for women, a white long-sleeved blouse, a colored skirt, and a white headscarf. They kept their hair long, according to custom, and were described in phenotypical terms as having a "white complexion with good and round-shaped face" (3). Men wore a *tirnu* ('suit') comprised of a long-sleeved shirt, long pants, and a hat. The hard-working character of the Eskaya was remarked upon. Their humble houses were kept in immaculate condition, and their toil produced an abundance of vegetables, rice, and fruit. A section of common land was set aside for the benefit of the community and was worked every Monday on a rotational basis.

FIGURE 3.5. Office for Southern Cultural Communities (OSCC) survey in Taytay ca. 1991 (photograph courtesy of the NCIP).

Eskayan was here categorized, relaying Abregana's exact words, as "the language supposedly of the pre-Spanish Boholanos" (1), but the OSCC document did not suggest an exotic origin of the language from outside Bohol. Until this time, the Eskaya, among other lately registered Indigenous Cultural Communities (ICCs), had not necessarily regarded themselves as a 'tribe' (or *tribu*), but the new bureaucracy required that they behave like one, at least on paper, in order to benefit from government services. Thus, a Tribal Council composed of Tribal Chieftain, was formed as an administrative necessity. One of Mariano Datahan's surviving sons, Juan, was appointed chieftain of Biabas and neighboring Lundag, Fabian Baja became chieftain of Taytay, and Julio Sajol was made chieftain of nearby Cantaub (Sisinio Amplayo, personal communication; see Map 4). Elpidio Palaca, a professed practitioner of prehispanic animist ceremonies, was later installed as the official Tribal Bishop or **biki**.

More than a mere mark on paper, the formal encoding of the Eskaya as a 'tribe' was to be a pivotal event that marked out a new terrain of political action. The recently appointed Eskaya leadership adopted their tribal identity with seriousness and used it as a mechanism for negotiating with the outside world. This important political moment brought into clarity the paradoxical character of tribehood that scholars have long remarked upon. Scott, for example, argued that the category 'tribe' is a more-or-less arbitrary designation that serves to reduce uncertainty and facilitate the governance of stateless people. For the disempowered members of such groupings, on the other hand, the tribe could become a "mode of claim-making" serving the same purpose as a "trade union, a corporation, or a craft guild" (Scott 2009, 257). Yet even if such groups may sometimes have more administrative than cultural coherence, there is no reason why the 'tribe' might not also become a genuine source of identity, the rallying point for an imagined community of others with shared experiences and goals. Eskaya leaders certainly invested in the concept of the tribe as a lived reality (see for example Fig. 3.6), but this came with its own disadvantages. Critics of the group now had a target to attack, while the Eskaya stood on territory that required defense. Moreover, the loaded term 'tribe' provided outsiders with a screen on which to project their own prejudices or fantasies of the tribal lifestyle, and the Eskaya were not always well equipped to challenge these characterizations.

As it happened, shortly after the new terminology was introduced, the legal status of the Eskaya as an Indigenous Cultural Community was disputed by the National Museum, prompting the editor of the *Bohol Chronicle* to commission a series of articles on the subject from Jes Tirol. In the first of these articles, "Eskaya of Bohol: Is it a tribe?," he argued that the National Museum had questioned the legitimacy of the Eskaya as a tribe simply because, in his words, they were "practically indistinguishable" from other Boholanos in appearance. As for the earlier accusation that the Eskaya were a cult, this was patently untrue. Instead, they were members of the Iglesia Filipina Independiente even if they practiced an "early revolutionary form of that church."

**FIGURE 3.6.** Eskaya teachers bearing the sign 'Tribal Leaders: Eskaya' marching at the Sandugo festival in Tagbilaran, ca. 1991 (photograph: courtesy of the NCIP).

Until this 1993 article, Tirol had never used the term 'tribe' to describe the Eskaya.[7] Here, however, he was at pains to point out that the Eskaya were not "a primitive tribe like the Aeta or Badjao but rather a highly developed tribe similar to the Biblical twelve tribes of Israel, which is practically the role model of the Eskaya." A few years earlier he was thanked in the introduction to a curious work of outsider history by Josemaria Salutan Luengo (1991) that suggested that *all* Filipinos were descended from wandering Semitic tribes and that the Eskaya of Bohol were merely the last to renounce their early tribal customs. Tirol nonetheless advised that the Eskaya did not use the word 'tribe' at all, preferring instead to be understood as a 'cultural minority', and to be called 'Bisayan Declarado' instead of 'Visayan Eskaya' or any other term. In essence, the Eskaya viewed themselves primarily as the original Boholanos who continued to practice early Boholano culture.

Three days after this was published, Zosimo Campos, the Regional Director of the OSCC, wrote a letter to Undersecretary Lorenzo Dinlayan at the Central Office of the OSCC in Manila (Campos 1993). His aim was to clarify rumors that the Central Office had obtained an "unofficial" report suggesting that the Eskaya were "not true ICC." Campos appealed to Dinlayan to intervene, drawing attention to the fact that if the Eskaya claim of indigeneity were proved untenable, resources directed toward their development could be more fairly allocated to other minorities in the region.

## A formal alliance and a lost report

The controversy ultimately failed to interfere with the fledgling partnership between the government and the Eskaya; in February of 1996 President Fidel Ramos himself formally presented the community with a Certificate of Ancestral Domain Claim (CADC), a document that granted negotiating rights over 3,173 hectares of land (see Map 4). A photo of the ceremony shows Fabian Baja in the embroidered headwear known as a *kupya* characteristic of village headmen in Mindanao, sartorially overpowered by the president's floral necklace ("Ramos' visit to Bohol," *Sun Star Daily*, February 7, 1996). By the following year, the Congress of the Philippines passed the Indigenous Peoples Rights Act (IPRA), which mandated the merging of the OSCC into a new entity called the National Commission on Indigenous Peoples (NCIP). The Act formalized a process for cultural minorities to gain rights over their ancestral lands, not dissimilar to Australia's Native Title Act. In essence, a group could make a claim over a territory on the basis of continued occupation, and this claim might subsequently progress to a Determination of Title. The Act also stipulated that any claim area that had been delineated by the Department of Environment and Natural Resources (DENR) *prior* to the enactment of IPRA—as per the Eskaya claim—would remain in place and was exempt from satisfying the new provisions contained in the Act.

Not long before IPRA's official enactment in September of 1997, the OSCC compiled a 105-page *Ancestral Domain Management Plan* (Office for Southern Cultural Communities ca. 1996; date is deduced from content), loaded with statistical data, development plans, and a long list of customary tribal laws. Of the 597 households surveyed in the report, only 24 were living above the poverty line. The causes of this poverty were itemized as follows: "usury or exploitation by businessman, lack of capital, outmoded agricultural tools and lack of courage" (Office for Southern Cultural Communities ca. 1996, 23). Consistent with the neoliberalizing development rhetoric of the era, the Eskaya were implicated in their own poverty, having "lost their initiative to improve their living" (Office for Southern Cultural Communities ca. 1996, 23). As an unfortunate consequence of this, they were engaging in environmentally destructive slash-and-burn swidden farming. The compilers of the report went on to explain that indigenous peoples throughout the Philippines were also responsible for their experience of discrimination: "They have been deprived of human rights and fundamental freedom due to the fact that they feel inferior to other members of society. This is due to lack of education and information among the IPs [Indigenous Peoples] regarding the inroad of civilization in the country." (Office for Southern Cultural Communities ca. 1996, 72–73). The document mentioned the formation of the Tribal Council, and shortly after its publication, new Eskaya chieftains were to be appointed for villages beyond Biabas and Taytay that had mixed Eskaya and non-Eskaya populations.

The damaging report that Zosimo Campos had referred to in 1993 never materialized, but the issue did not go away. In 2005, the new regional director for Region VII, Alfonso Catolin, wrote directly to Jesus Peralta at the Anthropology Division of the National Museum, pressing for more details.

Peralta responded:

Dear Director Catolin:

The National Museum's Anthropology Division did conduct a study on the Eskaya in Bohol some years back in which I was involved. The study was intensive and included documentation of whatever information and literature there are about the group. These materials are with the National Museum.

The general findings are that the Eskaya is a quasi-group/pseudo-group, more of a cult rather than a distinct ethnic group. What distinguishes an ethnic group primarily is the language that they speak, since language is the culture bearer. The people in their daily conversation use Boholano and their general culture is in fact also Boholano with central Visayan characteristics.

The so-called Eskaya language is only taught in their schools, and not actually used domestically. All languages in the Philippines at present belong to the Austronesian family of languages, specifically the Malayo-Polynesian branch. The so-called Eskaya language has no relationship whatever with this family of languages. Strangely enough even though the group is located in Bohol, their so-called language has no affinities with the surrounding languages—a situation that is rather incredible.

A lexico-statistical computer-generated modeling shows that Eskaya has an index of affinity with Boholano by only 0.1114865; and with Cebuano, only 0.0855019—which shows practically zero affinity. A cross-check on the word list done on this group by Mr. Ederick Miano of the Cebu Branch of the National Museum showed that there are no words in the list of at least 70 words common to Philippine languages. The language, in effect, is artificially devised, like a secret code by the core of a group of people.

The Eskaya script also has no relationship with any of the ancient forms of writing in the Philippines, nor even with those existing in the rest of Asia—which again makes it incredible. This writing was devised by one man named Pinay, by their own admission, which makes it an invention rather than being one that is evolved by a culture. [ ... ]

Nothing of their claims to a distinct ethnicity like, for instance, the Ifugao, Maranao, Cebuano, etc. can be validated anthropologically. *The people merely belongs to the Boholano ethnicity—a distinct segment of that due to their intimacy of contact with each other, and nothing more* [Peralta's emphasis]. The group can be regarded like the Moncado colony that existed formerly in Lanao del Sur. This is like saying that the Hanglulu or Yattuka are not distinct ethnic groups but are merely members of the Ifugao ethnicity.

[ ... ]

Best Regards.
Dr. Jesus T. Peralta
Consultant NCCA
(Peralta to Catolin, February 23, 2005)

By the time I interviewed Peralta in February 2006 the study he referred to in this letter could no longer be found in the archives of the Anthropology Division.[8] If this document had been acquired by the OSCC prior to 1987, the relationship between the Eskaya community and the Philippine government might well have followed a very different trajectory. Instead, Peralta's letter and the summary it contained became a tricky point of contention that developed between the Region VII office of the NCIP in Iloilo City, Panay, and the Eskaya Tribal Council in Bohol. Since a Certificate of Ancestral Domain Claim had already been issued by the DENR, the negotiating rights it entailed remained beyond dispute. But the Tribal Council's application for title became mired in stalemate as the status of the group vis-à-vis IPRA was reduced to a matter of minute legal interpretation.[9] The deadlock is unresolved to this day, despite a House Resolution submitted to congress by the Bayan Muna Party on January 20, 2009, "Urging the Committee on National Cultural Minorities to conduct an investigation, in aid of legislation, on the various controversies, including the decline of their linguistic and cultural traditions, that hound the indigenous Eskaya tribe, the cultural minority on the island of Bohol."[10]

## Eskaya responses and a new research agenda

To the dismay of many within the tribal leadership, the word 'Eskaya' has been adapted for local commercial ventures that have exploited its connotations of naturalness and the exotic. The most notable of these is the Eskaya Beach Resort & Spa, an ultra-exclusive resort in Panglao (Map 3) with a logo that incorporates the Eskaya script. The word has also been appropriated, without permission, as a brand name for a range of tiles and a style of bikini. A more welcome adaptation was proposed by Boholano actor Cesar Montano, who announced plans to produce a movie featuring the Eskaya, under the working title *Eskaya: The Quick Brown Fox*. The draft storyline concerns a wealthy American who is falsely accused of a crime and is forced to pursue the only witness into Bohol's forests, where he encounters the Eskaya tribe. Montano, who appeared in the Hollywood action feature *The Great Raid* (2005), was keen to enroll an A-list actor "like Brad Pitt or Tom Cruise," with Filipino champion boxer Manny Pacquiao in the lead role (Cruz 2009). Montano has discussed these plans with the Tribal Council though nothing has yet eventuated.

Eskaya voices are conspicuously scarce in media bulletins and government documents. From my interviews with Eskaya teachers it is clear that they were neither oblivious nor indifferent to the earlier attention surrounding their community and its language. Editions of *Bisaya* magazine and *Mabuhay* found their way to Taytay and Biabas at the time of publication, and the coverage was generally regarded as positive. However, core elements of theories suggested by Abregana and Tirol ran counter to prevailing orthodox views within the community. The ancestors of the Eskaya, for example, were unambiguously understood to have arrived from western Sumatra and not from far-flung locations in Europe or the Middle East. The language meanwhile was quintessentially Boholano, having been divinely transmitted to the people through the vessel of Pinay, recognized as their first **inmunsiktur** ('Pope'). These Eskaya perspectives are described in greater detail in Chapters 4 and 7.

However, the outsider views of Abregana and Tirol were never wholly rejected and are still considered by many Eskaya leaders as acceptable expansions of a fluid historical consciousness. Indeed, a framed copy of Tirol's "Eskaya of Bohol: Is it a tribe?" (1993) hangs in the schoolroom in Taytay to this day. For Hilario Galambao, current chieftain of Taytay, the views expressed in that article are not consonant with Eskaya beliefs, although he was hesitant to be specific. The importance of the text, for Galambao, lay in the attention and recognition it brought to his community. On the other hand, Logarta's article (1981) was experienced by many as a devastating betrayal, particularly her characterization of the Eskaya as a cult. More than a decade after her feature appeared, a researcher visiting Taytay commented that Logarta was remembered with great bitterness (Martinez 1993).

The formation under IPRA of a Tribal Council, headed by Col. Roberto Datahan, granted the community a mechanism for presenting a unified position in the face of public and governmental skepticism. A respected former police colonel, Roberto Datahan is a grand-nephew of Mariano Datahan, and although he was not raised within Eskaya culture, he has positioned himself as the principal advocate for the group since his retirement from the police force; under IPRA he takes the title of Federated Provincial Tribal Chieftain and in day-to-day life he has adopted the honorific *datu*, meaning 'chief' or 'headman.' His distance from the cultural activities of the community is not unusual, reflecting a division that has emerged in upland minorities elsewhere in the southern Philippines between 'cultural *datus*' and 'government *datus*': the latter taking responsibility for interactions with state bureaucracies (Paredes 2019).

Datahan has welcomed almost all the past commentary on the Eskaya, regardless of the contradictory positions. Like Galambao, he has not insisted on a single orthodox narrative, and he has been active in facilitating research in the Eskaya Ancestral Domain, including my own work. In his view, the more research that is completed, the better his community will be understood.

Jesus Peralta's perspective, as expressed in his letter to Alfonso Catolin, was not, however, accepted, and together with Tribal Bishop Elpidio Palaca, Datahan officially responded with an eight-page 'Joint Manifestation' that was sent to several branches of the NCIP in 2005. Together with their own personal testimonies, the two men rallied almost all previous commentaries on their community, no matter how speculative, in order to defend against the charge of being a cult. Above all, they were adamant that surviving shamanic practices in Bohol stood as evidence of a continuous indigenous culture that had been protected from colonial interference (see Chapter 2).[11] What is of special interest in both Peralta's letter and the rebuttal to it is the emphasis on language. As the "culture bearer," Peralta treated language in terms typical of sociolinguistic naturalism, asserting that it carried the burden of proof for ethnic identity and authenticity. Doubling down on this position, he argued that by using computational comparative methods, any language relationship could be statistically quantified and its speakers "validated anthropologically." Datahan and Palaca, meanwhile, did not reject the premise out of hand but had different criteria for linguistic validation. Their response treated the *script* as the genuine embodiment of language and associated it genealogically with the Egyptian, Phoenician, Arabic, Javanese, and Hebrew writing systems.[12] Just like Peralta they understood language to be a palpable and verifiable object, unaffected by human will and capable of revealing a social reality by neutral means (see Gal and Irvine 1995).

With encouragement from the Eskaya leadership, a number of Filipino graduate students with varying interests and experiences pursued further research in the Eskaya villages. Two of these stand out as being especially important, both for their serious engagement with Eskaya language and literature and their centering of Eskaya people in the research process. The first, Milan Ted Torralba, was a seminarian at the University of Santo Tomas in Manila when he began drafting preliminary grammatical and lexical descriptions of Eskayan through structured interviews with speakers. His aim was to investigate the history of the language and in particular to address the hypothesis that Eskayan was related to languages outside the Philippines (Torralba 1991a, 1991b). Keen to undertake a master's dissertation in linguistics, he later submitted a detailed thesis proposal (Torralba 1993). Sadly, his superiors urged him to abandon this work and pursue canon law instead, but he never lost interest in the question. The second graduate student was Cristina Martinez, whose comparative literature thesis of 1993 included a small amount of linguistic data but focused largely on the stories recorded in Eskaya manuscripts, which she analyzed as unique products of postcolonial folk literature. Her incisive and ethnographic analysis of this literature, in its Visayan-language versions, did not touch on the status of the Eskayan language itself, although she was prepared to hypothesize that it was "a highly acculturated linguistic phenomenon, probably overdetermined by an ideology of a single person, probable traces of some linguistic data that may have pre-hispanic origins, and a communal response to a post-colonial situation" (Martinez 1993, 145–146). The possibility of an artificial origin for Eskayan was described by Martinez in admiring terms: "If the language is a pure concoction, then the concoction is even more incredible. The highly consistent lexicon, the syntax, the texts. [ . . . ] The pure gumption that is involved in this highly elaborate, meticulously implemented agenda" (Martinez 1993, 68).[13]

Those lowlanders who independently tried to make sense of the Eskaya people and their language in the 1980s and 1990s generated a surprising array of perspectives, ranging from the fantastical to the dismissive to the scholarly. As I have shown, early theories that Eskayan was related to Hebrew among other "ancient" or exotic languages accorded with Spanish-era intellectual traditions of linguistic prehistory in the Philippines. Similarly, Abregana's hypothesis that Eskayan was the first language in the world was consistent with the earlier European views that all the world's languages were descended from a common tongue. Others with a less miraculous bent preferred to view the Eskayan language and its literary expressions as subjects of academic inquiry embedded in a more widely accepted historical context. In different ways, these positions and polemics informed the earliest interactions between the Eskaya and the national government apparatus and set the terms by which the group was to become legible as an administrative entity. They also provided a set of ready-made narratives for the Eskaya tribal leadership to draw on in their official representations and public defenses.

In Part II, which follows, all these competing characterizations are set aside in order to look more closely at the Eskayan language itself. I introduce the ways in which Eskayan is used today in its proper communicative context (Chapter 4), preceding a clear linguistic description of its formal features, from its sound system and writing system (Chapter 5) to its grammar and lexicon (Chapter 6). Finally, I describe and analyze the complex body of Eskaya literature (Chapter 7) in order to identify how the history of the Eskayan language is traditionally understood by Eskaya people in their own words. I show how these oral and written narratives are used to explain past conflicts, foreshadow future transformations, and to assert a special place in the world for the Eskayan language and its speakers.

## Notes

1. These were made available to me by Col. Roberto Datahan and can be accessed at http://catalog.paradisec.org.au/repository/PK2/08/PK2-08-GOV10.pdf.
2. All early media reports on the Eskaya are now digitized and available via PARADISEC at https://catalog.paradisec.org.au/collections/PK2/items/09, DOI: 10.4225/72/5703EABD74AF0.
3. "[ . . . ] kay ang mga butang nga karaan diin nahilambigit ang atong kultura sa kanhiay, angay mang masayran sa mga ulahing kaliwatan" (Amparado 1981, 55).

4. This was conveyed to me by Marianito Luspo (personal communication) and corroborated by Cristina Martinez, who described her as "a quaint old lady who has devoted almost an entire lifetime curating for a museum which contains artifacts with no national museum value" (Martinez 1993, 229).

5. Campos (1993).

6. Citation data is missing for this typed report kept in the NCIP service center in Bohol. In the report, the age of Fabian Baja is given as seventy-three. As Baja was born in 1918 it is likely that it was compiled in circa 1991. In the bibliography of Martinez (1993) there is an OSCC document dated 1989 with the title "An Eskayan Profile." I have been unable to locate this text, but it is conceivably the same document, incorrectly dated, or a forerunner to it. Surviving photographs of OSCC fieldwork are remembered by teachers in Taytay as having been taken in 1991.

7. In a previous essay entitled "Eskaya of Bohol: Traces of Hebrew Influence Paving the Way for Easy Christianization of Bohol" (1991) Jes Tirol wrote that the Eskaya "are recognized by the government as a tribal group or cultural minority," but he here chose to focus on proving that the community was a displaced Hebrew enclave as opposed to an indigenous Filipino tribe.

8. The actual date of the report is unknown. In the interview, Peralta told me he thought it was compiled sometime in the 1970s. This was also the recollection of Artemio Barbosa, curator of the Anthropology Division. Of the six pages in the possession of Col. Roberto Datahan, none are dated, but there is mention of a seventy-one-year-old man from Biabas referred to as "Mang Masyong." If his identity and birth year can be found, this would clarify the age of the report. The pages from Roberto Datahan's collection can be accessed at http://catalog.paradisec.org.au/repository/PK2/08/PK2-08-GOV10.pdf.

9. Within IPRA, ICCs and Indigenous Peoples (IPs) were defined in any of three ways: (a) a group of people who recognized themselves as a group and had continuously occupied an area of land while sharing language, culture, and traditions since time immemorial; or (b) those who had culturally resisted colonization to the extent that they had become historically differentiated from other Filipinos; or (c) those who were descended from prehispanic populations and who had retained some of their social, economic, cultural, and political institutions.

10. From House Resolution 943, introduced on January 20, 2009, by Bayan Muna representatives Satur C. Ocampo and Teodoro A. Casiño, Anakpawis representative Rafael V. Mariano, and Gabriela representatives Luzviminda C. Ilagan and Liza L. Maza. The text of the house resolution was copied almost entirely from the Wikipedia entry on the Eskaya, as it stood in 2009.

11. In their rebuttal (available at http://catalog.paradisec.org.au/repository/PK2/08/PK2-08-GOV03.pdf) Datahan and Palaca argued that Eskaya were the original settlers of Bohol from whom "mainstream" Boholanos had later split. The Eskayan script bore similarities to Egyptian, Phoenician, Arabic, Javanese, and Hebrew

writing systems, as well as the script found on the Butuan silver strip. Tirol's 1985 exploration of the Inambacan cave bore out these connections. As for known Filipino scripts, there were marked points of comparison with those reproduced in Paterno's "Cuadro Paleografico" (see Fig. 2.1). The language itself was connected to Sanskrit, and a short comparative table of Eskayan and Sanskrit numbers was provided to illustrate this. The "great leader" Mariano Datahan secured permission to teach in Eskayan from President Manuel Quezon in 1937. During the Spanish era, the authorities had a policy of arresting any practitioners of Eskaya culture as *insuriktus* ('rebels'), leading both Tamblot and Dagohoy to fight back and protect the native *babaylan* ('shamanic') religion. Because of the Dagohoy rebellion the territorial integrity of the present Eskaya Ancestral Domain survived intact. Further, this *babaylan* religion was still present in other parts of Bohol and witnessed in beliefs concerning the *tambalan* ('medicine men') and *diwatahan* ('nature spirits'). Babaylan chapels could still be found in Fatima, Timawa, and Balingasao, though many Eskaya had now converted to the Philippine Independent Church. Artifacts were held in the Museo Nacional in Madrid, proving that Boholanos had a distinct language and alphabet, and that they possessed ancient documents prior to the arrival of the Spanish. This was ascertained from the museum's director, during her recent visit to Bohol. No response from the regional office of the NCIP was forthcoming.

Several months later, Col. Datahan lodged a bid to extend the borders of the Ancestral Domain Claim into villages of mixed Eskaya populations. This was vigorously opposed by the Mayor of Candijay, who argued that Eskaya presence in these villages was due to recent intermarriage and that there was no evidence of long-term occupation. The issue was referred to the Committee on General Resolutions, which ruled against Col. Datahan ("Group Claims Territory in the Name of Eskayas" 2005).

12. This may be have been influenced by Aglipayan ideas. In his *Biblia Filipina*, the eccentric ilustrado Pedro Paterno positioned the Iglesia Filipina Independiente as the inheritor of the old literate traditions of "Assyrian Chaldea, Persia, Egypt, Syria, Phoenicia, India, China and other peoples as ancient as the Hebrews" (cited in Mojares 2006a, 329).

13. Other graduate students were Aida Hinlo (1992), Stella Consul (2005), Proceso Orcullo (2004), and Regina Estorba (2004), whose work is sometimes referred to in later chapters but is of less immediate relevance to the history of the Eskayan language and script. Hinlo's (1992) thesis was a proposal for a tribal education project aimed at raising literacy standards. Proceso Orcullo (2004) took a sociological approach to the Biabas community using quantitative survey methods, Stella Consul wrote the foundations of a sketch grammar (Consul 2005), while Regina Estorba's paper (Estorba 2006) was an ethnographic take on gender in Taytay.

# LANGUAGE, LETTERS, LITERATURE

*"You write in hieroglyphics! And why?"* the young man asked, doubting what he was seeing and hearing.

*"So that they won't be able to read me now."* Ibarra was regarding Tasio with attention, debating whether the old man was mad. He examined the book rapidly to see if the old man did not lie, and saw well-drawn animals, circles and semicircles, flowers, feet, hands, arms, and so forth.

*"And why then do you write if you don't want to be read?"*

*"Because I do not write for this generation. I write for other ages. If the present one were able to read me, they would burn my books, the work of a lifetime; on the other hand, the generation that can decipher these characters would be an educated generation; they would understand me and would say: "Not all slept during the night of our ancestors." The mystery, or these curious characters, will save my work from the ignorance of men, as the mystery and the strange rites have saved many truths from the destructive priestly class."*

*"And in what language are you writing?"* asked Ibarra after a brief pause.

*"In our own, in Tagalog."*

—JOSÉ RIZAL, *Noli me tangere* (1886)

# 4 HOW ESKAYAN IS USED TODAY

I remember the first time I heard Eskayan spoken out loud. It was on January 26, 2006, on the anniversary of Mariano Datahan's death, and I was seated in a cramped single room school in Biabas listening to speeches from leaders who had gathered from across the Eskaya villages. Visayan dominated these addresses, but when Eskayan was spoken by the more senior orators the assembled guests became still and parents hushed their children. I felt as fixated by the sounds of the language as everyone else. By that time my arrival in the uplands had already been delayed by three months, but I had profited from the enforced absence to explore archives and familiarize myself with lowlander debates and intrigues. To be hearing, at last, those mysterious words with their multi-syllabic roots and dense consonant clusters felt like a vindication. Here, on this bare hill, the much-mythologized language was alive and defiant.

In this chapter I will describe, in plain terms, the wider linguistic context of Eskayan and provide an overview of language use in the field site as I experienced it. My chief interest is in communication as a practice, with an emphasis on linguistic repertoires, channels, and domains. As I will show, the Eskayan language is used for highly circumscribed purposes. Spoken Eskayan is employed for teaching and learning, praying, singing, and speech-making. However, the most consistent domain of the Eskayan language use is in writing; it is through the reading and reproduction of traditional Eskaya literature that the language achieves its fullest expression. Eskaya people consider writing to be a true and sacred embodiment of their language to such a degree that altering Eskayan text is prohibited, even when the text contains errors. Given the importance of written practice, it is only briefly introduced in this chapter so that it can be described much more thoroughly in Chapter 5, where I analyze the Eskaya writing system, and in Chapter 7, which concerns Eskaya scribal activities and the interpretation of Eskaya texts.

*The Last Language on Earth*. Kelly, Piers, Oxford University Press. © Oxford University Press 2022.
DOI: 10.1093/oso/9780197509913.003.0004

In the present chapter I show how the Visayan language of the southern Philippines is made up of a number of dialects of which Boholano-Visayan is regarded as distinctive on lexical grounds, even though no substantial description of this dialect is available. Within Boholano-Visayan the sound [ʤ] is a marked regionalism that has come to index rural backwardness and informality, but also a more authentic and distinctly Boholano voice. In Bohol at large, English is used as a complement to Visayan in educational settings, administrative activities, media, church services, and formal speech-making. Tagalog, and other languages, have a more limited range. The island is also home to several ritual registers and playful varieties of disguised speech.

I point out that within the Eskaya villages, Boholano-Visayan is the dominant variety for most ordinary domains while full competence in English is relatively rare. The Eskayan language, meanwhile, is used for prayer, singing, speech-making, traditional education, and writing. In other words, it occupies the same space as English does in lowland settings.

Unlike Boholano-Visayan, which is acquired as a mother tongue, knowledge of Eskayan is learned through voluntary attendance at traditional Eskaya schools, and mastery of the language is considered a prerequisite for becoming truly Eskaya. In this way the acquisition of Eskayan is mediated through an ideological conception of language as a product of intellectual effort, and as an object to be attained through diligence and determination.

## Bohol in the Visayas

Prior to Spanish contact in the sixteenth century, Visayans were largely a coastal, seafaring people who maintained regular inter-island contact through trade, marriage, war, and slave raiding. Like other coastal groups of the Philippines, the Visayans engaged in fishing and swidden farming, importing luxury goods from Siam, South China, and India (Santiago 2003). The catch-all term 'Visayan'—or Bisaya' in the language itself—can be used to designate either a linguistic, ethnic, geographic, or administrative entity, though there is no neat correspondence between these categories. In its administrative sense, the Visayan archipelago includes the territory of the major central islands of the Philippines, namely, Panay, Negros, Cebu, Bohol, Leyte, Samar, and Palawan, as well as smaller islands in their vicinity.

The Visayan language, which is estimated to have at least sixteen million speakers, is usually understood to encompass the dialects of Cebuano-Visayan, Boholano-Visayan, Samar-Leyte-Visayan, and Mindanao-Visayan (Map 2).[1] Differences between these varieties are minimal (Wolff 1972a, vii); however, major languages of the Visayas such as Waray (spoken on Samar) and Hiligaynon

(Negros Occidental and Panay) can also fall under the designation *Bisaya'* despite a more significant distance in intelligibility. Visayan is used as a regional lingua franca throughout Mindanao, as well as the northern islands of Sulawesi (Map 1).

By present convention, many linguists use the term 'Cebuano' to refer to all the close Visayan varieties spoken on Cebu, Bohol, Negros Oriental, southern Leyte, and coastal Mindanao. Since the distinctions between these varieties are relevant to the present study, I am using the speaker-preferred term 'Visayan' (*Bisaya'*) to denote the language as a whole and am differentiating each dialect by region (Cebuano-Visayan, Boholano-Visayan, etc.; see Map 2).[2] Historical linguists agree that Visayan belongs to the Malayo-Polynesian branch of the Austronesian family. It is the most widely spoken language of the Bisayan subgroup of this branch (Zorc 1977). The linguistic classification is borne out by genetic and archeological evidence. Originally from Taiwan, the early Austronesians are believed to have moved south to populate Luzon, the Visayas, Mindanao, and Indonesia (5100 BP) then entered the Pacific (3550 BP) before reaching as far east as Rapanui (700–900 BP).[3] Evidence of the earliest human habitation of Bohol, however, is estimated to date from the Late Pleistocene (Santiago 2003), roughly 50,000 BP. Whatever language the ancient Boholanos were speaking, it could not have been genetically related to today's Boholano-Visayan, introduced by the settler Austronesians arriving from the north, although it may have had a substratum influence on the Visayan spoken in the region today.

Bohol's heavy limestone composition has resulted in a distinctive topography of conical, evenly sized hills in the island's interior. This limestone also accounts for the island's numerous underground cave systems and springs, and one popular explanation for the Bohol's name is that it is derived from the Visayan word *buhu'* ('hole'). Roads connecting inland settlements to the lowlands and to the major port towns of Tagbilaran and Guindulman were not constructed until the late nineteenth century, and travel by carriage was difficult even on the coastal roads (J.B. Tirol 1998, 13–15). Easy access to Bohol's two main ports of Tagbilaran and Guindulman remained out of reach for most Boholanos well into the twentieth century. Since the 1970s successive provincial governments have initiated road-building projects in the uplands around Biabas and Taytay for the dual purposes of counterinsurgency and poverty alleviation by means of improved transport infrastructure. However, travel through this rugged and landslide-prone region of Bohol remains difficult, especially in the rainy months.

Bohol's soil is not as fertile as that of neighboring islands, a fact remarked upon by the U.S. administration in the early years of its occupation (*RPC* 1901, vol. 3, 96).[4] Rice is still imported to Bohol from elsewhere in the Philippines to supplement demand. Although the island's main export is limestone, most Boholanos are employed in agriculture, and the primary crops are rice, corn, *kamuti*, and *ubi* (root vegetable varieties). About half of Bohol's population of 1.25 million lives below the poverty threshold. As in other parts of the Philippines, Bohol's economy receives additional support from Filipino overseas workers, known as *balik-bayan* (Tagalog: 'returnees'), who send remittances to their relatives at home. Tourism has recently emerged as a strong industry, particularly on the island of Panglao, which is joined to the mainland by a bridge near Tagbilaran (Map 3). The reefs surrounding Panglao (Map 3) are home to rare marine species and are popular with scuba divers from around the world.

Lying in the shadow of the more prosperous and culturally dominating island of Cebu, Boholanos like to emphasize their distinctiveness by elevating certain values they judge to be lacking in Cebuanos. The perceived fast-living lifestyle of Cebu, for example, is contrasted with the conservatism and Christian piety held to be characteristic of Bohol. It is a matter of regional pride that Bohol's Catholic seminaries 'export' priests to other islands, and it is frequently (but erroneously) asserted that the stone church at Baclayon is the oldest in the Philippines. In the two shopping malls in Tagbilaran, prerecorded Catholic prayers are broadcast over the speaker system for vespers at 6:00 pm; shoppers and retail workers stop still and bow their heads for the duration of the broadcast. Cebuanos, in turn, disparage Boholanos as parochial and are amused by the fact that there is a separate anthem for every major town of Bohol. Boholanos working on neighboring islands will often return home to celebrate a string of regional fiestas in May. It is a well-worn Cebuano joke that heaven itself empties on May 1, because all the Boholanos go home.

## Language use in Bohol

The lexicon of Boholano-Visayan is considered, by popular reputation, to have many terms that are not found in other Visayan varieties.[5] To date, no dialect survey of Bohol has ever been carried out; however, Boholanos often drew my attention to minor lexical variation within the island itself.[6] One short study (Tinampay 1977) divides Boholano-Visayan into eastern and western varieties, which are distinguished on phonological grounds.[7] The most socially marked of these distinctions is between the sound [y], and its variant [ʤ] (as heard at the beginning and end of the word 'judge'). Thus, for example, in the west of Bohol the pronoun *siya* ('she'/'he') is realized as [siya], while in the east it is typically, but not always, pronounced [siʤa]. The specific variation between [y] and its optional allophonic variant [ʤ] is witnessed only in word-medial environments.[8]

East Boholanos avoid [ʤ] in formal situations and will switch to [y] or use a mixture of the two. When reading aloud from a text, for example, it is common to favor [y], perhaps because standard Visayan orthography encourages this pronunciation. While doing transcription work, I noticed that consultants would use [dʒ] while providing an oral gloss for a Visayan word but would 'correct' to [y] when reading back over a transcription. In elite circles [dʒ] was once considered indexical of rural backwardness, but today Boholanos from both sides of the island are heard to comment that [dʒ] represents the authentically Boholano form, while [y] is a latter-day introduction from Cebu. Whatever the truth of this assertion, both east and west Boholanos who wish to emphasize their Boholano identity, such as folk singers or politicians, will make conspicuous use of [dʒ] as form of "covert prestige" (Labov [1966] 2006). Consistent with the sociolinguistic phenomenon of 'hyperdialectism' (Trudgill 1986), the sound is even hypercorrected into word-initial environments where it would not otherwise be phonologically predicted. The Visayan idiom *yamu-yamu gyud* ('really nothing at all'), for example, is commonly realized as [dʒamu dʒamu dʒud] as a humorous way of asserting a local identity. The conspicuous use of [dʒ] is reminiscent of how speakers of Xinca in Guatemala are observed to go 'hog-wild' with glottalized consonants that are perceived as exotic with respect to Spanish (Campbell and Muntzel 1989, 189), a situation that has led Woolard to comment that "subordinate languages in contact situations can acquire not only the functional but also some of the formal properties of antilanguages" (Woolard 1998, 20). In this case, an exotic feature of the subordinated Boholano variety of Visayan is overgeneralized to the point where it appears to mark out a kind of oppositional 'slang' register. In the west of Bohol I was told that [dʒ] is used as a softener for signaling intimacy and putting an addressee at ease. Thus, when *dayun* ('please come in') is realized as [dadʒun] it carries the pragmatic sense of 'Please come in and relax, we don't stand on ceremony here.'

Use of [dʒ] enters into orthographic play in local signage where multiple valences of the letter 'j' are exploited (see Figs. 4.1–4.2). In 1992, the governor of Bohol erected a sign at the main pier in Tagbilaran, reading 'Maajong Pag-abot!' ('Welcome!'). His use of 'j,' intended for realization as [dʒ], was designed to foreground the distinctiveness of Boholano speech, though at the time the sign was controversial among those who considered it too folksy or uneducated.

In the archaic Hispanic orthography of Visayan, one way of representing /h/ was to use the letter 'j,' and this is preserved in place names such as Maribojok [maribuhuk] and 'Jagna' [hagna], not to mention the name of the island itself, which was written as 'Bojol' in some Hispanic records (see, for example, de la Cavada Mendez de Vigo 1877). When Boholanos cheekily pronounce these as [maribudʒuk] and [budʒul] they are simultaneously referencing a Hispanic colonial past, while promoting their regional native authenticity—an inside joke lost on non-locals.

FIGURE 4.1. The 'Bojol Grill' chicken shop in Tagbilaran.

FIGURE 4.2. From left: Alma E. Aparece, Regina Estorba Macalandag, and Marla Reyes in front of a sign for the Boholana women's artists group 'Baji Arts Collective.' The organization takes its name from *bayi*, a contraction of *babayi* ('woman'), but emphasizes a Boholano identity in its spelling.

Inter-dialectal differences are not emphasized when Boholanos wish to proclaim the value of Visayan as a regional language in the face of its national rival, Tagalog. Several punning phrases make use of Visayan-Tagalog homophones to playfully denigrate the national language and demonstrate *ang kahawud sa atung pulung Binisaya* ('the superiority of our Visayan language'). The best-known of these is: '*Ang langgam nila gakamang pa. Ang atua galupad na*,' meaning 'Their ant crawls. Ours flies.' (The word *langgam* is 'ant' in Tagalog but 'bird' in Visayan.) Another is: '*Ang paa nila tiil naa sa ubus. Ang atua naa sa taas*,' meaning 'Their foot is located below. Ours is located higher.' (The word *paa* is 'foot' in Tagalog, but 'leg' in Visayan).

## Bohol's languages in their domains

In accordance with government educational policy, Tagalog and English are introduced as second languages in Bohol's elementary schools, to become languages of instruction as early as third grade. By secondary school these languages are officially the sole medium of instruction, though in practice Visayan is still used. In Bohol's two universities, Visayan is used for the humanities and English for the sciences. On the whole, textbooks and students' written production are in English. Although English is associated with education and social prestige, there is unequivocal local pride in the Visayan language. Indeed, for some time Jes Tirol (Chapter 3) has spearheaded a movement to make Visayan the sole medium of instruction at the University of Bohol. By contrast, at least two universities on the Visayan island of Negros have decided to turn their entire campuses into English-only zones.

English is used in the news reports of *The Bohol Chronicle* and *The Bohol Standard*, the island's two main newspapers; some columnists choose to write opinion pieces in Visayan. *Bohol Balita*, a smaller newspaper distributed in east Bohol, is in Visayan. Radio broadcasts are mostly in Visayan with regular English code-switching.

Popular songs on the radio, or in karaoke bars, are mostly in English or Tagalog. The national anthem is sung in Tagalog before film screenings, government-sponsored events, and at the flag raising ceremony that precedes the first class of the day in elementary school. Traditional folk songs, sung at work or among friends, or occasionally performed for an audience, are in Visayan.

In Catholic churches, prayers are said in English while hymns are sung in Visayan. Sermons may be in English or Visayan. In two parishes, Dauis and Baclayon, the Latin mass was recently revived in a limited way. In Bohol's two mosques, Qur'anic Arabic is used for prayers and religious teachings. The teachings are then repeated in Maranao, a language of the Lanao region of Mindanao;

if non-Maranao-speaking visitors are present, the imam may also deliver the teachings in English, Visayan, or Tagalog.

Tagalog is primarily heard on television and in schools. I have heard Boholanos spontaneously use Tagalog in the following circumstances: instructing elementary and secondary-school students, reporting dialogue from the television, addressing or mocking a Tagalog speaker, and establishing communication with an individual whose provenance is unknown to the speaker, although English is by far the most common contact language for this last purpose.

Code-switching between English and Visayan is common in Bohol, as it is throughout the Visayas. The term 'Ceblish' refers to a form of speech in which the mixing is habitual. No published study of Ceblish as used within Bohol is presently available. From my observation, Ceblish is used mostly by Boholanos in their thirties and younger, in casual conversation and in text messages. Formal speeches will often begin in English then switch to Visayan at the clause or sentence level; formal replies to speeches mirror this structure.

## Ritual languages and speech disguise

At least three distinct ritual registers are attested in Bohol. In the Inabanga region of north Bohol (Map 3), shamans known as *sukdan* perform chants that make use of formulaic phrases and archaic or obsolete lexemes in ceremonies of healing (Aparece 2003). It has been reported to me that a similar register is used by shamans in Anda (Map 3), though I have not observed this myself. Quite distinct from the *sukdan*, practitioners known as *urasiyunan* ('prayer-makers') make use of a ritual language based on corrupt Latin for purposes of healing, power, or romantic attraction. The *urasiyun* ('prayer,' 'spell') may be performed aloud but is often written on paper or cloth (Fig. 4.3). This written artifact may then be swallowed by the recipient or worn on his or her body.

The inland town of Loboc (Map 3) is famous for its troupes of musicians who are highly sought after as performers at important events. Loboc has a long history as a center of musical activity, and it is reported that a cant has developed among its traveling musicians. I have not been able to record any examples of its use, but I have been informed that it is a variety of veiled speech, laden with metaphor, and that it is used to exclude overhearers.

An elaborate form of disguised speech, known as Timuri or Timuri-Binali, is in use in a number of parts of Bohol but is particularly prevalent in the southeast, around Candijay and Cogtong (Map 3). A speaker of Timuri encrypts plain text in Boholano Visayan by means of the following cypher:

T   I   M   U   R   I
↕   ↕   ↕   ↕   ↕   ↕
B   I   N   A   L   I

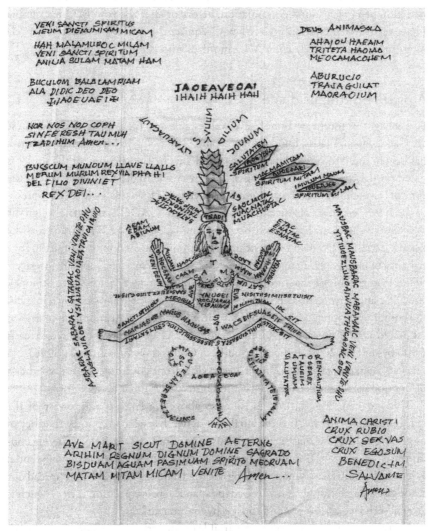

**FIGURE 4.3.** An *urasiyun* from Quiapo market, Manila. The inscribed cloth is secretly worn on the body to attract a lover.

This cypher tells the speaker to substitute the phoneme represented ortho-graphically by 't' with the phoneme 'b,' 'm' with 'n,' 'u' with 'a,' 'r' with 'l,' and vice versa (the letter 'i' is not substituted). Thus, the question *Unsay imung gibuhat gahapun?* ('What did you do yesterday?') is rendered as '*Amsuy inang gitahub guhupam?*' Timuri is learned in childhood and takes great skill to master. Talented Timuri speakers, both adults and children, are often requested to produce Timuri phrases on the spot. Timuri may also be written, although speech is the preferred medium. A far more common form of speech disguise involves the consistent insertion of a given sound combination, before or after the vowels. One example I have recorded in Guindulman (Map 3) requires the speaker to insert V (vowel) + /g/ prior to any vowel, where V harmonizes with the vowel it precedes.[9]

## A picture of the field site

Five villages in southeast Bohol have well-established Eskaya populations. These are Cadapdapan, Biabas, Lundag, Taytay, and Canta-ub (see Map 4). My fieldwork has been limited to Cadapdapan, Biabas, and Taytay. The selection of the sites was based on the fact that Eskayan linguistic activity was highest in these areas at the time of research. Of the three villages only Taytay and Biabas fall within the borders of the 1993 Certificate of Ancestral Domain Claim (CADC), and even though the outcome of the claim has not yet been determined, this zone is referred to as the Eskaya Ancestral Domain both within the communities and in the administrative parlance of local governments and NGOs. The Eskaya Ancestral Domain intersects the upland regions of the municipalities of Guindulman, Duero, Sierra Bullones, and Pilar and is thus situated within four local government jurisdictions. In 1990 the combined population of all villages within the Eskaya Ancestral Domain was estimated at 2,625, rising to 2,811 circa1996, at which time it was predicted to reach 3,000 by the year 2000 (Office for Southern Cultural Communities ca. 1996). No census has taken place since, and it is not clear from government data whether a distinction was made between Eskaya and non-Eskaya inhabitants.

Cadapdapan (Fig. 4.4), at 213 meters above sea level, is the lowest of the villages in the field site. It has a small but active Eskaya community that began migrating there from Biabas in the 1960s to profit from better rice-growing con-ditions. Like many of Bohol's smaller settlements, the village has no visible center. A handful of houses are lined up along the road, and the remainder are spread out among the surrounding fields. In Cadapdapan the principal crop is rice, which is grown both for subsistence and for sale in coastal markets.

A steep and arduous 6-kilometer trail leads directly from Cadapdapan up to Biabas (Fig. 4.5), which is perched on a plateau at 526 meters above sea level.

FIGURE 4.4. Cadapdapan.

From Biabas, there are magnificent glimpses of Bohol's famous landscape of conical hills, and large limestone caves are found a short distance from the village.
Rice is not easily grown due to the rocky soil and steep incline but is still produced in small quantities for local consumption. The longest established crop is
*abaka* (a form of hemp); other crops are *gabi*, *kamuti*, and *ubi* (root vegetables),
bananas, and cassava. The center of the village is built along a square grid of four
straight roads with a Philippine Independent Church (PIC) marking one corner
and the house of the late tribal chieftain, Juan Datahan, marking another. On a
slope that overlooks the village stands the Eskaya school where language is taught
on Sundays.

From Biabas, a 13-kilometer trail along a steep ridge leads to the Eskaya village
of Taytay (Fig. 4.6) at 742 meters above sea level. The higher altitude results in a
cool, crisp climate, and in the rainy season the village is often covered in fog, even
at midday. The altitude allows farmers to grow rarer crops such as strawberries and
peanuts, as well as ornamental anthurium flowers for displaying at festive events
or for decorating church altars. Root vegetables, onions, tomatoes, and eggplants
are grown and delivered to lowland markets twice a week in a community-owned
*jeepney* ('diesel bus'). The success of these crops inspired Taytay's official slogan
'the vegetable bowl of Bohol.' Rice is grown for local consumption only. Until the
1990s, the Taytay Eskaya practiced a form of semi-communal farming in which
one field was worked every Monday on a volunteer basis and the profits collected

**FIGURE 4.5.** Biabas.

**FIGURE 4.6.** Taytay.

for the benefit of the community. Now this occurs once a month. During my time in the area I did not notice any swidden farming, as had been reported by the OSCC (ca. 1996).

Taytay's houses are built in a circle along the ridge of a crater-like depression with an overgrown limestone cave at its depths. In the cleared area around the cave is an ornamental garden, a hut used by visiting employees of the Soil and Water Foundation (an agricultural NGO), an Eskayan language school, and a community hall. During my first long stay in Taytay in 2006, the Armed Forces of the Philippines maintained a small counterinsurgency detachment in Taytay, and soldiers could be seen resting in camouflage hammocks just below the community hall. The area surrounding the village is so densely forested that all the structures appear to blend into the foliage. When I entered Taytay by motorcycle during the rainy season, at a time when the rain and fog often obscured visibility, I sometimes failed to realize I had arrived at all.

Travel between these three villages is difficult. The steep, rocky trail between Cadapdapan and Biabas can only be traversed on foot or by water buffalo. Vehicles reach Biabas from Cadapdapan by making a long detour toward the coast then backtracking along the better roads that lead from Guindulman. The area around Taytay (toward Mayana) is prone to landslides, and roads are often impassable in the wet season. An 'Eskaya Highway' linking the villages was first proposed in the 1990s (Office for Southern Cultural Communities ca. 1996). Roving military graders began constructing new roads in the region in 2006 and 2007 but did not complete any of them.

Houses in all three villages are generally constructed in the local style from untreated Philippine mahogany timber, concrete breeze blocks, or a combination of both. Floors are dirt or paved in cement. Roofs are made from corrugated iron, or less commonly, thatched with *nipa* ('palm fronds') or *kugun* ('wild grass'). When the first survey of the Eskaya villages was made it was estimated that 96% of families lived below the poverty line (Office for Southern Cultural Communities ca. 1996) and little has changed since (Granada 2010); however, my Eskaya consultants tended to describe themselves as neither poor nor rich, identifying simply as 'middle class' (using the English term). As of 2009, a constant supply of electricity has become available in all the villages.

## The spoken and sung domains of Eskayan

Abregana's demand for Eskayan interpreters in 1980 and one graduate student's report of low second-language competence in Visayan in 1992 contrasted sharply with my own experiences. In the course of my fieldwork, no individual

I interviewed claimed to have been raised with Eskayan as their first language. Nor, when compiling genealogies, did anybody declare their parents or grandparents as mother-tongue Eskayan speakers. The principal language of communication in the field site was Boholano-Visayan. Most Eskaya under the age of fifty were able to speak and understand Tagalog and a little English. Two consultants (one in Tatyay and the other in Cadapdapan) were highly proficient in English. The most regular use of Eskayan was witnessed in the volunteer-run schools that operated on Sundays (Figs. 4.7–4.9). Outside the classroom Eskayan was used for praying, singing, speech-making, and the reading and writing of Eskaya literature.

Notably these domains are isomorphic with the domains of English usage in other communities of Bohol. In effect, Eskayan appears to have supplanted the special authoritative role of English in education, prayer, speech-making, and writing. Use of Eskayan in these domains is, I will later argue, indicative of the political context in which the language was recuperated.

More rarely, Eskayan was employed to exclude an overhearer. Some speakers at village meetings I attended, for example, would switch to Eskayan when the discussion concerned my activities in the community and the speakers did not want me to understand what was being said. For visitors and locals alike,

FIGURE 4.7. Singing the national anthem in Eskayan in front of the Eskaya flag before the commencement of class, Biabas.

**FIGURE 4.8.** Biabas children's class.

**FIGURE 4.9.** Adults' class in Taytay. Separated by a partition, the children's class is taking place in the background.

common imperative phrases were frequently rendered in Eskayan with a certain self-conscious jocularity, among them **griyu** ('come in!), **milyamun** ('let's eat!'), and **uchdirim** ('come and drink [alcohol]!'). In this way, these simple phrases mark Eskayan as a language that differentiates insiders from outsiders, while at the same time serving to include them, humorously, within a sphere of intimacy and solidarity. A similar process was identified by Jane Hill in her description of the ways that the way Mexicano (Nahuatl), as spoken in the Malinche Volcano region of Tlaxcala and Puebla in central Mexico, is used as a marker of intimacy in contrast to Spanish, which is set aside as the language of power and distance. Hill observed that Mexicano would be chosen when calling for more food or drink at a celebration, at major community rituals such as the blessing of newlyweds, and also as a light-hearted shibboleth to test the ethnicity of strangers encountered on the roads (Hill 1985, 727). In the Eskaya villages, use of such simple and formulaic expressions nonetheless often belied a far greater linguistic sophistication on the part of the speaker, as I was later to discover during elicitation sessions.

I have not undertaken any thorough survey of speaker numbers or of competency in Eskayan, although I did ask teachers in each of communities for their personal approximations. Based on their local reckonings, I in turn estimate that there are between 500 and 550 speakers of Eskayan today. This figure represents about a quarter of the total number of individuals who identify themselves as Eskaya. Though Biabas and Taytay were once exclusively Eskaya villages, today my impression is that Eskaya people make up roughly one-quarter of the Biabas population and about two-thirds of the Taytay community. Over the years I have personally encountered at least twenty individuals who have displayed a very high degree of linguistic competence, to the extent that they are able to speak, read, and write Eskayan with little hesitancy.

Those who call themselves Eskaya often point to their knowledge of the language, however limited, as an index of their identity. This is in contrast to the administrative requirements of the National Commission on Indigenous Peoples (NCIP): applicants who wish to be officially registered as Eskaya must first prove descent from recognized Eskaya forebears and have the genealogy validated by a local leader.

## Schools

All of the most fluent speakers of Eskayan attained proficiency through regular attendance at one of three volunteer-run schools in Taytay, Biabas, or Lundag. Built by the community, the single-room Eskaya schools host classes every Sunday, beginning after the morning church service and continuing until midday. In Taytay, classes run until 5:00 pm with a break for lunch. Attendance is voluntary, and typically there are about twenty children and ten adults on any given Sunday. Teachers are highly respected but not paid for their work. All classes begin with the Philippine national anthem sung in Eskayan. Other songs, such as the "Hymn of Bohol," may be sung after this. In Biabas, teachers wear embroidered berets, and female teachers wear dresses with puffed shoulders, as commonly worn by women in Bohol up until the early twentieth century. Men wear collarless shirts woven from pineapple fiber. In Taytay, all women (teachers and students alike) wear headscarves that resemble nun's habits and long flowing dresses with straight shoulders. These styles of formal dress are also worn on special occasions.

Separate classes for children and adults take place simultaneously at different ends of the room. Children from ages six to eleven years old learn the basics of the Eskayan script, principally the **abidiha**, a primary 'alphabet' of forty-six mixed alphabetic and syllabic characters. Teachers mostly use Visayan as a medium of instruction and ask students to chant responses in unison. This call–response technique is a common pedagogical method in Philippine schools.[10] Adults practice the **simplit**, the full syllabary of over one thousand characters that incorporates the **abidiha**. Teachers of the adult classes use a wider range of didactic techniques. One of the adult-class teachers in Biabas opted for a full immersion style and did not permit the use of languages other than Eskayan. Her classes encouraged spontaneous production of the language through games, quizzes, and naturalistic conversation. Once, when I arrived late to class in Biabas drenched and dirty from the motorcycle journey from Taytay, a student improvised a joking example question, which the teacher wrote out on the blackboard:

| Nadu | yan | gamirgamirdu | kus | yan? |
|------|-----|--------------|-----|------|
| why | 2.SG | very.dirty | Q | 2.SG |

'Why are you covered in mud?'

When I gave my excuse she condensed it as:

| Ditsu | kus | guwagu | nustra | dil | ya | Taytay |
|-------|-----|--------|--------|-----|-----|--------|
| because | be | big | rain | up.there | in | Taytay |

'Because of the heavy rain in Taytay.'

In Taytay, classes have recently begun to include Eskayan-to-English transla-tion drills, providing practice in both languages simultaneously. Basic arithmetic is also taught in Taytay, as well as names for local flora. Adult classes end with transcription of Eskaya stories, although this may also happen outside of class hours. Students consult one another or their teacher to assist in the transcription.

As of 2011, an Eskayan language component was introduced into the government-run elementary school in Taytay for the first thirty minutes of each school day for third to sixth grade students. Maura Galambao Jumawan, the first teacher to put the program into action, is an Eskayan speaker with nationally recognized teaching qualifications. Her classes rely partly on the call–response method used in government schools across the Philippines but are enlivened by games, competitions, and group activities.

The notion that one's native language is the ground on which authentic eth-nic identities are built is an ideological commonplace both within and beyond the Philippines. However, the fact the Eskayan language learning occurs delib-erately in an institutional setting, as opposed to 'naturally' via vertical trans-mission, is not experienced as a contradiction by either the students or their teachers. Just as all writing systems must be actively learned through deliberate instruction in institutional settings, Eskayan, with its emphasis on the written form, is likewise approached as a legitimate object of study. Language learning is, in itself, regarded as a key activity in the ongoing process of becoming prop-erly 'Eskaya.' This kind of processual attitude has been noted in the context of Hawaiian language–revitalization initiatives where the drive to learn one's heri-tage language is undergirded by the native value of *kuleana*, understood as a "a sense of 'responsibility' that is both a duty and a privilege to carry out" (Woolard 2016, 35, commenting on Snyder-Frey 2013). When *kuleana* is foregrounded, learners' anxieties about authenticity may be softened, even if a naturalized association between identity and language is retained. The particular Eskaya manifestation of this value is even prefigured in the myth of Pinay, the ances-tral patriot who created the language through his own intellectual labor. Yet it is also worth acknowledging that the Eskaya ideology of language-as-process witnessed in school environments coexists with a somewhat contrary ideology of language-as-object that surfaces in Eskaya literature (Chapter 7), where lan-guage is materialized as a bounded possession that is capable of being lost, repos-sessed, and defended.

## Church

Most Eskaya people belong to the PIC (formerly the Iglesia Filipina Independiente), and there are churches sited in Biabas and Taytay with non-Eskaya visiting priests. Prior to 1972, the liturgy was performed entirely in Spanish. In Biabas, the service is now performed in Visayan, though some of the hymns are in Tagalog. In Taytay, on the other hand, a priest visits only once a month for the Visayan Mass. When the priest is absent, the congregation performs a lay service of hymns, prayers, novenas, and litanies in both Visayan and Eskayan (Fig. 4.10). During hymns, men accompany the singing from the pews with saxophones, trumpets, and a bass drum. The service lasts for about an hour, and novenas continue in the school building prior to beginning Eskayan classes.

For entertainment, people occasionally gather at a house to sing songs in Eskayan with brass and guitar accompaniment (Fig. 4.11). These secular songs are almost all direct translations of patriotic Visayan anthems.

### Speech-making

On important occasions such as the arrival of a special guest, the celebration of a fiesta, or significant anniversaries such as the death date of Mariano Datahan (January 26), a respected elder may make a short speech in Eskayan. Eskaya speeches often open with formulaic phrases such as **Muygriyalu aga ridilyan sikwis** ('Good morning to everyone') and will proceed with acknowledgments and thanks to various members of the community, reminders of the importance of the occasion, and recapitulations of Eskaya stories or historical events in the context of wider Philippine history. A fragment of an Eskayan speech at a

FIGURE 4.10. Sung prayers in Eskayan, Taytay.

**FIGURE 4.11.** Secular songs performed at the house of Roberto Datahan, Cadapdapan.

farewell event can be viewed online where the speaker, Gaudencia Pizaña, says the following:[11]

**Ah, lamis samyal rimuy graban ya mudril Bisayan**
Ah, many thanks PL sibling LOC meeting Visayan
**ya chdiaru nungkasay Bisayan-Eskaya.**
GEN our:EXCL teachings Visayan-Eskaya.

'Ah thank you very much brothers and sisters at our Visayan meeting for our Visayan-Eskaya teachings.'

**Mun . . . chdiarukun . . . riluki arhitika ya chdiarukun kwirdidami . . .**
Now our:INCL continue we:INCL GEN our:INCL activities

'Now . . . our . . . to continue with our activities . . .'

**I gad rilki ya chdiaru kwirdidami uy risirla**
And next step-across GEN our:INCL activity one speech
**ya chdiarukun uy graban.**
GEN our:INCL one brethren

'And straight after our activity [an Eskayan song] is a speech from one of our brethren.'

| Insil | ri | ganti | | yi | **Anoy Datahan,** |
|-------|-----|-----------|--|-----|----------------|
| be | SBJ | grandchild | | GEN | Anoy Datahan, |
| **ya** | **chdiumpir** | **ya Biabas,** | | **yi** | **Basilio.** |
| LOC | hometown | GEN Biabas, | | SPEC | Basilio |

'He is the grandchild of Anoy [Mariano] Datahan from his hometown of Biabas, Mr. Basilio.'

## The written domains of Eskayan and ideologies of writing

Eskayan is principally a written language, and as a result literacy is a necessary precondition for full participation in the Eskayan speech community. Public signs displaying Eskayan text comprise part of the linguistic landscapes of Biabas and Taytay, and the language is very occasionally used for letter writing and text messages. However, written Eskayan is used most extensively for the reading and written reproduction of traditional literature. Throughout the fieldwork period, consultants generously loaned me thousands of pages of Eskayan text to photograph or scan, and these have formed the basis of my analysis of language in the chapters that follow.

This literature can be regarded as part of the "institutional paraphernalia of standardization" (Silverstein 2000, 123), namely, the set of authoritative texts that reify a language and codify its correct usage. As all consultants were second-language speakers of Eskayan, they were unable to produce grammatical 'intuitions' in response to my queries during elicitation sessions. More complex questions were addressed through a consultation of hand-copied Eskayan texts, or discussion with another speaker, and often a combination of both. These traditional texts are regarded as the ultimate authority on correct language, and the ability to read and faithfully copy the traditional literature is considered a primary marker of linguistic aptitude. Over time, as my language and literacy improved, I was encouraged to contribute my own judgments to the discussions.

The notion that the written word carries greater authority than speech is emphasized in Eskaya literature, where languages without writing systems are described as 'air in the mouth' (see Chapter 7). Though not unique to the Eskaya community, this ideology is exemplified in Taytay, where a framed copy of an article by Jes Tirol is placed on display, despite the fact that the article itself is contentious for Eskaya cultural leaders. As discussed in the Prologue, carved reproductions of the reply of Jorge Vargas to Mariano Datahan are displayed in Biabas and Taytay (Figs. P.1–P.4), where they are treated as official endorsements of the Eskaya educational program. As Martinez put it during her visit to Taytay in 1993,

> From that brittle yellow paper, the Eskayas by inscription on wood, seemed to have sought to establish continuation as well as legitimacy through the "written." Needless to say, the equivocation that is expressed in the letter has been totally disregarded and the woodblock has been prominently displayed as a "permit" handed through the generations, and across villages. (Martinez 1993, 114–115)

The primacy of Eskaya writing is further emphasized by the fact that speakers make no categorical distinction between the Eskayan language and its representation via the Eskayan script. As a result, Visayan or English words written in the script will be recognized as Eskayan.[12] In fact, the written representation is regarded as the genuine 'language' from whence the spoken form was derived. Differences between Eskayan and other languages were frequently explained to me in terms of overt features of their writing systems, and during my research I often had to remind my consultants that it was not simply the script that I was interested in but the phonology, grammar, and lexicon as well.

Crossing out, destroying, or trampling on Eskayan text is culturally proscribed, and Martinez reports that when she made photocopies of Eskayan documents, her consultant kept hold of all the misprints.[13] Belief in the integrity of Eskaya writing means that errors in the process of recopying traditional texts are almost always left uncorrected. In certain texts, the corrected word is often written adjacent the incorrect one, and it is left up to the reader to make the appropriate decision. This can require a measure of intuition, especially if the original transcriber has passed away. In those texts that include a Roman transliteration, the Roman text might be amended but not the script. As Eskayan is transmitted via written texts, and these are reproduced by hand, the prohibition against correction accelerates the diversification of Eskayan literature and is ultimately a driver of language change, a phenomenon I will return to in more detail in Chapter 9.

In Chapters 5 and 6, which follow, I describe and analyze the form of Eskayan in terms of its writing system, grammar, and lexicon, with a view to understanding its deeper history. Readers who have less interest in formal linguistic analysis may wish to skip to the conclusions of these two chapters. In Chapter 7 I zero in on the Eskaya manuscript tradition as the chief domain of Eskayan linguistic expression today. My evaluation of this literature will focus especially on how the history of the Eskayan language is characterized, and how Eskaya readers themselves interpret these traditional representations.

## Notes

1. This estimate provided in *Ethnologue* (Lewis, Simons, and Fennig 2021) is probably conservative since it is drawn from census data and probably does not take into account second-language speakers of Visayan, particularly in coastal Mindanao.

2. A U.S. report from the early twentieth century set a terminological precedent by distinguishing 'Bohol-Visayan' from Cebuano (*RPC* 1901, vol. 3, 95). Unfortunately, this was not sustained. In most English-language publications the term 'Cebuano' is a synonym for all Visayan varieties.

3. For date estimates of the Austronesian expansion see Greenhill, Drummond, and Gray (2010); Blust (2013); and Reith and Cochrane (2018).

4. This claim may have been overstated, as the Philippine–American War in Bohol (1899–1901) disrupted agricultural production and resulted in widespread hunger and disease.

5. *Ethnologue* notes simply, "Boholano [is] sometimes considered a separate language" (Lewis, Simons, and Fennig 2021). In the introduction to his dictionary Wolff also commented that "Approximately five percent of our data is not included for lack of reliable informants. These are mainly forms of only local currency, a large portion of them from Bohol" (Wolff 1972a, viii).

6. In his dissertation on Boholano literature, Victoriano B. Tirol noted an interesting folkloric interpretation of intra-island linguistic variation. The so-named *Incarnatis* who lived on the west of the island were regarded by the easterners as *buyagan* (people with the power to cause illness through praise). Although they were dominated and driven away by Sikatuna's forces, "[t]he descendants of the Incarnatis can be identified by the way they talk and pronounce some Visayan words: *kalayu* for *kayu* (fire), *siliboyas* for *siboyas* (onions), *palayong* for *payong* (umbrella), *kalanding* for *kanding* (goat), *kalabao* for *kabao* (carabao)" (Tirol 1968, 28).

7. Tinampay wrote, "There are two dialects of Cebuano in Bohol: the Eastern Bohol dialect (EB) and Western Bohol dialect (WB). The former is bounded by Lila, Dimiao, Valencia, Garcia-Hernandez, Jagna, Duero, Guindulman, Anda and Mabini. The latter is bounded by the towns of Panglao, Loon, Calape, Tubigon, Clarin, Inabanga, Buenavista and Jetafe." (n.p.). See Map 3.

8. I enclose all sounds in square brackets as opposed to slashes to avoid introducing a phonemic claim here. The phonological dynamics of this variation are explained in greater detail in Chapter 5.

9. These kinds of syllable insertion language games are reported in many parts of the world but have a long pedigree in the Philippines. In the early twentieth century, Pedro Laktaw (1910) compared Tagalog syllable reversal and syllable insertion games

to similar games among German speakers, reported by Ferdinand Blumentritt. He also drew attention to the incidental documentation of a Tagalog syllable reversal game in the eighteenth-century *Vocabulario de la lengua tagala* (de Noceda and de Sanlucar [1754] 1860, 97, under the entry for *dagá*).

10. Pardo de Tavera, in 1884, contended that although Filipinos had forgotten their native literacy, they had retained from pre-contact days a distinctive reading voice. Whatever the antiquity of this, I have indeed often heard students and teachers in Philippine classrooms reading out loud in a "monotonous manner [ . . . ] as if singing, as if they were unsure of their reading and with a nasal voice" ("manera monótona [ . . . ] como cantando, cual si estubieran inseguros de su lectura y con una voz gangosa") (de Tavera 1884, 30).

11. This can be viewed directly at http://onlinelibrary.wiley.com/doi/10.1111/taja.12005/suppinfo.

12. An interesting illustration of this is witnessed in the rendering of Vargas' reply into the Eskayan script, as reproduced in Fig. P.3. This text is actually a transliteration of the Visayan words in Fig. P.2 and not the romanized Eskayan of Fig. P.4.

13. The belief that ritual objects lose potency if stepped upon is recorded by Aparece, who reports that Boholano shamans in Inabanga take great pains to avoid stepping over their *habak* ('bottles') and ritual herbs (Aparece 2003, 162). Evidently this belief has survived in Bohol since at least the early seventeenth century. The Fr. Alonso de Humanos, Superior of Bohol, in 1604 described the case of a local priest in Loboc who publicly destroyed the ritual objects held by a local *datu*: "[ . . . ] upon arriving at the house the man himself had to take down and collect all the cups and jars, none of the Indians who were with him daring in any way to touch the objects lest they die at the touch. [ . . . ] But the Father, allaying their dread and disabusing them of their false forebodings, since he had touched them and remained alive, made them take the things out into the open and calling the young men to join him they all spat on them and trampled them (for these acts, among these people as among all other nations, denote the greatest contempt, abhorrence and dishonor)" (Chirino [1604] (1969), 384).

# 5 THE WRITING SYSTEM

In the face of mute and undeciphered Egyptian hieroglyphs, Renaissance scholars "translated" them into solemn religious odes inspired by their outward forms. So too, the Eskaya script was a literal inkblot test for early visitors who saw, in its tangle of lines and loops, visions of Phoenician, Hebrew, Greek, Etruscan, and Glagolitic writing (Chapter 3). Eskaya leaders themselves have contributed to the speculation, suggesting origins in Egyptian, Arabic, and Javanese scripts. Why such exotic comparisons? It is curious that no participant in this exercise has ever assumed a connection to the indigenous Philippine script. Nor is the Eskayan script a paleographic riddle awaiting its Champollion. It is a fully deciphered, living, and functional system.

In earlier chapters I described the day-to-day use of Eskayan by the inhabitants of Cadapdapan, Biabas, and Taytay and reviewed how these communities were reimagined by outsiders. In the decades after "contact," wide-ranging and often sensational theories on the history of Eskayan have proliferated, and these narratives have set the present terms of accommodation between the Eskaya communities and government institutions. But for the most part, written histories that were authored and reproduced by Eskaya people themselves were either sidelined, submitted to fanciful reinterpretations, or not taken into consideration at all. In these traditional texts, the figure of the Boholano pope Pinay is central to the origin story of the Eskayan language. As I will describe in greater detail in Chapter 7, Pinay was said to have created the Eskayan language and script out of a human body and transmitted his creation to the people of Bohol. Among Eskaya historiographers today, the historical status of Pinay continues to be a subject of speculative discussion. Like debates among classicists over the identity of Homer, some wonder whether he was a real individual or a mythological figure, whether "he" was actually a woman or, indeed, whether Pinay and Mariano Datahan were the same person.

*The Last Language on Earth*. Kelly, Piers, Oxford University Press. © Oxford University Press 2022.
DOI: 10.1093/oso/9780197509913.003.0005

In the present chapter and Chapter 6, which follows, I explore what the Eskayan language and its script might reveal on their own terms. For rhetorical convenience I will use the formula 'Pinay' to denote the putative linguistic creator even if the historical existence of an individual by this name in Bohol is unverifiable. Although Pinay is also an entity of uncertain gender, I apply the pronoun 'he,' as this is a default used by many Eskayan speakers when referring to Pinay in English—gender is not grammatically marked in Eskayan or Visayan. Further, images of Pinay in Taytay and Biabas depict him as a man (see Fig. 5.1). Despite these uncertainties, much can be understood about Pinay through a forensic dissection of the writing system, grammar, and lexicon he constructed. For a language held to have been fashioned from human flesh, the linguistic anatomy of Eskayan may well embody the image of its creator.

In this chapter I consider the form and function of the Eskaya writing system, how it maps onto the sounds of Eskayan words, and how its graphic structure relates to other scripts. I will show, at the outset, that the phonology of Eskayan contrasts in marked ways with that of Visayan in both its phoneme inventory and syllable structure. In turn, the Eskaya writing system employs

**FIGURE 5.1.** Pinay depicted on a chart of Eskaya ancestors, Taytay. The script transliterates as **Pinay inmunsiktur** ('Pinay the pope').

a wide range of techniques for modeling these sounds and sound combinations. A set of foundational letters presents as a direct cypher of a standard Spanish alphabet, while a much more expansive set of supplementary signs is available for encoding syllable shapes. Complicating this division are a number of alphabetic letters that have an optional inherent vowel, allowing them to be expressed as a consonant-vowel (CV-) sequence, a convention that characterizes the underlying system of the indigenous Philippine script (Chapter 2). In practice, Eskaya writers are presented with an extraordinary array of acceptable orthographic choices since a single word may be represented in a number of ways. A very small number of symbols are arguably logographic, meaning that they represent distinct morphemes of Eskayan, while others, such as those used in the numeral system, have conceptual or ideographic values. Moreover, the writing system includes signs for representing phonemes and syllable shapes that do not feature at all in Eskayan or Visayan. Learners of Eskayan also have to contend with the fact that sets of letters sharing a family resemblance in their core graphic forms do not necessarily correspond to sets of related sound values, and vice versa.

Despite this, iconicity is a central feature of the script. Writers of Eskaya consider certain signs to represent parts or poses of the human body. Many other signs display a kind of secondary iconicity in the way they resemble letters of the Roman alphabet or the Hindu-Arabic number system. All these correspondences point to the sources of inspiration that were available to Pinay and begin to tell a story of how the script first developed. Although the Eskaya writing system is characterized by exceptional complexity, hybridity, and redundancy, I argue that, at a fundamental level, it acts as a composite cypher for other writing systems and orthographies. In so doing, I argue that *the Eskaya writing system is produced through processes of substitution and elaboration, in which outward forms and structures are derived from other models while the actual content, in terms of sound or meaning values, is modified or replaced.*

In keeping with the narrative spirit of ethnographic history, and to remain inclusive of nonspecialist readers, I have tried my best to avoid lengthy and overly technical description of the script and its system. Readers who prefer a more extensive and analytical treatment of the language and script are referred to more detailed published articles on the subject.[1]

## Writing Eskayan sounds

Eskayan and Visayan share the same set of minimal sounds, or phonemes, but with one crucial distinction. Certain sounds in Visayan only turn up in *loaned* words from English or Spanish. For example, the 'ch' sound that appears at the beginning of the word *tsinilas* ('slippers') is borrowed from Spanish *chinelas*, or the 'j' sound at the beginning of *joker*, a now-naturalized Visayan word borrowed from English. In Eskayan, on the other hand, these borrowed phonemes turn up in loaned and non-loaned vocabulary alike. In other words, they are an ordinary part of the native Eskayan sound system. Furthermore, the phoneme /ʤ/ is conspicuously frequent in Eskayan words, a fact that lends weight to Woolard's observation that oppositional registers are sometimes formed through the overemphasis of culturally loaded features (Chapter 4). I once heard a boy in Cadapdapan mocking Eskayan by loading his caricatured speech with a /ʤ/ in every syllable, to the general amusement of his Eskayan-speaking audience.

A more dramatic difference between Visayan and Eskayan is in the way the sounds are organized within words. Native Visayan words do not contain any consonant clusters, that is, sequences of successive consonants, as seen, for example, in the first three letters of the word 'strike,' but follow a basic CV pattern. In Eskayan, on the other hand, dense consonant clusters are widespread, especially at the beginning of words. A comprehensive overview of Eskayan phonology and syllable structures is available in Kelly (2015). For the present chapter, I will look at how these sounds map onto the script and what these loaned or "foreign" characteristics index for writers of Eskayan.

Although many linguists do not view writing as having anything to do with grammar, or even with language, the Eskaya script has a determined relationship to Eskayan phonology and is thus integral to any understanding of Eskayan as a linguistic system. On the whole, Eskayan words are "seen and not heard," that is, their graphic representation in writing is regarded as the true form from which speech emanates. The belief that writing precedes and governs speech is found across many intellectual traditions, even if it is not a view defended by linguists today. It was even enshrined in the 1939 census of the Philippines, which defined 'dialects' in contrast to 'languages' as having little or no written form and "whose speech is thus changeable" (Commonwealth of the Philippines Commission of the Census 1941). But what counted as *legitimate* writing, for the Commission, was ultimately determined by political prestige. Thus, despite having a long-established Roman orthography and even a pre-colonial native script, Tagalog was identified in the census as a 'dialect' while English and Spanish were awarded the status of 'languages.'

In the case of Eskaya written practice, this literacy ideology is powerful enough to have effects on the language itself. Eskaya teachers regard the written form as the "correct" expression of language to the extent that grammatical "intuition" is judged by the degree to which an Eskayan utterance coincides with an orthodox representation in written records. This concept, which I term 'literality' (by analogy with 'grammaticality'), is held by English-language prescriptivists everywhere, but in the Eskaya case it is taken to a further extreme: no categorical distinction is made between script and language, meaning that *any* language— be it Visayan, Spanish, or English—is seen to *become* Eskayan by virtue of being written in the Eskaya script. The special material status accorded to the script is witnessed elsewhere in cultural proscriptions against crossing out, destroying, or trampling on Eskayan text. It can be controversial for a non-Eskaya person to write or circulate words in the Eskaya script, while speaking the language is accepted and even encouraged. In the course of fieldwork in Taytay, I was permitted to record sung performances of a sacred Eskayan hymn, described by its singers as a *nubina* (Visayan: 'novena'), but not to transcribe it in any form of writing.

This set of ideologies has specific relevance to Eskayan phonology and its relationship to the writing system. Since the written form provides the primary cues for pronunciation, the analysis of Eskayan phonology cannot easily be separated from its graphic representation. Like sign languages, the visible representation of Eskayan words can be understood as a kind of "phonology" whose structure has potentially significant effects on the language as a whole. Thus, for example, 𝒜𝑃𝒬𝒻 (<ʔa> <bi> <la> <ki>)—the written form of the greeting **abilaki** ('hello')—is not construed as a graphic model of its phonetic form /abilaki/, but quite the reverse: the utterance /abilaki/ is understood, in local ideology, as a phonetic byproduct of the "real" written word 𝒜𝑃𝒬𝒻.

I follow Coulmas' formal/functional distinction of a 'script' as a graphic set of written symbols, and 'writing system' as the system by which these symbols are applied and interpreted, e.g., as an alphabet, syllabary, etc. (Coulmas 1996, 454). For clarity, I will begin by reviewing the writing *system*: how it is organized, how it relates to the sound system of Eskayan, and how it works in actual practice. The actual form of the writing and its relationship to other scripts are discussed later, although form and function cannot always be separated descriptively.

Despite the ideological conflation of language and script, there are nonetheless a few Eskayan terms that are used to denote the script specifically. In the traditional literature (Chapter 7) the terms 𝒜𝑡𝒻𝓁𝑢 <atikisis> and 𝒜ℰ𝓈𝑆𝑆 <aspurmus minimi> are labels that refer to Eskaya writing, although I have never heard these terms used in contemporary speech. In Taytay, written characters are occasionally distinguished from the language as 𝓁𝑢𝑡𝒜·𝑃𝓂𝒹 <iskaya litri> or 'Eskaya letters.'

What is immediately evident about the Eskaya writing system is that, like Western alphabets, words are written from left to right and are separated by spaces. Further, Eskaya texts are punctuated with commas, colons, and quotation marks in a conventional Roman style, although the Eskaya question mark ૬ and the full stop ◡ have been elaborated slightly. This contrasts with the conventions of the prehispanic Philippine script in which words were usually written from top to bottom and were not separated by spaces or punctuation.

Eskaya people describe their writing system as being divided into an Abidiha ('Alphabet') of 46 letters and a Simplit ('Syllabary') of approximately one thousand letters. This division is realized in handwritten texts used as reference documents by Eskaya scribes. Each of the forty-six **litri** ('letters') of the Abidiha represents an independent syllable while some may be realized as either a syllable or as an alphabetic consonant, depending on a judgment made by the reader. Thus, although it is referred to as an 'alphabet,' the Abidiha is perhaps better defined as an alphasyllabary in its broadest sense, since it contains dual-purpose alphabetic and syllabic characters. The Simplit, meanwhile, has no alphabetic or alphasyllabic characters and amounts to an expansion of the syllable set.

## The Abidiha

The iconic relationship between letters of the Abidiha and the parts or arrangements of the human body they are said to be derived from is made explicit in classroom charts (Fig. 5.2).

Of the 46 characters in the Abidiha the first 25 are notionally alphabetic, though a large proportion of these have a dual alphabetic-syllabic value. What this means is that certain consonantal alphabetic characters may be realized either as a consonant (C) or as a CV unit, according to a judgment made by the reader. This contrasts considerably with the indigenous Philippine script in which consonants have an inherent -/a/ unless an alternative vowel is specified. In Philippine systems, consonant or semivowel codas are conventionally left off altogether, requiring the reader to infer these from the context. Thus, the Tagalog word *bantay* ('guard'), would be represented as $\mathcal{O}\Upsilon$ (<ba><ta>), a homograph of *bata'* ('child').

Within the Eskaya Abidiha the inherent vowel is not /a/ by default but corresponds to its recited alphabetic value. Thus, the characters ৪ and ゐ can represent [b] and [t], respectively, in the alphabetically written word ৪ℓ𝑞ゐ (<b><r><i><t>, **brit**: 'female plant or animal') but may be realized as [bi] and [ti] in the word ৪ゐ (<bi><ti>, **biti**: 'skilled'). These alternative syllabic realizations have the vowel [i] as a nucleus simply because [bi] and [ti] are the conventional pronunciations of the equivalent letter names in a recited Visayan or Spanish alphabet.[2] Such inherent alphabetic-syllabic flexibility is reminiscent of the way a Visayan speaker today might exploit the dual phonetic realizations in SMS messages such as "naa sa balay cla" (*naa sa balay sila*: 'it's at their house'); see also Fig. 5.3. When used syllabically, the alphabetic characters with two-syllable names—ƒ 'f' /iphi/, ℛ 'h' /ʔachi/, ℾ 'l' /ʔili/, ℬ 'm' /ʔimi/, ℬ 'n' /ʔini/, ℳ 'ñ' /ʔinyi/, and ℐ 'x' /ikis/—are

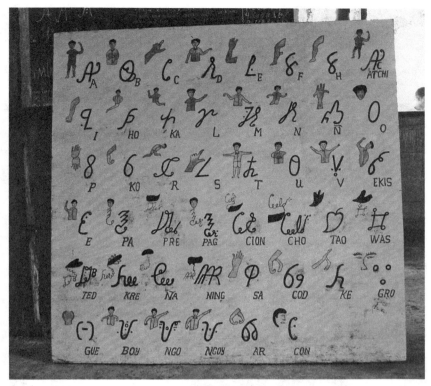

**FIGURE 5.2.** An Abidiha displayed on a wooden board at the Eskaya school in Taytay.

conventionally shortened to their final syllable when used as a component of a word: [hi], [chi], [li], [mi], [ni], [nyi], and [kis].

One striking feature of the Abidiha is its apparently redundant elements. For example, the phoneme /i/ may be represented by either of the signs ℓ or ꝗ while /u/ may take 0 or θ. An examination of Fig. 5.2 reveals that all four characters are clearly designated with different Roman letters: ℓ ('e') and ꝗ ('i'), 0 ('o') and θ ('u'), even if there is a formal resemblance between the shapes of the paired characters. Nonetheless, the orthographic distinctions within each pair do not correspond to a contrast in Eskayan or Visayan, let alone any meaningful phonemic contrast. It could be argued that the script has retained the representation of a historical contrast in the Eskayan language that is no longer meaningful in its present form. But to my mind, the most likely explanation for this "redundancy" is that the Abidiha is not representing a sound system, phonemic or otherwise, so much as *another writing system*. In other words, the Abidiha *is designed as a cypher for transliterating a Spanish alphabet or a Spanish orthography of Visayan*. This is

**FIGURE 5.3.** Sign to the caves known as Bugnao Sii (literally: 'very cold') on the Anda peninsula east of Biabas (Map 3). The East Boholano intensifier sii /siʔiʔ/ is represented as 'c, e,' referencing the pronunciation of these letters in an English alphabet.

borne out in other "foreign" elements of the Abidiha. The symbols ℱ ('f', /f/) and ⱴ ('v', /v/) are assigned to Roman letters representing sounds that are absent from the phonologies of both Eskayan and Visayan. Likewise, the Abidiha includes the symbol ℐₒₒ for transliterating the letter 'x', ℳ for 'ñ', and ℓ for 'q'—all letters that are absent from modern orthographies of Visayan but that do feature in English and Spanish alphabets, obsolete Hispanic-Visayan orthographies, and Philippine proper names of Spanish origin. The fact that the Abidiha faithfully follows standard Roman alphabetic recitation order in reference texts adds weight to this impression, although the absence of an Eskaya equivalent for the Hispanic and English letter 'z' is curious.

Table 5.1 lists the alphabetic-syllabic characters of the Abidiha accompanied by their phonetic realizations and their corresponding Roman transliterations:

The Abidiha does not effectively capture the full set of Eskayan sounds. Nowhere in this list are signs for the very common Eskayan phonemes /w/, /tʃ/, /dʒ/, /ŋ/, and /ʔ/. These are found only as components of syllables in later sets of the Simplit. Unusually, too, the Abidiha includes characters that stand for [f] and [v], two sounds that never appear in any Eskayan words. This suggests that the Abidiha was not devised with the Eskayan language in mind. If, instead, the Abidiha is understood as a mostly alphabetic system for transliterating a Hispanic Roman alphabet, then the system begins to make more sense.

The remaining twenty-one syllabic characters in the Abidiha, not shown in Table 5.1, include symbols for the commonplace Visayan affixes /pag-/, /ning-/, and /gi-/, as well as the particles /sa/ (sa 'to') and /pa/ (pa 'yet'), although curiously the more frequent Visayan particles ang (determiner, 'the') and mga (plural marker) are not represented. Typical Hispanic syllables are also found here, including /pri/, a Spanish verbal prefix; /kun/ for the morpheme con ('with'); /ar/, an ending for Spanish infinitive verbs such as vibrar ('vibrate'); and /sjun/ (transliterated as 'cion'), which is a common nominalizer (e.g., vibración 'vibration'). All this suggests that the Abidiha is more conventionally suited to the transliteration of Spanish, or of Visayan (using a Spanish orthography), than it is to the Eskayan language, a fact that is crucial to the investigation of its historical development.

## Syllabic characters

When Eskaya pupils have progressed to a sufficient level, they are introduced to the remainder of the Simplit, which comprises fifty-three syllable sets, each containing between nine and thirty-one characters, and two sets for numerals and fractions. There is no expectation to commit all characters to memory. Instead, students are required to transcribe an existing Simplit for reference. Through

Table 5.1. Abidiha (alphabetic-
syllabic characters)

| | | |
|---|---|---|
| 𝒜𝒫 | [a] | 'a' |
| 𝒬 | [b], [bi] | 'b' |
| 𝒞 | [s], [si], [k] | 'c' |
| 𝒹 | [d], [di] | 'd' |
| ℰ. | [i] | 'e' |
| 𝒻. | [f] | 'f' |
| 𝒻 | [g], [h], [hi] | 'g' |
| 𝒜ℛ | [h], [tsi] | 'h' |
| 𝓆. | [i] | 'i' |
| 𝒫 | [hu] | 'j' |
| 𝓀 | [k], [ka] | 'k' |
| 𝓇 | [l], [li] | 'l' |
| 𝓂 | [m], [mi] | 'm' |
| 𝓃 | [n], [ni] | 'n' |
| 𝓃𝓎 | [nj] | 'ñ' |
| 0 | [u] | 'o' |
| 8 | [p], [pi] | 'p' |
| 6 | [k], [ku] | 'q' |
| 𝒮 | [r], [ri] | 'r' |
| 𝓁 | [s], [si] | 's' |
| 𝓉 | [t], [ti] | 't' |
| θ | [u] | 'u' |
| 𝒱. | [b], [bi] | 'v' |
| 𝒻oo | [kis] | 'x' |
| ℰ́ | [y] | 'y' |

regular use and repetition the most frequent characters are soon memorized. With so many available syllables to choose from, scribes have a great deal of freedom in deciding how to transliterate any given word. Thus, **katsila'** ('Spanish') is attested in traditional stories as both 𝓀𝒜ℛ𝓆. (<ka><tsi><la'>) and 𝓀𝓁𝓆. (<kat><si><la'>), the latter form notionally dividing the digraph 'ts' (representing /tʃ/) onto separate characters.

While apparent redundancy and lack are found among the twenty-five characters of the Abidiha, the remaining syllabic symbols in the Simplit as a whole are characterized by excess. Of the 1,065 symbols found in the syllabary, only about 460 of them are actually needed to represent the possible syllables in Eskayan or Visayan words. Even among these letters there are a number of duplicate forms; for example, <ʔar> is represented as both 𝛿 and 𝒜ᵗ, <ri> as both ℱ and ℒ, <taw> as 𝒟 and 𝒜ᵥ, <was> as 𝒶ℓ and ℋ, among other examples. Further, the Simplit goes so far as to include characters for thirty-seven syllable shapes that are not found in *any* Eskayan or Visayan words at all (Kelly 2016b). In reviewing these unattested syllables, what is of immediate interest is the fact that the sound sequences are (theoretically) available in Spanish or English words even if they are not found in Eskayan or Visayan. This extraordinary state of affairs lends weight to the possibility that Pinay devised the Eskaya writing system primarily to replicate and exceed European systems, even at the expense of practicality. Consistent with prophecies that Eskayan will one day be spoken everywhere in the world, perhaps Pinay thought to compile a more exhaustive set of symbols to live up to a universalist ambition for the language.

## Inahan *and* sinyas

For a large number of the purely syllabic characters, Eskaya scribes distinguish between the *inahan* ('mother')—the central graphic component of the character, typically representing a (C)CV- onset—and the smaller *sinyas* ('gesture'), which stands for the coda and is generally composed to the right of the *inahan*. Interestingly, the term *inahan* harmonizes with the conventional terminology used for other Malay writing systems such as Volaŋ'Onjatsy, Batak, Buginese, and Had Lampung, where C(V) characters are referred to by their users as 'mothers' and diacritics as 'children' (Adelaar 2005). To illustrate this distinction with an Eskaya example, the *inahan* character ⱡ <lu> stands for a CV- onset. But with the addition of a *sinyas* standing for the coda –ʔ one can produce the CVC character ⱡₛ <luʔ>. In rarer cases, however, the *inahan* stands for a vowel nucleus while the *sinyas* indicates an onset. For example, in the case of the character 𝒜ᵍ <da>, the *inahan* is the portion that resembles a Roman 'A,' and the *sinyas* is the closed curl at its far right standing for the /d/- onset. Another *sinyas* can be added in the form of a second closed curl to make 𝒜ᵦ <dad>; the system here is reminiscent of Korean Hangul in which single characters stand for independent syllables, but these syllables are further broken down graphically into alphabetic segments.

In short, any Eskayan character with the shape CVC is decomposable into two components as CV- combined with -C, or sometimes "alphabetically" as three components C-, -V-, and -C. It is also worth pointing out that although Eskayan is written from left to right, a *sinyas* representing an onset will, in most cases, still be written to the right of the *inahan*, as in the case of 𝒜ᵖ <da>.[3]

Complicating this system is the fact that the *sinyas* components do not function as regular diacritics. Graphically identical *sinyas* may be associated with different consonant values in different sets. For example, the characters � (<la>) and �ₒ (<la?>) are distinguished by the feature ₒ; however, in the set that follows the same feature differentiates 𝘔 (<ma>) from 𝘔ₒ (<maw>). The *inahan* components may also be irregular: compare, for example, 𝒜𝓏 <dad> with 𝑈𝑟 <dan>. This irregularity accounts for the great difficulty in learning Eskayan characters and is analogous to the irregularity in Eskayan vocabulary with its abundant suppletive verbs, as I will show in the next chapter. While for the most part, Eskaya characters and diacritics represent single segments or syllables, there are two exceptions: the disyllabic 𝒬𝒞 <narin> (**narin**, 'I') and the trisyllabic 𝓮𝓵𝓾𝓻 <chdiyaru> (**chdiyaru**, 'our') are logograms that are not easily analyzable into syllabic components.[4] The letter 𝒟 <taw> is intriguing as a potential rebus-like logogram because it is derived from the stylized shape of a human heart (familiar from Catholic sacred heart iconography) and represents the Visayan word *taw* 'person.'

## Numbers

Eskaya numerals accord with the Hindu-Arabic decimal system such that the placement of the symbol in a sequence determines its value to the power of ten. Hence 𝑃𝑃 is read as '11.' The Eskaya numeral system uses the symbol 𝒞 for '0' even though there is no attested word for it, and the innovation of mathematical functions such as means that equations can be performed in Eskayan. Indeed, Eskayan arithmetic is taught in the traditional schools using the script (Fig. 5.4).[5] There is no question, therefore, that Pinay's numerals are a cypher for a post-contact decimal system, even if a base-ten counting system was in use in the Visayas prior to Spanish colonization.[6]

As well as taking inspiration from the Hindu-Arabic system, a peculiarity of certain Eskaya numerals is that Pinay appears to have been inspired by their graphic form as well. However, as can be seen in Table 5.2, Eskaya numerals do not necessarily have the same value as their ostensible Hindu-Arabic counterparts.

Note, for example, that the subtly varying forms of �7 ('3'), �7 ('6'), and �7 ('8') are apparently based on the Hindu-Arabic '7,' and that �4 ('5') resembles the Hindu-Arabic '4.' It is possible that Pinay took inspiration from the idea of the 'numeral' but not the value itself (in the way that the Cherokee script takes inspiration from

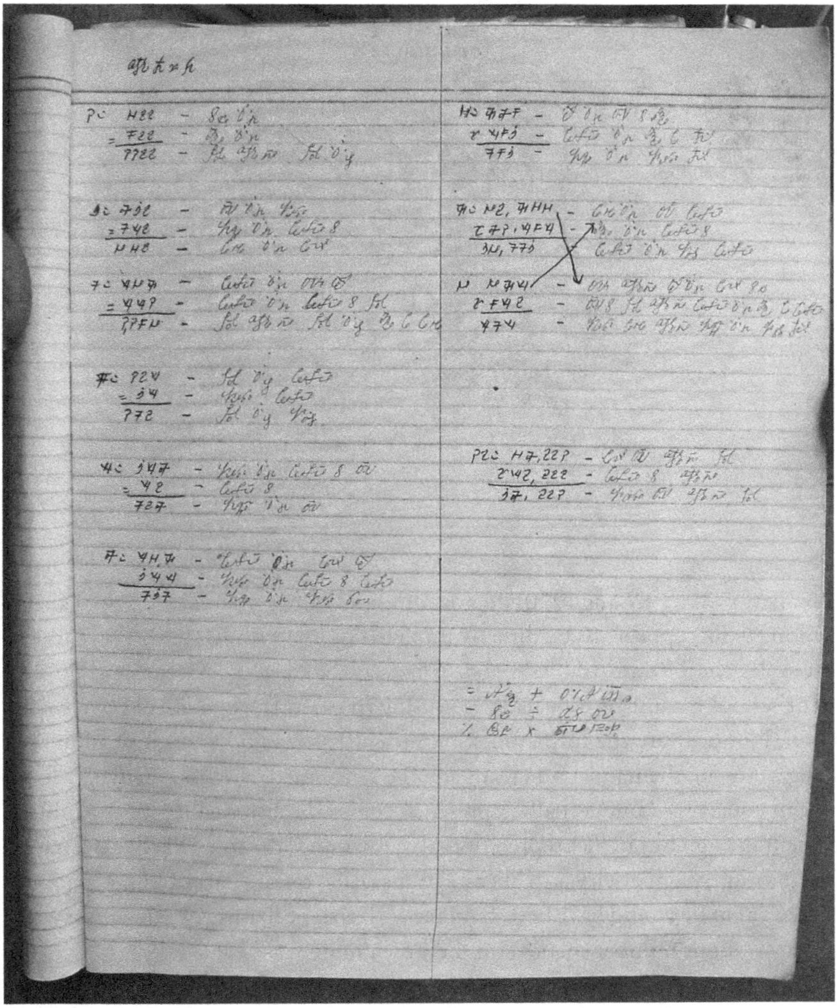

**FIGURE 5.4.** Page of equations using Eskayan numerals, Cadapdapan.

the form of certain Roman letters) or that there was a more conscious attempt at disguise or reassignment. It is interesting to observe that the Eskayan word for 'two' is **tri**, possibly inspired by English 'three' or Spanish *tres* while other numbers are less ambiguous borrowings from Spanish (e.g., **sing** from Spanish *cinco* 'five') or Visayan (**pan**, *upat*, 'four'; **num**, *unum*, 'six'; **pin**, *pitu* 'seven'; **wal**, *walu*, 'eight').[7] Similar reassignments of form and value are found in the Pahawh Hmong script, a writing system developed by the Messianic cultural revivalist Shong Lue Yang in 1959 in northern Vietnam. Although the system's biographers

Table 5.2. Eskaya symbols and words
for numerals

| 0 | ?' | [no word] |
|---|---|---|
| 1 | P | uy |
| 2 | ʃ | tri |
| 3 | ⁊ | kuy |
| 4 | f | pan |
| 5 | ५ | sing |
| 6 | ⁊ | num |
| 7 | H | pin |
| 8 | ⁊ | wal |
| 9 | ʮ | sim |

(Smalley, Vang, and Yang 1990) do not comment on the resemblance, the Pahawh Hmong 0 ('0') appears to be directly modeled on the Hindu-Arabic '0,' and ꞩ '2' resembles the Hindu-Arabic '3.' For those educated in a conventional government school it must be especially confusing to perform equations in the Eskaya script. Not only are the form and semantics of Eskaya numerals misleading, but some of the mathematical functions are also reassigned: the Eskaya glyph ▪ looks like an equals sign but actually represents +, and the Eskaya glyph ꙁ resembles a percentage sign but in fact represents ×. To my mind, the most likely explanation for this non-systematicity is deliberate obfuscation on the part of Pinay, since it is unlikely that he would have been familiar with the mechanics of a decimal system yet naive about number shapes and their meanings.

If deliberate obfuscation can be isolated in the numeral set, it raises the question as to whether other non-systematic elements within the Eskaya system were also engineered for the purposes of mystifying those who are not formally trained in the script. A similar, though less forceful, hypothesis has also been suggested for Cherokee. In his influential volume on writing systems David Diringer argued that since there is no single Roman-derived Cherokee symbol that has retained its "original" Roman phonetic value, the inventor Sequoyah must have intended to create a script that deliberately differentiated itself from the Roman alphabet (in which, by implication, he must have also been literate) (Diringer [1948] 1968, 129). The motives for such conscious acts of obfuscation are impossible to recover, and there are no traditional Eskaya explanations for Pinay's decision-making in this sphere. The strategy is nonetheless consistent with the processes of mimicry-and-rejection that, I argued, underpin the entire Eskaya creative enterprise. Pinay, in other words, decided to innovate forms that were familiar yet contrastive. When it came to Eskaya numerals and mathematical operations, however, he went a step further in his more radical decision to disguise one sign for another. This has the effect of misleading a naive reader instead of merely setting up a distinction. Although I have no reliable basis for this intuition, I can imagine that Pinay's trickster mathematics was, in this way, intended as a shibboleth for reinforcing an insider Eskaya identity defined by access to an exclusive knowledge system. The arcane lessons in arithmetic provided by the colonial lowland schools could, in this way, be countered by an even more esoteric system in the highlands.

## Script

The Eskaya script is transmitted through rote copying of the Simplit from teacher to student. As a result of ongoing intergenerational transcriptions there are minor differences between individual versions of each Simplet, just as there are slight variations in the rote-transcribed Eskaya literature. This method of transmission accounts for the survival, in reference form, of characters for syllables that are unattested in the Eskayan or Visayan languages and the fact that most Eskaya scribes are not conscious of these redundancies.

As shown earlier, the Eskayan system does not universally make use of an inherent vowel (except, to some extent, in the Abidiha) nor any consistent system of diacritics. For most of the hundreds of characters that make up the Simplit, each symbol stands for a distinct syllable and must be learned independently. A pictographic origin for certain Eskaya letter shapes bears some consideration. Although for Eskaya people the human anatomy is identified as the sole source of inspiration for Eskaya letters, it can be argued that body parts and poses were first and foremost a mnemonic prompt for those acquiring literacy in Eskayan, and that the traditional stories are a post hoc rationale for what is essentially a pedagogical strategy.[8] This anthropomorphism is nonetheless integral to the traditional view that that script is natural and "embodied," as opposed to arbitrary and frivolous; in Chapter 7 I will show how this ideology is made explicit in traditional texts that denigrate the "Spanish" (i.e., Roman) alphabet. Metaphors of personhood and the human body even enter the (Visayan) metalanguage for describing the Eskaya syllabary where the diacritic *sinyas* ('gesture' but more properly 'body signal') physically emanates from the *inahan* ('mother'). The Eskaya were not alone in associating Philippine writing with the human body. As interest in the Philippine script experienced a revival among nationalists in the years prior to the Philippine Revolution (1896–1898), the eccentric *ilustrado* Pedro Paterno surmised that the

Philippine symbols ◯ and ⋎ as in ◯⌢⋎ (<ba><ha><la>, *bathala* 'god') were imitative of the female and male sexual organs, respectively, and that ⌢ represented a divine ray of light uniting the two (Paterno [1887] 1915). Similar associations between letters and the human body are known further afield in other Indic literacy traditions. In the Hindu *Purana*, a goddess of writing (Lipidevi) is described as a "body made of letters," and some tantric rituals involve the use of letters that are characterized as organs of a divine body (Guillaume-Pey 2021). In a Sora religious community of East India, a set of sacred letters is worshiped as the embodiment of the god Jagannath (Guillaume-Pey 2014, 2021).

Whether anatomic resemblances preceded or followed the initial creation of the Eskaya script, the alphabetic characters of the Abidiha are represented as corresponding, with varying degrees of iconicity, to whole-body poses or arrangements of individual limbs or hands (Fig. 5.2). The non-alphabetic characters in the Abidiha are also associated with body positions; however, eleven of them are compared to or derived from internal organs. The letters ℓ <pa> and ℰ𝒾 <pag>, for example, are shown to represent the head and its connection to the esophagus and intestines, while a heart models the syllable 𝒟 <taw>, as discussed earlier. Eskaya consultants identified the letters 𝒫𝓎 <pri>, 𝒞ℰ <syun>, ℰ𝒮 <tsu>, ℋ <was>, 𝒥𝒫 <tid>, 𝒽𝓮 <kri>, 𝒞𝓮 <nya>, and 𝓂𝓀ℰ <ning> as internal body parts but were uncertain about which organs they corresponded to.

The anatomic iconicity of Eskaya letters is not, however, the only advantage available to learners of the script. It is clear that certain Eskaya characters are modeled on their Roman counterparts; in the Abidiha, characters that are evidently inspired by the Roman alphabet include 𝒜 'a,' 𝒞 'c,' 0 'o,' 𝒶 't,' and 𝒱 'v.' Although Eskayan "pseudo-diacritics" resist generalization, and thus ease of acquisition, there are helpful family resemblances between components of certain Eskayan syllabic graphemes and the Roman alphabet, just as there are in the Abidiha. For example, there are many Eskayan characters of which the *inahan* is comparable in both form and sound value to a Roman 'a' or 'o' in upper- or lowercase. These are too numerous to reproduce here, but by way of brief example: the *inahan* component of the characters 𝒶 <ba>, 𝒶𝒮 <bag>, 𝒶 <wa>, and 𝒶𝓃 <wang> has affinities with Roman lowercase 'a'; the letters 𝒜 <ga>, 𝒜𝓃 <nas>, 𝒜 <tag>, and 𝒜𝒮 <yab> with the uppercase 'A'; and the letters Ô <bu>, 𝒪𝒾 <duk>, and 𝒪ℓ <ul> with 'O,' among dozens of others. Certain onsets and codas are also represented with *sinyas* that resemble a corresponding Roman letter. Where this occurs, the form tends to be less arbitrary and is found to have the same value in more than one character. The sounds ℓ <i> and ℓ𝓇 <in>, become 𝒴ℓ <yi> and 𝒴ℓ𝓇 <yin> with the addition of a *sinyas* that resembles a lowercase Roman 'y.' The various *sinyas* for the coda -/t/ frequently resemble the crossed line in Roman lowercase 't,' as in 𝒜 <at>, 𝒶𝓍 <bit>, 𝒶 <dit>, 𝒻 <hit>, and 𝓂𝒶 <mat>.

Likewise, for many characters that represent syllables with the coda -/k/, the *sinyas* resembles a lowercase Roman 'k' or 'c,' such as ꞓk <kik>, Aк <nak>, ｸᶜ <lik>, and ꝺc <tik>, among many others. The use of *k* [-k] as a 'pseudo-diacritic' has implications for the historical development of the Eskaya script, as I will discuss in Chapter 9.

## The past and future of Eskayan writing

Of the precise origins of the Eskaya writing system, little can be learned from the documentary record, but the script itself lends clues to its own genesis. Whether chanced upon in a cave, given to Datahan directly by the ancestor Pinay, or retrieved through spiritual inspiration, the Abidiha, or primary alphabet, is likely to have emerged first. This was later followed by the twenty-one syllabic-only letters that are typically represented as a supplement to the Abidiha (Fig. 5.2). Last to be revealed was the remaining body of approximately one thousand additional syllables of the Simplit. The motivations for the script's development (or revelation), and the stages through which it passed, will be set out in more detail in Chapter 9. However, it can be briefly noted that its social and historical circumstances are broadly similar to those of other twentieth-century scripts in the region. Just like the many revealed scripts of mainland Southeast Asia (Kelly 2018a), the Eskaya system came to prominence in the context of extreme social upheaval and anti-colonial conflict—circumstances that gave impetus to radical religious change and a collective desire to rediscover and valorize ethnic identity. These circumstances are the subject of Part III.

The non-systematicity of the writing system and the elaborate form of many of the letters, even those representing common sounds, makes literacy acquisition especially laborious. Unlike other recent scripts of Southeast Asia such as Pahawh Hmong (Smalley, Vang, and Yang 1990), and Iban (Philip 2007), the Eskayan system never went through any stages of reform and simplification; if anything, it became more complicated as the Simplit expanded. Ironically perhaps, the very act of committing Eskayan letters to paper may have impeded its journey toward simplification. Crossing out or destroying Eskayan text is still disapproved of, making any act of drafting or reworking very difficult. It is, however, still possible that over time Eskaya scribes will consciously or unconsciously make changes in the system, simplifying elaborate characters, eliminating redundant or unattested syllables in reference documents, and formalizing a standard set of diacritics. The very fact that a majority of Eskaya characters in handwritten syllabaries are unused or no longer used is perhaps a sign that simplification is already under way. Certainly, such slow and unconscious processes of simplification can be detected in the histories of other scripts (Kelly et al. forthcoming).

However, if radical reforms to the system make the traditional literature unreadable to younger generations, as transpired with the reformation of the Shan script of Burma (Morey 2015) and the romanization of Turkish (Lewis 1999), they are unlikely to gain acceptance. One striking reform is already in evidence. Fabian Baja, like his mentor Mariano Datahan, was opposed to the learning and teaching of English, but since his passing in 2007 the Eskaya script is now used for writing English sentences for classroom exercises in the traditional Taytay school that combine script literacy with English-language acquisition.

The Eskaya writing system is unique among the world's scripts for the extent to which it combines various modes of representing linguistic structure. I have shown that Eskayan has alphabetic, alphasyllabic, and strictly syllabic features with an inconsistent system of consonant diacritics and more than 50 percent redundancy in its recorded syllable characters, including thirty-seven characters for representing phonotactic impossibilities. Such redundancy is echoed in the morphology of the script where graphic contrasts are overdetermined with no clear tendency toward a stereotyped orientation of strokes and loops (Kelly 2016b). Orthographic variation is also apparent in how individual scribes choose to segment words into syllables, consonants, and vowels: one word may have a number of acceptable spellings.

Eskaya alphabetic letters have a cypher-like quality as if they were designed for direct transliteration (or encryption) of Spanish, or Hispanic orthographies of Visayan. Arguably, although not unequivocally, the system shows a degree of logography (and perhaps pictography and ideography) in the Abidiha, or primary 'alphabet.' Less ambiguously ideographic, the numeral set is decimal and can even be used for performing equations but appears to include deliberately obfuscatory or misleading elements from the perspective of a scribe who has prior literacy in a Hindu-Arabic numeral system. This obfuscation, detected in the apparent incongruence between certain number shapes, their semantics, and their phonetic realizations, suggests the possibility of deliberate opacity in other aspects of the writing system. One such area is the Eskaya system of consonant pseudo-diacritics: one-off graphic elements that perform the function of differentiation only, with no combinatoric value. I propose, somewhat speculatively, that deliberate obfuscation across the Eskaya writing system as a whole was a function of Pinay's desire to generate an insider's code, a worthy adversary to the colonial knowledge systems that had encroached on Bohol's soil.

As for its inspiration, the script exhibits an influence from the Roman alphabet, while the writing system displays Hispanic alphabetic elements as well as inherent vowels reminiscent of indigenous scripts of the Philippines, even if Eskaya vowels display more variation in their default realizations. For all these reasons I have proposed that Eskaya is the *least* systematic writing system on record and in regular use today (Kelly 2016a). As I have shown here, this lack of systematicity is not so much about the relative depth of its orthography, i.e., the degree to which individual graphemes correspond to phonemes (Katz and Feldman 1983). Rather, it concerns its astonishing combination of variant systems and the marked superfluity of graphemes that are brought to the task of representing phonemes and syllables. In other words, Eskaya violates the maxim that there is an "underlying rationale of efficiency in matching a language's characteristic phonology and morphology to a written form" (Katz and Frost 1992). Indeed, Pinay's values were arguably *opposed* to efficiency on principle. Redundancy, complexity, and misdirection, it would appear, were all productive strategies to the extent that they generated opacity and increased the distance between knowledgeable insiders and uncomprehending outsiders.

Despite its extravagant non-systematicity the Eskaya script is not strictly arbitrary. Its relationship to the Roman alphabet, its putative derivation from the human body, and its application of various mechanisms (such as alphabetic letters, diacritics, and inherent vowels) point to serious deliberation in its creation. The thoughtfulness that went into its construction suggests that its unsystematic elements were not merely (or always) naive oversights. What is clearly at play is a strategy of substitution combined with elaboration, or what I have referred to in Chapter 1 in terms of "mimicry and rejection." Pinay wove together marked elements from other scripts and orthographies to build a complex heterographic system in which these features were combined to cooperate according a new logic. In Chapter 7 I will review how Eskaya people themselves make sense of their special script through an analysis of traditional Eskaya stories that specifically comment on it. As I will show, Eskaya writing is extolled as agentive and animate, in stark comparison with colonial alphabets that are disparaged in Eskaya literature as inert, arbitrary, and inadequate.

Indeed, the valued complexity of Eskaya writing may account, in part, for its successful transmission for over a century or more: the misdirection, redundancy, and inconsistency that make it opaque to outsiders may also serve to protect the knowledge and community identity it encodes in the Eskaya manuscripts. In the manner of Darwin's famous example of the impractical but desirable peacock's tail the Eskaya script's elaborate and almost calligraphic morphology may increase its appeal to students wishing to learn it. As the scholar of writing David Diringer once noted, in a Darwinian mode, "[t]he best fitted resists and survives, although sometimes the surrounding circumstances may bear a greater influence on the survival of a script than its merits as a system of writing" (Diringer [1948] 1968, 4–5). Indeed, the relative merits of systematicity might, in the case of the Eskaya script, have given way to the greater survival benefits of hybridity, redundancy, and *non*-systematicity. Part accident, part design, the Eskaya script is perhaps less a feat of engineering than a form of scribal art.

In the chapter that follows I turn at last to the language that the Eskaya script represents. I will show that the heterographia of the writing system is recapitulated in Eskaya morphosyntax and lexicon. The underlying grammar of Eskayan, for example, is a morphologically reduced form of Boholano-Visayan but has been populated with a unique lexicon. The vast majority of these Eskayan words are not borrowed from equivalent terms in other languages, and yet a widespread influence from Visayan, Spanish, and English can be detected in the syllable structure as well as certain crucial sets of vocabulary. In this way, Pinay's design template for the Eskayan lexicon is an extension of his ambitious strategy of mimicry, rejection, and elaboration.

## Notes

1. Eskayan phonology and the writing system are described in greater detail in Kelly (2015, 2016b), morphosyntax in Kelly (2012), and the lexicon in Kelly (2016c).
2. A precedent for this system of vocalizing recited letter names is found in the Type 2 variant of Caroline Islands Script (Riesenberg and Kaneshiro 1960).
3. J, Fraser Bennett writes, "Indic scripts generally place some vowels in positions other than to the right of the consonants which they temporally follow. [ . . . ] Compare also the Pahawh Hmong script which, like Kayah Li, is a Southeast Asian script of recent invention used for an open-syllable language. Pahawh Hmong places all vowels characters *before* the consonants which they temporally follow" (Bennett 1993, 12).
4. Note nonetheless that the leftmost graphic element of ჱ <chdiyaru> can at least be isolated as the syllable ჱ <chdi>. One Simplit includes a character for the sequence **tsudub** /tʃudub/, which does not have a known meaning and is not attested in Eskaya literature or wordlists.
5. Interestingly, Pahawh Hmong also has unique symbols for arithmetic functions, although the original Source Version did not include a zero (Smalley, Vang, and Yang 1990, 79).
6. This is evident from etymologies of Visayan numerals but is also noted in the historical record. Ignacio Francisco Alcina observed that "[the Visayans] did not have arithmetic or numbers which may correspond to ours in writing, although, it is certain they counted by tens as we do" (Alcina [1668] 2005, 91).
7. Jes Tirol argued that **tri** ('two'), **kuy** ('three'), and **pan** ('four') were derived from Sanskrit *tri* ('three'), *catur* ('four'), and *panca* ('five'), and that the Sanskirt *dua* ('two') had been dropped in Eskayan to bring about a recalibration of the numeral sequence (Tirol 1993b).
8. This presents another functional parallel to the Hangul system (created circa 1443) wherein consonant characters were designed to represent human speech organs as a mnemonic to their place and manner of articulation.

# 6 WORDS AND THEIR ORIGINS

In contrast to the vast majority of the world's lesser-known languages, Eskayan has the singular advantage of having been documented by its own speakers, who have produced reference syllabaries, wordlists, and a traditional literature for several generations without any mediation from outsiders. Given that handwritten text production is the domain of Eskayan language use with the most vitality today, my analysis of Eskayan grammar and words has relied heavily on this stable and growing corpus. Eskaya people themselves defer to the traditional manuscripts in order to adjudicate correct forms of Eskayan linguistic expression, via a principle I have referred to as 'literality,' by analogy with 'grammaticality' (Chapter 5).

In the present chapter I will draw on Eskaya texts primarily for insights into the form of Eskayan words and their sources of inspiration. Beyond providing a description of the Eskayan lexicon, my aim is to enter into the mind of the creator Pinay, to reconstruct the linguistic decisions that he made and to generate a linguistic and ideological profile of him.

I will show that the grammar of Eskayan presents as a kind of plaster cast of Visayan to the extent that it reproduces all of its major contours but with a systematic reduction of morphological complexity. Yet the simplification is deceptive since new forms of complexity are reintroduced in the guise of verbal irregularity, variable root length, and highly diverse syllable structures. Despite the strong syntactic relationship to Visayan, remarkably little Visayan *vocabulary* has entered into the Eskayan lexicon. Spanish, on the other hand, is powerfully evident in the Hispanic syllable structure of Eskayan words. This European "accent" makes spoken Eskayan sound like a caricature of a foreign language for those whose primary model of linguistic foreignness is Spanish. Eskayan vocabulary also includes a very small set of unambiguous Spanish and English borrowings. Some of these are predictable to the extent that they are used to lexify colonial products and ideas. For the most part, however, novel phenomena associated with colonial contact, such as modern technologies and administrative roles, are denoted with pristine Eskayan coinages. Meanwhile,

*The Last Language on Earth*. Kelly, Piers, Oxford University Press. © Oxford University Press 2022.
DOI: 10.1093/oso/9780197509913.003.0006

clear Spanish and English loans are found in surprising domains such as body part terminology, a rare state of affairs in natural languages.

The peculiar distribution of notionally foreign and "native" words conjures an image of Pinay as an individual who was intimately acquainted with Visayan, well familiar with Spanish, had at least some exposure to English, and was able to manipulate the interplay of all three. Whether Pinay is to be conceived of as a historical individual or a mythological construct, I maintain on this basis that he was plausibly a post-contact Visayan native, associated with the period of transition between Spanish-speaking and English-speaking colonial powers. Pinay created a distinctive language by innovating a new lexicon for Visayan that nonetheless relied on the available structures within his existing linguistic repertoire.

In this chapter, and in the chapters that follow, I argue that Pinay exploited this insider knowledge to replicate the literal terms of colonial representation and substitute them with authentic native alternatives. His inspired vocabulary was to become, in essence, the linguistic foundation for a more expansive literary program of substitution and realignment in which the innate foreignness of colonial narratives, lifeways, and belief systems was not so much opposed as creatively re-channeled for anti-colonial ends (Chapter 7).

## Eskayan grammar

Although I will not be plunging into the deep end of Eskayan grammar (a much more comprehensive treatment is available in Kelly [2012]), it is worth making a few introductory observations to frame the analysis of the Eskayan lexicon. A cursory review of bilingual Visayan–Eskayan texts indicates that the structural correspondences between the two languages are manifest at the level of the literary discourse all the way down to the individual word. This impression is emphasized by the fact that almost no line of Eskayan text exceeds or falls short of the number of words in its Visayan translation (see Prologue). As such, the parallel translations have the distinct quality of word-for-word calques, in the same way, for example, that the English terms 'earworm' and 'superman' are calques of the German *Ohrwurm* and *Übermensch*, respectively. Consider the following Eskayan (bold) sentences together with their Visayan (italics) counterparts:

(1) **Yi** **Omanad** **aripirna** **huntun** **kun** **Jomabad.**
    SPEC    Omanad   soldier    under    GEN    Jomabad

    *Si*    *Omanad*   *sundalu*   *ubus*    *ni*    *Jomabad.*
    SPEC    Omanad     soldier     under     GEN    Jomabad

'Omanad was a soldier under the command of Jomabad.'

(2) **Istu**  **dirisil**  **chdinchdiyumli**  **yi**  **Magellan**  **giyu.**
Istu   dirisil   chdin-chdiyumli   yi   Magellan   giyu
SPEC   sign   AV.RE.PFV-understand   SPEC   Magellan   at.once

*Ang*  *sinyas*  *ningsabut*  *Si*  *Magellan*  *dayun.*
ang   sinyas   ning-sabut   si   Magellan   dayun
SPEC   sign   AV.RE.PFV-understand   SPEC   Magellan   at.once

'Magellan understood the sign at once.'

At no point do the Eskayan or Visayan interlinear layers diverge, suggesting that the relationship between them is one of text to cypher-text in the same way that the primary Eskayan alphabet encodes Roman letters in a one-to-one relationship (Chapter 5). Even reduplicated Eskayan lexemes mirror their equivalent reduplicative forms in Visayan. Consider, for example, the symmetrical relationship between the Visayan terms *diyus* ('God') and *diyusdiyus* ('false god'), and their counterpart terms in Eskayan: **ara** ('God) and **araara** ('false god').

## Homophonic pairs

The structural equivalence is further reinforced by the symmetrical distribution of Eskayan and Visayan homophones, or terms that are phonetically identical but have different semantic values and etymologies. To give an English example, the words 'doe' (female deer) and 'dough' (unbaked bread) are homophonic, but we would not presume that terms meaning female deer and unbaked bread would also be homophonic pairs in languages other than English, except by coincidence. However, *every* homophonic pair of this kind in Visayan is lexified with a corresponding set of homophones in Eskayan. Thus, in direct contrast to the deliberate irregularity explored in the previous chapter, Pinay's lexification of Eskayan was *over*-regularized in the precision with which it has been mapped onto Visayan. If the putative creator Pinay had thereby merely grafted a new set of lexemes onto an existing Visayan rootstock, it raises the question of whether Eskayan is really an independent language, or whether it is simply a special way of speaking Visayan, a situation that has led Rupert Stasch to argue that Eskayan "blurs the typological boundary between 'register' and 'language'" (Stasch 2012).

## "Foreign" complexity

Nonetheless, the minor areas of *difference* between the grammatical systems provide meaningful clues about the historical development of Eskayan and the language ideologies that promoted and sustained it. Pinay appears to have developed highly variable syllable structures and verbal morphology that did not merely imitate colonial linguistic models but embellished them to the point of exaggeration. In effect, he exploited the perceived complexities of Spanish, and to a lesser extent English, as authentic exemplars of linguistic foreignness. In Pinay's creative practice colonial forms are not so much mocked as imitated and extended, suggesting an implicit respect for the power and potential of these codes.

One of the most striking examples of this tendency is the fact that Eskayan syllable structures are much more diverse than those of Visayan, exhibiting a high prevalence of dense consonant clusters that are more typically found in Spanish and English (Kelly 2015). These "colonial" clusters, in words such as **prindidu** ('tooth') and **istrapiradu** ('flower'), are so common as to suggest that Pinay found this feature to be a salient index of linguistic otherness.

On the whole, words in native Philippine languages are built from roots of one to two syllables. These simple roots are then inflected with a large number of affixes: that is, units added to the beginning, end, or middle of the root. Visayan roots, for example, tend to be of two syllables to which an array of verbal affixes might be attached in order to specify fine-grained information about tense, aspect, and mood. In Eskayan, on the other hand, the relationship between simple roots and variable affixes is flipped. Eskayan roots range widely in length from one syllable, as in **lu'** ('valley'), to as many as five, as in **wasnangpanudlu** ('think'). Meanwhile, there are just five Eskayan affixes available to do the work of fourteen Visayan counterparts. Superficially it would therefore appear that Eskayan verbs are hobbled in their capacity to express the same level of nuance as they do in other Philippine languages. However, many Eskayan verbs are irregular with unanalyzable covert morphology that appears to be implicit in the whole word. Such unanalyzable or 'suppleted' verbs are analogous to the way the English word 'went' encodes the past tense of 'go' without recourse to a productive segment such as '-ed.' Here is a clarifying example of such suppletion in Eskayan. The non-suppletive Visayan word *hikayun* ('be prepared') is composed of the root *hikay* ('prepare') and the affix *-un* for specifying the patient voice irrealis, essentially meaning that the action has not occurred or is hypothetical. The structure of *hikayun* is transparent and regular. However, this very same word in Eskayan is **kubit**, a word that cannot be carved up into a root and affix. In other words, the two neat components that are easily extracted and reassembled in *hikayun* are "baked in" to the suppleted word **kubit**. Eskayan-speaking consultants with a sophisticated grasp of both Visayan and Eskayan morphology are unable to point to which part of a suppleted verb is doing the inflection, responding simply that the word is "all in one."

This invites the hypothesis that Pinay's analytical focus was on orthographically discrete words and that engineering a consistent morphology was of secondary concern to his creative enterprise. Further, it raises the possibility that Pinay was deliberately including irregularity as a feature of his language. It is not clear if there is any categorical principle determining which kinds of Eskayan verbal roots are analyzable and which are not. However, it is worth noting that unanalyzable irregular verbs are more frequently found in Eskayan *wordlists* than in the traditional narratives. In terms of the actual structure of Eskayan morphosyntax this fact may be considered peripheral, but it nonetheless sheds light on the circumstances in which the Eskayan language was devised, and the relexification method Pinay may have employed to achieve his ends. As I will outline later, Eskayan wordlists, including older manuscripts belonging to deceased Eskayan speakers, provide crucial insights into how Eskayan words may have been assigned to Visayan equivalents.

In the bilingual traditional literature, the reductiveness in both morphology and semantics of the Eskayan layer points to the strong probability that the Visayan text was composed first before being shoehorned into a more rudimentary Eskayan mold. It is harder to explain a reverse trajectory whereby the Visayan text acquired more nuance and verbal complexity in the process of its translation from Eskayan. This suspicion is reinforced by a stylistic feature of Eskaya narratives. A number of texts include small digressions from the main story in which Eskayan-language words and phrases are glossed for the benefit of the audience. An example I will return to in the next chapter is:

(3) | **Istu** | **hirdu** | **kapitan** | **ya** | **Ispanyul** |
|---|---|---|---|---|
| SPEC | 'hirdu' | captain | GEN | Spanish |
| *Ang* | *hirdu* | *kapitan* | *sa* | *Ispanyul.* |

'[The term] **hirdu** is *capitán* in Spanish'

My supposition is that at the time these texts were dictated, the Eskayan language had only been partially recuperated, and the parenthetical explanations of Eskayan words and their meanings were provided as a foretaste for a language that was in the process of emerging.

## The lexicon

Regardless of how Eskayan is characterized, Pinay's vocabulary is a fundamental aspect of what makes Eskayan unique. There are at least three thousand items in the lexicon, as extracted from Eskaya literature and wordlists.[1] Of these words, approximately 1.5 percent are borrowed from Spanish or English, less than 1 percent have an identifiable Visayan origin, and the remaining words are "native" terms that cannot be traced to outside languages. Though fewer "borrowed" words are found in Eskayan, relative to Visayan, these terms have special diagnostic value; just how Pinay exploited the lexical raw materials available to him will be shown to conform to consistent patterns, and these, in turn, give depth and detail to the context of relexification. Further, the preponderance of words in particular semantic domains, such as the domestic sphere, and the relative scarcity of terms relevant to other environments and activities such as fishing and agriculture, provide further clues about the circumstances of lexification, a situation that is revisited in its historical context in Chapter 9.

Although many of the Eskayan lexical items analyzed in the present chapter are attested in the corpus of traditional literature, most have been sourced from Eskayan wordlists made available to me by speakers. These include the Visayan–Eskayan wordlists of Sisinia Peligro and Alberta Galambao (Fig. 6.1), and the Spanish–English–Eskayan lists attributed to Domingo Castañares (Fig. 6.2) and Fabian Baja, among others. A full glossary of Eskayan terms mentioned in this work is provided in the "Glossary of Eskayan Terms Used in This Volume" at the end of this book.

The traditional Eskayan wordlists have an added importance to the analysis of the Eskayan lexicon due to the fact that Pinay is likely to have relied on foreign

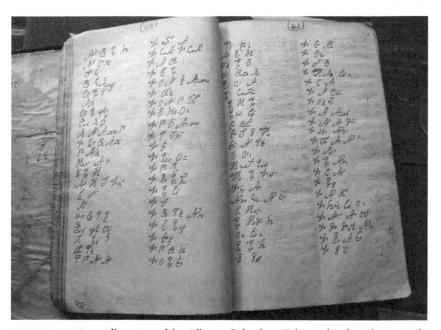

FIGURE 6.1. A wordlist penned by Alberta Galambao. Eskayan headwords are in the left-hand column of each page, with Cebuano glosses in the right-hand column.

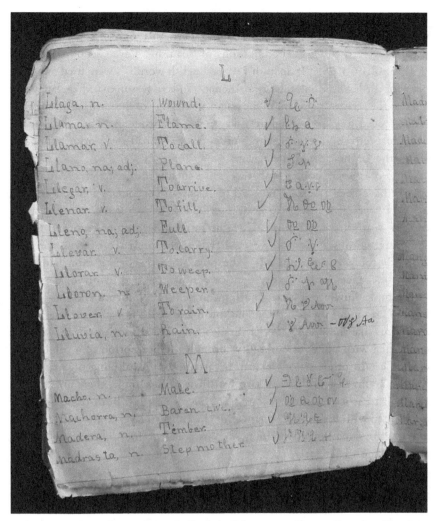

FIGURE 6.2. Pages from a Spanish–English–Eskayan wordlist attributed to Domingo Castañares (1912–1985).

wordlists as a template for lexifying Eskayan. The Castañares Manuscript (Fig. 6.2), a wordlist of uncertain age, appears to be a hand transcription of a Spanish–English–Visayan pedagogical text, in which the Visayan glosses have been wholly substituted with Eskayan alternatives. I have argued elsewhere that Eskayan verbal suppletion imitated the same conspicuous irregularity in English and Spanish verbs, and that this was part of a drive to represent Eskayan as comparable to colonial languages while simultaneously remaining exotic and opaque (Kelly 2012).

The practice of modifying existing wordlists to create pedagogical materials was not unique to the Eskaya community. Early textbooks used by American teachers were themselves modifications of Spanish–Visayan school textbooks (L.B. Tirol 1975, 251). If Spanish and/or English wordlists were used as a template for the lexification of Eskayan, then it stands to reason that these languages were, at the very least, present in the linguistic ecology of the lexification environment. Indeed, a Spanish–English–Eskayan wordlist would have been of little use to a prospective learner of Eskayan unless they also had some prior familiarity with either of these colonial languages.

It is necessary to point out that wordlists such as the Castañares Manuscript cannot have been the sole standard for Eskayan vocabulary items. Variation exists between wordlists that are transcribed by Eskaya students today, while certain words are attested in Eskaya literature that are not recorded in any surviving wordlist, and vice versa. Further, the presence of synonyms for basic vocabulary items points to the possibility that lexification happened in discrete stages or that more than one individual was involved. Consider, for example, **kuwir** and **iskrit** (both mean 'school'); **kabrum** and **hus** ('water buffalo'); **tap** and **uwis** ('peso'); and **dudu** and **bril** ('horse'). The survival of synonyms like these suggests that Eskaya language authorities have not been concerned with policing variability through the promotion of a single standard. Certain other synonyms can be attributed to calquing of Spanish or English terms in wordlists. In two wordlists, for example, there are Spanish headword entries for *luna* ('moon') and *mes* ('month'). Both these concepts are lexified with *bulan* in Cebuano, but the Eskayan layer follows the Spanish and English semantic distinction with separate terms for *luna*/'moon' (**kuldu**) and *mes*/'month' (**ngari**).

## Sources of inspiration

I use the term 'inspiration' to refer to words of "foreign" origin—including Visayan—and avoid misleading metaphors such as 'loan' or 'borrowing.'[2] Since Eskayan and Visayan phonologies exhibit strong similarities I have sought out Visayan-like patterns in the Eskayan lexicon to guide my identification of Visayan inspirations. For example, a regular alternation between Visayan /l/ → /r/ corroborates a relationship between the Visayan *arak* ('wine or liquor') and Eskayan **alak** ('wine or liquor') in Table 6.1. For identifying words of presumptive origin in colonial languages I have judged phonetic and semantic resemblance of roots, taking into consideration analogous processes in the phonotactic adaptation of Spanish or English words in lexicons of Philippine languages, e.g., /f/ → /p/. In the interests of thoroughness I have deliberately cast the net wide, and in some

Table 6.1. Visayan elements in Eskayan

| Visayan | Eskayan |
| --- | --- |
| *arak* ('wine or liquor'), ultimately from Arabic *araq* ('sweat'; 'juice') | **alak** ('wine or liquor') |
| *asa* ('where?') | **aya** ('where?') |
| *aswang* ('supernatural force that preys on human organs'; 'vampire') | **aswang** ('kind of bird whose call signifies the presence of a vampire'; 'a vampire') |
| *babaylan* ('shaman') | **babaylan** ('shaman,' 'priest') |
| *basak* ('field of wet-cultivated rice') | **basak** ('large basket for grain') |
| *buktun* ('arms') | **tingbuk** ('arms') |
| *bulbul* ('pubic hair') | **bulbing** ('hair,' 'pubic hair'; 'feather') |
| *buntag* ('morning'); Hiligaynon and Bikolano *aga* ('morning') | **aga** ('morning') |
| *higala* ('friend') | **gal** ('friend') |
| *kinsa* ('who?') | **kinya** ('who?') |
| *langgam* ('bird') | **langam** ('fly' [insect]) |
| *lumad* ('native,' 'native-born citizen') | **lumad** ('tribe') |
| *magtutudlo* ('teacher') | **tutulan** ('teacher') |
| *nanay* ('mother') | **nani** ('mother') |
| *paypay* ('fan') | **paypaypling** ('butterfly'); **tipaypay** ('small butterfly') |
| *pitu* ('seven') | **pin** ('seven') |
| *pulu* ('ten') | **pun** ('ten') |
| *sa* ('to') | **ya** ('to') |
| *siyam* ('nine') | **sim** ('nine') |
| *magtiayun* ('romantic couple') | **tiyunmiridu** ('romantic couple') |
| *unum* ('six') | **num** ('six') |
| *upat* ('four') | **pan** ('four'); **pansi** ('forty') |
| *uwak* ('crow') | **uwan** ('crow') |
| *walu* ('eight') | **wal** ('eight') |

cases my identification of possible lexical relationships is speculative; I have noted wherever the analysis is uncertain.

## Visayan in Eskayan

When submitted to a lexical comparative analysis, Eskayan vocabulary does not coincide significantly with the lexicons of Austronesian languages. Reviewing the

Eskayan lexicon as a whole, I have identified just twenty-four plausible Visayan inspirations, including one term of possible Hiligaynon or Bikolano origin. These are listed in Table 6.1.

The data are too minimal to make any kind of confident generalizing claim, but of interest here are the apparent cognates of six Austronesian number terms ('four,' 'six,' 'seven,' 'eight,' 'nine,' 'ten'), two body part terms ('arms,' 'pubic hair'), and one term apparently sourced from regional lexicons ('morning'). In a relexification scenario Pinay may have been sufficiently familiar with regional languages or dialect differences to appreciate the relative stability of these kinds of core terms across Philippine languages and be inspired to innovate a cognate-like lexeme. And yet, despite the ostensible inclusion of conspicuous cognates in core vocabulary, many Eskayan words like 'one' (*usa*, **uy**), 'hand' (*kamut*, **dapami**), and 'day' (*adlaw*, **abiya**) fail to be cognate.

Table 6.1 points to a strong pattern across foreign-inspired Eskayan lexemes: rarely is a word identical in both form and semantics between the Eskayan term and its foreign cognate. In other words, when lexemes like **balsa**, **basak**, and **lumad** are phonetically equivalent to their Visayan glosses, their semantics will differ, if only subtly, but where Visayan and Eskayan term have the same gloss, their *phonetic* forms will differ, as seen, for example, in **num** ('six') and *unum*, 'six.' Minimally, a cognate pair must differ in form, semantics, or both (as seen in Table 6.4 later). Here Pinay appears to be representing another salient feature of natural languages, namely, dialect variation, or more accurately, lexical variation where the difference in question is marked yet mutually intelligible between speakers of both varieties. The word **langam** ('fly [insect]') is arguably an overt nod to dialect difference. As discussed in Chapter 4, Visayans are conscious of the fact that *langgam* ('bird') means 'ant' in Tagalog, a fact that is jokingly exploited to demonstrate that Visayan is superior to Tagalog ('Their ant crawls. Ours flies.').

Pinay's tendency to maintain a kind of sound–sense complementarity is compatible with the observable symmetry between Visayan homophones and their Eskayan counterparts. An example given in Kelly (2012, 198) is the Visayan morpheme *ning* ('this [one] here'), an abbreviation of *kining*, and the bound verbal morpheme *ning-*, indicating actor-voice realis perfective (approximately meaning 'did'). Though these coincidental homophones have distinct etymologies, they are both lexified with the syllable **chdin** in Eskayan. What is emphasized, ultimately, is the integrity of any sound–meaning pairing within, but not between, lexicons.

For the most part the relationship between the glosses of apparent Visayan and Eskayan cognate pairs is one of either synonymy or metonymy.[3] Three of the terms in Table 6.1 that exhibit identical phonetic forms in both languages have cultural connotations of "nativeness" in the Visayas. In Peligro's wordlist, **aswang** is glossed in Visayan as *wakwak*, a name for a mythical bird whose call warns of the arrival of a flesh-eating creature known as an *aswang*, which is described in Philippine English as a 'vampire.' The *aswang* is important to Visayan mythology and is to some extent emblematic of prehispanic Philippine folklore (Gardner 1906; Torralba 1916; Ramos 1971).

Similarly, the *babaylan*, or 'shaman,' is a much-romanticized figure of prehispanic spiritual culture. Rebels such as Tamblot (referred to as 'Tumud' in Eskaya literature) and Francisco Dagohoy exploited the powerful mystique of the *babaylan* in the expression of their anti-colonial struggle, as did religious insurgents on Negros in the early years of the American occupation (*RPC* 1900, vol. 1, 179–180).

The Eskayan word **lumad**, meanwhile, is glossed as *tribu* ('tribe' via Spanish *tribu*, 'tribe'). In Visayan, *lumad* ('native') is often used in political discourse to index indigeneity, particularly in Mindanao. For Pinay, the use of unambiguously native words as metonyms of native-like concepts was perhaps preferable to foreign characterizations embodied in such Spanish-inspired Visayan terms as *bampira* (from Sp. *vampiro* 'vampire'), *pari* (Sp. *padre* 'priest'), and *indiyu* (Sp. *indio*, 'native'). Despite his free exploitation of foreign linguistic models elsewhere in Eskayan vocabulary, these words for concepts that are indexical of an intrinsic Visayanhood such as **aswang, babaylan, basak**, and **lumad**, retain their original Visayan forms. This could be considered an example of what Paul Kroskrity has termed "linguistic purism" (Kroskrity 1992), a language ideology concerned with promoting and maintaining 'pure' registers of non-borrowed forms for special activities and contexts. However, as I will outline next, the fact that such purism is *not* generally in evidence in Eskayan (notwithstanding these examples) indicates that Pinay was hardly beholden to purist principles and was content to embrace or reject colonial models as it suited him.

Other curiosities in Table 6.1 are the words **paypaypling** ('butterfly') and **tipaypay** ('small butterfly'), presumably derived from the Visayan *paypay* ('fan') by a process of analogy: the shape and movement of a butterfly being likened to the action of a fan. Indeed, in Fabian Baja's wordlist, the headword term '*abanicar* [Sp.]—to fan' is glossed in Eskayan as **muypaypay**, where **muy-** represents a multivalent verbal affix (Kelly 2012, 205). I have not been able to find comparable instances of metaphor being used as a lexifying strategy, but the term calls to mind the ending to the story "Pinay." The text will be analyzed more fully in the chapter that follows, but its concluding sentences are revealing of Pinay's indigenizing perspective. The story's narrator describes Magellan's sailing boat in full sail as a 'large raft' (**guwagu balsa**) and an 'eleven cloth house' (**puntri kul ga'up**). Both appear to be creative representations of an unfamiliar vessel relying on "native" concepts available to the speaker as points of reference. Similarly, Pinay's terms

**paypaypling** and **tipaypay** contain, perhaps, an implicit folk etymology of the Visayan *paypay* ('fan'), with the suggestion that Boholanos, traditionally viewed as having been speakers of Eskayan before shifting to Visayan, lexified the foreign import by means of a natural analogy.

## Spanish in Eskayan

While a number of dubious claims have been made about Eskayan's relationship to known languages (Chapter 3), the marked influence of Spanish on Eskayan attracted little comment. Eskayan words of Spanish inspiration, such as **miridu** ('husband,' from Sp. *marido* 'husband') and **kuyba** ('hole,' Sp. *cueba* 'cave'), are in evidence throughout the lexicon. Before entering into an analysis of these terms it is necessary to point out that a good many Eskayan lexemes display a markedly Hispanic syllable structure, regardless of whether or not they can be identified as Spanish inspirations (Kelly 2015). This makes genuine patterns of Spanish influence on the Eskayan lexicon challenging to map. I will briefly review this phonotactic "noise" before identifying and categorizing lexemes of plausible Spanish inspiration.

### Hispanic phonotactics

Certain Eskayan terms that appear to be directly inspired by Spanish are found to have little or no semantic commonality. For example, the words **ingratu** ('back of body'), **intimi** ('tasty'), **intindimintu** ('land'), **istar** ('short'), **kristal** ('owner'), **kulmar** ('door'), **mimurya** ('sky'), **mirkanti** ('old'), **sabana** ('stone'), **sigla** ('animal'), and **sirdu** ('director') have no obvious relationship to the comparable Spanish words *ingrato* ('ungrateful'), *íntimo/a* ('private,' 'intimate,' M/F), *entendimiento* ('understanding'), *estar* ('be'), *cristál* ('glass,' 'crystal'), *colmar* ('fill to the brim'), *memoria* ('memory'), *mercante* ('merchant'), *sábana* ('sheet'), *sigla* ('abbreviation'), and *cerdo* ('pig').

On the face of it, Pinay might appear to be engaging in a process of deliberate semantic substitution, but this would be to ignore the fact that many more Eskayan words have a marked Hispanic phonotactics without resembling any specific Spanish word. Terms such as **almurada** ('lay one's head on something'), **birurariyu** ('cry'), **gulusiha** ('vein,' 'blood vessel'), and **krisiyun** ('household') come across as phonotactic 'caricatures' of Spanish—no single Spanish word can be isolated as the source of inspiration. In light of this, apparent semantic substitutions such as **kristal** ('owner') for *cristál* ('glass,' 'crystal') cannot be positively validated beyond a coincidence of their phonetic forms. As I will show, semantic reassignment may have played a small part in Pinay's relexification project, but this was by no means systematic.

In order to arrive at a more confident identification of Spanish-inspired terms, I will be considering only those Eskayan lexemes that overlap with Spanish terminology in *both* their semantics *and* their phonetic shape. As an additional analytic principle, words of putative Spanish inspiration are further categorized according to whether the path of inspiration leads directly to Spanish, whether the term in question entered Eskayan by means of a Visayan intermediary, and whether the relevant semantic domain is associated with a pre- or posthispanic concept.

### Spanish via Visayan

Table 6.2 lists fifteen Spanish terms that have provided lexical inspiration for synonymous Visayan and Eskayan words; more will be shown in Table 6.3 later.

**Table 6.2.  Spanish terms in both Visayan and Eskayan**

| Spanish | Visayan | Eskayan |
|---|---|---|
| *balsa* ('raft') | *balsa* ('sled'; 'raft') | **balsa** ('wooden boat') |
| *bulto, figura de bulto* ('statue of a person,' ultimately from Latin *vultus* 'face') | *ribultu, bultu* ('sculpted human or animal used for sacred purposes,' 'statue') | **bultu** ('person') |
| *Castellano* ('Castilian,' 'Spanish') | *katsila'* ('Spanish') | **katsila'** ('Spanish') |
| *cinco* ('five') | *singku* ('five') | **sing** ('five'); **singpi** ('fifty') |
| *cueba* ('cave') | *kuyba* ('cave') | **kuyba** ('hole') |
| *cuña* ('wedge') | *kunya* ('wedge') | **kunyus** ('narrow,' 'inadequate in space') |
| *espíritu* ('spirit') | *ispiritu* ('spirit') | **tuispitduing, ispitduing** ('spirit') |
| *espiritual* ('spiritual') | *ispirituhanun* ('spiritual') | **ispitdu** ('spiritual') |
| *gris* ('gray') | *gris* ('coarse gray cotton cloth') | **griski** ('brown') |
| *lavar* ('wash') | *laba* ('wash clothing') | **laban** ('wash') |
| *maldición* ('curse') | *maldisiyun* ('curse') | **muldisiyun** ('war') |
| *original* ('original') | *urihinal* ('original') | **urinitril** ('original') |
| *secreto* ('secret'), *secretario/a* ('secretary') | *sikritu* ('secret'), *sikritaryu* ('secretary') | **sikrit** ('note,' 'short letter,' 'love letter') |
| *verde* ('green') | *birdi* ('green') | **wirdu** ('blue') |
| *viaje* ('journey') | *biyahi* ('journey,' 'to travel') | **biyabi** ('visitor') |

Table 6.3. Spanish elements in Eskayan with no Visayan intermediary

| Spanish | Eskayan |
|---|---|
| *así* ('like this/that') | **asi** ('in order to') |
| *astro* ('celestial body', 'star') | **astru** ('day', 'sun') |
| *cabrón* ('billy goat', 'bastard') | **kabrum** ('water buffalo'; also **hus**) |
| *con* (conjunction 'with') | **kun** (*ni*; personal GEN 'of [him/her]') |
| *culpa* ('fault', 'sin') | **kulpanu** ('proper behavior', 'code of behavior') |
| *esto* (DEM, 'this') | **istu** (*ang*; SPEC 'the') |
| *final* ('final', 'end') | **pinal** ('first', 'firstly') |
| *ligar* ('bind') | **ligar** ('surround', 'go around') |
| *marido* ('husband') | **miridu** ('husband'); also **tiyunmaridu** ('romantic couple') |
| *piel* ('skin') | **pil, piyil** ('skin') |
| *polvo* ('dust') | **purmu** ('ashes', 'dust') |
| *sellar* ('to seal') | **silyis** ('thermos bottle') |
| *sol* ('sun') | **sul** ('warm') |
| *y* ('and') | **i** (*ug*; 'and', 'if', NSPC 'some') |
| *yo* ('I') | **yu** (*ku*; 1.SG POSS/GEN 'of me') |
| *zapato* ('shoe') | **sapitu** ('calf of leg') |

Consistent with the Visayan terms discussed earlier in Table 6.1, Pinay has adhered to a general principle of what I have called sound–sense complementarity. Thus, wherever two terms are phonetically identical—e.g., *kuyba* ('cave') and **kuyba** ('hole')—their *glosses* vary subtly (but remain in the same semantic domain); where two terms have identical glosses—e.g., *singku* ('five') and **sing** ('five')—their phonetic *forms* vary. This is a minimal principle since a few terms in the table go further still and vary moderately in both form and semantics, e.g., *biyahi* ('journey', 'to travel') and **biyabi** ('visitor'), and the two color terms **griski** ('brown') and **wirdu** ('blue').

Since the words in the second column of Table 6.2 have been nativized in Visayan it is possible that Pinay was oblivious to their Spanish origins. Of particular note is the pair *balsa* ('raft') and **balsa** ('wooden boat'). In the story "Pinay" (Chapter 7), the word is presumably intended to evoke a native-like perspective with Magellan's vessel likened to a 'large raft' (**guwagu balsa**). If the Visayan word *balsa* were considered markedly Spanish, Pinay may not have chosen to exploit its rhetorical potential as a characteristically native word indexical of a native perspective.

Harder to interpret is the core vocabulary item **bultu** (*tawu*, 'person'), where, rather than being synonymous, the Eskayan and the Spanish/Visayan glosses are at one degree of symbolic remove ('person' → 'statue'). But the Visayan meaning offers some insight into Pinay's motives for using this term as a lexical model. William Henry Scott maintains that in the early colonial period Cebuanos accepted a continuity between European *figuras de bulto* ('carved figures') such as the Santo Niño and their own carved *diwata* ('spirits') (Scott 1992, 119–120). Among other names, the indigenous statues were called *tawutawu*, meaning 'little people' or 'pseudo-people' (from *tawu*, 'person') (1992, 127). Later, the Spanish word *bulto* came to be applied in the Visayan magical tradition to refer to a kind of voodoo doll used to inflict pain on enemies (Demetrio 1969, 106), a practice known in Bohol (Aparece 2003, 68) as well as Bicol.[4] Thus, it is plausible that Pinay was referencing the nativized Visayan meaning, with all its connotations of prehispanic indigenous tradition.

### Direct Spanish inspirations

Although Pinay may well have treated the Visayan terms in Table 6.2 as his primary lexical models and remained ignorant of their ultimate Spanish origins, I have identified sixteen Spanish-inspired lexemes in Eskayan (not including derivations) that have *no* Visayan intermediary, as shown in Table 6.3.

Thus, of the 54 total terms in the Eskayan lexicon that are evidently influenced by Spanish, there are at least 38 (or 70.4%) that have counterparts in Visayan (see Table 6.2 and Table 6.4), while 16 (or 29.6%) have no Visayan counterparts, suggesting an unmediated inspiration from Spanish. To put it another way, the mere fact that no Visayan cognates are available suggests that Pinay's primary reference point, for these terms at least, was Spanish.

Most significantly, however, the very fact that Spanish forms are used to lexify function words, among other items of core vocabulary that typically resist borrowing, is suggestive of conscious forethought in building the Eskayan lexicon. Even if Pinay wanted to reserve Visayan forms for a handful of distinctive indigenous concepts, he manipulated Spanish in ways that suggest a masterful understanding of its linguistic potential. Illustrative examples from the list are **pinal** (associated with Sp. *final* through the phonotactic filtering of /f/→ /p/) and **kulpanu** ('proper behavior'), which have antonymous relationships to their apparent Spanish cognates *final* ('final') and *culpa* ('fault', 'sin').[5] If comparable cases could be discovered elsewhere in the Eskayan lexicon, this would invite comparisons with other auxiliary lects, such as the Warlpiri initiation language described by Hale (1971), which rely on antonymy as a lexifying strategy. It is evident, however, that Pinay did not use this as a consistent technique, and the pair *final*/**pinal** ('final'/ 'first') is alternatively analyzable as a case where the dialect-like distance

**Table 6.4.** Eskayan terms of Spanish inspiration for colonial products and concepts

| Introduced product/concept | Spanish | Visayan | Eskayan |
|---|---|---|---|
| 'book' | *libro* ('book'), *libreta* ('notebook') | *libru* ('book'), *librita* ('book containing magic spells that are known in Visayan as *urasiyun*) | **librit** ('book,' 'notebook,' 'reading materials') |
| 'candidate' | *candidato/a* (M/F) | *kandidatu/a* (M/F) | **kandi** ('leader of a group,' 'political leader') |
| 'December' | *diciembre* | *Disimbri* | **Dibi** |
| 'flag' | *bandera* | *bandira* | **bandi, panubandi** |
| 'freedom' | *libertad* ('freedom'), *liberación* ('freeing,' 'liberation') | *libirtad* ('freedom'), *libirisyun* ('the period following the ouster of the Japanese and the achieving of independence, 1944–1946') | **libirsim** (*libirtad*, 'freedom'), also the non-cognate synonym **drusir** (*kagawasan*, 'freedom') |
| 'godfather' | *compadre* ('godfather of one's child or father of one's godchild'); *compañero* ('partner,' 'comrade') | *kumpari* ('father, godfather or father-in-law'); *kumpanyiru* ('term of address to intimates') | **kumpanitu** ('father, godfather or father-in-law') |
| 'ink' | *tinta* | *tinta', tintiru* | **liyir** (from Sp. *leer* 'to read') |
| 'Jesus Christ' | *Jesús Cristo* | *kristung hisus* ('Jesus Christ') | **kriyusisu** ('the word of Jesus') |
| 'Latin' | *latín* | *latin* ('Latin'; 'special kind of prayer with magical effects') | **latin** ('Latin') |
| 'letter [of the alphabet]' | *letra* | *litra* | **litri** |

## Table 6.4. Continued

| Introduced product/concept | Spanish | Visayan | Eskayan |
|---|---|---|---|
| 'lion' | *león* | *liyun* | **lindil** |
| 'March' | *marzo* | *Marsu* | **masu** |
| 'May' | *mayo* | *Mayu* | **maw** |
| 'miracle' | *milagro* | *milagru* | **milagral** |
| 'Monday' | *lunes* | *lunis* | **lini** |
| 'October' | *octubre* | *Uktubri* | **Uktubi** |
| 'Filipino' | *filipino* | *pilipinhun* | **pilipayin** |
| 'Pope' | *Monseñor* ('Catholic honorific for prelates and certain clergymen') | *Munsinyur* ('honorific given to higher-ranking Catholic or PIC clergy') | **inmunsiktur** ('Pope'; possibly from Sp. phrase *el monseñor*) |
| 'prayer' | *alabar* ('to praise') | *alabadu* ('say the final prayer in a novena on any day') | **alaba** |
| 'school' | *escuela* | *iskwilahan* | **iskrit** ('school'; from Sp. *escrito* 'written'); **kuwir** |
| 'September' | *septiembre* | *Siptimbri* | **Sitibi** |
| 'Thursday' | *jueves* | *huwibis* | **hubis** |
| 'tobacco' | *sigaru* ('cigarette', 'cigar') | *sigaru* ('cigar') | **apuysigaru** ('tobacco') |
| 'vicar' | *vicario* ('vicar') | *bikaryu* ('officer of the church') | **biki** ('cardinal') |

constructed between the two glosses was simply exaggerated to the extent that only a higher-order sense of 'positional order' was retained.

### Semantic domains and time depth

If Eskayan really was a natural language that developed without conscious intervention, as some early observers argued, its Spanish-inspired vocabulary could be explained in terms of natural accretion over a period of historical contact, in precisely the same way that Spanish has lexified approximately 17% of vocabulary items in Tagalog (Panganiban 1965). Alternatively, if Pinay was in fact a historical agent who generated Eskayan vocabulary in prehispanic times, there is every reason to imagine that the lexicon he devised would have expanded in the colonial era to include more and more items of Spanish provenance. However, an analysis of the Eskayan lexicon by semantic domain does not corroborate either view.

Spanish loans in non-creole Philippine languages tend to cluster in predictable semantic domains. Imported products, concepts, or species for which no suitable equivalent was available in the local lexicon were often represented with a Spanish-inspired term. For example, the Spanish word *caballo* ('horse') was universally adopted into regional Philippine lexicons to refer to the unfamiliar quadruped species brought from Europe. In the same way, adaptations of the Spanish words *tenador* ('fork'), *monasterio* ('monastery'), and *espada* ('sword') found their way into local languages along with the products or institutions they stood for.

Of course, this lexifying strategy is not so much an axiom as a strong tendency. In Visayan there are examples of native innovations for foreign products, such as *simbahan* ('church'), used in addition to the now-archaic loanword *iglisiya* (from the Spanish *iglesia*), and *tubig bagtuk* ('ice,' literally 'hard water') is found alongside the loan *yilu* (from the Spanish *hielo*, 'ice'). Conversely, examples can be found of words imported from Spanish where a suitable native equivalent already existed, such as *amigu/a* (M/F), used as an alternative to *higala* ('friend'). For the most part, however, words of Spanish inspiration are predictably found in those semantic domains that relate to post-contact cultural imports, and there are no instances of Spanish terms replacing items of core vocabulary such as body parts.[6]

In Eskayan, similarly, I have identified twenty-four introduced products, species, and ideas that are lexified with Spanish words, as shown in Table 6.4. Note that all these words have Visayan intermediaries.

The terms **iskrit** ('school') and **liyir** ('ink') are noteworthy for the oblique correspondence between the Spanish and Eskayan senses. The glosses 'written' → 'school' and 'to read' → 'ink' do not merely represent a shift in word classes, but their meanings sit in a metonymic relationship to one another, as seen earlier in words of Visayan origin such as **aswang**. But beyond these examples, glosses for Eskayan terms are not radically different from those of their Spanish/Visayan equivalents.

Viewed in isolation, the existence of Spanish-like cognate terms for post-contact ideas and products might lend the impression that Eskayan was a natural language, or that it had acquired foreign-inspired vocabulary since its creation, or at the least that Pinay deliberately reproduced similar patterns of colonial lexification found in other Philippine languages. However, these words are by no means representative of post-contact terminology in the Eskayan lexicon as a whole. In fact, contrary to expectations Pinay's lexicon includes many more post-contact-related terms (seventy-three in total) that are quite clearly *not* inspired by colonial vocabularies. These are listed in Table 6.5.

Table 6.5. Eskayan acculturation terms without Spanish or English cognates

| Introduced product/concept | Spanish | Visayan | Eskayan |
|---|---|---|---|
| 'airplane' | *avión* | *abiyun* | **kanis** |
| 'angel' | *ángel* | *anghil* | **pakan** |
| 'apple' | *manzana* | *mansanas* | **chdiyami** |
| 'archbishop' | *arzobispo* | *arsubispu* | **witsiktur** |
| 'bell tower' | *campanario* | *kampanaryu* | **huntun** |
| 'bishop' | *obispo* | *ubispu* | **insiktur** |
| 'blackboard' | *pizarra* | *balakburd* | **silmunsi** |
| 'bottle' | *botella* | *butilya* | **liksun** |
| 'chalice' | *cáliz* | *kalis* | **tarbu** |
| 'chamber pot' | *bacinica; orinal* | *arinula* | **labu** |
| 'Christmas carols' | *villancico* | *daygun [dalayig]* | **imur** |
| 'church' | *iglesia* | *simbahan* | **bisa** |
| 'clerk' | *escribiente* | *isklibinti* | **inpintir** |
| 'clock,' 'watch' | *reloj* | *urasan* (from Sp. *hora* 'hour') | **agahun; kayra** |
| 'cow' | *vaca* | *baka* | **damulag** |
| 'date' (of year) | *fecha* | *pitsa* | **pim** |
| 'dictator' | *dictador* | *diktadur* | **baganibagani** |
| 'district' | *barrio* | *bariyu* | **pruk** |
| 'drive a vehicle' | *manejar* | *pagmanihu* | **muynunung** |
| 'dynamite' | *dinamita* | *dinamita* | **prin** |
| 'editor' | *editor* ('editor'; 'publisher') | *iditur* | **wintiskis** |
| 'election' | *elección* | *iliksiyun, piliay* | **sikadu** |
| 'examination' | *examen* | *iksaminisyun* | **sawardit** |
| 'factory' | *fábrica* | *pabrika* | **pulpul** |
| 'February' | *febrero* | *Pibriru* | **hibinu** |
| 'fiesta' | *fiesta* | *pista, pyista* | **lam** |
| 'fork' | *tenedor* | *tinidur* | **kibir** |
| 'general' (military) | *general* | *hiniral* | **hibir** |
| 'go to confession' | *a confesarse* | *kumpisal* | **miyur** |
| 'governor' | *gobernador* | *gubirnadur* | **bansithi** |
| 'horse' | *caballo* | *kabayu* | **bril, dudu** |
| 'hour,' 'time of day' | *hora* | *uras* | **kayra** |
| 'incense' | *incienso* | *insinsu* | **ribus** |
| 'judge' | *juez* | *huwis* | **baganhunda** |

*(continued)*

## Table 6.5. Continued

| Introduced product/concept | Spanish | Visayan | Eskayan |
|---|---|---|---|
| 'kettle' | *pava, hervidor* | *takuri* | **turbati** |
| 'key' | *llave* | *yawi* | **limanus** |
| 'kilometer' | *kilómetro* | *kilumitru* | **ritilda** |
| 'king' | *Re* | *hari* | **sutbagani** |
| 'major general' | *comandante general* | *kumandanti hiniral* | **baganiring** |
| 'meter' | *metro* | *mitrus* | **biriil** |
| 'mile' | *milla* | *milyas* | **argas** |
| 'money' | *dinero* | *salapi* | **tindas** |
| 'nun' | *monja* | *mungha* | **sirdas** |
| 'office' | *oficina* | *upisina* | **hup** |
| 'paper' | *papel* | *papil* | **sampris** |
| 'pencil' | *lápiz* | *lapis* | **dutal** |
| 'peso' | *peso* | *pisu* | **tap; uwis** |
| 'photograph' | *fotografía* | *ritratu* (from Sp. *retratar* 'take a photograph,' *retrato* 'portrait') | **amirsim** |
| 'prayer' | *oración* | *urasiyun* ('special set of prayers in the liturgy'; 'magical Latinate formula') | **alaba** |
| 'queen' | *reina* | *rayna* | **biyarga** |
| 'railway train' | *tren* | *trin* | **giring** |
| 'refined sugar' | *azúcar* | *asukar* | **baruta** |
| 'rubber' | *goma* | *guma* | **kutik** |
| 'sacrament' | *sacramento* | *sakramintu* | **purchdidi** |
| 'schoolteacher (female)' | *maistra* | *maistra* | **isirdas** |
| 'scissors' | *tijeras* | *gunting* | **ilgatu** |
| 'shoe' | *zapato* | *sapatus* | **gulada** |
| 'slippers' | *chinelas* | *tsinilas* | **gulada** |
| 'small change' | *sencillo* | *sinsilyu* | **dilyun** |
| 'soap' | *jabón* | *sabun* | **punlas** |
| 'socks' | *medias* | *midyas* | **sapaw** |
| 'spoon' | *cuchara* | *kutsara* ('tablespoon') | **damuti** |

### Table 6.5. Continued

| Introduced product/concept | Spanish | Visayan | Eskayan |
|---|---|---|---|
| 'Station of the Cross' | *Estación de la Cruz* | *istasyun* | **agura** |
| 'student' | *estudiante* | *istudiyanti* | **istuwal** |
| 'Sunday' | *domingo* | *duminggu* | **lyunggu** |
| 'surname' | *apellido* | *apilyidu* | **lurim** |
| 'table' | *mesa* | *lamisa* | **lasiku** |
| 'town hall' | *municipio* | *munisipyu* | **lundu** |
| 'trunk', 'chest' | *baúl, cofre* | *baul, kaban* | **basiku** |
| 'Tuesday' | *martes* | *martis* | **mimati** |
| 'Wednesday' | *miércoles* | *mirkulis* | **mibul** |
| 'window' | *ventana* | *bintana* | **salay** |
| 'senator' | *senador/a* (M/F) | *sinadur* | **gadyus** |

As mentioned earlier, there is no compulsion for natural Philippine languages to take inspiration from contact languages when lexifying contact products. Indeed, three of the Visayan terms in Table 6.5 are also lexical innovations: *day-gun* ('Christmas carols') is a nominalization of the verb *dalayig* ('praise'), *sim-bahan* ('church') is derived from *simba* ('adore') and the location-making suffix *-(h)an*, and *piliay* ('election', lit. 'choosing', syn. *iliksiyun*) is derived from *pili'* ('choose') and the nominalizer *-ay*.[7]

Comparable processes of nominalization and metaphoric extension are harder to detect for the Eskayan lexical counterparts, but in the list as a whole, a number of morphemes are tentatively segmentable: **-iktur** may indicate 'high ecclesiastic rank' in **witsiktur** ('archbishop') and **insiktur** ('bishop'), while -**bagan**- specifies 'high political rank'; **agahun** ('clock', 'watch') theoretically contains the word **aga** ('morning'), and the root of **alaba** ('prayer') may be **Ara** ('God'). Other words of interest are **tindas** ('money'), a possible metonym of the Spanish *tienda* ('shop'), and **sapaw** ('socks'), which may well be inspired by the Visayan verb *sapaw* ('wear two things one on top of the other') as in the example sentence *Magsapaw ku ug midiyas* 'I will wear two pairs of socks' (Wolff 1972b).

Since the items listed in the first column of Table 6.5 were unheard of in prehispanic Filipino society, their Eskayan terms are necessarily lexical innova-tions, even if the structure is at least theoretically reconstructable for words like **agahun**. In Taytay, words for acculturation products were sometimes explained to me by Eskaya people as distortions of English or Visayan words, even if the resemblance was not obvious. Teachers in Cadapdapan maintained that Pinay was able to prophesy new technology before it had been created, and this was tendered as an explanation for words such as **kanis** ('airplane').

A contrasting phenomenon is witnessed in the presence of foreign-inspired terms where one would otherwise not be expected to find them. Eskayan has at least three words of Spanish origin in its core vocabulary: **bultu** (*tawu*, 'person'; from Sp. *ribultu*), **piyil** (*panit* 'skin'; from Sp. *piel*), and **purmu** (*abug* 'dust'; from Sp. *polvo*). In natural languages these kinds of core concepts—relating to people, body parts, and the environment—tend to resist lexical replacement. Thus, if the Spanish-inspired words in core vocabulary and the acculturation terms in Table 6.5 can be plausibly explained as examples of deliberate lexical innovation, there is no reason to suppose that innovation was limited to these domains. To put it another way, the non-predictable distribution of foreign versus "native" terms across semantic domains points to the probability that the entire Eskayan lexicon was innovated in more or less one hit.

### English in Eskayan

An analysis of phonotactics (Kelly 2015) suggests that Eskayan permits the kinds of syllable structures found in English loans to Visayan. But the possible influence of English on the Eskayan lexicon is harder to pin down. Table 6.6 lists twelve words conceivably inspired by English terms.

#### Table 6.6. Potential English inspirations

| English | Eskayan |
| --- | --- |
| 'clear' | **klir** ('make space for') |
| 'drink' | **drinkir, drikis** ('hot chocolate drink') |
| 'hang' | **wirhang** ('hang') |
| 'horse' | **hus** ('water buffalo') |
| 'joker' | **chdiyukir** ('poor,' 'destitute'; perhaps via Visayan *dyukir* 'one who jokes,' 'one who made a ludicrous mistake') |
| 'lad' | **lad** ('child') |
| 'lip' | **lup** ('lip,' 'lips') |
| 'major' | **midyu** ('person holding an office'; via Visayan *midyur* 'major in military or police') |
| 'medical' | **midikil** ('doctor'; also Sp. *medico* 'doctor') |
| 'miracle' | **mirikilyu** ('doctor') |
| 'onion' | **unyada** ('onion') |
| 'three' | **tri** ('two'; see also Sp. *tres* 'three') |

The least ambiguous of these are **drinkir** ('hot chocolate drink'), **klir** ('make space for'), and **lup** ('lip'). This last term joins **piyil** ('skin') and **bulbing** ('pubic hair') as examples of body part terms inspired by 'foreign' lexemes. Others in the list are more speculative. It is tempting to argue that the European appearance of **midyu** ('major'), **midikil** ('doctor'), and its synonym **mirikilyu** ('doctor') reflects a historical fact that these roles were traditionally occupied by Spanish or American foreigners in Bohol, or by Hispanicized Boholanos. By contrast, the European-style roles of 'bishop' (**insiktur**) and 'senator' (**gadyus**) have manifestly un-European forms.

### Other languages in Eskayan

One of the most striking "foreign" words in Eskayan is **Ara** ('God'), which is immediately reminiscent of الله ('Allah') and suggests an Arabic influence. The correspondence is reinforced by the fact that in Visayan, /l/ is optionally realized as [r] between vowels of the same quality. I have not been able to find other plausible Arabic, or indeed Semitic, influences in the Eskayan lexicon.[8] The word **alak** ('wine or liquor') in Table 6.1 cannot be considered a direct Arabic loan from *araq* ('sweat'; 'juice') in view of the fact that the more proximal Arabic cognate is available in Visayan, namely, *arak* ('wine or liquor'). One possibility is that **Ara** is modeled not on الله but on the Spanish *ara* ('altar'; from Latin *ara* 'altar'), which would be consistent with the pattern of metonymic relationships established between Eskayan glosses and those of their foreign lexifiers. In any case, there is no reason to imagine that Pinay would only have drawn from one source of inspiration per word.

## Pinay's lexical agenda

In this chapter I have identified the principles of language building that Pinay employed and his sources of inspiration. Pinay used Visayan as a grammatical template and repopulated it with innovated Eskayan coinages. The productive affixes on Visayan verbal inflections are not, however, always represented as a straightforward substitution and are often indicated with suppleted forms similar to those encountered in Spanish and English. Further, the strong morphosyntactic consonance between Visayan and Eskayan is not reflected in Pinay's lexicon, which includes very few items of Visayan inspiration. More consistent is the influence of Spanish on Pinay's lexifying project. Spanish had a significant role in the development of Eskayan syllable structure: many Eskayan words have the phonotactic "look and feel" of Spanish words without being positively traceable to a Spanish term; others are superficially recognizable as Spanish cognates but with clearly different semantics. Yet out of this noise a more coherent Spanish signal can be detected. Numerous Eskayan terms have transparent origins in Spanish words, but for a large proportion of these, Spanish has lexified both the Eskayan and its corresponding Visayan term. Consequently, Pinay's most proximal source of inspiration was not necessarily Spanish so much as the Spanish loanwords into Visayan. However, a smaller subset of Spanish-inspired lexemes has no Visayan intermediary, and these reveal that Pinay was likely to have had direct exposure to Spanish and some proficiency in it. In short, Pinay's lexical imagination, though bold, was constrained by the available sounds and sequences in both Visayan and nativized terms of Spanish origin. That is, he could access and exploit the novel structures available in introduced colonial languages but could not overstep their inherent structural constraints. Even today, speakers of Eskayan are conscious of the Spanish influence on their language, despite the fact that there are no longer any Spanish speakers in the Eskaya community.

The semantic domains in which Spanish-inspired Eskayan lexemes are found, or not found, have a bearing on time-depth estimations. A large number of post-contact items, such as **amirsim** ('photograph'), **huntun** ('bell tower'), and **lurim** ('surname'), do not show a resemblance to their associated terms in colonial contact languages. Likewise, names for administrative centers established under Spanish rule have pristine Eskayan equivalents.

If we were to accept the evidence for free innovation in Eskayan acculturation terminology we would have to assume that these lexemes were coined by Pinay sometime after Bohol came under colonial rule and thus came into regular contact with new products, species, governing systems, and above all a new language. Of course, in contact situations there is no necessity for speakers to borrow terminology for an introduced item from the language of the group that supplied it. However, lexical innovations for acculturation products often have a degree of transparency since they rely on overt strategies such as metaphoric extension. In Eskayan, on the other hand, lexical innovation is widespread in acculturation terminology while the process of innovation remains opaque. Meanwhile, certain items of Eskayan core vocabulary, a domain considered to be reasonably stable in natural languages, show evidence of inspiration from Spanish. Together, these two circumstances—the conspicuous Hispanic lexification of core vocabulary and *non*-Hispanic lexification of many introduced items—indicate that these words, at the very least, are products of conscious post-contact innovation. A plausible English influence on Eskayan vocabulary conveys the strong impression that this innovation may have happened after the arrival of English-speaking administrators and educators to Bohol. Accordingly, I maintain that the creative ancestor Pinay was a native speaker of Visayan with an awareness of Visayan dialect variation, facility in Spanish, and at least some familiarity with English.

Beyond these circumstantial aspects of Pinay's historical identity, what might any of this tell us about his ideological motivations and design principles in the development of a "declared Visayan"? On a superficial reading it would be tempting to argue that he had been hoodwinked by colonial languages and that his creation was an imperfect derivative of Boholano-Visayan and Spanish, with a smattering of terms from English and other languages thrown in for good measure. Yet, just as I have shown with regard to the Eskaya writing system, there is clear evidence of serious planning and forethought. Pinay's relexification of Boholano-Visayan was rule governed to the extent that he ensured that any Eskayan words that shared a phonetic form with Boholano-Visayan would differ obliquely in their semantics, and those that shared a semantic gloss would differ with the same degree of subtlety in their phonetic realizations. In other words, it is as if Pinay wanted to ensure that Eskayan remained in dialogue with Boholano-Visayan at a dialect-like distance. The pervasive Spanish influence is perhaps harder to unravel. It is evident that Pinay had knowledge of Spanish in view of the fact that he developed terms of Spanish inspiration that were not already available as nativized loanwords into Visayan. It also is clear that he made use of this knowledge in the way he generated a Hispanic syllable structure for typical Eskayan words. The overall effect would have been to make spoken Eskayan "foreign" sounding, an outcome that would have been reinforced further by his insertion of Spanish- and English-inspired lexemes. After all, these were the two foreign languages to which Boholanos were most regularly exposed and that may have influenced their perception of stereotypical "foreignness."

Pinay's introduction of exotic verbal irregularity was similarly intentional since it would have been easier to simply substitute one Visayan affix for a new Eskayan equivalent than to create a whole series of one-off suppleted verb forms. This is in direct contrast to other planned languages invented by a single individual—like Esperanto or Volapük—that were designed to be regular and morphologically transparent on the assumption that this would make them universally accessible and learnable. From an ideological perspective it could therefore be argued that Pinay was not concerned with universality or learnability so much as creating a language that could "out-foreign" the foreigner. As with the misdirection encoded into the Eskaya writing system (Chapter 5), it appears that Pinay was not merely participating in a push and pull of "accommodation and resistance" (Tsing 1993, 71) but, paradoxically, constructing an insider code through a strategic appropriation of colonial languages.

At the same, such a reading contradicts the traditional narratives of the language's origin and history. For Eskaya people, Pinay is recognized as a foundational ancestor whose distinctly Boholano language did not just precede the introduction of Spanish and English to Bohol, but also the arrival and continuing hegemony of Visayan. Beyond the view that Pinay, as a future-oriented prophet, could predict future technologies and was thus in a position to supply preemptive native terms for them, speakers had little interest in rationalizing, for example, the surprising influence of Spanish and other languages on Eskayan. In the famous case of the Turkish language reforms that were enacted in the 1930s, state language planners felt compelled to justify the retention of Arabic and Persian-derived terms by arguing that Turkish was the source of all languages, thus effectively denying the possibility that *any* word in the language could be loaned (Heyd 1954, 33–44, cited in Jernudd 1989, 2). In this way, an overriding principle of linguistic purism could be maintained without having to disrupt the existing Turkish lexicon too severely. But beyond policing its *written* materiality (Chapters 4 and 5), Eskayan speakers I spoke with showed scant concern for purism with regard to the grammar and lexicon of their language. This laissez-faire attitude requires no serious explanation if it is understood that Eskaya people operate within an ideological frame that regards language as simultaneously natural *and* artificial, an embodied and primordial reality that springs from the human creative impulse.

Be that as it may, Eskaya traditional literature does emphasize the prior cultural and linguistic legitimacy of Pinay and his descendants on comparable grounds to those espoused by the Turkish language reformists. As I will describe in the chapter that follows, Pinay is unambiguously situated in a *pre*colonial context while his successors are understood to have resisted assimilation until Tugpa's last stand in the early nineteenth century and beyond. In this extraordinary body of work I will explore the ways in which Pinay's project of radical substitution was concerned with anticipating and exceeding the foreign products, systems and ideologies implanted by colonizers, rather than merely reflecting them. The calquing of sounds, letter signs, and words that I have just described is projected at a larger scale into a set of literary narratives and expository texts, outlining a parallel and utopian vision of Eskaya society.

## Notes

1. Since beginning my research I have been compiling Eskayan words in a database. To date I have collected 2,948 individual terms; these are available at http://catalog. paradisec.org.au/repository/PK2/01/PK2-01-DICT.txt.
2. This term is intended to reflect Pinay's creativity but is also, to my mind, a more accurate analogy for what actually takes place when words are "borrowed" between any languages. After all, no word is ever transplanted between one language and another without undergoing a degree of phonological realignment, or, in some cases, radical reassignment of semantics or word class. It is simpler to assume that

so-called borrowings merely take foreign lexemes as their primary influence and are thus already automatically nativized the moment they come into meaningful use. This is a circumstance pointed out by Haugen (1950), who suggested 'mixture' and 'adoption' as alternative metaphors. More recently Robbeets and Johanson (2012) have attempted to establish 'copy' as a terminological convention to replace 'loan' or 'borrowing.'

3. Note that I am using the term 'cognate' in its loosest sense to signify the relationship between any lexemes of shared origin regardless of whether the terms in question are genetically related or were introduced by a contact language.

4. Lucetta Ratcliff's informant in Bicol related, "One Easter I went into the mountains to hunt deer, as I said, but really to look for a doll. My father had told me that one must search during Easter. If you desire a *bulto*, doll, you must go to the forest at this particular time. As soon as it is three o'clock in the afternoon, you take a bolo [machete] and cut every little shrub which you see. From one of these shrubs drops of blood will fall as soon as the bolo cuts it. This shrub is the one which you must take to make your doll. At the proper time I went about cutting shrubs until I found one with a bloody juice. This shrub I carried home and shaped it into the doll which I now have. [The man stopped to fetch the doll.] You see these holes? If you wish to kill anybody, you fill the holes with different materials. The person whom you wish to kill will surely die, because the spirit will move to the person." (Ratcliff 1951, 234)

5. It is also possible that **klus** ('pry open') is derived antonymically from English 'close,' or it may be inspired by Catalan *claus* ('keys').

6. The presence of Spanish number terms in Visayan vocabulary does not represent a case of lexical replacement in core vocabulary. Spanish numbers are reserved exclusively for counting money and telling the time, both of which are post-contact practices.

7. The terms *takuri* ('kettle'), *salapi* ('money'), and *gunting* ('scissors') are probably not lexical innovations. The word *gunting* is a Malay loan of unknown ultimate origin. I have been unable to trace *takuri* and *salapi*, but these too may be loans.

8. In Kelly (2006, 71–80) I tagged the most likely Hebrew suspects in Swadesh vocabulary as **aya** ('where'; Hebrew *'ay*), **giru** ('bone'; Hebrew *gerem*), **kuryu** ('cold'; Hebrew *qor* [M]), **nima** ('mother'; Hebrew *'em*), **rakilan** ('road'; Hebrew *macillah*), and **tima** ('worm'; Hebrew *rimmah*). I did not, however, judge these to be words of genuine Hebrew origin. They were generously marked as cognates in a Swadesh comparison for the purposes of addressing the Hebrew hypothesis promoted by Tirol and Abregana (see Chapter 3).

# 7 ESKAYA LITERATURE AND TRADITIONAL HISTORIOGRAPHY

A hardwood bas relief carved with vines and flowers once greeted visitors to Bohol's Provincial Museum in Tagbilaran. In its center was the image of a female monkey framed by two large combs. The label that accompanied the artifact read simply: "Wooden tablet showing evolution according to Eskaya." When the museum relocated in 2007 the bas relief was put into storage and its caption revised to "Wooden carving from Dauis." The provenance of the bas relief remains undetermined, a fate common to many objects sourced from informal excavations, but it is rumored to have been first recovered in the 1970s from the beaches of Dauis on the opposing shore to Tagbilaran (Map 3).

From what evidence was the original caption composed? Whoever wrote it must have been sufficiently well versed in the literary tradition of the Eskaya to know of the story of the **balinsiya**, the female orangutan who gave birth to the first human pair, Idam and Hidam, and another monkey. Without the archeological context, however, we may never be sure whether this interpretation has validity. If the carving really was a prehispanic ornament that referenced Eskaya creation mythology, it would be the earliest positive evidence that the Eskaya predated Spanish contact. Presumably the staff who revised the label in 2007 rejected such a possibility out of hand.

"The Eskayas know," wrote Cristina Martinez, "that if a people do not construct, someone else will construct for them" (1993, 237). As I have outlined in Chapter 3, Eskaya narratives were subjected to reinterpretation by others who promoted alternative, often idealized visions of Bohol's history. In short, Eskaya literature was a medium for imagining possible pasts that were awaiting discovery in the present. But while the fantasies projected onto Eskaya people from the outside offer useful insights into the cultural context of their reception, these accounts have failed to give due recognition to Eskaya subjects as historiographers in their own right.

*The Last Language on Earth.* Kelly, Piers, Oxford University Press. © Oxford University Press 2022.
DOI: 10.1093/oso/9780197509913.003.0007

In this chapter I do my best to restore Eskaya-centric perspectives by describing the history of the Eskayan language and script as it has been narrated and interpreted by Eskaya people themselves. As I have shown in my analysis of the language, an important process underpinning Pinay's creative agenda was the subversive copying, elaboration, and repositioning of foreign forms, as instantiated in letter shapes, syllable structures, verbal morphology, and borrowed terms. In the traditional literature this dynamic takes on a narrative reality. Throughout Eskaya texts, triumphalist colonial myths of conquest and progress are turned on their heads. Concepts, products, and technologies that readers might associate more immediately with European colonization are reimagined as indigenous. Further, the native iterations of these categories are represented as primordial, and as more authentic and superior to their imported counterparts.

Here I limit my analysis of Eskaya literature to seven key texts that I have selected for examination because of their special bearing on Eskaya linguistic history and language ideology. These stories reveal the ways that language is fundamental to Eskaya claims of comparability and superiority to outsider equivalents. For the Eskaya, languages are understood as material and technological artifacts that are produced through human creative effort and cannot be separated from their visual representation in writing. Moreover, languages are efficacious in their power to effect changes in the world or to project a political claim to territorial sovereignty. Languages can nonetheless change over time, become disassembled or lost, but also resuscitated, reassembled, and deployed as weapons. In all these particularities, Eskayan is not represented as *distinct* from languages such as Cebuano, Spanish, or Latin in any categorical way but is seen instead to enact these intrinsic qualities of language with greater power and virtuosity.

The foundational Eskaya origin story of a patriotic ancestor who devised the language and script, later to be recuperated by Mariano Datahan, is hard to reconcile with common understandings of how languages evolve and are transmitted. However, for Eskaya narratives to be explicable to non-Eskaya readers a process of careful translation is necessary, not just of the semantic content of the literature but of the terms by which it is consumed, reproduced, and made relevant to the lived experience of Eskaya people today. In this vein I argue that Eskaya literary practice is an auto-historical discourse that is most productively elucidated through local norms of interpretation.

If critical theorists have struggled to delineate the ambiguous borders of such categories as 'history,' 'folklore,' 'myth,' and 'literature,' these are not meaningful distinctions for Eskaya readers and writers who describe all the traditional documents as *pagtulunan* ('teachings') or more broadly as *balasahun* ('texts'; literally 'readings'). According to Fabian Baja, the word 'Eskaya' itself, attested for the first time in Taytay, originally meant *pagtulunan sa mga tawo* ('the people's teachings'), a reminder of the centrality of the traditional literature to Eskaya identity. That is not to say that each text is assigned an equivalent status. A small subset of stories is considered to be important enough to be included as part of the traditional school curriculum; the remainder does not require formal study and is not expected to be recopied by all students. Crucially, the traditional literature is written for a small and select audience—an audience, moreover, whose cultural identity is partly informed by the very ability to read and recreate the texts. Thus, a serious ethnographic history of the Eskayan language and script necessarily requires a dialogue with traditional Eskaya historiography as a "truthful but different mode of history," in Hokari's memorable phrase (2011, 263).

The production and reproduction of Eskaya texts is relevant to the history of the language in which they are written. Not only does this substantial body of work represent the most significant domain of Eskayan language use, but both the language and its documentation are contingent on one another for their survival and meaning. It is through Eskaya texts that the language is taught to children, who are made to recite and reproduce them in writing, while the texts themselves are only decipherable with reference to other texts, in the form of wordlists and syllabaries, or by accessing linguistic knowledge acquired through their meticulous study. In this way, the Eskaya texts form a self-sufficient corpus. Indeed, "corpus" is an apt designation as the body of literature is depicted as a literal body (*balasahun sa lawas sa tawu*, 'literature from a human body'). This might be seen as a logical extension of the Eskaya metaphor of language-as-body: individual letters are derived from distinct organs, but together they form a unified agent with natural and generative power.

The critical importance of *writing* to Eskaya history and cultural identity defies any easy association of minority Philippine communities with oral tradition.[1] As discussed in the previous chapter, writing is vital to the creation mythology of Eskayan. The ancestor Pinay is held to have developed writing from the human body, and it was by means of a written channel that Pinay's creation was said to have been imparted to Mariano Datahan. According to the text known as "Visayan teachings," a language without writing is simply *hangin sa baba* ('air in the mouth'), while cultural legitimacy hinges on the form this writing takes. Even today, claims and counterclaims over the antiquity and authenticity of the Eskayan language in Bohol's media are most frequently oriented to the script and tend to presuppose that writing is the true essence of the language. These debates reflect an ongoing preoccupation in the Philippines with pre-contact literacy as an index of cultural sophistication, and with paleographic remains as material evidence of indigenous civilization. As discussed in Chapter 2, it is believed by many Filipinos today that Spanish missionaries destroyed all the native archives upon their arrival to the islands in order to make way for their own governing structures and scriptural traditions. A variant of this narrative is expressed by Eskaya people in relation to their own historical literacy, as I will show.

## The origins and scope of Eskaya literature

Before I first visited Bohol in 2005 the only information I had concerning Eskaya literature came from two staff members at the University of Melbourne's Centre for Cultural Materials Conservation. They informed me that the most sacred artifacts of the Eskaya were a series of blue-lined exercise books, known as the Old Books, which contained Eskayan stories written with a ballpoint pen. Shortly after I began my internship at the local office of the National Commission on Indigenous Peoples (NCIP) in Tagbilaran (Map 3) I was introduced to Riche Datahan, a great-great-grandson of Mariano Datahan's brother Marcos. Riche brought with him two blue-lined notebooks filled with Eskayan text for me to examine. Believing these to be the Old Books, I scrutinized them with great reverence, transcribing as much of the unfamiliar script as I could. Riche did not know where they came from, and a few weeks later I was dismayed to learn that he had misplaced them. Not until I visited Taytay early in the following year did I realize how commonplace such notebooks were. Every Eskaya individual who had attended a traditional school kept a personal hand-copied exercise book of the literature and most households had several stored away.

Nonetheless, the existence of the so-called Old Books remained an open question. On one of my first visits to Biabas I was shown a series of wooden tablets described as faithful copies of the scriptures discovered by Mariano Datahan. In the 1980s and 1990s, local journalists routinely referred to secret *karaang mga libru* ('old books'), imagined as wooden tablets, stone slabs, or leather-bound volumes. Whether these books were material or metaphorical entities remained unclear.

The stories transcribed as part of the traditional school curriculum, including texts named "Pinay," "Daylinda," and "The Itch-mite Tumaw," are held by many younger Eskaya to belong to the corpus of ancient scripture encoded in these Old Books.[2] Yet neither Juan Datahan, the late chieftain of Biabas, nor Fabian Baja, the late chieftain of Taytay, gave credence to this view. For them, the stories themselves represented an authentic record of ancient experience, but these were first dictated for transcription by Mariano "Anoy" Datahan in the twentieth century ("Anoy" is the affectionate name for Datahan, derived from the last syllables of his first name). In Baja's understanding, as told to his son-in-law Hilario Galambao, the ancestor Pinay did not write anything down, and Anoy Datahan was the first to record his wisdom. Since Datahan had such detailed knowledge of the past, as well as the ability to predict the future, Baja and his fellow students surmised that their revered mentor was none other than Pinay himself.[3]

Datahan's former scribes were identified for me by Juan Datahan as Eleuterio Castañares, Victorio Cagas, Patricio Carias, Domingo Castañares (1912–1985), Espredion Degracia (ca. 1909–1959), Eleuteria Viscayda (1924–2009), and others that he could not recall. The first three individuals were remembered by Juan Datahan as Anoy's "first generation" of teachers, but no birth or death dates could be retrieved for them, either from memory or from parish records.[4] Of these scribes and teachers I had the privilege to meet an elderly Eleuteria "Faustina" Viscayda in Lundag in 2006. Blind, bedridden, and smoking a banana leaf cigar, she was not alert enough to be interviewed for more than a few minutes; she would pass away in 2009.

Cristina Martinez took care to distinguish popularized versions of the origins of the texts from speaker accounts. While Fabian Baja had reportedly seen these original books, he told her that *gikan ni Datahan ang mga sinuwat* ('the writings came from Datahan') (Martinez 1993, 49–50). Eleuteria Viscayda was even more straightforward:

> Asked where the narratives like "Daylinda" and "Pinay" came from, Viscayda says, 'gikan sa ulo ni Anoy pangadtu sa akong papel' (from the head of Anoy to my piece of paper). She recounts how Anoy Datahan would sit through the night and narrate tales in Ineskaya [Eskayan], and how she, then a young lady, would copy them down. (79)

When I posed the same question to Viscayda, some thirteen years later, she was visibly confused and answered that the stories simply came from Bohol. Making a rough calculation from the year of her birth, the texts she transcribed as a "young lady" would have conceivably been dictated between the late 1930s and early 1940s.

The canonical literature is always reproduced with an accompanying official translation such that Eskayan is found on the left page of the notebook with its Visayan rendering on the facing page, or vice versa (see Fig. 7.1). In my own assessment of these facing-page documents, it is apparent that the Eskayan text is actually a translation from a Visayan original and not the other way around. I base this claim on the fact that the Visayan text displays a greater diversity of synonyms for common items of vocabulary and more specificity in its verbal affixation (for an explanatory analysis of this, see Kelly 2012). It is hard to explain how a translated text might regularly acquire *greater* detail and precision in the process of its translation. Likewise, many stories contain passages that explicate the meanings of individual Eskayan words. These passages are coherent in Visayan, but when

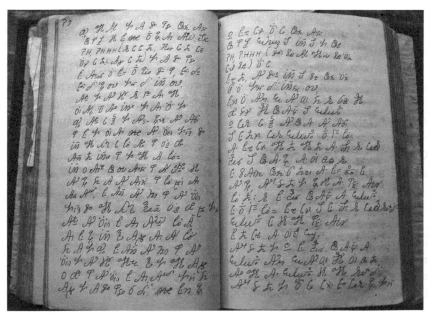

**FIGURE 7.1.** Eskaya literature from the notebook of Alberta Galambao. The left-hand page is in Visayan and the right-hand page in Eskayan.

read in Eskayan "translation" they are virtually nonsensical. More detail on the possible methods by which Eskaya literature was first developed, transcribed, and diffused is provided in Chapter 9.

## A preliminary note on variation and intelligibility

Like traditional Boholano folklore, Eskaya stories are today treated as author-less texts, a fact that has implications for their reproduction and modification. Despite the value placed on scrupulous copying, no two Eskaya texts are identical. Confusingly, it is often impossible to know where one text ends and another begins. From notebook to notebook, near-identical stories may go by several different names, while texts with the same name can differ considerably in their content. To take one example, a list of prehispanic ancestors and their roles in Boholano society is sometimes appended to "Pinay," at other times to "The Spanish and Eskayan Alphabets." Certain texts, including "Atikisis"and many of the songs, have no Visayan translation or transliteration. Others such as "Visayan Teachings" and most versions of "Pinay" are in Visayan only. Errors abound, including accidental transpositions of Visayan words into the Eskayan layer and vice versa, incomplete sentences, direct speech attributed to the wrong character in dialogues, and paragraphs that appear to be haphazardly repunctuated, resulting in awkward fragments. Few of the texts are wholly intelligible, even to erudite Eskaya teachers.

In her essay on the recorded tales of the Jacob and Wilhelm Grimm, Joan Acocella drew attention to the problems that the brothers faced when attempting to document orally dictated stories for the first time, as spoken narratives rely on very different communicative conventions. As she noted, "oral tales, when transcribed faithfully, are often barely readable." Thus, in a subsequent edition of Grimms' tales, the stories were deliberately rewritten to make them more literary and intelligible.[5] It is possible that the early scribes were determined to be faithful to Mariano Datahan's words and that stylistic features of spoken Visayan were reproduced at the expense of clarity for the reader. This may account for the difficulty in ascertaining which character is speaking in dialogues, information that may have been more easily signaled through the natural pauses or voice modulations of a speaking narrator. In fact, sometimes the ambiguity is "repaired" in the text, as for example, in this pair of consecutive sentences from "The First People in the Land of Bohol" (Eskayan in bold, Visayan in italics):

**Muywiri narin ya damu larak i tim yan. Bultu ya bintud ya Loon karku.**

*Magatanda aku sa akung basak ug hinug naba. Tawu sa lungsud sa Loon kana.*

'I will inspect my ricefield if it is ready for harvest.' That's a person from Loon speaking.

One teacher in Cadapdapan gave an alternative explanation of how such opacity emerged, attributing it to an unusual transcription method supposedly adopted by Mariano Datahan's first three secretaries. As Datahan spoke they would each copy down a single word in sequence. Thus, for example, the first scribe would write "*Ang,*" the second scribe "*kabaw,*" and the third "*habilin.*" The final product is then meshed together to create the sentence '*Ang kabaw nahabilin*' ('The water buffalo was left behind').[6] Errors, the teacher argued, were the result of a failure to reconstitute the three texts in the right way. This account leaves the integrity of the original words intact while preserving the literality principle; those who copy the texts today can justify the existence of mistakes while faithfully reproducing the same errors. Naturally, the kinds of errors that surface within the traditional literature can just as easily be explained in other ways. Mistakes have plausibly accrued as a result of inaccuracies in retranscription and accelerated by a proscription against crossing out text.[7] Even if the secretaries were transcribing unfragmented speech, this would have resulted in as many versions of the stories as there were scribes.

I have not been able to detect any consistent "regionalisms" between texts kept in Taytay and those held in Biabas and Cadapdapan, or across generations of transcribers, but considering the relative isolation and independence of Eskaya settlements from one another, such consistent differences are very likely to exist. Today, most of the active transcription takes place in Taytay, where the literature is always written using the Eskayan script alone. In Biabas, a few wordlists and shorter texts have been produced in the Roman script while in Cadapdapan I have had access to a notebook written by Viscayda herself, which includes a Roman layer alongside the script; a digital version is now archived online.[8] The present custodian of the book, Gemina Palma, informed me that this particular document represented part of Viscayda's attempt to standardize Eskaya literature. Palma recalls that after the local government issued the community with blank notebooks in the 1990s, Viscayda decided to hand-copy her own notebook multiple times. But even among Viscayda's own scrupulously reproduced notebooks, marked variations can be found and obvious errors are left untouched. Be that as it may, this book is the guiding reference for my analysis of Eskaya literature even if a certain amount of ongoing "standardization" has been necessary in order to describe the stories effectively and to distinguish between what readers themselves determined to be "correct" or "incorrect."[9]

## Texts

A full translation and evaluation of all Eskaya texts made available to me, in the vicinity of twenty-five thousand words, would far exceed the scope of this book. Nonetheless, certain texts are considered more important than others. Eskaya teachers in Taytay and Biabas told me that the two reference texts, namely, the Abidiha and Simplit (see Chapter 5), are the first to be introduced, followed by the narrative texts "The Itch-mite Tumaw," "Pinay," and "Daylinda."[10] These three narratives are clearly identifiable as stories that unfold as a chronological sequence of events with occasional asides that evaluate the morality of a protagonist's actions.

Less canonical narratives include "The First People in the Land of Bohol," an account of the original settlement of Eskaya people in Bohol under a chief by the name of Dangko; "The White Bell," which dramatizes the Bohol-wide legend of a bell salvaged from a church and hidden in a river; and "Hurayhaber's Dream," a story about an ancestral prophet. Although I will make reference to the linguistic elements of this last text, it is not given a full analytic treatment here. The final text that Datahan dictated is an autobiographical statement that brings Eskaya traditional history into the sphere of recent events, casting light on the circumstances in which the language and script were recuperated; this will be discussed in Chapter 8. Certain pedagogical documents for practicing basic numeracy and literacy are also reproduced and circulated. Among those that have now fallen out of use is a Spanish–English–Eskayan wordlist with pedagogical explanations of Spanish grammar in Visayan, and a religious text in Eskayan directly translated from a nineteenth-century Visayan-language catechism; these will be discussed in Chapter 9.

## Hermeneutics and oral historiography

The proliferation of differences across texts does not seem to have generated any conflict over which represent the "true" or orthodox versions, though Juan Datahan has expressed the view that the texts in Biabas are the most authentic as they are more proximal to Datahan (Martinez 1993, 78). Nevertheless, it was in Biabas and Cadapdapan that I encountered the most liberal interpretations of Eskaya literature. In these villages, spontaneous hermeneutic discussions of Eskaya texts that took place during school or elicitation sessions were far from dogmatic. Participants raised questions over the gender of Pinay, whether Jesus of Nazareth had really visited Bohol, and the extent to which the narratives indicated appropriate ways to behave. During a discussion of the text "The First People in the Land of Bohol," two teachers made the following exchange, which I did not record but have approximated here from my notes:

> "Were there people in Bohol before the arrival of Dangko?"
> "Yes, there were . . . No, Dangko was first."
> "I think the dates here in this story are not right."
> "Of course it is impossible for Sikatuna to have been there at that time.
> But I believe Pinay was a real person."

This segued into a discussion of where the first Mass was said in the Philippines, a popular historical debate throughout the country. In the manner of a theological debate, the text itself was considered the ultimate source of knowledge even if its correct interpretation remained unsettled. Indeed, theology was occasionally invoked as an interpretive device. On another occasion in Biabas, a question was raised as to how Sunu could be both the Santo Niño ('Holy Infant') and the adult Jesus, and this was resolved by analogy with the divine unity of the Holy Trinity.

In Taytay it was not customary to discuss the meanings of texts in a group, and it was my impression that an individual's relationship to the literature was considered to be a relatively private matter. Eskaya consultants in Taytay were nonetheless happy to answer my questions about stories, but their opinions tended to be narrower, less variable between readers, and expressed with more confidence.[11] But while Biabas readers preferred to analyze each text on its own terms, for students in Taytay the traditional literature had a great deal of intertextual coherence. It was far more common in Taytay to hear oral recapitulations of Eskaya narratives (discussed later), and narrators often situated the stories within a broader sweep of Philippine history, recounting, for example, the exploits of Pinay alongside those of José Rizal.

Certain oral interpretations of Eskaya literature are relatively consistent across communities in both hermeneutic discussions and recapitulations. Nowhere in the literary corpus is there any mention of Eskaya records being burned by the Spanish, nor of Eskayan-inscribed tablets hidden in a cave for protection. Nevertheless, these events are universally regarded as factual and even self-evident—the cave in question lies a short distance from Biabas.

To my mind these contextualizing stories, despite being orally transmitted only, have become integral to the corpus of Eskaya literature. Other oral stories concern the exploits of Mariano Datahan and his supernatural talents. Often prefaced by distancing or equivocal remarks, villagers told me that Datahan was able to travel great distances by leaping from mountain to mountain in a single bound, to make himself invisible and to be adept at *antinganting* ('amulet magic'). When food was scarce during World War II he is said to have cast a line from his window and hauled in fish from the jungle.

## Prophecies

The prophecies attributed to Mariano Datahan are another important category of orally transmitted texts. When I elicited Datahan's prophecies they were always preceded with the phrase, *Muabut ang panahun* . . . ('The time [or season] will come when . . .'), and faith in their accuracy was widespread even if interpretations differed and variations were accommodated. Among those prophecies that are considered to have been fulfilled are the following: the time will come when one will be able to touch a wall and a light will appear (i.e., electric light); when metal will float on water (i.e., steamers); when metal will fly (i.e., airplanes); when a man will step on the moon; when goods will be very expensive—a bunch of bananas will be more than five pesos, and a water buffalo will cost P1000 (a water buffalo now costs around P20,000); when women will try to compete with men and men will become like women.

Prophecies that are yet to be fulfilled include the following: there will come a time when rice grains will be as small as the spikelets from *amursiku* (a kind of crab grass); when Biabas will become a town and then a great city—if one were to lay a banana trunk on the road to Biabas in the morning, by evening the constant traffic will have worn it down into hemp; when the oil in the Middle East will be depleted and the Philippines will be a supplier of oil; when foreigners will till the soils; when the Philippines will become a center of world politics; when Christ will reign over the Philippines; when a golden boat will be seen; when the hills will collide and a volcano under the sea will erupt bringing forth a golden church. During my first visit to the field site, a landslide in nearby Mayana was interpreted by some in Taytay as a forewarning of the destruction predicted by Anoy.

Concerning language, Datahan foretold that there will come a time when Eskayan will be the national language of the Philippines (see Prologue), or that it would one day stand alone as the last language on earth. In Taytay it is remembered that Datahan predicted the imminent demise of the English language, which is why he urged the study of Eskayan. Tribal Bishop Elpidio Palaca told me a prophecy that every letter of the Eskayan script would one day be paid for. My presence in Cadapdapan was considered by some to fulfill a prophecy that scholars would come and take great interest in the language. In Cadapdapan it was also said that one day Mariano Datahan will be resurrected and the scattered Eskayan language would be gathered together again in his body.

Not all Eskaya prophecies can be positively attributed to Datahan. In 1983, José Datahan, a grandson of Mariano's brother, was dying, and he called all the students and teachers in Biabas together. He asked Nida Salingay to embroider a flag based on his drawings of a Santo Niño holding a Katipunan icon of the sun, similar to the one that appears on the Philippine national flag. Traditionally the national symbol of the sun has eight rays representing the provinces that first took arms against the Spanish: Manila, Cavite, Bulacan, Pampanga, Nueva Ecija, Tarlac, Laguna, and Batangas. Nida asked José why his sun had nine rays, and he replied that she would know the answer to this one day. Much later she saw an article on the Internet about a campaign to add a ray to the Katipunan sun to represent Mindanao and wondered if this was the fulfillment of José Datahan's vision.

Jes Tirol, of the University of Bohol (see Chapter 3), has formulated at least two Eskaya-related prophecies, but these are not today considered orthodox in the Eskaya communities: that the "Semitic" culture of the Eskaya suggests that Bohol will be the site of a new Jerusalem, and that the Eskaya will one day be led by tall white men with beards. Though these are not analyzed here, Tirol's predictions underscore the fact that the articulation of prophecies is by no means an exclusively Eskaya practice.

## Performance

As outlined earlier, songs and prayers in Eskayan are expected to be performed at specific times and locales. The performance space of the traditional literature is less rigorously defined. Reproduction via transcription is an important aspect of literary performance, and this may take place in the schools or at home. On at least one occasion "The Itch-mite Tumaw" was performed as a play by children in Taytay (see Fig. 7.2).

Although no single text makes explicit reference to another in the literature, and no protagonists other than Pinay feature in more than one story, Eskaya readers consider all the narratives to belong to a cohesive intertextual corpus. This intertextuality is expressed through brief oral retellings in Visayan that amount to short summaries of significant events in the stories. Summarized accounts were related to me personally by community members and were embedded in speeches made by teachers at special events. Oral retellings, which may be preceded by formulaic Visayan phrases like *Sa wala pa muabut ang mga katsilang tawu* . . . ('Before the Spanish arrived . . .'), emphasize the themes of prehispanic culture (including language), anti-colonial resistance, and the exploits of Eskaya ancestors and Philippine national heroes. Such retellings are illuminating in several ways. They represent an attempt to synthesize the narratives into a more accessible form (e.g., for children or visitors); they serve to remind listeners of the

**FIGURE 7.2.** Children performing the story of the Itch-mite Tumaw (photograph: Zoë Bedford, Taytay, ca. 2004).

important elements of a well-known tale; and they draw attention to what the performers of Eskaya literature themselves consider salient (e.g., war, resistance, and pre-contact culture).

The section that follows begins with a summary and synthesis of key events of Eskaya linguistic history as it is retold by Eskaya narrators. In the subsections that follow I provide summaries, in italics, of the individual texts that inform this history, followed by my own analysis. These summaries have been condensed for brevity, but the source documents are available in the PARADISEC archive.[12]

## Language history in Eskaya literature: A summary and analysis

In the spirit of the many oral recapitulations I have heard concerning the history of the Eskayan language and script, the following is my own composite narrative of Eskaya language history, as I have attempted to reconstruct it in my own way.

Before the arrival of the Spanish, say Eskaya narrators, a chieftain by the name of Dangko with his eleven sons and one daughter sailed from west Sumatra to Bohol and intermarried with the locals. The migrants maintained a distinct culture under the leadership of Pinay who is described as the first **inmunsiktur** ('Pope') in the Philippines. Pinay was divinely instructed by a being known as Sunu ('Santo Niño') to create the Eskayan language and to base its form on a human body. This is why Eskayan letters resemble a body in various poses, or individual body parts and internal organs. Pinay taught this language to the people; the language they spoke beforehand is unknown. His Eskayan language, which was then called Bisayan Declarado ('Declared Visayan') was used throughout the island. Well-known figures of Boholano history, such as chief Sikatuna, who made a famous pact with the conquistador Miguel de Legazpi in 1565 (Scott 1992), and the rebel fighter Francisco Dagohoy (ca. 1724–ca. 1782) are claimed as ancestral speakers of Eskayan. Use of the language continued until the Spanish established a sustained presence in Bohol. Intent on destroying the indigenous culture, the Spanish suppressed Eskayan by systematically burning all the native records. In the meantime, 'Cebuano' was introduced into Bohol from Cebu's printing presses and took root. Fortunately, records of Eskayan were hidden in a cave until they were discovered by the rebel soldier Mariano Datahan. In another version, it was Mariano Datahan who received direct linguistic inspiration from the ancestral past, and he wrote down the language on wooden tablets, which were then stored away for protection in a cave by his followers. In any event Datahan is credited with the feat of reanimating the Eskayan of Pinay and of retransmitting it to his followers. Some stories describe a community of mother tongue speakers of Eskayan who left Bohol for Mindanao at the time of Spanish contact; in some accounts this migration happened during the lifetime of Mariano Datahan.

Within oral retellings, such the as the version I have reproduced, the Eskayan language is as firmly associated with its mythic progenitor Pinay as it is with Datahan. Fabian Baja described Datahan to me as a linguistic genius, fluent in every language in the world, and it was Baja's belief that Pinay and Datahan were the same person. Indeed, the unity of the two figures is perfectly exemplified in the prophecy that Pinay's language, created through a dissection of the body, would one day be restored into the body of a reincarnated Mariano Datahan.

Understandings of local language history vary from person to person and are subject to hermeneutic debate. When I asked about specific events, replies would sometimes be prefaced by distancing remarks such as 'The old people say . . .' or 'Some people believe . . .' Not all Eskaya readers automatically think of Mariano Datahan as the ultimate author of these tales, but he is nonetheless acknowledged to be their privileged mediator. For this reason I reserve the name 'Anoy' to refer to the *mediator* of the texts, personified by Mariano Datahan. The distinction between the author construct 'Anoy' and the historical Mariano Datahan is maintained here in order to avoid coercing the origin story of Eskaya literature into a single authoritative narrative.

What follows are analyses of the *linguistic* motifs in the most widely reproduced Eskaya texts in my English translation; other no less important themes within the literature must remain the concern of another study. My descriptions are based largely on the versions found in Viscayda's "standard" notebook with missing fragments provided by other manuscripts and from oral retellings. Shorter texts are reproduced as free translations while the longer narratives (some exceeding five thousand words) are described in summary.

### "The Itch-mite Tumaw"

With its intimations of a deep biblical past, this is a creation story that accounts for the origins of all animate beings in the world. It is also a narrative that develops the theme of deliberate naming, and the generative potential for names to reproduce the world and to substantiate kinship and belonging. As such it introduces what will become a consistent concern of Eskaya literature: the creative power of language to both represent and influence reality.

*At the time of Noah's flood, a butterfly and a butterfly's egg became the parents of the Itch-mite Tumaw. When he was one year of age he went off through the fields, mountains and forests in search of his parents. Finally he came to rest on the vein of a leaf from where he spied a lion and a lioness.*

*He was permitted to ride on the back of the lioness on the sole condition that he would give her a name and thereby save her life. Itch-mite gave her the name Liyuna and gave the lion the name Lindil (Liyun). He urged them both not to forget their names and as a reminder he gave them the affectionate nicknames Lino and Liyunsya. The lion then asked him for his name, and Itch-mite replied that first he was the egg of a butterfly but now that he was grown up he was simply 'Itch-mite.' He had gone in search of his parents but could not find them. The lion and lioness said that he could claim them as his new parents and Itch-mite replied that he would feed on the lion's fur like an infant. He would not feed on the lioness's fur because he intended to use it as a blanket to keep him warm by day and night. Presently Itch-mite mounted the lioness and entered her womb. He was reborn again after some months as a* **balinsiya***, a creature with the appearance of a female orangutan. This orangutan discovered that she could eat food that was poisonous to others and declared that she would live by her wits, stealing food and giving it to her relatives. The orangutan later gave birth to a human male child called Idam, a female child called Hidam and another monkey. At the age of eleven, Idam and Hidam gave birth to four children who began to have knowledge of God, recognized as the creator of the first butterfly. Their human offspring are called 'Tumaw' from Itch-mite's family name. The children named the first butterfly Ipilis Iribilis and had more children of three kinds to inhabit all parts of the world—*ipilis *('real people'),* iribilis *('animals') and supernatural beings.*

In Eskayan this tale is given the title **Nuku Tumaw**, where **nuku** is glossed as *kagaw* in Visayan, a word that is conventionally translated into English as 'germ.' I have translated it into English as 'itch-mite' (*Sarcoptes scabiei*) since this meaning is recorded in earlier Visayan dictionaries including Martín (1842a, 84, 1842b) and is a more likely interpretation given the fact that Itch-mite feeds on fur and uses it as a blanket.[13] But when Itch-mite enters the womb of the lioness, the word appears to overlap with its meaning in the term *kagaw nga lalaki* ('sperm,' literally 'male germ'). The word *tumaw*, meanwhile, is attested in Filipino folklore as a synonym for *anitu*, a helpful invisible being that inhabits special sites, but it is not a word that has currency today.

There are no discernible correspondences between "The Itch-mite Tumaw" and other known creation stories from the Visayas, although the biblical influences are unambiguous: it is introduced as having taken place at the time of 'Noah's flood' while at the same time we learn that the first human beings are named Idam and Hidam; in another version of the same text they are called Idam and Iba. The name of the butterfly Ipilis Iribilis also has an intriguing similarity to the figure of Iblis (إبليس), an angel who appears in the Qur'anic version of the Adam and Eve narrative, and who is cast out of heaven for refusing to prostrate himself before God. Finally, the Eskaya story alludes to the theft of forbidden food on the part of the female ancestor.

As hinted at in the label on the unsourced bas relief in the Provincial Museum, the descent of humanity from a monkey resonates with popularized narratives of Darwinian evolution. This was a topic of great interest for the early Aglipayan church to which the Eskaya community had converted. Aglipayan theologians distinguished themselves from their Romanist forebears by promoting a "scientific" catechism that embraced evolutionary thinking. The Aglipayan audience for this story was made up of individuals who had at first been exposed to creationist theology and were later asked to accept new evolutionary knowledge that may have been challenging to assimilate (Chapter 8). Personified in the **balinsiya**, the ancestral monkey who gives birth to humans seems to accommodate both perspectives.

The principal linguistic theme in the story concerns the power of naming, and it is my impression that the relevance of the Book of Genesis to "The Itch-mite Tumaw" runs deeper than an identification of Idam and Hidam with Adam and Eve. In the King James version, Genesis verses 19–20 are as follows:

> And out of the ground the lord God formed every beast of the field, and every fowl of the air; and brought them unto Adam to see what he would call them: and whatsoever Adam called every living creature, that was the name thereof.
>
> And Adam gave names to all cattle, and to the fowl of the air, and to every beast of the field; but for Adam there was not found an help meet for him.

In the Eskaya origin story, Itch-mite names the lions while searching for a companion (or 'help-meet') with whom he can reproduce. Reproductive power is inherent in his progenitor, the first butterfly whose name is analyzed as a composite of two Eskayan words that stand for 'real people' and 'animals' while his own name 'Tumaw' is passed on to his human offspring. The notion that referents are assigned signifiers through deliberate processes of naming—so-called Adamic naming (Dawson 1992; Siegert 1996)—is a theme that underpins much of Eskaya literature. Eskaya readers I consulted did not have a view as to why Itch-mite was able to save the life of the lions by giving them names, but conceivably Anoy regarded naming as an event that brings the referent into material existence, just as elsewhere in the Bible, words are described as becoming flesh (John 1:14), or of granting eternal life (John 5:24).

It is worth noting that, aside from 'Tumaw' itself, the names in "The Itch-mite Tumaw" have a distinctly foreign tone to a Visayan ear. Itch-mite names the male and female lions Lindil and Liyuna, or *Liyun* ('Lion') and *Liyuna* ('Lioness') in the Visayan translation, and gives them the nicknames Lino and Liyunsiya. Not only are these names inspired by the Spanish *león* ('lion'), but they take what appears to be Spanish gender in the endings -/u/, -/a/, and -/sya/, represented in Spanish orthography as '-*o*,' '-*a*,' and '-*cia*'; gender is not grammatically indicated in either Visayan or Eskayan. The Eskayan word **paypaypling** ('butterfly') does, however, have a plausible origin in the Visayan word *paypay* ('fan'; see Chapter 6), but the syllable -**pling** is phonotactically unattested in native Visayan words. In essence, the narrator Anoy was addressing an audience of Visayan speakers for whom Spanish was a prototypically 'foreign' language. Instead of relying on arbitrary sound combinations, Anoy conjured a particular brand of linguistic otherness that was specific to his context, a phenomenon discussed in the previous chapters with respect to the Spanish influence on Eskayan lexemes.

## "The First People in the Land of Bohol"

In contrast to the Genesis narrative of "The Itch-mite Tumaw," this text is an account of a more specific *ethno*genesis that explains how the ancestors of the Eskaya first laid claim to Bohol and how they opposed the domination of later-arriving Spanish invaders.[14] There are no obvious linguistic motifs in this tale, but it is significant to the extent that it provides a mythical frame for mimicry-and-rejection and establishes a heroic anti-Spanish lineage for Eskaya people:

> *The first Visayans arrived in Bohol when a chieftain by the name of Dangko, together with his wife Luneta and their children set sail from western Sumatra.[15] Upon arriving in Bohol, the family settled on the island of Tambu in the region of Talibon (Map 3). Here the children of Dangko and Luneta intermarried with the dark-skinned local inhabitants. Later, in the year 1777, a successor of the early settlers by the name of Tugpa rose up against the Spanish. Tugpa established his rebel camp at Cansungay in the district of Inaghuban (Map 3) declaring that he and his men represented the last descendants of the Visayans. He urged his followers to pledge their last breath for the motherland or be enslaved again by white people from the west. Tugpa warned that Guindulman had already fallen to the Spanish and that Cansungay would soon follow but would always retain its Visayan honor. After this speech the Spanish troops arrived and there were many casualties on both sides. Rebel soldiers, women and children were slaughtered in a cave, and young girls were raped by Spanish troops. A rebel captain acted as*

*a decoy and pretended to ally himself with the enemy. He helped them haul the houses to the mouth of the cave to be set on fire. His wife, Gaka, was raped while their only child managed to escape into the jungle. Then the captain and his wife threw themselves onto the fire, crying that they would rather burn than submit to the Spanish. The story ends: "This was the omen of the seventh year of the seventh month on the seventh date, April 17, 1777."*

The tale of Dangko and Luneta's voyage, introduced at the beginning, has parallels with a popular belief that the ancestors of modern-day Filipinos arrived in the archipelago from Sumatra (see, for example, de los Reyes y Florentino 1889, 69, 72). Indeed, José Rizal himself was a proponent of this theory. In an annotation to an 1890 edition of Antonio Morga's *Succesos de las islas Filipinas*, he wrote:

Ancient traditions place the origin of the Filipinos in Sumatra. These traditions were lost, along with the mythology and genealogies of which our ancient historians spoke, thanks to the zeal of the religious orders in eradicating our national, native and idolatrous memories.[16]

An "out-of-Sumatra" narrative was revisited by the anthropologist H. Otley Beyer, who popularized the long-discredited theory that coastal Filipinos had emigrated from islands to the south. Beyer and others maintained that southern Malays had colonized the coasts, pushing the more "primitive" Filipinos into the mountains (for a summary of these views see Scott 1994, 10–11). In the Eskaya story, by contrast, the Malay tribe represented by Dangko, Luneta, and their offspring intermarries with the prior inhabitants of Bohol, giving rise to a glorious legacy that would end with the rebel Tugpa. Thus, Tugpa could identify himself and his followers as the "last of the Visayans" whose lineage reached back to the founding colonists.

Even more interesting is the fact that Mariano Datahan, who first dictated the story, was born Mariano *Sumatra*. Although both he and his brothers were to change their family names to Datahan, for reasons that will be explored in Chapter 8, his birth name was known to his audience, and toward the end of his life he was to reinstate it, identifying himself as Mariano Datahan Sumatra. An implicit correlation is thus established between the narrator of the story, the founding patriarch of Bohol, and his heroic successor in the person of Tugpa.

An individual named Tugpa is, in fact, known to mainstream Boholano history as the younger brother of the rebel Francisco Dagohoy (see Chapter 2). Baptized Maximinio, he went by the aliases Handug, Hantud, and Tugpa and led rebel camps in Catagdaan and Inaghuban (Map 3; Misa 1970; Romanillos 1997). Tugpa was said to be among the 395 insurgents killed in 1829 when Dagohoy's eighty-five-year resistance was finally put down. Spanish troops lit a fire at the entrance to the cave in which the remaining rebels were hiding, suffocating them to death. Today, the cave is named 'Tugpa' in his honor. A shaman I met in Valencia, who was introduced to me by the official Eskaya *biki* or tribal bishop, claimed direct descent from one of Tugpa's trusted comrades.

The idiom *kaliwat ni Dagohoy* ('Dagohoy's people') is still used to designate Boholanos as a population (Chapter 2). This collectivizing term is a reflection of the scale and longevity of Dagohoy's insurrection, in which a majority of Bohol's inhabitants participated over several generations (see Map 5). In like manner, the Eskaya story readily exploits a colloquial association of Dagohoy with the inhabitants of Bohol. With the genealogy of the *kaliwat ni Dagohoy* traceable to a founding Sumatran voyage, the reader is left with the impression that Boholanos had never submitted to colonial rule and had maintained a proud independence until the Dagohoy rebels' last stand. Even the name of the Sumatran matriarch alludes to national resistance—Luneta is the site in Manila where José Rizal was executed in 1896, and a shrine was erected there in 1913.

Eskaya readers could not provide insight into the story's cryptic final line— "This was the omen of the seventh year of the seventh month on the seventh date, April 17, 1777"—but the date certainly alludes to the narrative of "The White Bell," which recounts another anti-colonial struggle set in this year. Possible parallels between elements of this battle and local World War II history are detailed in Chapter 9.

The language spoken by the early Sumatran colonists is not mentioned in the story, but presumably it was not Eskayan since this was to be wholly created on Bohol by Pinay. Nonetheless, by Tugpa's era Eskayan appears to have taken root, and the story includes a few Eskayan words that are left untranslated in the Visayan text. The attack on the rebel fortifications is described in Visayan as *unang binuhat sa gahum ni* **Ara** ('the first deed of Ara's power'). The Eskayan word **Ara** denotes 'God' and may be inspired by Arabic الله ('Allah') or Spanish *ara* ('altar') as discussed earlier in Chapter 6. This meaning is not explained in the text, but two other words are given Spanish glosses. In the final part of the story, the heroic captain is introduced thus (from the Visayan):

A certain **hirdu** stayed in the uppermost part of the cave. The word **hirdu** is *capitán* ['captain'] in Spanish. This **hirdu** acted as the *pahuy* ['scarecrow', 'decoy'] for the troops, or *guardia* ['guard'] as they say in Spanish.[17]

Clearly **hirdu** is an Eskayan word, and Anoy provides the reader with a Spanish, rather than a Visayan, gloss. But the unambiguous Visayan term *pahuy* is also glossed in Spanish. Neither gloss adds any vital information to readers with a knowledge of Spanish. Instead, Anoy seems merely to be emphasizing the fact that Boholanos possessed native terms for Spanish military roles, with the implication that complex social-military systems existed prior to colonization.

## "Pinay"

"Pinay" is the sole written text to refer to the creative ancestor responsible for the Eskayan language and script and is thus of central relevance to Eskaya beliefs about language and language history. It is sufficiently short to reproduce a free translation in full. Although at least one Eskayan-language version of "Pinay" exists, the text of the story does not sit well in Eskayan translation. Like "The First People in the Land of Bohol," a number of lines embed Visayan explications of the meaning of Eskayan words that are coherent in Visayan but are nonsensical when reproduced only in Eskayan. The very deliberate switches to Eskayan with accompanying explanatory context suggest that "Pinay," like the stories discussed previously, was probably dictated for transcription before fully translated Eskayan texts were in common circulation. In the following I have translated the Visayan text into English but kept the original Eskayan words in place in order to preserve the polyglot character of the story. Where their meanings are known, glosses for Eskayan words are added by me in square parentheses:

> The **inmunsiktur** ['Pope'] Pinay created **Bisayan** ['Eskayan'] which is now called **Buul** ['Boholano']. The native power of the Philippines was created in the year 600 from the birth of Jesus. He was the first wise man here in the Visayan islands. He was the custodian of the created Filipino flag, the **planu** ['flag'] leaf of the land of the Filipinos. Without knowledge, without a flag, without a leaf, there is no native flag. The Spaniards say *bandera*. In **Bisayan** it is **planu** or **bandi**, our native knowledge. In England they say 'American flag.' In the Visayas it is the Philippine leaf. Through our own native knowledge, the flag is the strength of independence. The independence of a nation is the mark of its nationhood. They say 'American flag' in England, *bandera* in Spanish, **planu** (**bandi**) in **Bisayan**.
>
> From the year 55 from the birth of Jesus, Pinay was the first Pope to be created. Jesus is the third part of the whole world's faith. Here in the Philippines a native faith existed 32 years after the birth of Jesus. Our native faith was born here in the **Buuw** ['Bohol'] Visayas, Salvador Mono, the native land of **Marabuyuk** ['Maribojok'], Booy, Dauis. The mother was Guadalupe, the father was Lumono.
>
> A citizen of Portugal, Magellan travelled towards the island of Australia before the arrival of the Spanish. His second journey was

to Singapore, the last island of Sumatra. The third journey was to the Visayas, Moraho and Zamboanga. The fourth journey was to **Buuw**. Magellan fled to the island of **Pangaw** ['Panglao']. Magellan went roaming with his companions. Magellan passed through the city of **Pangaw** whereupon he went straight up to the house of Angaw. Since between Spaniard and Visayan there was no understanding of the one called Angaw, Magellan asked what the island was called, whereupon Angaw replied, 'My name is Angaw.' The Spaniard said 'Angaw, Angaw, Angaw.' The Spaniard returned to his **guwagu balsa** ['large wooden boat'], the white **puntri kul ga'up** ['eleven cloth house'] **sapi** ['bamboo ladder'] **duylan ya balsa guwagu.**

Translated from **Bisayan** ['Eskayan']: 'They boarded their large wooden vessel.'

As mentioned earlier, the gender of Pinay is a matter of debate. Though he is understood as a 'Pope,' the *-ay* suffix is typical of female nicknames in the Visayas and the Philippines at large, just as *-oy* is a typical suffix for male nicknames. More precisely, names of this kind are formed by taking the final two syllables of a Hispanic given name and adding *-y*. Hence, Mariano becomes 'Anoy.' By means of the same derivational process, the word *pinay* coincidentally means 'Filipina' throughout the contemporary Philippines, and the word has patriotic connotations (the masculine form is *pinoy*). Just like Luneta in "The First People in the Land of Bohol," the name 'Pinay' indexes Filipino nationalism.

At the beginning of the text, several apparent anachronisms are introduced. Pinay, of 600 CE, is an **inmunsiktur** ('Pope') and the owner of a Filipino flag. He is also described as the creator of **Bisayan** ('Eskayan'). The term 'Bisayan,' thus spelled, is in fact an English rendering of *Bisaya'* ('Visayan') as applied by the early American colonists, and it is here used by Datahan to denote the language of Pinay. Only after Datahan passed away in 1949 did the word 'Eskaya' and its derivatives come into circulation. Thus, the application of the word **Bisayan** to encode Pinay's language is significant in two ways: it situates Eskayan as central by appropriating the dominant term (*Bisaya'*), while the **-n** suffix takes this appropriation one step further by both referencing and redefining the terminology of the U.S. colonial administration ('Bisayan'). Thus, the **Bisayan** ('Eskayan') language as created by Pinay is emphasized as primary, and the regional language presently used throughout Bohol and its surrounding islands is a deviation or displacement of it. There are several further hints of this implied linguistic shift. Bohol is rendered as **Buuw**, and Boholano-Visayan (*Bulanun*) as **Buul**. The town of Maribojok, on Bohol's west coast, is **Marabuyuk**, and the island of Panglao is **Pangaw**.

The hints at a past, pre-contact moment are clear. Bool is the name of a district near Tagbilaran, and some believe the island as a whole derived its name from it. A popular folk etymology relates that a kind of tree known as *buul* grew in this area. When the Spanish first came ashore, they pointed to the island to ask its name. Thinking that they were pointing to the tree, the locals offered the reply /buʔul/, and, because the Spanish could not pronounce the glottal stop, they assimilated it as /buhul/, which they wrote as 'Bohol.' In "Pinay," language change as a product of miscommunication or mispronunciation is similarly illustrated in Magellan's visit to Panglao, an island just off the coast of Tagbilaran (Map 3). In this case, the misunderstanding associates the name of an occupant of the island with the island itself. Thus, the reader is led to conclude that the toponym 'Panglao' (/panglaw/) came from Pangaw (/pangaw/), which in turn was derived, mistakenly, from Angaw (/angaw/).[18]

These "earlier" place names embody characteristics that are considered to be marked features of Boholano-Visayan, albeit via a certain amount of orthographic punning. Visayan speakers from Cebu often contend that Boholanos have a habit of replacing /l/ sounds with /w/ sounds, and hence **Buuw** /buuw/ might be conceived of as an authentically provincial realization of 'Bohol.' This is partly true insofar as intervocalic /l/ is optionally realized as /w/ in Bohol in words like *ulan* ('rain') and *sulat* ('write'), which become *uwan* and *suwat*. There are, however, no cases of word-final /l/ to /w/ alternation in Boholano-Visayan, and thus /buuw/ for 'Bohol' is something of a hypercorrected "Boholanoism."

The conspicuous insertion of "pre-contact" names for Bohol's significant towns, and of their misnaming by European visitors, serves to emphasize the primordial sovereignty and legitimate authority of Boholanos over their island. This, needless to say, is in direct contrast to the historical record, which shows that these towns were planned by Spanish administrators who hoped to centralize Bohol's populations into more easily governable settlements (a policy known as *reducción*). But a pre-contact history for Bohol's administrative centers is given further literary impetus in the person of Pinay, whose papacy in the year 55 is conferred, not by the Catholic Church, but by Jesus himself, who, it is alleged in oral commentary on "Pinay," visited the Philippines in AD 32, i.e., the year before his Crucifixion according to Christian texts.

Pinay is identified as the custodian of a national flag projected as the consummate symbol of nationhood, independence, and linguistic cohesion. All nations are represented by a flag, the name for which is denoted in the national tongue. Indeed, Datahan's nationalist isomorphism of flag, country, and language is made all the more stark by his mistaken attribution of an 'American flag' to England. The existence of a Philippine flag and of a "Bisayan" language draws attention to the fact that Bohol is the same as other nations and satisfies the requirements of nationhood. But it distinguishes itself from the flags of European nation-states by its characterization as a *dahun* ('leaf'), an organic embodiment of native belonging. Thus, any notion that flags and nations are European artifacts of recent introduction is preemptively undermined by Anoy's historical revision and cultural nativism.

This drive toward difference is developed linguistically in the final lines of the story. Magellan's boat is a **guwagu balsa**, an Eskayan term that is translated into Visayan as *sakayan nga daku* or 'large wooden boat without a sail.' However, *balsa* is also a Visayan word that means 'raft' (from Sp. *balsa*) in coastal areas but 'water buffalo sled' in upland regions: Eskaya people I interviewed were familiar with the 'sled' but not the 'raft' meaning. Thus, a sense of linguistic continuity is established between Eskayan and Visayan. In like manner, the characterization of Magellan's boat as a 'large raft' allows the reader to inhabit the linguistic perspective of Angaw, who, unfamiliar with European maritime technology, perceives it in terms of the nearest cultural approximation. The ultimate strangeness of Eskayan is brought home in the phrase **puntri kul ga'up sapi duylan ya balsa guwagu**, translated into Visayan as *Nanguli sa ilang sakayan nga daku* ('They boarded their large wooden vessel'). This is by no means a literal translation of the Eskayan phrase. The word **duylan** cannot be decoded by Eskayan speakers, but of the remaining text, an awkward but more accurate translation is 'house of eleven cloths, bamboo ladder **duylan** the large wooden vessel.' Ultimately, this has the effect of doubly defamiliarizing the action of Magellan boarding his vessel and of foregrounding the semantic relativity. Amid a haze of arcane words, the Eskaya reader may just distinguish a man climbing a bamboo ladder to a house with eleven cloths (i.e., sails) resting on a large raft.

### "The White Bell"

Boholano folklore is rich in recuperation narratives in which a lost artifact is hidden by a heroic ancestor in order to be retrieved by a future hero, usually with the prohibition that the object must not be reclaimed before the appointed time or disaster will ensue. The Eskaya story of a hidden white or silver bell (Fig. 7.3) elaborates this theme in its identification of the folkloric bell as a trophy of religious and linguistic preeminence:[19]

> *The Spanish arrived in the Philippines between AD 600 and AD 677. By 1777 a war broke out which by 1804 had become a battle between the indigenous* **biriki** [pari, *'priests'*] *and the Spanish friars. The two sides had different belief systems. The* **biriki** *believed in miracles and venerated an entity known as Salbadur Sunu, whom the Spanish denounced as* **araara** [dyusdyus, *'a*

**FIGURE 7.3.** Painted panel in an Eskaya chapel in Balingasao, depicting a scene from "The White Bell."

*false god*]. *During this conflict, an indigenous priest known as Tumud the Shaman received a vision of how to capture a white bell hanging in the tower of a Spanish church in Malabago. He climbed the tower with a small rope and tied one end to the foot of a bird, and the other to the loop of the bell. The local population, divided between baptized Christians and followers of the indigenous religion, gathered on the floor of the church to witness Tumud's daring. Using his faith in Salbadur Sunu, Tumud intoned the 'language of God* [**Ara**].[20] *The parish priest, Fr José Maria, counters this with his friar's faith in Christianity and uses Latin, the 'language of Christ.' Tumud's words prevailed and the bird took flight, towing the bell aloft. It flew to where a* *creek known as the Abatan flowed into the river at which point the iron fetter of the bell's clasp turned to water and the bell sank into the depths. The worshippers of Salbadur Sunu, who had not submitted to baptism, rejoiced at the capture of their bell and vowed to die in defense of their motherland. Tumud sent his followers into the forests to fight against the friars. He told them that the bell could only be recovered from the river when those who have died for it are resurrected. If anyone were to try to obtain the bell before this time, a mighty flood would issue from the bell's clasp bringing death to thousands.*

The story of a bell hidden in the depths of the Abatan River (Map 3) is well known to Boholanos (see Chapter 3), but the tale itself is not original to the Eskaya and is in fact relatively well known in other communities throughout the island. In its simplest form, a silver bell belonging to the native people is said to have been requisitioned by Spanish priests, who hoisted it into the bell tower of a church. But the bell was reclaimed by the local people, who took it to the Abatan River and let it sink so that the Spanish would never again be able to get hold of it. A more detailed local variant, on which the Eskaya story seems to be based, casts the rebel shaman Tamblot (see Chapter 2) as the hero. Tamblot, also known as Lumud, lived in the old settlement of Malabago in the upland region above Cortes (Map 3). Tamblot had been given a white or silver bell by the Spanish authorities, but when a priest wanted to take it back to install in Malabago's church he refused and hid it in a large bend of the river. To this day, it is said that the bell can be seen glinting under the water's surface at dusk. At least one attempt was made to retrieve the bell from its presumed resting place by an archeological expedition in the 1930s. In variants of this narrative that are known beyond Bohol, the bell is either buried or sunk in a lake or bay, to be hidden from priests or Moro pirates and may only be retrieved under the right conditions (for an overview of the bell cycle in Philippine folklore see Kelly 2016a).

"The White Bell," as told by Anoy, presents a clash of civilizations between locals and colonists. The Spanish are followers of Christ while the Boholanos, under Tumud, follow Salvadur Sunu, a being who is nonetheless understood as a kind of indigenous proto-Christ.[21] The Spanish faith is portrayed as deficient, and the friars as incapable of belief in miracles. Yet Tumud's native epistemology is unencumbered by Spanish dogma, and he is able to access the miraculous. During the standoff there is last-ditch contest between languages. The language of God, presumably but not explicitly Eskayan, is pitted against Latin, the language of Christ.[22] Tumud's language prevails and the bell is miraculously reclaimed.

Other traditional tales circulated within Bohol follow the same narrative structure: a precious object that is seen to have been misappropriated by colonists is recaptured and hidden, awaiting rediscovery at the hands of a virtuous native. Dagohoy's treasure, ransacked from church estates, is said to be buried in caves in the cliffs of Kailagan, but anyone who seeks it will die unless they use it to fight for the freedom of the Boholano people. At sunset, you can still see glints of gold in the cliff face (V.B. Tirol 1968, 53). A more recent recuperation narrative concerns the World War II occupation. Japanese soldiers are said to have buried bars of gold at Mt. Puwawan, but those who have gone in search of them have often lost their lives. It is said that a group of American engineers planned to bulldoze the mountain to find the treasure but some members of the group died from mysterious illnesses, so the project was canceled (Aparece 2003, 104).[23]

The most significant Eskaya parallel to the recovery of the white bell is the suppression and recuperation of Pinay's language, carved on wooden tablets and stored in a cave. Like Tumud, Pinay wrested the artifact from Spanish authorities, and, with a flair for the miraculous, Datahan was able to restore it. Of relevance is the description, in "The Spanish and Eskayan Alphabets," of Pinay as the first **mirikilyu** ('doctor'), a word that is plausibly inspired by the English 'miracle' (see Chapter 6).

Eskaya readers in Cadapdapan identified the bell as a symbol of Eskaya culture and language but were also inclined to think of it as a literal bell that would one day be recovered. It is my view that such tales have a special importance for colonized people coming to terms with cultural dispossession (Kelly 2016a). Culture, in these narratives, is a powerful and even dangerous object that can be suppressed by outsiders but never wholly obliterated. Its retrieval must be performed with great care lest it wreak misfortune on the unworthy. Among the unworthy, in the Eskaya narrative, are the colonizers with their impoverished Latin and their weak epistemology that leaves no room for the marvelous. In Chapter 3 we saw a similar contest of epistemologies that was played out by Brenda Abregana and Jes Tirol, both of whom characterized Eskayan as a lost treasure and adopted a miraculous view of its speakers and history. Indeed, Tirol's subterranean discovery of Eskayan in the Inambacan cave is an elegant recapitulation of the discovery of Pinay's tablets.

## "The Spanish and Eskayan Alphabets"

This text represents an insider account of the origin and significance of the Eskayan writing system and is therefore of particular interest to this study. The first part of the text is a comparison of the Roman and Eskayan alphabets, while the second part introduces the creator Pinay along with a brief genealogy of other Eskaya ancestors.

*Visayan knowledge was imprisoned in Spanish letters which are derived from a wide variety of domestic objects. Eskayan letters, on the other hand, come from a single human body. It was Pinay, ruler of the Visayas in the year 600, who revealed Eskayan letters known as* **aspurmus minimi**.

*The first of these was A̅ ('A') which represents the Visayas. The letter C ('Kun') represents half of a human head and is composed of the letter C ('C') with a full stop in the middle of it. It represents Pinay's brain.*

*The letter (-) ('G') is taken from two ears. These letters are from a human body. The foreign Spanish letters come from wood, iron and animals.*

*The Spanish letter 'A' is taken from the shape of a festive archway erected over a thoroughfare. The lowercase letter 'g' is taken from an animal's tail, the letter 'X' from a pair of steel scissors, the letter 'I' from a candlestand and the lowercase 'a' is a cup for drinking chocolate at fiestas.*

*Pinay was the first doctor* [**mirikilyu**] *in the Philippines. From the year 677 he began to teach his compatriots. Pinay's home town was Canlaas, once part of Loon but now part of Antequera. He is still remembered in that part of Bohol, such that if you ask a person heading to Loon where they are going, they will reply that they are going to Pinay's town. Another pre-Hispanic ruler was Sirol who was married to Kurang.*

*In Sirol's administration Sikatuna was king and he was married to Datag. Dagohoy's mother was Booy and his father was Duya. Pinay's mother was Bas and she was married to Kangkay. The town of Malinggay was Candungaw which is now Calape; the town of Amgay was Bowasa within Inabanga. Sitio Kamangay is now a part of Colonia Carmen. Alburang's town was Agbunan, now Catigbian. The town of Dangko was Puwang Yuta, now Tambo Talibon. The town of Tugpa was Kansungay Lisun, now Candijay. The town of Malta was Tubowan, Loon. The town of Paulit was barangay Kangable in Loon. The town of Sira was barangay Bungku, Loon. The town of Sikatuna was Bow, a barangay that is now within Tagbilaran. The town of Datag, wife of Sikatuna was Kambujud Sikatuna. The town of Dagohoy was Buuy, now a part of Dauis.*

*Kurarang was a* **sirdas**, *or 'nun'; Malta was* **isirdas** *or 'female teacher'; Paulit was* **hining sirdas**, *'a nun of the third rank';* **birsirdas** *were 'female teachers'; Pinay was* **inmunsiktur** *or Papa ['Pope'] in Spanish; Sikatuna was* **sutbagani** *or hari ['king'] in Spanish (sic). Dagohoy was* **bagani hibir** *or* general *in Spanish; Dangko was* **baganibagani** *or* dictador *in Spanish; Amgay was* **bansithi** *or* gobernador *in Spanish; Alburang was* **baganhunda** *or* juez *('judge') in Spanish; Tugpa was* **baganiring** *or* comandante general *('major general') in Spanish.* **'Minalki biki Pilipin Visayas'** *means* Maung dagkung mga punuan Pilipin Visayas ('There were a great number of leaders in the Philippine Visayas').

"The Spanish and Eskayan Alphabets" emphasizes the iconicity of two writing systems that are evaluated on the basis of their origins. The Eskayan alphabet was "revealed" to Pinay, expressed in Visayan with the word *nagabandira* (**dilplanu**), literally 'put in full view' from the Spanish *bandera* ('flag'), reinforcing the association of language and writing with national symbols. Indeed, Anoy explains that the first letter of the Eskayan alphabet stands for the Visayas itself, situating the islands as primary. Other letters have self-evident origins in the human body, in direct contrast to the Spanish system, which takes its inspiration from inconsequential objects. However, these superficial foreign letters have held Visayans to ransom. Anoy declares that the "teachings of the Visayan islands were bound and chained to the letter of Spain," a theme that he returns to in "Declared Visayan," where he laments the representation of the Visayan language in Roman letters by Cebu's printing presses. The second part of the story lists Eskaya ancestors and their places of origin, beginning with Pinay, who is from Loon—a fact of some significance to Eskaya readers since Loon is the hometown of Mariano Datahan. Like "Pinay" the text ends with a micro-lesson in Eskayan: the Eskayan names for the ranks of these ancestral heroes are given with glosses in Spanish, and a full Eskayan sentence is provided with an accompanying Visayan translation. Again, this state of affairs suggests that the entire text had been written in Visayan first before an Eskayan translation was added.

## "Atikisis"

"Atikisis" is presented as an illustrated reference text in which the letters of the **abidiha** or primary Eskayan alphabet (Chapter 5) are personified as the cultivators of different edible plants and exhibit varying degrees of industriousness. In contrast to the inanimate Spanish letters reviewed in the previous story, Eskaya letters are agentive and morally responsible, reinforcing a view of Eskayan writing as conscious, creative, and human phenomenon:

> *The letter ᴁ ('A') declares itself to be a hard worker who plants capsicum and tomatoes. Its right hand is particularly industrious and performs any kind of work. The letter ᴂ ('H') plants sweet potato, bananas, onions and yams, it is subordinate to the command of the letter ᴁ ; the letter ƒ ('F') represents thievery—it is lazy and does not know how to cultivate anything; the letter ℬ ('B') plants ginger and garlic, taking orders from letter ᴂ ('H');*

*the letter ໄ ('C') plants tobacco and taro, and represents the left hand of let-*
*ter Ϸ ; the letter Ꝣ ('D') plants corn and rice and represents a human face,*
*the 'object of a word'* [**gonsadu ya uy gwadrid;** butang sa usa ka birbu],
*and the writings of an Eskayan person; letter ໄ ('E') plants green squash and*
*cabbage; the letter ſ ('Hi') plants coconut, fruit and squash varieties known*
*in Visayan as* patula *and* sikwa—*it keeps to the left side of Ꝣ ('D') in order*
*not to become indolent or resort to thievery; the letter Ꝙ ('I') represents the*
*word of a person and plants cocoa and coffee; the letter ſ ('J') represents the*
*body, hands and feet of half of the letter Ϸ and plants water spinach and a*
*tree with edible leaves known as* malunggay, *working hard and skillfully to*
*avoid becoming a bandit; the letter ⴕ ('K') represents the feet and hands of*
*the letter Ϸ and symbolizes hard work and power; the letter ꝳ ('M') plants*
*bitter melon and paddy oats, and does any kind of work on the land and*
*sea. It is the first letter to issue from the letter Ϸ, and is part of the original*
*Boholano alphabet that came from Pinay's mind. ꝳ is also the source of all*
*Eskaya literature, representing all kinds of words. It is adept at teaching,*
*reading and study. The letter ꝳ ('N'), plants* lanzones *and the bell-shaped*
*fruit known as* tambis; *the letter ꝳ ('Ñ') plants starfruit and Java apple;*
*the letter ໄ ('O') plants mango and pomelo, representing both the brain and*
*wisdom; the letter 8 ('P') plants jackfruit and breadfruit; the letter ϐ ('Q')*
*plants seedless breadfruit and bamboo; the letter ſ ('R') plants tangerine*
*and bitter orange; the letter Ꝉ ('S') plants grapefruit and* calamansi *(a type*
*of lime); the letter ⴛ ('T') plants* jambul *(Java plum) and shaddock and*
*represents the fact that there is no other true writing except that which comes*
*from an entire human body; the letter Ꝟ ('V') plants water spinach and*
*cloves; the letter ſoo ('X') plants peppers and avocado, representing the hard-*
*ship of work and of remembering.*

Unusual among Eskaya texts, "Atikisis" is always written in Eskayan with
no accompanying Visayan text, and each letter introduces itself to the reader in
the first person. There is no evident sound symbolism between the letters of the
alphabet and the names of the fruit, nor between the shape of the characters and
the form of the plants.

The word **atikisis** is not glossed in this story, but an ambiguous explanation appears as the first sentence of "Declared Visayan": 'The letter is *índice*
['index,' 'sign'] in Spanish, **atikisis** in Eskayan.'[24] My suspicion is that **atikisis** is
formed from the letter sequence A, Ti, Kis ['X'], Si, on the same model as other
Visayan words for 'alphabet,' like *alibata* from the initial sequence of the Arabic
alphabet: Alif, Ba, Ta; and *abakada* from the traditional recitation order of the

Philippine Script: A, Ba, Ka, Da. An Eskayan precedent for this kind of formation is in the word **abidiha**, from A, Bi, Di, Ha, and in the text "Atikisis" itself
where the letter 'M' is described as originating in the original **abisi** (A, B, C) of
Pinay's mind.

The letters in "Atikisis" express the importance of hard work and the perils
of indolence. The morphology of Eskayan letters in the Abidiha is occasionally
explained with reference to the body, but for the most part the letters are personified as individual cultivators with distinctive characteristics. If the letters of
"The Spanish and Eskayan Alphabets" are mere parts or poses of a human body,
the letters of "Atikisis" are fully formed social subjects with roles in a subsistence
economy. Of these, the only letter without redeeming features is 'F,' the personification of thievery. Arguably, 'F' is selected for denigration because the presumptive sound it represents, /f/, is not available in Eskayan or Visayan phonologies
(see Chapter 5) but *is* a feature of the colonial languages Spanish and English.
However, the same could be said of 'V,' who nonetheless diligently plants water
spinach and cloves.

The other letter that stands out from the rest is 'M.' Not only does 'M' do all
kinds of work on land and at sea, but it is particularly adept at reading and writing, expressing the admonition that "if one does not study hard at school one
cannot learn to read." 'M' is also the only letter specifically associated with "the
mind of Pinay." Once again it appears that Anoy is subtly associating Pinay and
pre-contact literacy with the historical *M*ariano.

### *"Declared Visayan"*

This is a short text that serves as a succinct manifesto on the superiority of Eskayan
language and writing, on the basis of its human characteristics. The unfortunate
dominance of Cebuano-Visayan on Bohol is here explained as a result of printing
technology accessed by Cebuanos who were acting in the interests of the Spanish:

> *The Eskayan script is superior because it is based on a divided human body
> and is therefore easy to learn. Literature in Eskayan was produced from the
> right hand of a human body. Spanish letters have indiscriminate and non-
> human sources of inspiration: the letter 'g' from the head and tail of a mon-
> key, 'X' from a pair of scissors and 'A' from an archway at a fiesta, the letter
> 'C' from an eel. The Visayan language is spoken in Bohol but is represented
> through Spanish letters. When the Spanish began colonizing the Philippines,
> the first classroom teacher [**tutulan**, maistra] to be appointed in Cebu called
> the language 'Cebuano-Visayan' and it issued from the hand of an individual*

*known as Anapulco Santiago. From there it passed through a typewriter and a printing press before taking over the whole of the Philippines. Bohol's language managed to retain some of its original form but was mostly overwhelmed by Cebuano-Visayan with its corrupted elements, like the use of Spanish numbers for counting up to one thousand. Governor Felix Gallares, born in Madrid, was able to speak Cebuano-Visayan by accessing its Latin form, but he could not speak the real Visayan of Bohol. True Boholano words have survived, like* **guwagu** *for 'big,'* **bilik** *for 'beautiful,' and* **Aya sam?** *for 'Where are you going?' Tumud the shaman captured the white bell and led a revolt against the Spanish.*

Assumptions about the nature of language and its modes of acquisition are here illustrated in several ways. Not only is language again firmly conflated with its writing system, but the nature of the script also determines how easily that language is committed to memory. Thus, the reader learns that Eskayan is easily acquired because it is based on a human body, while Spanish is difficult and arbitrary since its shapes are derived from trivial and unrelated objects. Though Pinay is not mentioned, Eskayan is described as "our own creation" (**bayis binwir**, *kaugulingun pagmugna'*), and its literature is produced from the right hand of a body. Eskayan is subsequently contrasted, not with Spanish, but with Visayan—specifically, Cebuano-Visayan. This language is attributed to the hand of one Anapulco Santiago, and its diffusion began with the first classroom teacher in Cebu. Interestingly, the teacher in question (**tutulan**, *maistra*) is female, perhaps calling to mind the prototypical elementary school teachers familiar to readers. With the aid of a printing press, (Cebuano-)Visayan was able to take over the Philippines, a circumstance that accounts for its presence in Bohol. As already discussed in Chapter 2, the rise of 'Cebuano' as the prestige dialect of Visayan was facilitated by the fact that Cebu was the administrative hub of the Visayas. It was in Cebu that Visayan was first described, and printing presses produced formal grammars of the language that relied on the grammatical categories of Latin. Although the Philippine script had entered the region around the time of colonial contact, literacy was not widespread, and Spanish printers insisted on a Roman script and a distinctly Hispanic orthography. For Anoy, Bohol's forgotten language—uncorrupted by Spanish, Latin, or the printing press—has remained inaccessible even, or especially, to erudite foreign administrators. The appended reference to Tumud and the white bell draws attention to the underlying metaphorical resonance of this myth with the Eskayan language. Like the white bell of legend, Eskayan is an indigenous artifact that escaped manipulation by a foreign power. Hidden from view, only true patriots can be granted access to it.

## Discussion

Eskaya narratives contain a number of tropes typical of the regional oral folk-lore. A founding tale of Eskaya colonists arriving in Bohol from Sumatra echoes a nationwide legend that the ancestors of Filipinos today were originally from Sumatra. The figure of the trickster monkey, a literary entity found elsewhere in the Philippines (see, for example, Behrens 2007), appears as a peripheral charac-ter in the story "The Itch-mite Tumaw," a tale that also combines themes from the biblical Genesis. Accounts of Ferdinand Magellan's (historically unattested) visit to Panglao island are still circulated within Bohol (Añasco 2000), and one version of this tale is embedded in "Pinay." Meanwhile, "Daylinda" is an almost wholesale retelling of a popular Visayan potboiler of the same name (Osorio 1913) and was actually performed as a play in Datahan's hometown of Loon in 1914. A well-known Filipino story of a concealed bell is dramatically recounted in "The White Bell." This and other "recuperation" narratives from Bohol, in which lost objects are predicted to be retrieved by future heroes, foreshadow the tale of Mariano Datahan's discovery of hidden Eskayan documents.

And yet beyond these relatively minor concurrences, Eskaya literature does not appear to be substantially informed by the better-known literary traditions of Bohol or the region at large. To the best of my knowledge there are no Visayan folk tales that feature lions, an evidently nonnative animal, or itch mites. Nor are the place names or ancestral leaders from "The Spanish and Eskayan Alphabets" attested elsewhere.

Unlike regional Boholano folklore, Eskaya literature conveys an aura of historical authority through the frequent use of dates. Yet the presence of spe-cific historical dates in Anoy's texts appears largely to emphasize "pastness," like the English storytelling formulas "Once upon a time . . ." and "Long ago . . ." Moreover, these dates reinforce a contrast between *written* Eskaya literature with its linear historicity and consecutive ordering of historical events, and *oral* Eskaya literature, with its repertoire of prophecies that frame the future itself as a history waiting to be written down and reified. In effect, this is the essential structure of a recuperation narrative: the hope of regaining lost knowledge is oriented toward the future, but this future is accessed only by reaching back into a mythical past. As Karl Mannheim noted in his reflections on utopian Christianity, the "promise of the future" for the millenarian is "merely a point of orientation, something external to the ordinary course of events from where he is on the lookout ready to take the leap" (Mannheim [1936] 1979, 195).

To plot the extent to which Eskaya literature intersects with, or diverges from, other regional literary traditions is to demarcate the range of cultural associations accessible to Eskaya readers of these stories. Indeed, the relationship between the familiar and unfamiliar, the revealed and the concealed, is crucial. Even as the names in "The Itch-mite Tumaw" are redolent of foreignness, the narrator encourages his readers to identify these words as native and uncorrupted by foreign influences. Similarly, the administrative ranks in pre-contact Bohol, listed in "The Spanish and Eskayan Alphabets," are given explicit Spanish glosses, but the contrast between Eskayan and Spanish governance roles is merely lexical; there are no intimations of a cultural distinction between indigenous and foreign categories of social organization. From what is known of pre-contact Visayan society, local authority rested in village headmen and their offspring, who extracted various kinds of labor from the populations they governed through an array of often temporary labor bonds (Borrinaga 2010). The complexity of these arrangements was not understood by Spanish chroniclers, who tried to force Filipinos into familiar categories. As Benedict Anderson has noted,

> [ . . . ] wherever in the islands the earliest clerics and conquistadors ventured they espied, on shore, *principales, hidalgos, pecheros,* and *esclavos* (princes, noblemen, commoners and slaves)—quasi-estates adapted from the social classifications of late mediaeval Iberia. The documents they left behind offer plenty of incidental evidence that the "*hidalgos*" were mostly unaware of one another's existence in the huge, scattered, and sparsely populated archipelago, and, where aware, usually saw one another not as *hidalgos,* but as enemies or potential slaves. [ . . . ] [T]he "class structure" of the precolonial period is a "census" imagining created from the poops of Spanish galleons. Wherever *they* went, *hidalgos* and *esclavos* loomed up, who could only be aggregated as such, that is "structurally," by an incipient colonial state. (Anderson [1983] 2003, 167)

What is fascinating about Anoy's literature is that these imported categories—be they of social structures, writing systems, permanent settlements, or religious cosmographies—are not imagined from the poops of Spanish galleons but are projected back at the visitors from the native shore. Even the act of foreign colonization by an incipient colonial state is prefigured in the founding voyage of Dangko and his settlement in Bohol. Like the Spanish occupation, Dangko's was a colonization event that would also be enacted linguistically.

The practice of simultaneously nativizing and otherizing imported colonial categories has been commented on in other contexts. An early observation of this tendency can be found in Edmund Leach's seminal ethnography of the Kachin, where he remarks that the highlanders "are constantly subject to contradictory pressures both to *imitate* and *oppose* their valley dwelling neighbours" (Leach 1954, 20; my emphasis). In his account of the Tikopians, Marshall Sahlins described a "structural dynamic that makes foreign identity a condition of indigenous author-ity" (2012, 141) and appeals to Bateson's notion of "symmetrical schismogenesis" (Bateson 1936) by which a colonial category is countered with an equivalent-yet-superior indigenous one. Similarly, Anna Tsing writes of "accommodation and resistance" in her ethnography of the Meratus (Tsing 1993) while Rahul Rao's critique of Partha Chatterjee describes a postcolonial tension between "mimicry and rejection" (Rao 2010). In each analysis, the social legitimacy of a given colo-nial structure, category, or dynamic is taken for granted. What is challenged is its authority over a preeminent native equivalent, or as Sahlins succinctly put it, "anything you can do I can do better" (Sahlins 2012, 141).

A tension between sameness and otherness, or mimicry and rejection, lies at the heart of Eskaya cultural expressions. As I have shown in Chapter 3, the Eskaya community today continues to demonstrate an ability to accommodate to his-torical demands. In its interactions with government structures the community acceded to outsider categories of "Indigenous," "Tribe," "Tribal Council," "Tribal Chieftain," and "Ancestral Domain," all of which were foreign to the group prior to 1991. And yet these administrative constructions have been thoroughly reclaimed and reimagined by Eskaya political leaders today.

Within Eskaya literature, languages and their scripts are judged according to the authentic and grounded values of native-born Visayans, values that nonethe-less derive legitimacy from their commensurability with the foreign. In almost every text, languages are described in material or corporeal terms and are not dis-tinguished from their means of representation in writing. Moreover, the alphabet of a language points to its sources of inspiration in the human creative intellect. Like a national flag, language is symbolic of sovereign political power. But like sovereignty it can be suppressed and reaffirmed. Language changes, or is cor-rupted, over time, and it has its own agency and magical power. What makes Eskayan superior to Spanish, Latin, or Cebuano is that it possesses all these quali-ties to a greater degree: it is more human and natural than Spanish (its writing system is inspired by the body) and more authentically national (the flag is a leaf or *dahun*); it is more magical than Latin and purer than Cebuano. The corporeal-ity of Eskayan means that it is a bounded entity capable of being dissected and suppressed but also of being reassembled and miraculously reanimated.

The various assumptions about linguistic and cultural difference elaborated in Anoy's traditional literature are wholly reflected in the design features of Eskayan, as discussed in the previous chapters. Within its script, grammar, and lexicon, Eskayan displays a kind of "mimicry and rejection" with respect to colo-nial languages, particularly Spanish. In each of these areas, "typical" European linguistic features are imitated and elaborated to the extent of caricature. This presents a perception of a language that outshines its colonial rivals on their own terms while paradoxically representing the epitome of native alterity. After all, what is "foreign" from the perspective of a mother tongue Visayan speaker is informed by the models of otherness available in colonial contact languages. To offer an example of this peculiar dynamic, Eskayan vocabulary has *non*-borrowed words for such concepts as 'railway train' (**giring**) and 'airplane' (**kanis**), just as pre-contact "indigenous" terms for Spanish administrative categories are faithfully listed in "The Spanish and Eskayan Alphabets." With his precolonial creation of Eskayan, Pinay preempted the technologies and social structures that would later dominate his island in the hands of destructive and unenlightened foreigners. The Eskayan language and script were not simply a strategic counter to the linguistic imposition of colonial languages but a matrix for an independent political vision.

As I will explore in Part III, the "speaker profile" that emerges from Eskayan vocabulary is consistent with that of the rebel leader Mariano Datahan (ca. 1875–1949), a Spanish-educated man living in early twentieth-century Bohol at the time of its occupation by the United States and the introduction of English. If Datahan is understood as the foremost interpreter of Pinay, Fabian Baja's insistence that Datahan could speak "every language in the world" is a view consistent with the presence of foreign-inspired lexemes (particularly Spanish) in core vocabulary and elsewhere. And if Pinay (or Datahan) were tasked with creating a new language, the resulting product has embodied his folk-linguistic preconceptions about what "language" is. The relative symmetry between Eskayan and Visayan morphosyntax and the asymmetry of their respective lexicons suggest that, for Pinay, language is primarily a lexical artifact. Similarly, the dialect-like features in certain Eskayan terms notionally draw on a supposition that "linguistic variation" is lexical as opposed to grammatical. In short, the form of the Eskayan language appears to demonstrate that even the most radical linguistic utopians cannot easily escape their own skins, relying for their constructive project on raw materials that are easiest to grasp and closest to hand. Just how this was achieved, and what it tells us about our human relationship to language, is discussed next.

## Notes

1. In her discussion of whether Eskaya literature fits classic definitions of 'folklore,' Martinez wrote that "[t]he Eskayan texts are definitely not amorphous bodies of oral narrative floating around in peasant villages waiting to be documented/written down by folklorists from universities" (Martinez 1993, 82).

2. Writing about her fieldwork on the *Pasion* narrative epic of Bicol, Fenella Cannell described similar circumstances: "While I was conducting fieldwork, I was haunted by the constant mention of two particular texts that were cited as additional sources

for the construction of the Passion play and as objects of supernatural virtue. These two texts, the *Tronco del Mundo* and the *Martir de Golgota*, were, however, never actually produced for me to see, as everyone always claimed to have lost them. [ ... ] The conclusion to draw from this proliferation of texts and virtual texts is that it was not only the content of a particular text which defined its arcane power, but also the context in which that translation was made and the book used" (Cannell 2006, 157–158).

3. From an undated recording made by Zoë Bedford of an interview with Fabian Baja, Riche Datahan, and Maura Galambao in Taytay in circa 2004.

4. A teacher in Cadapdapan believes that the first three secretaries were Domingo Castañares, Espedrion de Gracia, and Patricio Caria. Eleuteria Viscayda recalls that her first teacher was Aryujeño Boses (spelling uncertain).

5. Joan Acocella (2012).

6. This example sentence was supplied by my consultant. It is not attested in Eskaya literature.

7. My observation is at odds with the experience of Martinez, who observed that Eskaya texts are highly regular: "Folk literature, generally characterized by fluidity, variability and a resistance to fixity [ ... ] cannot be congruent with the Eskayan text in its inscripted sacral form, and its standard texts and translations. On this issue of dynamism in folk form, the Datahan texts are sharply contrastive in their almost fossilized form. No innovation nor alteration is allowed to play on these sacred texts. So meticulous is the transcription of these texts that if a single student makes a mistake, the teacher simply marks out the entire page and asks the pupil to repeat" (Martinez 1993, 82). It should be remembered, however, that Martinez was working in a single field site, Taytay, at a time when Eskayan classes were under the strict authority of Fabian Baja.

8. This text can be accessed at http://catalog.paradisec.org.au/repository/PK2/04/PK2-04-MANCAD05.pdf.

9. Much of my work with Gemina Palma and her cousin Decena Nida Salingay involved the elucidation of difficult passages of this text, with the pair suggesting corrections to obvious errors.

10. All Eskaya written texts are identified by titles, which may or may not be included in manuscripts, depending on the scribe. Some stories are conventionally referred to by their Visayan names, even though Eskayan translations of their titles are available. Others are always identified by their Eskayan names. The stories known as "Pinay" and "Daylinda" are named after their protagonists, and the titles cannot therefore be assigned to one language or another. Since I am here analyzing the content of the stories, rather than the language in its own right, I have rendered their titles in English wherever possible, with their Visayan and Eskayan names (and variants) recorded in explanatory endnotes.

11. Cristina Martinez, whose field site was Taytay, was more emphatic. She wrote that "[The Eskaya] all consider the tales/myths/artifacts as authoritative and 'true.' They

all consider the texts as 'unang Pagtulun-an sa Bisayas' (the first Bisayan system of beliefs). And on these beliefs, they have based their very lives" (Martinez 1993, 85).

12. Original Eskaya manuscripts are at http://catalog.paradisec.org.au/repository/ PK2/, items 2 to 5. Annotations to Eleuteria Viscayda's notebook are available at http://catalog.paradisec.org.au/repository/PK2/01/PK2-01-LIT.txt.

13. Martín's definition of *cagao* [*kagaw*] is "Little mite known as 'ploughman.' Is created in rashes, scabs and wounds—it is unclear whether the former causes the latter" ("Piojito llamado arador. Se crea en las erupciones, sarnas y heridas, quiza es el que causa las primeras segundas") (Martín 1842a, 84). In another volume *cagao* is defined as "Ploughman [*Arador*]: *cagauon*, those that have them are *nahigagao*, remove them if they are sore or causing a skin aggravation [*empeynes*]" ("*cagao* p.c. Arador: *cagauon*, el que los tine *nahigagao,* sacarlos aunque sean de empeynes, ó llaga") (Martín 1842b, 91). Presumably the action of the mite producing eruptions in the skin is likened to ploughing. Both Moliner (2007) and the Real Academia Española (2004) define *arador de la sarna* (literally, 'scabies ploughman') as a common name for *Sarcoptes scabiei*, referred to in English as the 'itch mite.'

14. This story is popularly referred to by its Visayan name *Unang Tawu sa Yuta sa Bohol* and has a number of variant titles, including *Unang tawu sa Bisaya sa Bohol* ("The First Visayans in Bohol") and the *Katukiban sa Unang Tawu sa Yuta sa* **Buuw** *sa Pakigbugnu' sa Lumalangyaw Katsilang Tawu* ("Accounts of the First People of the Land of **Buuw** ['Bohol'] and of Their Struggle Against the Spanish Foreigners").

15. Martinez and Tirol cite versions of this story that state explicitly that Dangko and Luneta had eleven sons and one daughter. I have not had access to versions that include this detail (see Martinez 1993; Jes Tirol 1990a, 1990b,1993a, 1993b). There is a possible parallel here with the biblical Jacob, who had twelve sons and one daughter.

16. "Las tradiciones antiguas hacían de Sumatra como el origen de los Indios filipinos. Estas tradiciones se perdieron completamente así como la mitología y las genealogías de que nos hablan los antiguous historiadores, gracias al celo de los religiosos en extirpar todo recuerdo nacional, gentílicio ó idólatra." This annotation was affixed to a passage of Morga's speculating on the origins of the Malay race (Morga [1609] 1890, 259).

17. The original Visayan text reads "*Ang usa ka* **hirdu** *nia nagpuyu sa ibabaw sa gipuyan sa kadaghanan nga kuyba. Ang* **hirdu** *kapitan sa Ispanyul. Kining* **hirdu** *maung pahuy sa trupa, matud guwardia sa Kinatsila.*"

18. Miscommunication in first contact interactions is a frequent theme in Philippine folk etymologies. According to legend, the town of Loboc (Map 3) was so named after a Spaniard arrived there and saw a woman pounding rice with a mortar. He asked her the name of the place, but she assumed he was asking what she was doing, to which she replied '*Lubuk*' ('pounding rice'). Similar stories are told of Bulacnin

in Batangas, said to be from Tagalog *bumubulak na ang kanin,* 'the rice is almost cooked.'

19. An alternative title is "The Story of the Old Philippine Visayas" (**Witim ya rimuy miriklan Visayan Pilipin**; *Kasugiran sa mga karaan Visayan Pilipin*).

20. In the Viscayda document, the phrase **bidaryu ya Ara** ('language of God') is actually translated into Visayan as *pulung sa Diyus* ('word of God'), as opposed to *pinulungan sa Diyus* ('language of God'). It is possible that the Eskayan text is erroneous and should have been rendered as **bidar ya Ara** (*pulung sa Diyus*), but the context of the story, in which one language (Latin) is compared to another, suggests that the error is in the Visayan layer and that **bidaryu ya Ara** (*pinulungan sa Diyus,* 'language of God') is the correct form. The terms *pulung* and *pinulungan* are never treated as synonyms in Visayan.

21. In transcriptions of the text **Salbadur Sunu** ('Santo Niño,' or Holy Child) is sometimes written '**Salbadur Munu,**' and often the two spellings can alternate within the same document. I have been assured by Eskaya readers that this nonetheless refers to the same entity. What it suggests, however, is a derivation from the Spanish *salvador del mundo* ('savior of the world'). Equally, 'Sunu' could be understood as a contraction of 'Santo Niño.'

22. Wolff (1972b) defines the Visayan word *latin* as "1 Latin. 1a special k.o. [kind of] prayer with magical effects [ ... ]." Both senses (1 and 1a) are apparent in the context of its use in "The White Bell," where the friar's prayer is presented as discursively equivalent to the shaman's spell. See also the discussion of ritual languages in Chapter 4.

23. Of course, recuperation narratives are not peculiar to Bohol. Reynaldo Ileto, for example, describes the popular story of Bernardo Carpio in Luzon, frozen inside a mountain in Luzon, awaiting "a redemptive event that will bring about his freedom" (Ileto 1979a, 125); this story was to become symbolic of peasant aspirations for independence in the late nineteenth century.

24. **Istu litri indisi ya katsila', atikisis ya Bisaya** (*Ang litra 'indisi' sa katsila', 'atikisis' sa Bisaya*).

# INSURRECTION AND RESURRECTION

*What do the laws of physics and chemistry demonstrate?—They prove to us, jointly, that nothing is destroyed, nothing disappears: neither energy nor matter—all things will be reborn, probably in forms other than the present ones (though related to them), because the circumstances that attend their formation will be different. But everything will rise again. Worlds are born every day, while others die, but all are instantly reborn in a transformed state, because the power of God is inexhaustible.*

—"RESURRECTION," FROM *The Catechism of the Iglesia Filipina Independiente*, Fr. Gregorio Aglipay (1912)

# 8

## FROM PINAY TO MARIANO DATAHAN (AND BACK AGAIN)

For Eskaya people, it is a matter of received knowledge that the pope and patriot Pinay created Bohol's true native tongue in a distant time long before the island was colonized by Spain. Taking the human form as inspiration, Pinay devised a writing system that was a literal embodiment of language; sound and script materialized together as indistinguishable aspects of an externalized symbolic system. It is further believed that Eskayan became the language of a proto-national Bohol until foreigners arrived and decided to stay. Suppressed alternatively by Spanish priests and their Cebuano lackeys, Pinay's revealed language remained dormant until its heroic reawakening in Biabas by Mariano Datahan.

Incredible as this account may seem, the notion that Eskayan was the inspired creation of a human individual is reconcilable with the linguistic analysis, as I have already outlined in Part II. The mythic association of the creator Pinay with his Biabas spokesman is strong, and some Eskaya consultants went so far as to describe Pinay as a contemporary and colleague of Datahan. Indeed, the direct parallels between these heroic figures are so striking—both were "men of letters" who hailed from Loon, and both were gifted prophets who spearheaded religious institutions—that it is easier to imagine that the two individuals are embodied in the same entity. In other words, Pinay can be recognized as a projection and a prophetic foreshadowing of Datahan's radical linguistic program. The late Fabian Baja, a favored student of Mariano Datahan, concluded that the two individuals were one and the same. In Baja's understanding Pinay did not write anything down, and Mariano Datahan was the first to record his words. Since Datahan had such detailed knowledge of the past, as well as the ability to predict the future, Baja and his fellow students surmised that their revered mentor was none other than Pinay himself.

In Part II I probed the structure of the Eskayan language and its script, drawing out a narrative of its genesis and development on the

*The Last Language on Earth.* Kelly, Piers, Oxford University Press. © Oxford University Press 2022.
DOI: 10.1093/oso/9780197509913.003.0008

basis of linguistic evidence, and identifying consistent processes of substitution and elaboration. Following this, I introduced Eskaya literature as a privileged site of Eskayan language use and described how speakers themselves make sense of their language and its history in a symmetrical yet oppositional relationship to colonial languages and institutions.

In Part III, I hope to extend this account by re-situating the Eskayan language in a more widely recognized historical context and considering its theoretical implications. As a point of departure, I review the life history of Mariano Datahan (Chapter 8), before examining the likely circumstances in which Eskayan was revealed, codified, and transmitted (Chapter 9). Finally, the concluding chapter of the book delves into the global relevance of Eskayan as a cultural and linguistic phenomenon, with informative parallels to be found elsewhere in Bohol, the Philippines, and Southeast Asia.

## Datahan and the origins of the Biabas encampment

Although the existence of the Eskayan language he revealed was not widely known until the 1980s (Chapter 3), Mariano Datahan achieved a small degree of notoriety on Bohol in his lifetime. A 1948 portrait photograph describes him, in an etched caption, as "the famous Supreme leader of Biabas barrio" (Fig. 8.1). He is mentioned briefly in Maria Caseñas Pajo's thesis on Bohol's folklore (1954, 153), the World War II diaries of Col. Esteban Bernido (1981, 386), and Simplicio Apalisok's history of Bohol (1992a, 42–43). All of these sources treat him as an actor of some consequence in southeast Bohol, though none mention the language and writing system that he promoted. A larger-than-life figure, today it is still claimed by Eskaya and non-Eskaya alike that he was able to be present in two places at once, to die and be resurrected at will, and to make himself invisible, and that he survived to an improbably great age. In the present chapter I set aside linguistic and literary analysis in order to return to Mariano Datahan and review his life story as it unfolded in his own written words, as well as through the records and recollections of others. I describe his early education, his military conflicts, and his eventual migration from the west coast of the island to the wild interior of the southeast at the head of a large group of settler families. I then consider how he subsequently transformed into a radical religious leader and launched a new cultural and linguistic program in Biabas prior to the Japanese occupation of the Philippines. Finally, I explore the schisms in Biabas that arose after Datahan's death in 1949, preceding the founding of Taytay and the resurgence of Eskayan language activity in the new settlement.

FIGURE 8.1. Mariano Datahan in 1948[1]

Within his lifetime, Mariano Datahan made efforts to promote a legendary mystique. Living through one of the most transformative periods in Bohol's history, he cast himself as an active player in key events, recording a heroic legacy in the autobiographical statement he dictated shortly before died. "The Virtues and Experiences of Mariano Datahan Sumatra" (*Ang mga Hiyas ug Kaagi ni Mariano Datahan Sumatra*), relates, in Visayan, his life as an altar boy, small landholder, and soldier, and his participation in numerous battles from engagements with Moro forces in the early 1890s to the Philippine Revolution (1896–1898) and the Japanese occupation of Bohol (1942–1945). According to this document, Datahan was born in Loon (Map 3) to Juan Sumatra and Dominga Presentes.

Christened Mariano Sumatra, his family name resonated with the legend of past Filipino migrations and foreshadowed the Eskaya foundation myth he would later articulate (Chapter 7). The earliest anecdotes concern two near-death experiences in childhood. At the age of seven he drowned and was revived, and later in the same year he was gored by a water buffalo. Having miraculously survived both events, he attended school for one year before becoming a caretaker and sacristan for various priests throughout Bohol. In his late teens, Sumatra left the church with a handsome payment from his employer, which he used to buy land in the west of Bohol. Soon after he was drafted into the colonial army to fight against Datu Pakpak in Mindanao. During the Philippine Revolution he claims to have served in Malabon and Samar as a soldier of the Katipunan, the secretive insurgent organization that sought to overthrow the Spanish in the 1890s and that eventually gave rise to the revolutionary government of Emilio Aguinaldo (see Chapter 2). During the Philippine–American War he fought in Bohol, confronting American soldiers in Carmen (Map 3). The autobiographical statement concludes with mention of Datahan's fourth war as a proponent of the Iglesia Filipina Independiente. He describes it as a war against Rome, "without committees or soldiers," and recalls having established twenty-seven "camps" for the church. The final war in his memoir was waged against the Japanese. He set up an insurgent camp in Cabagnan, Biabas, in 1942 but was drafted the following year by an American officer to serve in the Butuan region of Mindanao for the remainder of the war.

To treat "The Virtues and Experiences of Mariano Datahan" as a straightforward contribution to the historical record presents a number of problems. Chronologies of events are confused and contradictory. The revolutionary actions Datahan describes, and his role in them, are historically improbable on many grounds, and his supposed activities during the Philippine–American War seem to place him everywhere at once, in tune with his fabled capacity for translocation. On the other hand, a number of excerpts contain small but crucial details that are almost certainly the product of first-hand involvement in the events described, and that can be corroborated from other sources.[2]

The many inconsistencies of location and chronology might easily be attributed to the failing memory of a man in the last years of his life who was trying his best to maintain control over a legendary legacy. But to judge the "The Virtues and Experiences of Mariano Datahan" solely for its relevance—compromised or otherwise—to Visayan history is to misconstrue its value as *localized* history. The author of the document has clearly assumed a degree of shared knowledge on the part of the reader, suggesting that the intended audience is limited and perhaps known personally. Only a Boholano could be expected to recognize the names of the various outlying barrios in small rural villages, while the Battle of Kabantian

Pass, one of the most celebrated in Bohol's war with the United States, is merely alluded to in passing, an implicit acknowledgment, perhaps, of the fact that the event would already have been well known to his readers. In effect, despite its many contradictions and abstruse details, I maintain that Datahan's written life story is first and foremost a product of Eskaya historiography, subject to the same principles of interpretation that constrain the reading of the Eskaya literary canon more generally (Chapter 7). For Eskaya readers, other access points to Datahan's life, via memory, prophecy, or oral history, are understood as independent to this text rather than as a challenge to it. In other words, what an Eskaya reader needs to know about Datahan's account of himself is bound up in "The Virtues and Experiences of Mariano Datahan": there is no reflexive need for intertextual validation.

This is not to suggest that the document is inaccessible to an outsider, nor that the text is entirely irrelevant for more generalized historical purposes. In the following section I trace the lives of Pinay and Mariano Datahan as variously represented in Datahan's autobiography and oral histories, and reinforced through genealogies and the archival record, drawing attention to points of convergence and divergence. My aim is not to establish an empirical account of the two figures so much as to chart, as clearly as possible, a layered map of the biographical terrain.

## Interpreting Datahan's memoirs: The early years

Like the examples of Eskaya literature discussed earlier, dates and descriptions of events in Datahan's autobiography do not coincide with widely accepted historical narratives and are often internally contradictory. From the outset Datahan informs his readers that he was born in 1845. Since parish records in Biabas indicate that he passed away on January 26, 1949, this would make him at least 104 years old at the time of his death. Researchers have cited 1842 (Jes Tirol 1993c) and April 1, 1844 (Orcullo 2004) as alternative dates of birth without any indication of their sources; in the Loon cathedral, the baptismal registers for the latter half of the nineteenth century are incomplete and no entry for Mariano Sumatra can be found among those that are available. Born to a poor fishing and herding family in an outlying barrio of Loon, it is conceivable that neither his date of birth nor his christening was documented at all. Indeed, no birth dates have survived for any of his eight known siblings (only one of whom, Francisco, is referred to in his memoirs). There are, however, several indications that Datahan was born later than the 1840s. He mentions, for example, that he was transferred to Anda with the first curate to that parish in 1854, when in fact Anda's first curate began service in 1885 (Anda had no church until that time). As a soldier in the Spanish army, he relates that he was deployed to Iligan, Lanao, on February 5, 1861 to fight against Datu Pakpak of Marawi, and that Spanish conscription was interrupted by the revolution in 1867 and 1869. Philippine military history mentions only two engagements between Spanish forces and Datu Pakpak, occurring in 1891 and 1895. Likewise, it is well established the Philippine Revolution took place between 1896 and 1898. Thus, using a projected distance of approximately thirty years between Datahan's dates and those of known historical events, one might infer a notional date of birth as circa 1875 and his life to have spanned roughly 75 years, as opposed to 105. This projection is corroborated by Simplicio Apalisok, who recalled him in 1942 as "an old man in his 70s" (1992a, 42).

On its own, this ad hoc recalculation adds little in the way of clarity to Datahan's life history. Longevity is often attributed to legendary figures of Boholano history from the elderly Sikatuna and his wife, who were supposed to have had "perhaps two hundred and thirty years" between them (Chirino [1604] 1969; see also Luspo 2005), to Francisco Dagohoy, who was believed by many to have lived for over a century (Misa 1970) or to have been immortal (V.B. Tirol 1968).[3] Datahan and his adherents may have wished to amplify his age as a means of positioning him within the pantheon of Bohol's long-lived legends. Similarly, the tales of his two near-death experiences in his early years ought to be interpreted in the context of the traditional belief in Bohol that children who have thwarted death are marked by fate for a special purpose. Today, Boholano apprentice shamans are still selected from among those who successfully staved off life-threatening events in their childhood (Aparece 2003, 95).

Datahan recounts that after both his parents died he traveled to Tubigon (Map 3), aged ten, to find his brother Francisco. It was here that he became a sacristan to serve a priest by the name of Fr. Dionicio Franco. When Datahan turned nineteen, he was transferred to Catigbian on orders from Fr. Felix Gallares, and shortly after to the newly established parish of Anda as a sacristan for Fr. Vicente Gallares. This period would have been crucial to Datahan's education and literacy. As a sacristan he would have been introduced to Castilian Spanish and Latin under the tutelage of Spanish priests who had acquired Visayan as a second language. Further, the dialect these priests were first exposed to was Cebuano, the prestige variety used for vernacular catechisms and other printed religious materials distributed to Bohol's congregations. In the register at the Anda cathedral there is no record of a curate by the name of Vicente Gallares or Felix Gallares—the earliest priest assigned to that church was Fr. Julian Cisneros, who served there from 1885 to 1888. However, it is recorded that a certain Fr. Felix Guillén was the resident priest of the parish church of Loon, Datahan's hometown, from 1895 to 1898 (Jose 2008). It is thus reasonable to assume that the "Fr. Felix Gallares" was actually Fr. Felix Guillén, whose name was imperfectly recalled. Significantly, Guillén was a missionary linguist who in 1898 published his *Gramática Bisaya para facilitar el estudio del dialecto Bisaya Cebuano* (Visayan Grammar for Assisting in the Study of the Cebuano-Visayan Dialect). If Guillén were responsible for the young Mariano's spiritual and linguistic education, as is probable, it would go some way toward explaining the passion for language that would later manifest itself in Datahan's programmatic revelation of Eskayan.

The sum of 50 pesos given to him by Gallares-Guillén provided Datahan with his first taste of independence. Establishing himself in Tubigon, a town where Guillén served as parish priest in 1877 and 1890–1893, he reports that he used this capital to employ workers and cultivate the land, soon becoming a successful agriculturist. It was in this period that he acquired his *dagnay* ('nickname' or 'pseudonym') of *Datahan*, meaning 'one who receives loan repayments' (see Trosdal 1990, 101). According to local practice, a *dagnay* is inserted between the Christian name and family name, which is why his autobiography is signed "Mariano Datahan Sumatra." But in 1901, his *dagnay* had displaced his family name entirely. Records indicate that he took to calling himself Mariano Datahan, and the new family name would later be inherited by his offspring. A few teachers in Biabas believe that he dropped the name Sumatra because he was wanted as an outlaw by the Spanish authorities. Juan Datahan told me of how his father was fond of using aliases particularly during periods of conflict.[4]

Datahan's brief service as a conscript in the Spanish army primed him for the Philippine Revolution, which would soon erupt in Luzon and devolve into the Philippine–American War. These were his defining years: his memoir devotes more space to the details of battles than to any other events in his life. For the most part, his descriptions of war cannot be augmented from other sources; however, the names of two of his former comrades—Juan Beronilla and Eustaquio Daligdig—do appear elsewhere. Beronilla, whose *dagnay* was Pilimon ('Philemon'), was an officer in the Boholano insurgent army, stationed in Guindulman, and his exploits are still recounted in the region. A story is told of how he wrestled with an *agta* ('dark skinned supernatural entity') for possession of an *antinganting* ('amulet') (Pajo 1954, 152–153). Having obtained it, he cut his right arm below the armpit and sewed the *antinganting* under his skin. The charm granted him the powers of invincibility and invisibility. Many years later, after the Japanese occupation ended in 1945, he was said to have disappeared to rule over the spirits of the other world. Maria Caseñas Pajo's research into Boholano folklore notes that Beronilla became the friend and bodyguard of Pascual Datahan, who "lived in the mountains of Duero as a barrio king with vassals at his command" (153). The name "Pascual" is likely to be an error; Pajo's description of the "barrio king" in the "mountains of Duero" tallies well with that of the "Supreme leader" who rose to prominence in that area.

Datahan reported that his first battle with Americans in Bohol took place in the vicinity of Carmen on August 17, 1901. No other record of this engagement is available. Luspo notes, however, that the rebels successfully routed the Americans in Cambaliga, Carmen, the previous month and that the battle of Kabantian Pass, of which Datahan describes the aftermath, took place almost a year earlier than this (Luspo 2005). In Datahan's account the chronology is reversed. He neglects to mention his more certain involvement in the failed ambush at Lonoy (Map 3) on March 8, 1901, in which hundreds of Boholano soldiers were killed. After this attack, the Boholano forces held a court martial, and one Francisco Alcala was charged with tipping off the Americans.[5] The other accused were Antonio Balili for arson, Eusebio Deliman for robbery, and Mariano Datahan for "*contra la union de los revolucionarios*" (Apalisok 1999). This latter charge was a military crime codified in an 1898 congressional decree of the Philippine revolutionary government: "The following are also deemed to have committed military crimes [ . . . ] Those who threaten the union of the revolutionaries, provoking rivalry amongst leaders and forming divisions and armed factions."[6] All three were found not guilty. The specifics of Datahan's alleged troublemaking are not noted in insurgent records. It is clear, however, that by this time "Datahan" had become his nom de guerre, entirely replacing the Sumatra family name.

## Eastward migration, circa 1900–1902

A rich source of genealogical material relevant to Biabas is archived at the service center of the National Commission on Indigenous Peoples (NCIP) in Tagbilaran in the form of standard genealogy paperwork filled out by those applying for recognition as an Indigenous Person (IP). The Eskaya community and the NCIP granted me permission to use this data for the present study. This material includes the names, relationships, ethnic affiliations, and places of origin of those who have successfully applied for indigenous status as Eskaya. The same information is also provided for the applicants' immediate ancestors, living and dead, going back as far as five generations in some cases.[7] An additional source of documentary information has come from parish records kept by the Philippine Independent Church (PIC) in Biabas. Roughly a third of the PIC records that I photographed were illegible due to termite damage or difficult handwriting. Many more were reported to me to have been destroyed by a typhoon in the 1960s. However, these parish archives, which include birth, marriage, and death dates, are an invaluable supplement to the NCIP material, which does not include dates at all. Where more detailed information has been necessary, I have elicited the data directly from descendants of the families in question. This method was particularly useful for researching the immediate family of Mariano Datahan, the pioneers of Taytay, and the migrants who settled in Cadapdapan. The resulting genealogies, comprising 1,704 individuals from 154 separate sources, are too extensive to include in an appendix, but at the request of the community the data are now online, and printed copies are kept with the relevant families.[8]

Past migrations of Eskaya people are traced by comparing the birthplaces of parents with those of their children and calibrating these with available dates for births, deaths, and marriages. The picture that emerges is of an exodus from Loon at the turn of the nineteenth century. At least sixty individuals from families represented with the names Baratas, Barbarona, Bastasa, Caleste, Carnece, Castañares, Cuadra, Esquilla, Labastilla, Lanzaderas, Manuero, Nilugao, Palma, Piscos, Rosalinda, and Sumatra left Loon to settle in Biabas or its immediate vicinity, where they had children who would remain there. The true number of migrants cannot be accurately estimated from the records but was certainly greater than sixty: those who did not have children or who would eventually settle elsewhere are not detectable in the available data. Out of this group of Loon pioneers, Olimpio Castañares, Isteven Cuadra, Mariano Datahan, Marcelina Labastilla, Nemesia Manuero, Calexta Nilugao, Julia Sumatra, and Santiago Sumatra would all choose spouses who lived in or near Biabas and have children with them. Intermarriages between Loon and Biabas did not cease after the resettlement, and there are instances in which descendants of Biabas-born individuals found spouses in Loon and remained there to have children. Even though Loon was the most significant source of early migrants to Biabas, the genealogies show that people settled in Biabas from other regions of Bohol. Taking only the great-grandparent generation and earlier (relative to Ego, i.e., the applicant), the most common place of origin for Biabas settlers, after Loon, is Tambongan (Map 3), with minimally twenty-two ancestral individuals who would settle permanently in Biabas and have children there. Members of Tambongan families were also more likely to marry migrants from Loon. After Tambongan, the most common regions of origin for migrants who would have children in Biabas are Pilar (nine individuals), Sierra Bullones (eight individuals), Jagna (seven individuals), Talibon (six individuals), Candijay (six individuals), and Tubigon (five individuals).[9] The pattern of migrations to Biabas is represented in Map 6.

Local folklore relates that a *biyabas* ('guava tree') once stood at the site of the present village, marking a place of rest for those traveling on to other towns and that this is the origin of the name Biabas. It is unclear when Biabas was first registered, but the earliest available listing of it in a published source is from 1877 (de la Cavada Mendez de Vigo 1877, 275). The population of Biabas before Datahan and his followers established themselves there is hard to reckon. But within the NCIP archive there are thirty-four individuals of the great-grandparent generation or earlier whose place of origin is recorded as Biabas. In other words, these

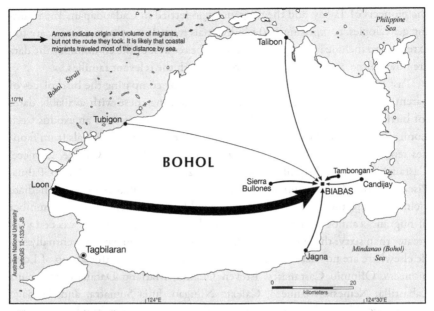

**MAP 6.** The origins and relative scale of migrations into Biabas from the great-grandparent generation and earlier.

individuals were resident in Biabas before the arrival of migrants from Loon and elsewhere in the early twentieth century.

Of course, considering that the collected family data is not comprehensive—an ambitious outcome for any genealogical research—the figures have been used here merely to show broad patterns and relationships, and to draw attention to other historical questions of interest. Why, for example, did so many leave Loon at the same time? And why did they choose Biabas as a place of settlement? For the inhabitants of a coastal village, a relocation to the mountains would have involved a significant change in circumstances, not least in the primary means of subsistence. Oral histories vary. Panfilo Datahan of Cadapdapan told me that the families left Loon to escape an unknown disease that was killing both people and livestock. Bobby Sumatra believes the crops in Loon were failing, so the pioneers set out for more fertile ground. Juan Datahan maintained that people evacuated Loon to escape the U.S. invasion and that others were attracted to Biabas from elsewhere because of the protection from the Americans promised by Mariano Datahan. Eskaya teachers in Biabas said that Datahan and his brothers were on the run from the Spanish authorities; they staked a hideout in Biabas and later returned to retrieve the rest of the family.

All of these explanations, save perhaps for the last, accord with other historical accounts.[10] The turn of the century was a time of enormous hardship in Bohol. As the last of the Spanish evacuated the island in December 1898, the Junta Provincial de Bohol formally took charge of the province, establishing the famous "Gobierno Republicano de Bohol" (Scriven 1900, 103). At this time, Bohol's population was about 250,000 (Romanillos 1997, 49). The American invasion of the island in March 1900 and the ensuing war, which raged from September 1900 to December 1901, devastated the entire province. Almost all of Bohol's towns were burned to the ground in the scorched-earth policy ordered by General Robert P. Hughes. Loon was targeted for near-total destruction by the nineteenth regiment on May 10, 1901; only the church survived the onslaught.

Division Superintendent LT Gibbens recalled in his report to the Philippine Commission:

Thousands of horses, cattle, and carabaos were shot and left lying where they fell, to vitiate the atmosphere and pollute the streams of water. Following closely after these events, rinderpest became epidemic among the remaining cattle and carabaos, while surra and glanders played havoc with the surviving horses. These facts have been commented upon in previous reports, but it is thought appropriate to again note them since their effects will be noticeable in this province for many years to come. (*RPC* 1903, vol. 3, 740)

Following the surrender of General Pedro Samson's forces, a serious cholera outbreak swept the island (as it had elsewhere in the Philippines) and did not begin to abate until the middle of 1903. Over six thousand cases were reported, and Loon was among the worst affected towns (Carter 1905, 65). Between the latter half of 1905 and the beginning of 1906, rinderpest—a deadly disease affecting cattle and water buffalo—returned to Bohol. Loon bore the brunt of the outbreak with forty-one reported cases and seventeen deaths, resulting in an emergency quarantine of the whole town (*RPC* 1906, vol. 7, 205). With dwindling herds, the threat of starvation contributed to the internal displacement of Bohol's population. Gibbens reported that "the natives [of Bohol] have been compelled to change their occupations, and many of them have removed nearer to the mountains, where the water supply is more available for the cultivation of rice, camotes, and other articles of first necessity" (*RPC* 1903, vol. 3, 740).[11] Needless to say, there were many incentives for Datahan and his followers to leave the devastation of Loon and settle in the uplands of Guindulman.

It is probable that the Mariano Datahan arrived in Biabas sometime between his court-martialing in Jagna in March 1901 and his re-emergence as a fanatical speech-maker in Biabas in January of 1902.[12] The destruction of Loon and the surrender of the Republic in this intervening period suggest powerful push factors. In the early years of the twentieth century, Bohol had few roads, and an overland journey from Loon to Biabas would have been an epic and dangerous undertaking, particularly in a time of conflict. (I was told in Biabas that Mariano and some of his brothers came first, and that they were aided by a supernatural ally who allowed them to traverse vast distances in the blink of an eye.) Interior roads were virtually nonexistent in Bohol at the turn of the nineteenth century (*RPC* 1901, vol. 3, 96; Luspo 2005, 13), and even where coastal roads were available it was often easier to travel between lowland towns by sea (J.B. Tirol 1998, 18). In all likelihood the refugees traveled east by boat, relying on their considerable seafaring expertise, as Loon's fishermen were reputed to travel as far as Palawan and the Turtle Islands (Añasco 2000). Perhaps the most demanding part of the journey would have been from the landing on the east coast to the uplands of Biabas. The Eskaya traditional story "The First People in the Land of Bohol" (Chapter 7) describes Bulawan, an area of land stretching between Guindulman and the foothills of Biabas, as "virgin forest" (**marasikaniyan maras**; *kagulangan lasang*); today it is almost entirely denuded.

According to his memoirs, Datahan had scouted out the Biabas region during the conflict, naming it the *yutang natawhan* ('motherland'). Perched on a plateau rising above thick forest, Biabas was surrounded by natural defenses and would have presented an excellent vantage point for spying on any approach by outsiders. Indeed, Biabas would later serve as a firing line in World War II, and until recently the area was a strategic redoubt for New People's Army (NPA) rebels. However, the new settlers were not to remain isolated in their jungle hideout. Having established a base, Datahan and his followers made forays into the surrounding villages as advocates for a new and radical ideology.

## Aglipayan missionization period, 1902–1925

In the early years of the Biabas resettlement Datahan initiated a missionary program on behalf of the newly established Iglesia Filipina Independiente (IFI; see Chapter 2). The nationalist church, headed by Fr. Gregorio Aglipay, had made few inroads into the Visayas, but it had struck a chord with Datahan, who, in the wake of the Boholano defeat, was intent on waging his "war against Rome." In 1902, the same year the IFI was founded in Luzon, Datahan built a church in Biabas, and together with other community leaders he wrote to Aglipay asking for priests to be sent to Bohol, as the Biabas church was served by a single layman (Moreno 2005). In 1904, Fr. Terencio Najarro was installed, and by the following year, the Aglipayan parish of Biabas, the first of its kind in Bohol, was officially founded. Biabas would soon become the center of IFI missionary activity in the province.[13]

Datahan's brand of Aglipayanism did not strictly follow the doctrine and dogma of the IFI. Fr. Gregorio Aglipay was supposedly laissez-faire when it came to questions of public morality, a fact that detractors claimed was a major source of his popularity with the masses. Unsympathetic American Protestants, such as Homer C. Stuntz, despaired that Aglipay tolerated the leisure activities enjoyed by Filipino men, such as cockfighting, drinking, and gambling (Stuntz 1904).[14] Datahan, on the other hand, enforced a strict code of propriety, which he linked to spiritual self-discipline and codified in a text known as *Pamatasan* ('proper behavior'). He prohibited gambling, drinking, idleness during work hours, working on Sunday, and dancing. Women were forbidden to wear trousers or to cut their hair short (Moreno 2005).

These austerities did not, however, lessen the popularity of his movement. His impact on the region, particularly the town of Candijay, was considerable. In 1925, Fr. Licinio Ruiz wrote in his *Sinopsis histórica*,

[Candijay] is like a black stain on a field of purest white snow.

It is one of the few towns of Bohol in which Aglipayanism has laid down deep roots, dragging with it a considerable part of the town. The phenomenon (for want of a better word) observed in Candijay, a town in the near vicinity of other models of faith, is easily explained when one is acquainted with the manner of being a poor Filipino: ever submissive, if not a slave, to Mr Big. Here is the explanation for this phenomenon. In these parts there has been a captain who, either by arrogance or some other reason, raised the first Aglipayan flag, built his church, installed a priest—or more accurately as they say in this country, a *Padre-Padre*; that is, one who has the appearance of something but isn't anything at all—and many of the inhabitants followed the captain out of fear.[15]

The label *Padre-Padre* was no trifling insult; the reduplicated form carries the sense of 'pseudo-' or 'inauthentic,' and it's one of several slurs leveled at Biabas residents to this day. The order of service for the centennial celebrations of the Biabas parish, a full eighty years after Ruiz's report, carried this lament:

Since the inhabitants of Biabas are Eskaya and Aglipayan, they are ridiculed and called 'ultra-superstitious' [*sobrang nagpatootoo*] and 'cult members.' Many names are used to mock them: 'infidels' [*mga erehes*], 'Rizalians,' 'fakes' [*mini*], 'pseudo-priests' [*paripari*] and 'ignoramuses.'[16]

The passage points to long-standing hostilities directed at the Eskaya community that have persisted into the twenty-first century and that go beyond mere sectarian rivalry. Even Bohol's own Aglipayan clergyman, who owe a historical debt to the foundational efforts of Mariano Datahan, have expressed unease at the supposed unorthodox practices of the Biabas congregation.[17]

Certainly, the systems of belief and behavior developed by Mariano Datahan and his followers took only partial inspiration from the teachings of Aglipay. The very existence, not to mention the content, of Datahan's codified dictates ran contrary to the liberal and modernist spirit of the Philippine church. "The law makes the sin," declaimed José Ferrándiz in the prologue to the official IFI catechism of 1912, which went on to accuse the papacy of generating myriad legal "inventions" to oppress people with feelings of unworthiness and keep them in a state of terror (Ferrándiz 1912, xix–xx). For early Aglipayan thinkers like Ferrándiz, the papacy was inherently flawed as an institution. It was incapable, not only of separating church from state but of viewing itself as anything other than a superstate in its own right. By contrast, Datahan's severe new society restored ultraconservative norms of behavior, and his literature did not oppose the institution of the papacy per se. Pinay, after all, was introduced as the first pope in the Philippines, even if he would also be the last; no other pope, or **inmunsiktur**, is recorded as having succeeded him. Datahan's presumed association with pulahan "popes" on neighboring islands would likewise indicate that he was at peace with the notion. The implied objection is that a foreign and illegitimate pope should rule in Bohol, in place of a native one. From this perspective, the battle cry of Datahan's "war against Rome" was not so much "Down with the papacy!," as "Down with *your* papacy!."

Significantly, too, the IFI insisted that Latin be abandoned as a language of liturgy in favor of local languages (Aglípay y Labáyan 1912, 100). But in the recollection of elderly congregation members in Biabas, local IFI priests continued to say mass in Latin right up until the 1970s, even after the Catholic Church itself had transitioned to the vernacular. Perhaps Datahan, as the chief evangelist for the IFI in Bohol, was too invested in the mystical opacity of a sacred language to let it be abandoned so lightly. Just as it was recounted in "The White Bell," the revealed Eskayan language with all of its sacred power was represented as a counterpoint, rather than a replacement, to Latin.

Such a crypto-utopian agenda is altogether consistent with Datahan's program of nativizing colonial categories and promoting a localized alternative as both historically prior and superior. His see-you-and-raise-you strategy helps to elucidate other contradictions with Aglipayan doctrine. The Eskaya veneration of the Santo Niño (Chapter 7), for example, would have been construed by orthodox Aglipayans of the early twentieth century as a manifestation of Romanist propaganda and premodern superstition (Ferrándiz 1912, xviii). Nativized as

Suno (ᵈᵒᵛ) the Biabas community was able to reclaim the icon as a prehispanic object of veneration.[18] Similarly, the tropes of apocalyptic calamities and resurrections that surface in Eskaya oral literature (Chapter 7) are at odds with Aglipayan dogma that vigorously denounced apocalyptic theology and beliefs in the miraculous, insisting that the prayer book and catechism be accompanied by nothing other than Science (Aglípay y Labáyan 1912, xvi). But what the Eskaya and orthodox Aglipayans shared was a narrative of emancipation. Where the modernizing Aglipayans saw themselves as rejecting the tyranny of tradition to enter a brave new future, the Biabas community under Datahan preferred to sabotage oppression at its historical source through a radical rescripting and reclamation of the past. In other words, while the Aglipayan church favored iconoclasm, Datahan insisted on revision.

One unusual point of apparent convergence between Aglipayanism and "Datahanism" was on the question of human evolution. Gregorio Aglipay was unequivocal in his acceptance of the scientific consensus. In a chapter of his *Catequesis* entitled "Desarollo y no Creación" ("Development, not Creation") he wrote, "[j]ust as [ . . . ] small monkeys transformed into large monkeys, man could have originated from the improvement and development of the latter," noting in a footnote the existence of "monkeys without tails that go about on two feet."[19] He was nonetheless at pains to explain that humanity was not directly descended from apes but shared with them a common ancestor. Both Martinez (1993, 187) and Bedford (2004, 30) have suggested that "The Itch-mite Tumaw" (Chapter 7) might be read as a Darwinian allegory. The Itch-mite ultimately begets a monkey who gives birth to Adam and Idam, understood as representing the biblical Adam and Eve. Arguably, the narrator Anoy was detoxifying the modern anti-creationist views of the IFI by synthesizing Darwin with Genesis.

Datahan's syncretic Aglipayanism was effectively a strategic articulation of his own brand of radical nativism with the nationalist program of ecclesiastic self-determination advocated by the IFI. He emphasized aspects of Aglipayan doctrine that were useful to his program—nationalism, indigenous self-determination, and the rejection of foreign papacy—while ignoring the reformist and modernizing elements of the new church. For Datahan, possession of a native and prior system of laws, iconography, cosmogony, scripture, and above all language was in itself evidence of cultural and political legitimacy.

## The return of militant cults, 1902–1922

Aglipay's church was by no means the sole source of inspiration for Datahan's revisionist ideology. Between 1902 and 1906, militant sects were rife throughout the Philippines, and these so-called *dyusdyus* (literally 'false god,' often written as 'dios-dios') and *pulahan* ('reds') movements were a far graver annoyance to the U.S. authorities than Aglipayanism (see Chapter 2 and Ileto 1979a). Contrary to Philippine Commission reports that associated pulahan rebellion with anti-U.S. sedition, the movements predated the American occupation by some years and were already a familiar cultural phenomenon. In his 1889 compilation of Filipino folklore and customs, Isobelo de los Reyes produced the ficitonalized tale of Isio, an innocent fugitive from the Spanish authorities who takes refuge in the mountains, where he manipulates the belief systems of the local Igorots, beguiling them with his magic tricks, prophecies, and technological knowledge (de los Reyes y Florentino 1889). Rising to the status of a charismatic despot he instills the value of education, takes multiple wives, and leads an unsuccessful attack on the Spanish.[20] Certainly, militant cult disturbances as well as plain banditry continued to rise from 1890 onward; the revolution and war with America simply gave them greater impetus (Sturtevant 1976, 118). The first movement that was referred to as *dyusdyus* rallied in Samar in 1884 under an individual known as Anugar whose leadership later passed to a "Pope Pablo" (Arens 1959). In 1887, a certain Pope Faustino Ablen was arrested for organizing a *dyusdyus* movement in Leyte, a setback that did nothing to stem the rise of attacks across Samar in 1894. *Dyusdyus* leaders at this time were also known to call themselves *baybaylans* ('shamans'), a term that hearkened back to their nativist motivations (de los Reyes 1889, 266). In 1902, the ranks of the *dyusdyus* in Samar were boosted by those ex-soldiers of the revolutionary government who had refused to accept surrender to the United States. According to Arens, it was in the years following the Philippine–American War that movements of this kind acquired their label *pulahan* on account of the red (Visayan: *pula*) uniforms worn by their members. In this period pulahanism spread to the islands of Masbate, Panay, and Cebu (*RPC* 1903, vol. 3; Arens 1959; Mojares 1976), while similar rebel outfits flourished in Luzon. In Samar, pulahan uprisings persisted up until World War II and after.

Early American administrators famously classified their guerilla opponents as *ladrones* ('bandits'), *ladrones políticos* ('political bandits'), and *ladrones fanáticos* ('fanatical bandits'), depending on whether they were identified primarily as bandits, insurrectionaries, or cult warriors, respectively (*RPC* 1903, vol. 3, 100). But this last designation grossly simplified a complex situation. The disparate *pulahan* movements of the early twentieth century did not comprise a cohesive organizational whole. At most, they operated as "semiautonomous units in larger, less formal coalitions" (Sturtevant 1976, 129). Yet despite their relative isolation, the ideologies and social practices from one group to the next were remarkably similar. Pulahan organizations were typically governed by charismatic "Popes" who made liberal use of *antinganting* ('amulet magic') to confer powers of invulnerability, particularly against the bullets of the Philippine

Constabulary (*RPC* 1904, vol.1, 610). Amulets were the exclusive property of a pope, or they were sold by the pope to his followers who may also have been obliged to pay a kind of tax known as a *cedula*. Beyond *antinganting*, pulahan leaders were reported to keep disciples in their thrall through the performance of sleight-of-hand illusions.[21] Popes were revered as gifted prognosticators, predicting everything from calamitous end times to changes in the weather. Pulahan leaders enforced strict gender norms that specified styles of dress and prohibited dancing. Local supremos such as Felipe Salvador of Luzon and Kubalan of Samar had numerous wives.

Pulahan mysticism was inextricably fused with nationalist aspirations. The rebel communities were known to create their own flags, and many revered José Rizal as a divine being whose resurrection or reincarnation was imminent. Certain pulahans of Samar even took to referring to themselves as Katipuneros, i.e., members of the revolutionary army that opposed Spanish rule at the turn of the century. This was experienced as a keen outrage to their compatriots, particularly after the neo-Katipunan warriors chose to ally themselves with the Japanese during the occupation of the island in World War II.

### Parallels between Visayan pulahans and Datahan's movement

I have not been able to uncover any evidence in U.S. archives that pulahanism ever took root in Bohol. It is of some note, however, that the single report of Mariano Datahan's fanaticism, issued by the Assistant Chief of the Philippine Constabulary, was made in the context of Visayas-wide cult militia disturbances. Briefly introduced in Chapter 2, the paragraph in question is worth citing in full:

> The beginning of the new year [1902] and throughout the month of January brought forth reports from nearly all provinces of the existence of agents of the dios-dios or pulijan [sic] sect. Antique had its dios-dios organization back of Tibiao, where frequent meetings are reported to have been held. The lieutenant of the barrio of Biaba [sic], pueblo of Guindulman, on the island of Bohol, is reported to have made some fanatical speeches that gained him considerable followers on the island of Bohol. Dios-dios cedulas continued to be sold in Capiz. On the island of Cebu the existence of regular societies of dios-dios in the northern end of the island and on the west coast opposite the city of Cebu was reported. There was apprehension in other provinces of danger from pulijans, but the higher classes of natives attributed most of the talk to the discussions concerning the Aglipay Church, and the preliminary organization of its followers from various sections. Aglipay's expected visit to the southern islands was looked forward

to, and some of the church people feared riot and bloodshed would come
with him. (*RPC* 1903, vol. 3, 116)

Beyond the concurrence of pulahan troubles across the Visayas in January
1902, what is striking about the Philippine Constabulary report is the association of pulahanism with the IFI. Yet fears of violent clashes with Aglipayans were
probably misplaced. Despite his radical religious agenda and disputes over the
ownership of church property, Gregorio Aglipay rejected extremism, accepted
U.S. sovereignty, and pursued legitimacy within the new order. By the time
this report was published, the Philippine Constabulary was beginning to concede that the IFI was not a threat to the peace (*RPC* 1903, vol. 3, 74, 79). The
Philippine Commission did not identify the Biabas fanatics as Aglipayans but
as local agitators in the mold of other Visayan pulahan movements. Unlike the
other groups mentioned in the report, Datahan's movement was not seen to be
engaging in violent resistance to U.S. rule. A later political disturbance can, however, be attributed to the Biabas community. The first elected civil governor of
Bohol, Don Salustiano Borja, reported to the Philippine Commission that dis-
gruntled veterans of Bohol's army had formed a resistance movement with influence across southern and central Bohol.[22] Among the disturbances described by
the governor was an attack on Carmen (Map 3) planned for May 15, 1906. Borja
himself entered Carmen with an armed escort and the danger was averted, but
it was rumored that the rebels—who set out to sack the town and kidnap its
officials—were resident in Biabas, the very village where Mariano Datahan had
attracted "considerable followers" just four years earlier. Evidently, the old republican soldier was not only resisting U.S. rule on his island but coordinating with
other disaffected comrades in the southern and central towns.

It has been proposed, on the basis of colonial records, that Visayan pulahan
or *dyusdyus* movements spread across the Visayas from a common source in
late-nineteenth-century Samar (Borrinaga 2009), and thus the possibility that
Datahan had direct contact with one or more of these organizations and took
inspiration from them cannot be easily dismissed. After all, Visayan cults were
known to address their leaders as "Pope" or "First Teacher," and these are honorif-
ics that recur in Eskaya literature. Overt *dyusdyus* sympathies can even be detected
in a passage of "The White Bell": "The Spanish priests were not capable of the
same faith in miracles that the **biriki** had in their god Salbadur Sunu. The Spanish
called this a 'dios-dios' belonging to the pagans of the Philippine Visayas."[23] Jes
Tirol even reported that Datahan was arrested for rebellion after World War II
for having sheltered pulahans from Leyte and Negros "whose beliefs were similar
to the Eskayas" (Jes Tirol, 2000). It was this event that prompted Datahan, in his
final years, to employ Tirol's father as a lawyer.[24]

However, in his inversion of colonial power and his channeling of ritual objects, Datahan was not only adopting pulahan cultural practices but re-enacting the behaviors of Visayan revolutionary peasant leaders from earlier times (Chapter 2). Present-day residents of Biabas and Taytay, for example, recall that he was in possession of several amulets. One of these protected him from bullets and machetes; another, which took the form of a *librita* ('magic book'), granted him powers of divination. He was said to hang a charm known as an *awug* on fruit trees so that thieves would be left with a stomachache; other amulets were used to guarantee a good harvest. As discussed earlier, locals invested Datahan with the power to make himself invisible, appear in two places at once, levitate, travel great distances in the blink of an eye, and make himself die and come to life at will. Though *antinganting* is not described as the source of his supernatural talents, these are the kinds of powers that are widely associated with amulets. Elpidio Palaca, the tribal bishop for the Eskaya community, once showed me his own personal *librita* but insisted that *antinganting* had nothing to do with the official religious system of the Eskaya.

Sleight-of-hand illusions, as practiced by pulahan popes in Samar, are also attrib-uted to Datahan. Jes Tirol's father, Victoriano Tirol, once entertained Datahan by performing a trick in which he made a coin disappear. Not to be outdone, Datahan responded with an impressive trick. Arranging himself under a sheet, he stepped into a rice mortar in such a way that his talking head appeared to be disembodied. He later performed tricks in which he made cutlery disappear. From this Jes Tirol deduced that Datahan used illusions to keep people in awe and attract followers (J.B. Tirol, 1993c). (Much later, Elpidio Palaca impressed me with an illusion in which he made a stone appear like a bird's egg and later asked me to bite down hard on a leaf only to reveal that my teeth had left no trace on it.) Also awe-inspiring were the prophecies in which Datahan predicted millenarian calamities, the emer-gence of technologies such as electric light, and social movements like feminism ("when women will try to compete with men"; see Chapter 7).

While several millenarian leaders at this time had sexual access to numerous women, it is unclear whether these arrangements were formalized "marriages." Datahan's partners, however, belonged to one of three designations. His first wife, Catalina Bernales, was recognized as his "legal" wife, while the rest were either *asawa* ('wives'), or *uyab* ('girlfriends'). Estimations of the number of Datahan's wives vary but Eskaya people gave me figures of eleven, forty-two, and ninety-nine.[25] Genealogical data indicates that there were fourteen women with whom he had children and who would also inherit the name Datahan; two women had children by him who did not inherit Datahan's name but took the family name of their mothers. Other men in the community did not have polygamous relationships.

A more direct connection to Samar might be drawn from Datahan's claimed association with the Katipunan. Datahan recounts in his memoirs that his Katipunan-related operations took place in Samar, an island where he reported that he stayed for almost two years. However, given that this probably occurred after the Philippine Revolution, it is more likely that Datahan was involved with the *neo*-Katipunan pulahan movements of Samar than with the Katipunan itself.

Although Martinez reported seeing a statue of Datahan in a military uniform similar to those worn by Katipunan soldiers (1993, 66), there is no evidence that male residents of Biabas wore uniforms as a practice. Brenda Abregana (1984) wrote that Datahan almost always wore a *bahag* or traditional sarong, an anachronistic garment associated with pre-contact Filipino society. The impressive photograph of him from 1948 (Fig. 8.1) depicts him wearing a *bahag* together with a U.S. army shirt, a juxtaposition that appears to encapsulate the paradox of "native modernity" witnessed in his literary reimagination of precolonial military roles (Chapter 7). The traditional dress observed today in Biabas and Taytay (see Chapter 4), of which the *bahag* is not a feature, is likely to have been innovated sometime after Datahan had passed away. Surviving photographs of Biabas' residents from the 1960s, taken on religious occasions, do not reveal evidence of a distinctive dress style (one of these photos is shown in Fig. 8.2; for a contrast see Fig. 8.3).

### Parallels with Laureano Solamo's colorum in Bucas Grande

By October of 1907, all key leaders of pulahan movements in Samar and Leyte had been captured or killed in battle and the movements went into rapid decline. Taking their place were less belligerent cult communities, which came to be known as colorums, supposedly from the coda to many Latin prayers, *per omnia secula seculorum* ('for ever and ever'; literally 'in all ages'). The most successful of these was directed by one Laureano Solamo, who coordinated his activities from Cebu. Learning that the inhabitants of the island of Bucas Grande in Mindanao had converted en masse to Aglipayanism, Solamo decided to establish an encampment there toward the end of 1918. The Bucas Grande Aglipayans, recent apostates of the Catholic Church, proved receptive to Solamo's more radical message, and new converts soon flocked to the island from Bohol, Cebu, Leyte, and Samar; migrants from the latter two provinces were believed to include former pulahans (Sturtevant 1976, 143). By 1922, the Provincial Commander of Surigao was beginning to have concerns over the rapid rise of the colorum and its spread to the adjacent islands of Siargao and Socorro, bolstered by a flood of converts from Bohol and Leyte (Juan 1922). Like their pulahan antecedents to the north, leaders of Solamo's colorum were addressed as "Pope." In certain key respects

**FIGURE 8.2.** Photograph taken of Biabas residents in front of the church during the May festival of Flores de Mayo, ca. 1964.

**FIGURE 8.3.** Eskaya members of the Biabas congregation in 2004, displaying Eskaya and Aglipayan flags. Juan Datahan, to the left of the priest, is wearing a raffia shirt and an embroidered *kupya*.

the Bucas Grande colorum had more in common with the Biabas community than it did with the Visayan pulahan movements. Members were governed by prohibitions against drinking, dancing, and gambling, and gender segregation was strictly enforced. One month out of every year was set aside for construction labor or agriculture for the benefit of the whole community (Sturtevant 1976, 143). Felix Bernales (known as Lantayug) rose to prominence as the supremo of the Bucas Grande colorum with his predictions of calamity followed by a shining era of Philippine independence ruled over by José Rizal. As Sturtevant put it, "millennium and independence had come to mean one and the same thing" (157).

I have not been able to chart the genealogies of Bucas Grande families to discover whether or not they intersect with families in Biabas. One coincidence of peculiar interest is that Mariano Datahan's first wife, Catalina Bernales, shares a family name with Bucas Grande headman Felix Bernales. It is also recorded that Maria Datahan (d. 1964), the sole daughter of Mariano Datahan and Luciana Patentes, was born in Surigao del Sur in the approximate region of Bucas Grande. Furthermore, certain Eskaya oral histories that are told to explain why there are no native speakers of Eskayan on Bohol relate that the original Eskaya people migrated to Mindanao (Hinlo 1992, 66; Bedford 2004, 17; see also Payot 1981). In some accounts, this mass migration occurred at the time of Spanish contact; in others it is supposed to have taken place sometime after the arrival in Biabas of Mariano Datahan and it was his students who migrated. Abregana even suggests that the migration occurred after Mariano Datahan passed away in 1949 (Ramos 1980).[26]

## The persistence of millenarianism

Whether parallels between the early-twentieth-century Biabas community and neighboring pulahan and colorum movements indicate direct historical contact between the groups is open to debate. Of more immediate relevance is the fact that their overlapping values, imagery, and practices point to shared concerns of national and spiritual self-determination. In the face of a new colonial occupier, Datahan and his radical contemporaries sought to reconstitute Filipino society from Year Zero. Drawing freely from indigenous tradition, Christian and clerical iconography, and nationalist revolutionary rhetoric, the *ladrones fanaticos* defied easy interpretation and were regarded by the U.S. administration as a cultural idiosyncrasy. But as Sturtevant has ably demonstrated, syncretic nativist movements of this nature recur throughout post-contact Philippine history from Tamblot's religious rebellion of 1621–1622 to Valentin de los Santos' Manila-based Lapiang Malaya movement of the 1940s–1960s (Sturtevant 1976; Ileto 1979a). That such social movements are typical of Bohol is clearly shown in the distinctly "pulahan" character of the Tamblot and Dagohoy rebellions. Indeed, the periodic emergence of charismatic leaders with supernatural skills has become culturally routinized in certain rural communities of Bohol (Aparece 2003, 70), and this pattern is observed across the region at large.

Rather than focusing narrowly on historical precedents and regional connections, such movements may be better understood in terms of their political dynamics and intrinsic appeal. James C. Scott has pointed out that millenarian organizations have regularly arisen among disconnected communities right across upland Southeast Asia. In response to extreme hardship, he has argued, local peasants are attracted to such movements since the "disprivileged have the least interest in maintaining the current distribution of status and wealth and potentially the most to gain from a radical reshuffling of the social order" (Scott 2009, 297). Moreover, he has noticed that highland cult leaders are almost always "culturally amphibious translators": just like Datahan they are usually educated cosmopolitans who speak several languages, have wide networks, and can move easily between worlds (Scott 2009, 309). This depiction accords with Herminia Meñez Coben's observation that indigenous Filipino verbal artists are often arbitrators of cultural change who rise to leadership roles. Moreover, they are seen to become active agents in the making and remaking of traditional histories via an "adaptive poetics" of "resistance and accommodation" (Coben 2010, 360).

What differentiates Datahan's movement, in comparison with others in the Philippines or highland Southeast Asia at large, is its impressive longevity. While religious militia movements inevitably came to blows with the lowland administrations and disintegrated after the death or arrest of their leaders, the Biabas community avoided confrontation and was able to adapt its demands to changing social circumstances, and it has continued to do so to this day. In this light, Datahan's miraculous recuperation of a lost language, script, literary tradition, and social organization is, perhaps, an exceptional example of what Phelan has referred to as the Filipino capacity for "creative social adjustment" (1959, viii, 133) in the face of colonial pressures. Datahan was able to articulate a desirable alternative to colonial rule, yet as a culturally amphibious translator he was in a position to adjust the levers of accommodation and resistance to avoid an overwhelming confrontation.

## Accommodation with the U.S. regime, circa 1914–1937

After the quashed ambush of Carmen in 1906, no more threats to the U.S. occupation of Bohol were to emanate from Biabas, and Datahan's ideological program was to shift away from defiant isolationism toward a more institutional solidity. Across the nation, guerilla attacks and local uprisings went into decline as the new administration initiated a more conciliatory period of rule. High on the agenda was land reform, and from 1903 Governor William Taft began acquiring lands held by the Catholic orders for redistribution to Filipinos. In the same year, the Homestead Act was introduced as a means of allowing ordinary farmers to lay claim to uncultivated interior territories, a policy that remains to this day (Hayami, Quisumbing, and Adriano 1990, 42–43). Although progress on land reform was slow and frequently exploited by large landholders, by the 1910s a significant number of Filipino farmers gained title to small plots of land and paid an annual tax to the administration.

Inland territories of Bohol that had been occupied by conflict-displaced populations were now surveyed, titled, and taxed by the provincial government. Records of the Provincial Assessor's Office in Tagbilaran show that in the period of 1914–1918, Mariano Datahan is officially listed as the owner of at least forty-five separate land titles ranging from P10 to P1140 in taxable value; a further two with a combined value of P30 are listed under the name Mariano Sumatra. In most instances, the land claim is listed as a new declaration, meaning no taxes had previously been paid on the land in question by the stated owner. In the same period a number of small landholders in Biabas are recorded as having their tax obligations canceled, presumably because their land had been sold. According to these records, by the end of 1918 almost all the land in Biabas was in the hands of Mariano Datahan; the rest largely belonged to Francisco Datahan and to members of the Ampoloquio and Gule clans, at least as far as the tax authorities were aware. Gregorio Aglipay is recorded, in 1918, as the owner of a tax-exempt portion of land valued at P10, presumably the site of the church. One of the more curious entries is of a certain Pedro Samson, whose tax obligations on a portion of land in Biabas worth P120 ceased in 1918; directly following the entry is a new declaration for Mariano Datahan on land worth P360. It is extraordinary to think that the surrendered general of the Bohol Republic had owned a relatively significant amount of property in Biabas up until 1918. Datahan's memoirs mention a meeting with Samson in the early stages of the Philippine–American War in Bohol, but there is no suggestion of his connection to Biabas. Could the *yutang natawhan* ('motherland') have been chosen as a resettlement site because General Samson was already landholder there? Or did Samson, who died in 1940, join Datahan's movement after his surrender to American forces in 1901? Oral histories do not contribute any clues to this conundrum.[27]

Precisely when Datahan began marrying multiple women in the community is unrecorded, but the birth dates of his children offer a very general indication. With the majority of his wives he had only one child, and those of his children for whom birth dates are recorded were born in 1914 (Clotilde Datahan), 1916 (Pedro Datahan), 1927 (Juan Datahan), and 1941 (Sisinia Datahan). What this may suggest is that Datahan had begun consolidating his place in Biabas through multiple marriages at about the same time that he was legally acquiring land.

As a tax contributor to Bohol's administration, and a wealthy one at that, Datahan had effectively abandoned his principled resistance to the new regime by this time. In Roberto Datahan's opinion, his great-grand-uncle Mariano renounced anti-U.S. insurgency when he was confident that the Americans were building schools and were no longer engaging Boholanos in open conflict. Whether the Biabas community ever was seriously opposed to American rule is an open question. From the very beginning of his resettlement in Biabas, Datahan may have even achieved legitimacy within regional governance structures by acquiring the role of barangay captain.[28] With local political influence and landholdings at stake, Datahan would have had little incentive to openly challenge the prevailing power structure.

I speculate that Datahan's decision to reconcile with the new administration preceded a flowering of cultural activity in Biabas. Just as his Aglipayan crusade was described as a "war without soldiers," Datahan was to prosecute an ambitious cultural campaign that left behind a remarkable linguistic and literary legacy. By at least October of 1937 this labor had come to full fruition when Datahan prepared a notebook in "Boholano dialect" (Prologue) and sent it to President Manuel L. Quezon, a leader who embodied renewed nationalist aspirations for an independent Philippines. Just like Datahan, the Spanish-educated president had fought against the U.S. regime in the Philippine–American War, only to achieve success as an influential player from within the system he had earlier opposed.

A logical sequence of steps that Datahan may have followed in recuperating Pinay's language is proposed in the chapter that follows. Though the reconstruction itself is hypothetical, the timing of it is more certain, and it appears likely that Pinay's linguistic and literary legacy was fomented in this period of relative peace, stability, and national optimism. But the bold march toward self-determination, in Manila as much as in Biabas, was soon to be interrupted by yet another formidable colonial aggressor.

## Datahan's final war and posthumous legacy

On May 22, 1942, Japanese troops took command of the key ports of Guindulman and Tagbilaran. The Bohol Provisional Battalion was officially disbanded, and various unattached resistance groups sprouted in its place. At this time, the pulahan movement on nearby Samar was also resuscitated. Biabas, which had served as an impenetrable haven for refugees some forty years earlier, once again found itself in a strategic military position. Stationed in defensible hills overlooking occupied Guindulman, the residents of Biabas under the elderly veteran Mariano

Datahan engaged in resistance efforts against the Japanese. Three war histories make passing reference to the actions of the "Biabas Force" in the early part of the occupation. Pio Ferandos (1981), Col. Esteban Bernido (1981), and Simplicio Apalisok (1992a) all concur that the Biabas contingent did not cooperate with other resistance groups and was considered to be a rogue element. In his war diaries, Bernido notes that in 1942, reserve arms and ammunition of Bohol's disbanded infantry were hidden in caves around Biabas for safe keeping under Datahan. Before long, Datahan formed a recalcitrant guerrilla faction and illegally assumed rights to the arms (1981, 15–18). The commander, an appointee of Datahan, was unable to discipline his soldiers who used their weapons for petty banditry and the intimidation of civilians. In Bernido's account, soldiers abused locals, stole their livestock, and soon became "more feared by the people than the Japanese" (15). A number of resistance agitators who had fled Guindulman had been compelled to surrender to the occupying forces, believing themselves safer in the hands of the Japanese than at the mercy of the Biabas guerrillas. The reports prompted the Mayor of Guindulman, Maximo Castrodes, to convene a secret meeting in which it was agreed that the Biabas soldiers were disorganized, cowardly, and unable to defend the civilian population from Japanese abuses. Juan Beronilla, Datahan's comrade in the Boholano–American war, persuaded Bernido to negotiate with Datahan to allow Bernido to assume military leadership of the Biabas soldiers. Talks between the two men continued all night in Biabas, but Datahan refused to relinquish his authority (Bernido 1981, 15–18). Ferandos writes that the Biabas guerrillas were soon defeated by the Japanese in September 1942, resulting in the enemy capture of "several rifles, one machinegun (complete) and one machine gun (tripod)" (Ferandos 1981, 169). As a direct consequence, the Biabas Force was disbanded a mere four months after the Japanese invasion.

The recollections of veterans such as Col. Esteban Bernido cannot be treated as neutral observations since rivalry between guerrilla factions was commonplace during the occupation; indeed, Ferandos dedicates an entire chapter to the subject in his history of the Japanese war in Bohol (1981). Regarding these incidents, Datahan's side of the story is not available, and only a few lines in his personal memoirs record his experiences at this time:

> I had my own camp in Cabagnan, Biabas Guindulman Bohol in the year 1942. In 1943, I was drafted by an American by the name of Captain Norch [Knortz]. The 15th of March was the day I arrived in Midina Talisayan, Misamis Oriental. It was there that I served for three years against the Japanese in the province of Butuan Agusan. My service here

in Bohol within my own camp began on June 5, 1942 until the 12th of March, Captain Norch had already come for me.

That Datahan, by now an "old man in his 70s" (Apalisok 1992a, 42), was drafted by an American for service in Mindanao seems unlikely, but this is in fact corroborated by Ferandos, who records that, "[o]n March 12, 1943, a party of 225 armed soldiers under a certain Colonel McClish, a Capt. Knortz, and a Lt. Jaradic arrived at Duero from Butuan, Agusan, and picked Auditor Roman T. del Bando and Mariano Datahan and took away 7,500 rounds of ammunition" (Ferandos 1981, 84). Presumably 'picked' is intended as a synonym for 'drafted.' A number of independent war memoirs identify Corporal William Knortz and Major Ernest McClish as U.S. soldiers who evaded the Japanese and went to serve under Colonel Wendell Fertig in the Butuan region of Mindanao (Keats 1963; Mapes 2000; Zincke 2003). Knortz escaped from a prisoner of war camp in July of 1942 (Zincke 2003, 50) and died in action in September 1943 (Mapes 2000, 226).[29] McClish, a Native American Choctaw of Oklahoma, managed his own guerrilla force of three hundred before joining Fertig's joint Filipino–American unit (Holm 2007, 48). Fertig's campaign in Mindanao was frequently beset by shortages of ammunition (Keats 1963), and the 7500 rounds in Datahan's possession would have been a welcome prize. Since Mariano Datahan was already in his seventies at the time he was recruited, it is possible that the American guerrillas brought others under Datahan's command such as Pablo Arcamo of Panglao, Fausto P. Cirunay of Dauis, Galu Sajulga of Jagna, Datahan's cousin Teodulo Datahan, who had been a lieutenant in the U.S. army, and Fabian Baja, all of whom are recorded as having served under Datahan's command as guerrillas during the war (Apalisok 1992a, 42; Orcullo 2004, 111–112).

Toward the end of the occupation, Datahan returned to Biabas. Juan Datahan remembers cooperating with American troops at this time to secure a firing line from Biabas toward Guindulman. One day he showed me a copy of his United States Air Force in the Far East (USAFFE) orders and complained to me that he had not been recognized as a war veteran by the provincial government.

Meanwhile the pulahan "Katipuneros" on Samar were not only accused of outrages against civilians but of active collaboration with Japanese forces. As mentioned earlier, pulahan members fleeing prosecution after the war were sheltered by Mariano Datahan, an act for which he was arrested and tried on charges of sedition. Sadly, no records of the trial or arrest can be discovered to throw further light on the relationship between the groups. In the month before Datahan passed away he appointed eight men to succeed him as language teachers (Orcullo 2004, 112).

## Datahan's death and its aftermath

Parish records indicate that Mariano Datahan died in Biabas on January 26, 1949.[30] The culture to which he dedicated much of his life went into rapid decline as feuding erupted among Datahan's sons and Biabas was subjected to anti-colorum army raids (Martinez 1993, 50). Unable to tolerate the situation, several committed students of the traditional literature abandoned the village to inaugurate a new Eskaya settlement in the densely forested mountains above Biabas.

Datahan's legacy in Biabas was soon to be threatened not only from internal divisions but also from rival movements. During the late 1960s, in Juan Datahan's reckoning, the Philippine Benevolent Missionaries Association (PBMA) established a compound in Biabas a few kilometers from the village center. A popular Visayan religious movement, the PBMA, was founded in 1965 on the island of Dinagat in Mindanao. Their national leader was Ruben Ecleo, a former Aglipayan who made predictions about the future and claimed fluency in Hebrew, Aramaic, Arabic, and Sanskrit. Adherents pray the "Revised Latin Rosary" consisting of twelve secret "Aramaic" words of divine inspiration.[31] Like Datahan, Ecleo enforced an ascetic lifestyle on his followers (which Ecleo himself did not adhere to), instituted a system of voluntary labor, had numerous "spiritual wives," was believed to be able to be present in two places at once, and made use of *antinganting* amulets. Held by his followers to be the reincarnation of both Rizal and Jesus Christ, Ecleo communicated with the spirit of a deceased warrior who was said to have led pulahan rebellions in Cebu in the early twentieth century (Vitug 1995).

According to Juan Datahan, the town of Lundag was established in the 1940s by Zenon Balaba as a Bisayan Declarado settlement under the direction of Mariano Datahan. However, after Datahan passed away, Balaba was to become a committed convert to the Philippine Ecumenical Christian Church, an organization that espoused the divinity and imminent return of José Rizal, beliefs incidentally shared in various ways by the "Katipunan" pulahans of Samar (Arens 1959, 346) and the Moncadistas of Cebu, Mindanao, and the Filipino diaspora (Cullinane 2000). Balaba's son-in-law Terry "Aser" Escalera rose to become a supremo of the movement, taking sixteen wives and issuing *antinganting* to his armed followers (Guingguing, 1975e, 8). During a leadership struggle with his father-in-law, members of Aser's faction initiated a campaign of intimidation, kidnap, and murder in the hills around Lundag. Matters came to a head in September 1975 when a police patrol killed a member of his group in armed confrontation and six others were taken into custody. Reports soon emerged that Aser and his remaining men had kidnapped about a thousand civilians and were holding them hostage in a cave. After talks with government negotiators, the rebel faction surrendered in October; the hostages had already escaped.[32] During the conflict, Juan Datahan recalls that the people of Biabas were evacuated to Cadapdapan and that an emissary was sent from Biabas to mediate peace with the Lundag rebels.

Meanwhile, those Eskaya who had already left Biabas for higher ground in the 1950s had succeeded in clearing an area of jungle near the peak of a mountain, where they established subsistence crops. The village was named Taytay (Visayan: 'ridge') in reference to the ridge line track leading there from Biabas, and the settlers attracted new followers from the surrounding area, particularly Bangwalog, which Datahan had earlier established as an IFI parish. Under the military-style leadership of Fabian Baja (Agbayani 1990, 18), Eskaya culture experienced a remarkable revival in Taytay. Sunday lessons in Eskayan began in his house in about 1951, and in the late 1960s a dedicated two-story school was built with six volunteer teaching staff (Orcullo 2004, 103, 106). The classes continued all day with a break for lunch and were so popular that students would walk the 13-kilometer uphill trail from Biabas just to attend. In Taytay, new traditions and dress codes were developed, including the distinctive headscarves worn by the women. Here too, the language expanded its domains, becoming the preferred medium for formal speech-making and the singing of nationalist and Aglipayan hymns translated into Eskayan.

But a large part of its renewed appeal can be attributed to its reinvention as a ritual and devotional language. Baja incorporated Eskayan into the Aglipayan liturgy with special prayers that could only be reproduced in writing by selected initiates; even more restricted was its use in prayer for secret women's rituals (Martinez 1993, 73–74). Teachers in Taytay say that the word 'Eskaya' once referred exclusively to the spiritual system developed at this time by Baja, only later becoming conflated with the language and its speakers. Baja himself said that the true meaning of 'Eskaya' was *pagtulunan sa mga tawu* ('the people's teachings'). When he was interviewed by Cristina Martinez in the early 1990s, Fabian Baja expressed his motivations for promoting Eskayan in terms that recapitulated the monoglot idealism of early Spanish and American administrators (Chapter 2):

> Unlike other countries, the Philippines remains undeveloped. Because we have too many languages. Unlike the Americans, they have only one. The Japanese, the Russians—only have one language. But us, we have too many and this is why we are very confused. When someone tells to speak in a different direction [*binali*] we obey and speak in a different direction. Unlike the Americans who have one language, we have many.[33]

If rampant linguistic diversity posed a threat to good governance, political unity, and economic development, Baja wanted to proffer Eskayan as a solution, just as Spanish, English, and Tagalog had earlier been promoted as auxiliary languages on the same grounds. By learning their true language, the people of Taytay would not be compelled to obey others by speaking in a contrary direction. Thus, like many other language activists around the globe, Baja's language ideology fused a Herderian ideal of linguistic nationalism with the quest for linguistic authenticity. It is nonetheless no exaggeration to say that without the efforts of Fabian Baja—and perhaps others of the Biabas diaspora like Faustina Viscayda— the Eskayan language would never have survived the death of its first prophet. In many ways, Baja was a figure in the mold of the celebrated Hebrew revivalist Eliezer Ben-Yehuda. Although he did not go so far as to raise his children exclusively in Eskayan, as Ben-Yehuda had done for Modern Hebrew, he created stable spoken and written domains for the language. I was fortunate enough to meet and interview Baja on several occasions shortly before his death, but the importance of his language-planning work only became apparent to me toward the end of my research. Only then did it become clear that the period of Eskayan's revelation had occurred in the twilight of Mariano Datahan's life and that for most of its history, Eskayan has been a living language of Taytay and not of its homeland of Biabas. Future studies may explore the history of Eskayan in Taytay in more detail.

At the very least, it is evident from oral and written sources that after Datahan's death, Taytay became the new center of Eskaya culture. For a full thirty years the population thrived in relative isolation such that by the early 1980s, Eskayan teaching and language use had reached the height of popularity. On Sundays the whole village turned out in traditional dress, and the school building was filled to capacity, with some students hiking long distances to attend. It was at about this time that the Taytay community began to attract the attention of the outside world. Taytay's relatively high altitude (742 m above sea level) made it conducive to the cultivation of a variety of new crops; cabbage was introduced in 1980 following a visit from representatives of the Ministry of Agriculture and Food (Orcullo 2004, 133). Reports of the unique culture and language of Taytay spread to the lowlands, sparking the curiosity of journalists, archaeologists, anthropologists, tourists, and mystics who were determined to discover the Eskaya on their own terms. Some of the outsiders believed they had encountered a magical native people; some saw a cult with a clandestine agenda; others still found themselves on the threshold of a lost prehispanic world.

Mariano Datahan's articulate vision of a restored Visayan culture was now in the eyes of new beholders.

# Notes

1. Rolando O. Borrinaga has suggested to me that "G.C.A." in the caption to this photograph might represent the initials of Gregorio C. Aglipay.

2. To take one example, the name of one of Datahan's supposed comrades during the Philippine–American War, Eustaquio Daligdig, is recorded in the archives of the Philippine Supreme Court, where his whereabouts correspond to details recorded in Datahan's statement. Daligdig was charged with murder and brought to trial on August 26, 1902 (Torres 1903), having been accused of ordering the deaths of two unidentified persons in Langaran, Misamis, in February 1901. Placards were allegedly placed on the victims' bodies reading "Traitor to the nation." He was acquitted on the grounds that this action was political in nature and had taken place while he was an officer of the revolutionary army engaged in conflict with the United States. Datahan's account also places Daligdig in Langaran at the time he was alleged to have ordered the executions.

3. Filipinos in the early colonial period were unlikely to have known their age, but this did not stop European chroniclers from making improbable calculations. As well as inflating Sikatuna's age, Chirino also reports that Father Alonso de Humanes, an early seventeenth-century Superior of Bohol, baptized two men of Bohol who were over one hundred years old (Chirino [1604] 1969).

4. According to Juan, one of these aliases was "Amoy," a name that was barely distinct from his favored epithet. "Amoy" was coincidentally an alias of a contemporary con man who impersonated José Rizal and whose actions destabilized Bohol in the period between the evacuation of the Spanish and the formation of Bohol's independent government. Of Amoy, also known as Amoy-Amoy and Pareng, one Don Vicente Elio wrote on January 28, 1899, "He pretended to be no less (what infamy!) than the well deserving Dr. Rizal. . . . The rascal "Pareng" committed crimes and griefs with defenseless and honorable citizens. For this he was made the terror of the province of Bohol . . . " (cited in Tirol 1998, 65). Amoy was eventually captured in Calape, where he was beheaded.

5. Apalisok argues persuasively that Alcala was innocent of this crime, and he lays the blame squarely on the poor strategy of the Boholano command.

6. "Cometerán también delitos militares: [ . . . ] Los que atenten contra la unión de los revolucionarios, provocando la rivalidad entre los Jefes y formando divisiones y bandos armados" (Aguinaldo y Famy 1898).

7. The structure of these forms is such that after the parent generation (relative to Ego) only the immediate ancestors on the patriline of each parent are recorded. As a result, the information does not represent a complete picture of the forebears of Eskaya-identified people known to the NCIP. Further, if an Eskaya couple from an earlier generation were married but remained childless, their data would not be recorded in the genealogy forms. Likewise, if the couple had had children who

had not applied for IP status, the family line would not be on record. Indeed, early twentieth-century tax records from Biabas include names of some resident landowners who are not found among the genealogical materials. Nonetheless, there is a great deal of overlap between records such that members of the great-grandparent or great-great-grandparent generation (relative to the applicant) may be attested in four or more separate genealogy forms. As a result, the matrilines from the grandparent generation and earlier can be reconstructed in the database even if individuals without descendants may remain invisible.

8. All geneaological data is available at PARADISEC: https://dx.doi.org/10.4225/72/5705AEDCBC2F2.

9. I have listed municipalities of origin rather than the specific barangays within those municipalities in order to present a broader overview of migration patterns. In the case of Pilar, however, all nine ancestral individuals were from Lundag.

10. Although no record has come to light indicating that Mariano Sumatra was a wanted man, the inhabitants of Loon had apparently established a reputation for disappearing into the mountains to avoid the law. The entry for Loon, in a Spanish gazetteer of 1851, included this curious observation: "The character of these natives [of Loon] does not belie that of their ancestors on the island. They are very unruly and some are in the habit of running off with the *remontados*, those Indians who penetrate the interior of the island, living in the mountains and the wilds of the forests" ("El carácter de estos naturales no desmiente el de sus antepasados de la isla, son muy indómitos, y algunos suelen fugarse con los remontados, que son aquellos indios que se internan en la isla, habitando los montes y espesuras de los bosques") (Buzeta and Bravo 1851, 167–168).

11. Reynaldo Ileto's brief history of the cholera epidemic in the Philippines argues that emergency sanitation measures were experienced by Filipinos as a continuation of the Philippine–American War. Ileto points out that in many cases, quarantine restrictions in Luzon made it difficult to sell harvests, encouraging field laborers to resort to banditry or outright insurgency. Further, cholera epidemics gave impetus to mystical healers "who attracted villagers away from town centers" (Ileto 1995).

12. Church records indicate that a certain Bonifacio Datahan was born in the Guindulman region in 1901. Bonifacio may have been a son of Mariano Datahan or of one of his brothers who took on the Datahan name. The record appears in FamilySearch.org batch B05298-4, source film 1969164. In any event, all those in Biabas with the family name of Datahan are related to Mariano.

13. In the first decade of the new century Datahan established parishes in Catagdaan, Bagacay, Bayong, Cantaub, Nan-od, Matin-ao, Boctol, Mayana, Laca, Bangwalog, Botong, Omjon, Capurao, Cadapdapan, and Tambongan. He also had a hand in establishing parishes in Loon's barrio of Biasong and in Candijay (Map 3; Moreno 2005), which was later to become the headquarters of the IFI in Bohol. Juan

"Pilimon" Beronilla and Tomas Tambayaon were among other former rebel leaders of Bohol who became advocates for the independent church at this time (L.B. Tirol 1975, 273).

14. Stuntz clearly disapproved of Aglipay's Church on doctrinal grounds and cannot be considered an impartial observer, but he was not altogether dismissive of Aglipay, whose anti-Rome stance was ultimately seen as beneficial to the American missionary project.

15. "El pueblo de Candijay es una excepción, es como una mancha negra en aquel campo de blanquísima nieve. Es uno de los pocos pueblos de Bohol, en que echó profundas raíces el Aglipayanismo, arrastrando consigo a una parte considerable del pueblo. Este que podríamos llamar fenómeno, observado en Candijay pueblo vecino a otros modelos de fe, tiene fácil explicación, cuando se conoce la manera de ser del filipino pobre, siempre sumiso, por no decir esclavo, del Sr. Principal. He aquí el por qué de ese fenómeno. Hay allí un Capitán pasado que, bien por soberbia, bien por lo que sea, levantó desde un principio bandera por el Aglipayanismo, construyó su Iglesia, puso su Sacerdote o el más propiamente llamado en el País, Padre-Padre, o sea, uno que tiene apariencias de algo y no es nada, y tras de el Capitán se fueron por el temor muchos de sus habitantes" (Ruiz 1925, 742–743).

16. "Sanglit ang mga lumulopyo sa Biabas mga Eskaya man ug Aglipayano, sila gibugalbugalan nga kuno sila '*sobrang nagpatootoo*' ug mga '*culto*.' Daghang mga ngalan ang gibugalbugal kanila '*mga erehes*,' '*mga rizalistas*,' '*mini*,' '*paripari*' ug *mga ignorante*'" (Moreno 2005).

17. One specific cause for consternation was the appointment of an unordained man to the newly established role of *biki* or 'tribal bishop.' In April 2006, I attended a meeting addressing this issue that was convened by Bohol's Aglipayan supremo, Monsignor Robespierre Moreno. The meeting brought PIC priests to the church's Summer Camp in Tambongan, and Col. Roberto Datahan was invited to speak. Datahan explained that all the land in the vicinity was part of the *yutang timawa* ('land of unsubjugated people') and that Tamblot (see Chapter 2) was the first priest of Boholano's indigenous religion. Thus, he argued, the new "tribal bishop" belonged to a lineage that predated the Iglesia Filipina Independiente (IFP) and was in no way associated with the present clergy.

18. Across Oceania there are many comparable instances of Christianity being reimagined as a primordial and indigenous religion that predated colonial missionization. See. for example, Tomlinson & Makihara (2009).

19. "De aquí se deduce que, así como los monos pequeños parece que provinieron de la transformación de los lemúridos; y que los monos pequeños se transformaron en los monos grandes, el hombre pudo haber provenido del mejoramiento y desarrollo de los últimos. [ ... ] [Footnote:] El gorila es de mayor estatura y fuerza que el hombre; y hay monos sin cola que andan con dos pies" (Aglípay y Labáyan 1912, 23).

20. Strictly speaking, this tale is neither folklore nor historiography but a fictionalized piece of social criticism aimed at exposing the corruption of Spanish officials. For an excellent exegesis of it see Thomas (2012, 132–137).

21. Arens (1959, 363) wrote of a pulahan organization in Samar, "[ . . . ] the leader would say: 'Come back next week, your name will be submitted to Christ, if he accepts you, you will be a member.' When the day of final decision came, the applicant was led to a room with a curtained crucifix. This crucifix had been rigged up in such a way that by pulling a string the head of Christ would nod, or his leg jerk. The leader would submit the name of the applicant in a loud voice to Christ. After a while of anxious waiting, during which Christ was 'deliberating the case,' suddenly the head of Christ would nod. For the simple mountain people this was a tremendous experience [ . . . ]."

    In another example, "A cross was placed in a glass filled with water. The leader would say: 'Come back next week, if Christ accepts you, the cross will have grown to its double size in the glass.' Coming the following week the 'miracle' had happened, the cross had grown (replaced by a bigger cross in a bigger glass, bought in Manila), the applicant was accepted and contributed his little earnings to the exploiting leader, at the same time becoming a fanatical follower" (363).

    According to Reynaldo Ileto, José Rizal was also something of an illusionist, and his tricks were misconstrued as evidence of supernatural power (1982, 314).

22. "The present political conditions of this province are scarcely different from those of the year before. Complete peace and tranquility prevail. The only disturbance was the work of certain persons belonging to a group of discontented ex-insurgents who under the pretext of protecting the rights of their fellow-citizens against the vexations that might be caused them by the authorities and for the purpose of concocting cabals have formed a sort of party from among some of the residents of Dimiao, Valencia, Carmen, Bilar, Sevilla, Loboc, Garcia Hernandez and Jagna, the true purposes of which I have not yet been able to find out, though the presumption is that one of its ends is to exploit the ignorance and guilelessness of the people. They avail themselves of peaceful means and soft words to attract people to their ranks, and once the latter are members of the party they have contracted an obligation to obey all orders of the leaders and faithfully to continue members of the party forever afterwards, on pain of death. In view of this terrible menace persons tiring of the party and wishing to leave it desert by emigrating to other provinces" (*RPC* 1906, vol. 1, 201).

23. **Istu muy biriki ri Ispanyanhun kidi muy narilya ya muntun ya rimuy milagrul laning ya muntun ya biriki kun Ara puy Salbadur Munu amanu ya rimuy katsila' Ara Ara ya rimuy huganu ya Visayas Pilipin.**

    *Ang mga pari nga Ispanyanhun dili makahimu sa tinuuhan sa mga milagrus maingun sa tinuuhan sa biriki nga diyus kang Salbadur Munu ingnun sa mga katsila' diyusdiyus sa mga huganu sa Visayas Pilipin.*

24. Tirol has succeeded in unearthing the record of Datahan's release but not his arrest. The relevant archives have now been moved to Cebu City, and I have not been able to corroborate the finding; however, there is no reason to doubt Tirol's testimony on this matter.

25. Tirol has reported twelve wives (J.B. Tirol 1993c), and Orcullo ten (Orcullo 2004, 114).

26. Fabian Baja (born 1918) told Margarita Logarta that as a young man he had encountered an Eskaya speaker by the name of Tomas in Malaybalay, Mindanao. Tomas, who claimed to have been a former servant of José Rizal, encouraged Baja to return to Bohol and join Datahan's movement (Logarta 1981).

27. Marianito Luspo told me that Boholano leaders like Pedro Samson and Sabas Ligones were marginalized under the American regime and ended up as small-scale farmers. Luspo has conjectured that Samson acquired the Biabas property under the Homestead Act, but as for a possible friendship or alliance between the two men, he remains skeptical. As Samson was a well-educated lowlander, the gulf in social class would have presented a serious barrier.

28. This is clearly intimated in the report of January 1902, which describes him as "[t]he lieutenant of the barrio of Biaba," and in the *Sinopsis histórica* (Ruiz 1925), where he is described as a *Capitán*. The *Teniente del Barrio* (Spanish: 'district lieutenant') was the appointed leader of a local district, or barangay, and the executive of a small governing committee. Under American rule *tenientes* were subject to election, and the position was renamed *Capitán del Barrio* or 'Bario Captain.' This structure of local governance continues to the present where the position is now officially termed *Punong Barangay* ('Barangay Head'), although *kapitan* remains the preferred term in common Visayan usage.

29. The Japanese commanders punished the escape of William Knortz and his fellow escapees William Johnson, Robert Ball, and Jas S. Smith by executing three prisoners. Victor Mapes reports that in response to this retaliation Knortz became reckless in his tactics. On September 11, 1943, he approached a pier guarded by Japanese soldiers. When he was discovered, he escaped into the water but drowned under the excessive weight of his ammunition (Keats 1963, 304; Mapes 2000, 226).

30. The document in question records his mother's name simply as "Maria" (her actual name was Dominga Presentes) with no details of his father. According to Fr. Ted Torralba, it is common for death records to contain errors because the details are not usually completed by members of the grieving family. That Datahan was born of "Mary" with no natural father is thus not evidence that his followers believed him to be divine.

31. This information is taken from the official PBMA website http://allaboutpbma.webs.com/informationfaq.htm, accessed April 7, 2020.

32. The events were reported by C.B. Guingguing (1975a–f).

33. The interview appears within Martinez's documentary *Eskaya: Letters, language and the fourth war*, available at https://youtu.be/gAPRchgdjUo. Additional footage can be retrieved from PARADISEC via https://dx.doi.org/10.4225/72/587e317766add.

# 9 ESKAYAN REVEALED

## A SCENARIO

If the ancestor Pinay created Eskayan, how did his lost language return
to Bohol? In this chapter I direct my attention to the critical period
that followed the end of the Philippine–American War in Bohol and
the successful establishment of a universal public education system on
the part of the U.S. administration. This era of relative political stability was also a time of cultural introspection and national imagining. In
defiance of the new English-based education system, the veteran rebel
Mariano Datahan turned to the task of retrieving the *true* Visayan
language and script of Pinay, and of creating a canonical literature in
it. I make the case that a relatively small subset of Eskaya letters was
revealed to Datahan and his followers first, followed by a handful of
basic vocabulary items. Subsequently, the lexicon of Eskayan expanded
dramatically while the syllabary enlarged to over one thousand signs,
allowing the language to be fully functional for speech and writing.
At every stage, the painstaking retrieval of Eskayan was guided by the
familiar set of interdependent language ideologies encountered in earlier chapters: the precedence of writing over speech, the notion that
language is a conscious and natural product of the human intellect,
that it confers natural political rights, and that it is a bounded and
material object that can be lost and rediscovered.

How the process actually unfolded requires careful reconstruction. In Part II, my analysis of the Eskayan script, grammar, and
lexicon led to conclusions that are reconcilable with the traditional
understandings of the language's creative origins. The relative symmetry of Visayan and Eskayan grammatical systems, taken together with
the asymmetry of their lexicons, invites the supposition that Eskayan
lexical items were the result of deliberate innovation. This hypothesis
is reinforced by the strong evidence for a European influence in the
Eskayan writing system, phonotactics, and lexicon. In other words, if
Eskayan was the planned creation of Pinay, mediated or personified by

*The Last Language on Earth*. Kelly, Piers, Oxford University Press. © Oxford University Press 2022.
DOI: 10.1093/oso/9780197509913.003.0009

Mariano Datahan, then this would satisfactorily explain the form and structure of the language as it is found today. Although Pinay is described by some Eskaya as a pre-contact historical figure, the overwhelming evidence for *post*-contact innovation in Eskayan cannot be ignored. Either Datahan's reconstruction of Pinay's language resulted in extensive interference, or—as I have argued together with Fabian Baja—Datahan and Pinay are alternate manifestations of the same entity.

The previous chapter examined the life story of Mariano Datahan from his birth in Loon to his death in Biabas and its aftermath. Precisely how and when Pinay's language was revealed to him in the context of this narrative is harder to demarcate. What follows in this chapter is an attempt to integrate the archival and genealogical record with the Eskayan language and its associated literature, both oral and written. I argue that all these various sources bear the traces of Eskayan's revelation, even if there is no single "smoking gun" that points to the concrete circumstances in which the language came to light. For this reason, the present chapter presents a hypothetical scenario that is consistent with the available evidence, rather than a definitive or authoritative reconstruction. To put it differently, I have ventured a chain of plausible actions that could conceivably be contradicted by an alternative analysis of the same data or invalidated with the emergence of new evidence.

Although the dating of events surrounding the resurrection of Eskayan is hard to posit, the *order* in which elements of the language were revealed can be made with slightly greater confidence. Hilario Galambao supposed that Datahan first dictated Pinay's literature to his secretary Espredion Degracia (ca.1909–1959), followed by the alphabet. In my reconstruction I propose, conversely, that the primary **abidiha** was made known first and that it was used for writing in Visayan and, possibly, Spanish. The alphabet was used for recording the earliest traditional literature in Visayan as dictated by Anoy. After this, the lexicon of Eskayan was made known to Datahan, and this necessitated the translation of the existing Visayan texts into Eskayan. Of course, these stages in the process of revelation are not so much sequential as thematic. There is no reason to assume that all of the literature was created first, followed by a systematic translation into Eskayan; a certain amount of overlap and revision of earlier work must have taken place.

## The rise of English in Bohol as a catalyst for Eskayan

As recounted in the previous chapter, Datahan attended an elementary school in Loon in about the 1880s and was able to continue his education into his teenage years in the care of Spanish priests (Chapter 8). Being one of nine children in a poor fishing and herding family, his exposure to education was a rare privilege.

Literacy, as well as linguistic competence in Spanish, the Cebuano dialect of Visayan, and, arguably, liturgical Latin, was the likely byproduct of his work as a sacristan. If he had served the linguist Fr. Felix Guillén, as is probable, he might have been introduced to the basics of Latinate linguistic analysis. Guillén's pedagogical work *Gramatica Bisaya para facilitar el estudio del dialecto Bisaya Cebuano* was published in 1898 and thus may well have been in preparation while Datahan was his sacristan. Conceivably Datahan himself was an informant for the grammar.

Figures are hard to come by, but school education was limited in Bohol in the 1880s and 1890s. Public schools were located in the major towns, and a handful of religious schools offered education to no more than two thousand pupils (L.B. Tirol 1975, 250). Nevertheless, Datahan's acquisition of Spanish was reflected in a nationwide trend that saw Spanish-language competence triple in his lifetime, even if actual numbers remained small as a proportion of the population.[1]

Be that as it may, U.S. control of the island brought far more dramatic changes to education and the linguistic ecology of the Philippines. In August of 1901, the USS *Thomas* docked in Manila with around five hundred American teachers who were destined for employment in the newly established Department of Public Instruction. The so-called Thomasites, as these and subsequent waves of U.S. teaching staff were known, were entrusted with the task of delivering mass public education to the Philippines. Although a Spanish public education system had been in place since the 1860s, the U.S. administration greatly expanded the reach of public schooling and introduced a new curriculum with English as the medium of instruction.

Perhaps due to the fact that the Philippine–American War (September 1, 1900–December 23, 1901) was still playing out in Bohol at this time, none of the first contingent of Thomasites were assigned to Bohol. Within weeks of the war's end, however, two U.S. teachers arrived on the island to begin the work of retraining Boholano teachers for the new curriculum. The first municipal elementary school under the American system was opened in 1902 in Tagbilaran. U.S. schooling was soon rolled out across the island, and "night schools" for adults were also established and staffed. English instruction proved popular, such that by 1904 a full 20 percent of Bohol's town-based population, both adults and children, were enrolled in a school (L.B. Tirol 1975, 250). Teachers adhered to the curriculum used in the United States, but this was soon adapted to the needs of Filipino students. In addition to English, arithmetic, and literacy, children received "moral education" in the form of edifying stories read in class. Within adult classes, women were given instruction in domestic skills while men learned agricultural techniques and animal husbandry.

Disease and famine, dual legacies of the Boholano–American War, presented impediments to the progress of school expansion and English-language education. Almost all towns closed their schools in September 1902 due to a cholera outbreak, and some were not to resume until January of 1903 (*RPC* 1903, vol. 3, 740–741). Two years later, famine forced the closure of forty-two schools while rinderpest necessitated the quarantine of entire towns (*RPC* 1906, 203, 205). Between 1902 and 1906 numerous outbreaks of smallpox afflicted the island (L.B. Tirol 1975, 264). Despite these early hardships, the appetite for learning English in the new system grew sharply as Spanish lost its former appeal as a language of the educated Filipino elite. Nationalist claims that Spanish-language policy had been designed to oppress Filipinos were now being amplified in U.S. propaganda that promoted English as a more politically inclusive alternative. At the time of the 1903 census it was estimated that 10 percent of the general Filipino population could speak Spanish. Levels of English-language competence are unknown for Bohol, but by the time of the 1941 census, an estimated 27 percent of the national population spoke English as a second language while competence in Spanish had fallen to just 3 percent (Gonzalez 1980, 26).

It is likely that the first Biabas residents to receive English instruction were educated in or near Guindulman, which opened its first public school in 1902. New graduates of the school, and of other institutions that were later constructed in the surrounding barrios, were in an unprecedented position. In many cases they would have represented not only the first literate generation in their families but also the first to acquire competence in the language of administration.[2] Before long, children would have been asked by older family members to decode government documents and to facilitate interactions with American administrators. In this way, reading, writing, and basic legal literacy were firmly associated from the outset with the English language and with political power.

## How Pinay's language was revealed

Mariano Datahan was a linguistic rarity. Among Bohol's rural poor he would have been one of the very few who was literate. What's more, he was a speaker of Spanish with access to the prestigious Cebuano dialect of Visayan as well as the ritual language of liturgy. No doubt he would have watched this gradual cultural encroachment from the lowlands with a feeling of unease. With the steady rise of literate graduates in the southeast, including adult attendees of night classes, his position as the most educated man in Biabas was challenged. Here were peasants, like himself, acquiring both literacy and linguistic competence in a foreign language that now offered more prestige than Spanish. English was also on the rise on nearby Cebu, but at the same time the gradual rise of printed materials in Cebuano-Visayan, a process that began in the 1890s, was reaching its high-water mark with the publication of nationalist Cebuano-language newspapers and popular novels like Amando Osorio's *Daylinda* (see Chapter 7). Writing and publishing in the vernacular was both a relatively new experience and an act of political defiance.

Rather than confront the threat head-on, he chose to beat the Americans and Cebuanos at their own game. Datahan would have been aware that Filipinos were literate prior to Spanish contact, and no doubt the popular account of how the Spanish destroyed all evidence of native writing was also familiar to him. For Datahan, this period of great cultural insecurity demanded a return to a heroic and precolonial past whose robust native traditions were summoned to overcome the suspect knowledge systems imposed by foreigners. Now was the opportune moment to retrieve the true language of the island and restore it to prominence. Datahan offered the doubly colonized Boholanos—lowly speakers of "bad Cebuano"—an irresistible alternative to the exclusionary Spanish, the elitist Cebuano, and the interloping English. Here was a forgotten but distinctly Boholano tongue, wholly inaccessible to colonial administrators and their local collaborators.

## The script

Whether chanced upon in a cave, given to him directly by Pinay, or retrieved through direct inspiration, the **abidiha**, or primary alphabet, was to emerge first. Its outward form was both exotic and familiar: the letters $\mathcal{P}$ ('a'), $\mathcal{C}$ ('c'), $\mathcal{O}$ ('o'), $\mathcal{t}$ ('t'), and $\mathcal{V}$ ('v') appeared to be archaic reflexes of their Roman equivalents, while other symbols such as 'ñ' $\mathcal{M}$ were entirely out of the ordinary. Yet in its order and structure, the **abidiha** was in every way the measure of the alphabet that had been imposed by the Spanish. For each letter in Hispanic orthographies of Visayan there was a corresponding symbol in the **abidiha**, making it purpose-built for transliterating written Visayan, or indeed, Spanish sentences. In Spanish reference documents, indigenous Philippine alphabets (see Chapter 2) were arranged in a conventional order that placed $\mathcal{V}$ <a> at the beginning of the series, followed by $\mathcal{O}$ <b(a)>, $\mathcal{I}$ <k(a)>, $\mathcal{C}$ <d(a)>, etc. This gave rise to the term *abakada* in reference to Philippine writing systems, just as the Greco-Roman system is designated as an 'alphabet,' from the sequence Alpha and Beta. The term *alibata* has also been used for Philippine scripts, derived from the initial sequence of the Arabic alphabet: Alif, Ba, Ta.[3] The Eskayan word **abidiha** clearly follows the same etymological pattern as 'alphabet,' *abakada* and *alibata*, in that it is a compound made up of the three sequential letters of the Eskayan alphabet, even if they are not all contiguous: $\mathcal{P}$ [a], $\mathcal{B}$ [bi], $\mathcal{J}$ [di], and $\mathcal{H}$ [h]. If Pinay was the author of both the writing system and its systemization, then his coining of the term **abidiha** was perhaps calculated to invite comparisons with known alphabets and to assume for it an equivalent historical status (see also the words **atikisis** and **abisi** in Chapter 7).

The strong resemblance between the consistent pseudo-diacritic *k* [-k] and the Roman letter 'k' suggests that Pinay had access to Roman scripts that included it. In Hispanic orthographies of Philippine languages the sound /k/ was represented with 'c' prior to 'a' /a/ and 'u' /u/ and in syllable-final position, and with 'qu' prior to 'i' /i/. These conventions are still adhered to by older Boholanos; reformed Visayan orthographies that included 'k' for /k/ were never to become mainstream within the lifetime of Mariano Datahan.[4] The pseudo-diacritic *k* could well reflect the influence of English in its written form, post 1901. Even today, many older Boholanos use the letter 'k' for English words only.

I conjecture that the alphabetic characters of the **abidiha** were first put to use for representing Visayan before the lexicon of the Eskayan language had been fully revealed. After all, the restored alphabet included characters designed specifically for imitating orthographic features of written (Hispanicized) Visayan that cannot have been inspired by any phonemic analysis of Eskayan (Chapter 5). The twenty-one syllabic-only characters of the **abidiha** were a later addition, as were those recorded in the **simplit**. In the absence of dated historical texts in Eskayan there is no way to confirm this scenario, nor to ascertain whether the transition occurred over the space of a week or two decades, but it is the sequence of invention that requires the least explanation. It shows, moreover, that *writing* was likely to have been a central focus of the Eskayan project from the very beginning, and that language was secondary to it, a state of affairs consistent with Eskaya language ideologies that see writing as the primary and sacrosanct embodiment of language (Chapters 4 and 5).

Residents of Biabas say that the first Eskaya school was constructed in the 1920s and that prior to this time, lessons took place in Datahan's house. Just as the **abidiha** relied on the structure of Spanish orthography, Datahan's school system was a direct, if subversive, reproduction of the American model: students were divided by gender, and separate "night classes" were held for adults (Prologue). Classes in the Biabas school focused primarily on literacy in the writing system. Like his Thomasite rivals in the lowlands, who made use of "charts showing pictures of objects with the names of each, written below" (L.B. Tirol 1975, 251–252) (Fig. 9.1), Datahan or one of his aids made use of a chart or a blackboard to deliver the lesson, indicating each letter with a bamboo pointer as the pupils recited its name in unison.

My surmise is that in the early years, most of the traditional literature was not yet available for use in pedagogy, but texts like "Atikisis" and "The Spanish and Eskayan Alphabets" were ideally suited as literacy materials. Importantly, the letter symbols that are explicitly mentioned in these texts all belong to the **abidiha** and not the **simplit**, which, I argue, was yet to be developed. The content of the two texts appeared to both mimic and mock the American teaching method that mnemonically associated letters with either the objects they resembled or words

FIGURE 9.1. A classroom in Luzon, early twentieth century. The top line of the chart reads 'This is my [hat] and my [cup]' (American Historical Collection, Ateneo de Manila; precise date and location unknown).

that they stood for. Consider how the following passage from "The Spanish and Eskayan Alphabets" (Chapter 7) echoes, in rhetorical form, the iconicity of letters in pedagogical charts:

> The Spanish alphabet has many different sources. There is a letter that represents a pair of steel scissors. Another is a candlestand from a church, another the heart-shaped sinker on a plumb line used in carpentry [ . . . ] Their first letter is the letter 'A,' taken from the festive archway erected over a thoroughfare [ . . . ].

Meanwhile, moral education, of the variety favored by the American school system, is paired with alphabetic literacy in "Atikisis," where each letter is the personification of various virtues and vices. The letter *ᴪ* ('a'), for example, "stands for industriousness and strength. Lazy hands lead to robbery, dishonesty, deceit, fraud, banditry and transience." The persistent references in this text to the value of hard work, planting, and good nutrition is perfectly consistent with the American educational program, which took great pains to emphasize the dignity of agricultural labor and healthy eating (Racelis 2001, 10–11). Appropriately, the letter *ᵯ* ('m'), perhaps for 'Mariano,' is described as "the source of all Bisayan [Eskaya] literature, representing all kinds of words. It is adept at teaching, reading and study."

In time, Datahan's pupils would have gained full literacy in the **abidiha**, and it is possible that those of them who did not also attend American schools were literate exclusively in this system. In more recent times, Fabian Baja was reported to be literate only in Eskayan (see Chapter 3), and Hinlo observed in 1992 that literacy rates in Taytay were higher in the Eskayan script than the Roman alphabet (Hinlo 1992, 89).

Once the alphabetic characters of the Eskayan writing system had been developed, Anoy dictated more Eskaya literature, and the Eskayan lexicon began to be revealed. This process will be tentatively reconstructed later, but the probable effect of lexification on the expansion of the Eskayan writing system is worth reviewing in brief. As more Visayan stories were dictated and new and exotic words came to light, the twenty-five letters of the **abidiha** began to seem inadequate. At first a set of twenty-one syllabic symbols were appended to the original alphabet, some of which would have facilitated the transcription of Visayan stories since they stood for common Visayan function words like *sa* ('to' $\mathcal{P}$ ) and verbal affixes like *ning-* (AV.RE.PFV; *fife* ) and *gi-* (PV.RE.PFV; *(-)* ). These alone, however, were soon deemed insufficient for the wide range of syllabic shapes found in the emerging Eskayan vocabulary. Thus, the **simplit**, a greatly expanded set of almost one thousand syllabic characters, was revealed. Again, a surplus of forms was preferable to a deficit. Variation exists among **simplit** reference documents used today, but the larger examples include up to six hundred characters for syllable shapes that are unattested in Eskayan words of which at least thirty-seven represent sound combinations that are not even permissible for Eskayan as it is used today (Chapter 5). Perhaps it was imagined that the revelation of Eskayan would be an ongoing process, and these symbols were recorded in order to preempt unforeseen syllable shapes for words that had not yet come to light.

## The lexicon

For the **abidiha** to be meaningful it required expression in more than mere teaching materials, and so began Anoy's recitation of stories. There is compelling evidence that most if not all of the stories were written in Visayan first, as I have mentioned in Chapter 4. Indeed, the reduced affixes and verbal suppletion for number and voice are so impenetrable at times as to make the accompanying Visayan text indispensable. Even more tellingly, the traditional narratives in Visayan include embedded Eskayan words and phrases that are designed to exemplify how the language used to be spoken in former times. When rendered in Eskayan, these passages become nonsensical on their own terms. Further, the "sneak preview" examples of Pinay's language resist satisfactory morphological analysis, even with the aid of an accompanying translation (Chapter 6). All this suggests that Eskayan was not fully developed at the time Anoy's literature was dictated, and that these embedded examples were offered as tantalizing fragments of a nascent language. Table 9.1 is a list of the Eskayan words that are explicitly glossed or otherwise explained in Anoy's literature and thus could be regarded as among the first Eskayan lexemes to have been revealed to Mariano Datahan. Of

**Table 9.1. The earliest Eskayan words and phrases**

| | |
|---|---|
| **aspurmus minimi** | 'name of the letters' |
| **aya sam** | 'where are you going?' |
| **baganhunda** | 'judge' |
| **bagani hibir** | 'general' |
| **baganibagani** | 'dictator' |
| **baganiring** | 'major general' |
| **balinsiya** | 'female orangutan' |
| **bandi** | 'flag' |
| **bansithi** | 'governor' |
| **bilik** | 'beautiful' |
| **birsirdas** | 'female teachers' |
| **Buul** | 'Boholano' |
| **Buuw** | 'Bohol' |
| **guwagu** | 'large' |
| **guwagu balsa** | 'large wooden boat' |
| **hibir** | 'major general' |
| **hining sirdas** | 'a nun of the third rank' |
| **inmunsiktur** | 'pope' |
| **ipilis** | 'real people' |
| **iribilis** | 'animals' |
| **isirdas** | 'female teacher' |
| **Marabuyuk** | 'Maribohok' |
| **Minalki biki Pilipin Visayas** | 'There were a great number of Philippine Visayan leaders' |
| **mirikilyu** | 'doctor' |
| **nuku** | 'itch-mite' |
| **Pangaw** | Panglao |
| **paypaypling** | 'butterfly' |
| **planu** | 'flag' |
| **puntri kul ga'up** | 'eleven cloth house' |
| **sapi duylan ya balsa guwagu** | 'They boarded their large wooden vessel' |
| **sirdas** | 'nun' |
| **sutbagani** | 'king' |

interest is the fact that most of these primary lexemes are nouns. Perhaps it was the case that their perceptual concreteness made them more accessible for early recuperation.

When Eskayan (or Bisayan Declarado, as it was then known) began to coalesce it was necessary to find lexical items to populate the vocabulary of the foundational Visayan-language texts. In this phase of development it was not just Anoy's dictated literature that was used as literary fodder for translation. A section of the Castañares Manuscript is a direct translation into Eskayan of part of a Cebuano-Visayan religious text. I have been able to identify the specific source as Fr. Gaspar Astete's 1885 catechism *Ang tocsaon sa pangadyeon nga cristianos* ('The catechism for Christian prayer'; Figs. 9.2 and 9.3). No other Eskayan versions of this catechism are known to me, and the text never became part of the Eskaya literary canon. Perhaps the Castañares translation was nothing more than an intellectual exercise, an application of Pinay's newly restored writing and language to a practical task.

Like the **abidiha**, the newly revealed Eskayan lexemes were poised between familiarity and strangeness. Most Eskayan lexemes had the appearance of Spanish or English borrowings into Visayan in both their syllable structure and their root length. For native speakers of Visayan, whose primary models of linguistic otherness were Spanish and English, the forgotten Boholano language would have conformed to a very local stereotype of "foreignness" but with enough phonological resemblance to Visayan to allow it to be pronounced with intuitive ease. I have linked this process of adopting and reconfiguring marked foreign features to postcolonial theorizations of "mimicry and rejection" (Chapters 1, 5, and 7). On a more localized scale, Eskaya techniques of creative coinage resonate to some extent with Zuckermann's account of phono-semantic matching in Israeli (Modern Hebrew) and other languages, in which neologisms are cleverly coined with input from more than one linguistic source. The result is a kind of subversive pun, which has the effect of either denigrating and excluding the referent, or of reclaiming and nativizing it (for examples see Zuckermann 2003, 2006).

Pinay was certainly familiar with Spanish and English, as demonstrated by the fact that certain Eskayan words are clearly inspired by counterpart lexemes in these languages, with no intermediaries in Visayan borrowings (Chapter 6). On the other hand, it is also plausible that the literary narrator 'Anoy' was an imperfect speaker of Spanish given that he misidentified *hari* ('king') as a Spanish word (Chapters 6 and 7), and his confusion of language and place in the story 'Pinay' ("In England they say 'American flag'") points to a naive understanding of the homelands of English speakers, if not the language itself.

The difficult process of extracting the new lexicon was mitigated by the structural correspondences between Eskayan and Visayan grammars. This meant that

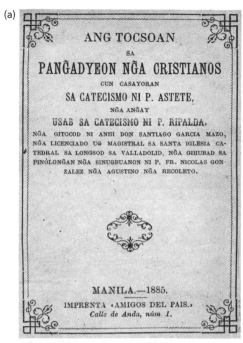

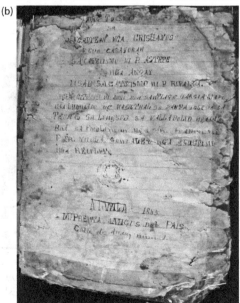

**FIGURE 9.2.** Frontispiece of Astete's catechism (Panel A) and its reproduction in the Castañares Manuscript (Panel B).

(a)

## PAHAMATNGON SA MAGABASA.

Ingon ca matahom ang Religion nga cristianos
nga dili gayud mahimo nga dili higugmaon sa naila
na siya. Capatan ca tuig sa canunay nga pagpa-
maidpaid co,. nagpacaquita canaco nga matood
gayud quini. Gitinguha co gihapon ang pagsaysay sa pagtolonan nga cristianos sa mga longsod,
nga gipacurahan canaco, ug sa canunay gayud
naquita co nga ang pagbigugma sa atong Religion
magaagad gihapon sa pagila niana, ug sa paghibalo sa iyang mga pagtolonan; ug nga ang
pagtuman sa mga sogo niya magaagad usab sa
paghigugma niana: maingon nga, batoc niini,
naquita co usab nga ang dili pagtuman sa mga
sogo sa atong Religion, ug ang pagpasipala ca-
niya magacadaco nga agad sa pagcadaco sa
caculangan sa paghibalo ug pagila sa mga pagtolonan nga cristianos. Quini, nga naquita co
gayud sa acong duha ca mata, maoy nacapasi-
but canaco, nga magadayon aco sa pagsaysay sa

(b)

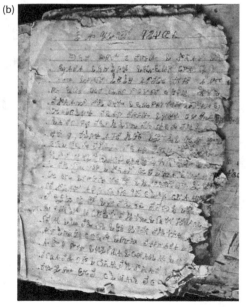

FIGURE 9.3. An early page of Astete's catechism. In the Castañares version (Panel B),
the heading is a direct transliteration of the Visayan words *Pahamatngon sa magabasa*
('Advice to the reader') while the ensuing text is a translation into Eskayan.

recovered Eskayan words could simply be substituted for Visayan words and occupy their equivalent semantic space. Nonetheless, the scribe would have had to make sure that any given Visayan word was consistently represented with the same lexical item across texts. This might have been reasonably practicable with high-frequency words like *ang* (**istu**; 'the'), but rarer lexemes would have been harder to keep track of. The question of morphology would also have presented an early challenge. Should Visayan morphemes be provided with consistent counterpart morphemes? How should the relationship between Visayan cognates be reflected in Eskayan? And what would constitute a correct and sufficient segmentation of Visayan in the first place?

Several solutions presented themselves. The first was to compile wordlists to serve as a database for the emergent Eskayan vocabulary. Here the revelation of Eskayan followed a precedent set by the early Thomasite teachers. As discussed in Chapter 6, the very first American teachers in Bohol worked closely with native teachers who had been trained under the Spanish system. New course materials were produced by taking the bilingual Visayan–Spanish texts from the previous curriculum and adding an English translation (L.B. Tirol 1975, 251). Documentary evidence suggests that Datahan, or his scribes, took a similar approach with the Eskayan lexicon. Indeed, one of the earliest Eskayan wordlists available, attributed to Domingo Castañares, appears to be a modification of an already modified Spanish–English–Visayan document. However, the vocabulary made available through such ready-made templates both exceeded the task of relexification and fell short of it. Predictably, there were words in the list that were not attested in the traditional literature, while many lexical items found in the literature did not feature in the wordlists. The chief goal of relexification was the translation of Anoy's Visayan literature into Pinay's language. Lexical items that could not be found in the Visayan wordlists to hand would have needed to be identified, extracted, and assigned Eskayan counterparts. Rather than isolate the root in such morphologically dense Visayan words as *gipuslan* ('was taken on'; Chapter 6) and provide them with equivalent Eskayan segments, it was easier to represent them with a relatively arbitrary and unanalyzable counterpart such as **bintaal**. After all, the Spanish and English words in available wordlists did not seem to follow any morphological patterns that were intuitive to a speaker of Visayan. Eskayan "suppletion" was thus, at least in part, a practical response to the problem of how to deal with complex morphology in the relexification process. Similarly, Eskayan needed only five verbal affixes in order to represent, minimally, twelve counterparts in Visayan. Thus, the problem of how to analyze a morphologically complex verb could be solved with recourse to multipurpose Eskayan affixes that collapsed more than one function (Chapter 6).

A related principle of relexification was to treat the phonetic form of the word as having a direct and regular relationship to its referent. Thus, homophonic pairs in Visayan were represented with dual homophones in Eskayan. No Eskayan word was permitted to have the same phonetic shape as a Visayan word unless the semantics differed. Equally, there could be no semantic equivalence between lexemes in each language unless the phonetic form was changed (Chapter 6). In such a way, the lexicons were like two sides of a single coin, allowing no scope for cross-lexical ambiguity.

But even with careful oversight, errors and redundancies were always going to arise. Despite the grid-like overlay of the two lexicons, certain Visayan glosses ended up with more than one Eskayan synonym. In some cases, the use of colonial wordlists as relexification aids was to blame. In Spanish and English, the words *luna* ('moon') and *mes* ('month') are both covered by the Visayan term *bulan*; however, Eskayan lexicographers reproduced the European distinction—**kuldu** ('moon'), **ngari** ('month')—probably because they were influenced by the template they were working from in this instance (Chapter 6). Many other synonyms such as **iskrit** and **kuwir** for 'school,' **dudu** and **bril** for 'horse,' and **kabrum** and **hus** for 'water buffalo' are more likely the result of the difficulty in monitoring the expansion of the lexicon: it is possible that Pinay revealed different words to more than one scribe, or that a single lexicographer was unable to effectively cross-reference the growing body of literature. Redundancies would soon have become apparent, but having a surplus of Eskayan words was always preferable to a deficit. In one curious example, an Eskayan scribe was confronted with the problem of translating the following Visayan sentence from Anoy's story "The First People in the Land of Bohol":

| *Ningbansag* | *Tugpa* **baganiring,** | *kumandanti hiniral* | *sa kinatsila* |
|---|---|---|---|
| ning-bansag | Tugpa baganiring | kumandanti hiniral | sa kinatsila |
| AV.RE.PFV-name | Tugpa baganiring | kumandanti hiniral | GEN Spanish |

'Tugpa was named **baganiring,** or *comandante general* in Spanish.'

The term *comandante general* ('major general') presented a dilemma. In order to retain the sense of the sentence, any Eskayan translation would have to preserve the term in its original Spanish form. To insist on an Eskayan-only text would result in a nonsensical literal translation, along the lines of 'Tugpa was named **baganiring** or **baganiring** in Spanish.' Instead, the translator found a surplus synonym **hibir**, perhaps to avoid resorting to obvious Spanish or Spanish-inspired Visayan words in this instance:

| **Chdinripuwir** | **Tugpa baganiring** | **hibir** | **ya kinatsila.** |
|---|---|---|---|
| chdin-ripuwir | Tugpa baganiring | hibir | ya kinatsila |
| AV.RE.PFV-name | Tugpa baganiring | hibir | GEN Spanish |

'Tugpa was named **baganiring** or **hibir** in Spanish.'

But by lexifying the Spanish term with an Eskayan equivalent the logic of the phrase collapsed in translation. Further, the principle of finding Eskayan equivalents for foreign lexemes at all costs was violated moments later by a failure to lexify the Visayan word *kinatsila* ('Spanish,' formed via Spanish *Castilla* 'Castile' and the language-making infix *-in-*) with an Eskayan alternative. Rebuilding the traditional literature with Pinay's language was clearly no easy task, and linguistic purism was not a reliable guiding principle.

Literary translation and the annotation of foreign wordlists were not the only methods used for releasing vocabulary. The Peligro wordlist begins with a heading 'Signs for the names of kitchen items' (*Timaan sa mga ngalan butang sa kusina*; **Intira ya rimuy rilangis ya gawpir ya sudalpu**) followed by a Visayan–Eskayan wordlist of over thirty common domestic objects and activities. Among these are terms with no straightforward Spanish or English equivalents such as **kuchda'ung** (*hungut*, 'bowl made out of three-quarters of a coconut shell') and **iklawkus** (*lalan*, 'to eat food unaccompanied by staples'), suggesting that lexification of these terms was not prompted by Spanish or English wordlists. Further, the inclusion of so many domestic items and the relative scarcity of Eskayan words relating to agriculture and animal husbandry point to the possibility that relexification occurred in a domestic environment and may well have been largely the responsibility of women. After all, in addition to his fourteen wives, Datahan had a least one female scribe in the person of Faustina Viscayda. The fascinating inclusion of the expression **warma** ('Don't lose it!') in the Peligro wordlist may corroborate this view. Its Visayan gloss is *wad-a*, a derivation of *wala'* ('none'), belonging to a Visayan 'baby talk' register used almost exclusively by mothers to their young children. The unsegmentable term **salwis** is glossed as *midyasi* ('put your socks on!'), a distinctly maternal command. One final, curious example of an Eskayan term that was neither prompted by a wordlist nor derived from literary translation is **grumpir** (*nagpanaku* [root: *tuku*]), of which the Visayan gloss means 'for a girl to keep her partner at arm's length in dancing' with a secondary meaning of 'to be hesitant to do something out of propriety.'

In Bohol, and probably elsewhere, Filipino students in the Thomasite schools used "copybooks" as a literacy development technique. These books displayed passages in English to be recopied line by line in an exercise book (Borja 2001). Those of Datahan's students who had attended American schools would already have had some practice in the faithful transposition of an authoritative text to a fresh page.

However, the fact that Pinay's emerging language was immediately recorded in writing did not mean that it was frozen in time. As I have shown, transcription errors are a driver of language change in Eskayan (Chapter 6), and wordlists exhibit curiosities that point to possible misreadings. For example, in the Peligro wordlist the term **purmu** is glossed as both *abug* ('dust') and *abut* ('arrival'), suggesting a mistaken decipherment of the final letter at some point in the recopying process. In the Castañares Manuscript, the item '*niño,ña*—child' is glossed in Eskayan as **sabana** 'stone,' a likely misreading of the supplanted Visayan gloss, which was probably *bata* ('child') and not *batu* ('stone'); it is of course possible that the error was made in the source document and not the annotated Eskayan version. On one occasion I was able to witness this kind of lexical replacement happening before my eyes. When working on a translation of the Castañares Manuscript from an enlarged and printed scan, a consultant was critical of the entry 'quemar—to burn—*ꝉȯ C ở* [**yuwisu**].' Violating the proscription against crossing out, he ran a line through *ꝉȯ C ở* and replaced it with *ℓꝗ ꝗ Ȯ Ȯ* [**iklabultu**] ('be born'). It is easy to confound 'burn' and 'born' since 'u' and 'o' represent the same phoneme (/u/) in mainstream orthographies of Visayan. No doubt my own documentation of Eskayan vocabulary and literature over the years has been imperfect and may in time contribute to the ongoing process of lexical replacement and diversification.

As Eskayan lexemes have undergone change and diversification, some of their Visayan glosses have remained fixed in time. One example, discussed in Chapter 7, is the Visayan word *kagaw* (**nuku**), which has long ceased to mean 'itch-mite'; today its primary meaning is 'germ,' and no Eskaya scribes I interviewed were aware of this earlier sense recorded in nineteenth-century dictionaries. Other Visayan words in Anoy's literature, like *higupanan* (**mubir**; 'something from which one sips a liquid') and *banus* (**chdinchdin**; 'always'), are understood but recognized as archaic. The word *masisiwa* (**arira**), which features in "The Itch-mite Tumaw" has gone out of use entirely, and no person or text has been able to illuminate its meaning. The presence of archaic and obsolete Visayan terms in Eskaya literature indicates that the stories could not have been dictated recently, but just how old they are is harder to judge as corpus-based historical studies of Visayan vocabulary are not available. Nonetheless, the actual content and the apparent sources of inspiration for Eskaya literature lend insight into the historical circumstances that preceded its dictation.

## Prophecy, prolepsis, and time depth in the revelation of Eskayan literature

In the turbulent years that followed the U.S. occupation, pulahan and colorum leaders in Luzon, Samar, Leyte, and Mindanao were given to making prophecies of imminent natural or social calamities followed by spiritual redemption. These messages were appealing. Having endured war, famine, and disease on a scale not seen in living memory, followers of apocalyptic movements could well imagine the terrors described to them and were primed to expect more of the same. Above all, rural prognosticators were able to make mass tragedy appear both meaningful and inevitable. The traumatic waste of life and livelihood could be framed as a shared sacrifice for higher patriotic and spiritual rewards.

I conjecture that Anoy's dissemination of oral prophecies (Chapter 7) began before his written literature was produced. His predictions of earthquakes and volcanic eruptions (perhaps the material of his "fanatical speeches" in 1902) were of a piece with the prophecies issued by contemporary pulahan popes. With the arrival of the Americans, his warning that foreigners would one day till the soils would have been persuasive. Anoy's claim that water buffalo would become exorbitantly expensive was similarly topical. Due to rampant rinderpest across the Philippines, the value of water buffalo had increased tenfold in 1901 alone (Hurley 1938). Meanwhile, successful predictions of turn-of-the-century technologies—metal floating on water, light commanded from a switch—lent credibility to his more fantastical and apocalyptic visions.

But for Anoy, as for his pulahan contemporaries, future catastrophes were merely the birth pangs of a great spiritual renewal. One of his most oft-recalled prophecies is of a time when the hills would collide, and the eruption of an undersea volcano was to bring forth a golden church and a golden boat. While the church surfacing from the ground might well be a metaphor for the grass roots Aglipayan movement, this particular prophecy also recapitulated motifs of regional folklore. In local stories, a golden boat is said to be seen in some creeks of Bohol bearing a cargo of cocoa and coffee destined for an enchanted city (Aparece 2003, 105); versions of this tale are circulated in Cebu (Alburo 1980). Likewise, the emergence of a golden church from the earth perpetuates the theme of a subterranean treasure and its glorious retrieval (Chapter 7).

In this way, Anoy's oral prophecies appealed to shared contemporary experiences and well-known narratives as a means of explaining the present and anticipating the future. However, his much larger body of written literature, as dictated in Visayan to his scribes, enacted a complementary process. Long forgotten experiences of war, displacement, and cultural contact were unearthed from an ancestral past to be mediated via the imperishability of the written word. Whether discovered on carved wooden slabs, or retranscribed by divine inspiration, the written word was emblematic of deep cultural memory that had a profound prophetic relevance to the present. Anoy's stories acted as a cogent mnemonic to lived history. The ancestral Eskaya people under Dangko are described as coming from the west of Sumatra to intermarry with the native population of

Bohol, just as the Eskaya under (Mariano) Sumatra were to come from the west of Bohol to intermarry with the people of Tambongan and Biabas. The capture of Guindulman by the Spaniards in "The First People in the Land of Bohol" was to be recapitulated by the American and Japanese occupations of Guindulman, perhaps fulfilling the 'omen' (**ripuwir;** *bad-un*) hinted at in this tale. The direct evangelism of the Holy Child in AD 32 preceded the degenerate Catholicism brought with the planting of Magellan's cross in Cebu. And Tamblot's religious war against Spanish Christianity, as told in "The White Bell," prefigured the *dyus-dyus* conflicts of *ladrones fanaticos* directed against American colonizers. Even Tumud's recovery of the bell may have been partially inspired by an actual event. In 1908 it was reported to the Philippine Commission that Aglipayan activists in Quimaya, Mindanao, had removed the bell from their local Roman Catholic church and installed it in their own church, where it remained until American administrators intervened (*RPC* 1908, vol. 1, 205). Whether Datahan was ever aware of this parallel incident may never be known.

If the written literature is ultimately a proxy for present events, then this raises the question of when the stories were dictated. Any notion that the tales are pristine pre-Hispanic accounts, as maintained by Abregana and others (Chapter 3), is easily dispensed with. After all, almost all the stories mention conflict with the Spanish and include such post-Hispanic historical figures as Tamblot, Dagohoy, and Tugpa. Even the origin myth "The Itch-mite Tumaw" is decidedly post-contact in its inclusion of Christian imagery and nonnative animal species such as lions.

If certain of the narratives took inspiration from recent historical events of local significance, such as the flight from Loon, pulahan conflicts, and Japanese occupation, then it can be presumed that these accounts were written after the events that informed them. One narrative in particular can be positively dated as post 1913. "Daylinda," not analyzed in the present study, is a tragic love story set against the backdrop of Magellan's landing. In many of its particulars it is influenced directly, inspired by the Cebuano-Visayan novel *Daylinda: Ang walay palad* [Daylinda, the ill-fated], published by Amando Osorio in 1913 and performed as a play in Loon the following year (Osorio 1913). Accordingly, Anoy's retelling of Osorio's novel, which he restaged in Bohol rather than Cebu, could have been penned any time after 1913 but not beforehand.

My reckoning is that many of Anoy's surviving texts were written down for the first time as late as the 1930s and 1940s, as implied by the recollections of his longest surviving scribe, Eleuteria "Faustina" Viscayda (1924–2009). In Viscayda's account, as documented by Martinez, "Anoy Datahan would sit through the night and narrate tales in Ineskaya, and [ . . . ] [Viscayda], then a young lady, would copy them down" (Martinez 1993, 79; Chapter 7). Since linguistic evidence indicates that the stories were written in Visayan first, my supposition is that Viscayda was referring to the Eskayan script as *Ineskaya* and not specifically the language. As discussed earlier, a local literacy ideology holds that script and language are one and the same; thus, any words written using the script are regarded as "Eskayan" (Chapter 5). Since Viscayda was born in 1924, her transcription is unlikely to have taken place before the mid-1930s, as she would have been too immature to be employed as a competent writer, even if literacy was skewed toward the younger generations. When Brenda Abregana later claimed that, according to her informants, the "Old Books" had not been seen since 1932 (see Chapter 3), she may well have been inadvertently reporting an approximate date of origin for the texts.

What all this suggests is that if Anoy's literature was still being transcribed by the likes of Viscayda in the mid-1930s, and these documents were written in Visayan, then the revelation of the Eskayan lexicon is more likely to have occurred at about this time or after, even if a writing system was already available. Such an estimation would accord with the earliest datable reference to "Boholano dialect" in the letter of Jorge Vargas of November 1937. Notably too, the subsequent transcription of his reply involved at least one positive lexical innovation. The placename 'Manila,' attested in the Eskayan translation of Vargas' letter as **Mandi** ('Mande,' Fig. 1.4), has no precedent in any Eskayan story, suggesting that lexical revelation was still occurring in this period.

## Summary

The speculative scenario I have outlined here cannot be verified in all of its particulars, but at the very least it suggests that the first encoding of the Eskayan language and script was a fraught undertaking. Since we know the identities and ages of Datahan's key scribes, it is possible to estimate that the traditional literature was dictated at a time when English-language education was expanding in Bohol. At this time, Datahan began to channel traditional stories and histories, and within these emergent Visayan-language texts, individual Eskayan words and phrases slowly came to the surface. Soon it would become necessary to back-translate the entire corpus of texts into their authentic and original language and script. When the Eskayan alphabet, or **abidiha**, was first revealed it was used for representing Visayan and Spanish words, but it was soon joined by over a thousand syllable signs. As full-scale linguistic revelation took place, scribes began entering the new Eskayan words into wordlists that were modeled on Spanish and English pedagogical texts. Other words and phrases came to light in a domestic environment without support from existing templates. This was a collaborative task and one that was difficult to coordinate. Standardization was not consistently enforced, if at all, and many referents ended up with more than one acceptable lexeme. The script, too, exceeded the task it was designed for and expanded so fast that it incorporated many more signs than were strictly necessary for representing Eskayan and Visayan syllables. The resulting language and script were arguably imperfect and in many ways overwrought, but they were also a monumental accomplishment. Ushered into the world at the hands of humble farmers and fisherfolk, whose families had never had the benefit of formal education, Pinay's language became their defining intellectual legacy, a worthy testament to Boholano ingenuity and cultural resilience.

## Notes

1. The census of 1870 noted that 2.46 percent of the population were speakers of 'Castilian.' By the time of the 1903 census this figure had risen to 10 percent (Hau and Tinto 2003).
2. In the 1860s, a mere 5 percent of the population would have had access to formal literacy, but by 1918, 49 percent of the population was classed as literate, and by the time of the 1948 census this figure had jumped to 61 percent (Kelly 2016c).
3. It is regularly asserted that the term *alibata* arose out of a mistaken belief that the Philippine script has an Arabic lineage. In fact, the term can be reliably attributed to Paul Rodriguez Verzosa, who claims to have coined it in 1914 by "basing it on the three MAGUINDANAO (Moro) arrangement of letters of the alphabet after the Arabic: ALIF, BA, TA (Alibata) 'F' having been eliminated for euphony sake" (Verzosa 1939, 12). Verzosa was, moreover, aware of the Indic origins of the script, and the Arabic sequence was adopted merely as a ready-made convention.
4. Rizal himself advocated spelling reform of Tagalog in 1890, and his phonemic orthography included the letter 'k' for /k/. Rizal's use of 'k' was exotic enough to be derided by one Manila journalist as a "German" imposition (Thomas 2012, 157).

# 10  CONCLUSION: THE FIRST LANGUAGE AND THE LAST WORD

Just eight years before Brenda Abregana had encountered what she believed to be a lost civilization in the highlands of Bohol, an anthropological discovery of far greater international consequence had been made less than 300 km to the south. Deep in the impenetrable jungles of Mindanao a millionaire playboy and high-ranking government advisor announced the discovery of an uncontacted "Stone Age" tribe. The territory that the tribe occupied in the South Cotabato province could only be accessed by a vertiginous rappel through high jungle canopy from a hovering helicopter, a fact that did nothing to dissuade visits from gung-ho international journalists, and celebrities such as Charles Lindbergh and Gina Lollobrigida. Extraordinary images of the Tasaday, as the group came to be known, were soon published in the pages of National Geographic and elsewhere, enchanting an international public weary of the daily traumas in Vietnam (Fig. 10.1). Wearing only banana leaves and using hafted tools, the tiny community of less than thirty individuals was depicted in a state of harmony with the environment. For sustenance they harvested insects, lizards, and frogs and were ignorant of the world beyond their jungle domain. Among the specialists who observed and described the group was Jesus Peralta, head of the expedition that would later visit and assess the Eskaya. Trained linguists did not interview the Tasaday, but it was nonetheless reported that their language had "no words for war" (MacLeish 1972, 226, 242; Nance 1975, 75).

## Imagining indigeneity from above: The view from the helicopter

The media love affair was cut short in 1976 when the Marcos regime closed the Tasaday territory to outsiders by presidential fiat. Although researchers had had less than six months to observe and comment

*The Last Language on Earth*. Kelly, Piers, Oxford University Press. © Oxford University Press 2022.
DOI: 10.1093/oso/9780197509913.003.0010

**FIGURE** 10.1. An NBC film crew visiting a cave of the Tasaday in March 1972. In the bottom right is Manuel Elizalde, the millionaire who first publicized the contact event. Republished with permission from the Estate of John E. Nance.

on the community, the authenticity of the group as a remnant pre-contact society was abruptly called into question. There were accusations of unscrupulous anthropological practices and high-level meddling. Critics declared the Tasaday to be a government-sponsored hoax, an elaborate and bizarre contrivance whose only purpose was window dressing for an unpopular regime. It was alleged that local Manobo farmers had been paid to present themselves as tribespeople and perform for the cameras. Those who had researched the group were characterized as unwitting dupes at best and conspirators at worst. The ensuing controversy over the anthropological status of the Tasaday continued to bubble long after the conjugal dictators were deposed, and taking "sides" became less about the most satisfactory interpretation of the limited data than it was a matter of political allegiance.

Later investigations have problematized the "real" versus "fake" binary that continues to dominate the Tasaday debate. Linguist Lawrence A. Reid analyzed tapes of spontaneous Tasaday speech, and his evaluation of the evidence is consistent with the hypothesis that the Tasaday community had split from Manobo speakers and remained in isolation for around 100–150 years (Reid 1992, 1996), a view supported by genealogical evidence (Nabayra and Rogel-Rara 1992). If not exactly ancient, the Tasaday were nonetheless a genuinely isolated community and could not have simply been contrived as such for a gullible audience. In true Zomian style, Tasaday oral histories also maintained that their ancestors had fled to the jungle to escape a lowland epidemic, the same circumstance that would later motivate the ancestors of the Eskaya to evacuate Loon and rebuild their lives in Biabas. Robin Hemley's (2004) compelling book about the affair brought to light the complex and often confused motives of early Tasaday critics, as much as it questioned the idealized representation of the Tasaday to a public that was all too eager to indulge in romantic fantasies of premodern innocence.

These important counter-criticisms to the standard "hoax" narrative have permitted a degree of complexity to enter the Tasaday debate. For many social scientists, the locus of enquiry has, by way of consequence, shifted away from the Tasaday and back onto their would-be ethnographers. Who exactly was it that we needed the Tasaday to be? And why were we so disappointed when they failed to occupy the cherished categories we had built for them? In addressing these questions anthropologist Jean-Paul Dumont went so far as to declare that "there are no Tasaday per se, but only a social and symbolic relationship, and it is the only analysable reality here," urging an exploration of "the semiotic conditions that lead to the inevitability of such a 'discovery'" (Dumont 1988, 267). Regardless of where you stand, he argued, the Tasaday remain a discursive construct of our own making.

Publicity for the Eskaya could never hope to reach the same sensational heights as the Tasaday story. First championed by a reclusive mystic of limited means, the Eskaya failed to interest a wide audience; even within Bohol news of the Eskaya was poorly disseminated. Nevertheless, when the people of Taytay first became an object of scrutiny in the early 1980s, the reactions echoed, to some extent, popular responses the Tasaday discovery, and both events even had overlapping dramatis personae.[1] Disconnected from town centers and coastal networks, the isolationist community of southeast Bohol become a screen onto which lowlanders projected their fantasies of an uncolonized and uncorrupted Boholano society. As custodians of indigenous texts in an inscrutable language and script, the Eskaya were imagined as all things at once. They were backward and uncorrupted, innocent and wise, intrinsically Boholano and exotic. Their language was alternatively Greek, Hebrew, or indigenous, and their writings were both sacred scriptures and historical documents.

But just as the Tasaday had been "outed" by critics, the Eskaya were very quickly accused of participating in an anthropological confidence trick, albeit on a smaller scale. As it happened, both the Eskaya and the Tasaday communities came to light during the Martial Law period (1972–1981), at a time when the virtues of truth and innocence were in short supply. Anyone could be suspected of running an ulterior agenda and indeed, in the case of the Tasaday, both the supporters and detractors of the "Stone Age" narrative overreached dramatically in their depictions of the situation. What all the various players had in common ideologically, however, was an appreciation of indigeneity as an authentic mode of being, a much-desired counterbalance to the perceived artifice of modernity. Ultimately, it was the failure of the Tasaday and the Eskaya to live up to the demands of indigenous authenticity, as defined by lowlanders, that provoked a crisis. To this day, the association of a counterfeit Tasaday tribe with an illegitimate regime remains dominant, and there is still widespread resistance throughout the Philippines to any alternatives to the hoax narrative. Similarly, the persistent question "Is Eskayan real?" (Prologue) can be seen as a product of the political disenchantment that prevailed at the time of the Eskaya "discovery," as much as a reflection of a lingering anxiety that isolated mountain communities might not occupy the subordinate roles assigned to them. Perhaps to their detriment, the Eskaya have always insisted that their language, if not their culture as a whole, is the product of the human creative intellect. If, ultimately, we accept this to be true of *all* cultural phenomena, there ought to be nothing radical or disturbing in such a proposition.

## The form of Eskayan and the identity of Pinay

My attempts to reformulate the question in more nuanced terms—"What story does the language tell us?," "What does this story mean?"—take a different point of departure to the real/fake or legitimate/illegitimate binaries imposed on the Eskaya from outside. From the outset, my study has sought to restore and examine traditional emic understandings of linguistic history as recorded in handwritten documents and oral testimony. As I have described, Eskaya historiographers contend that the language and script were created by the ancestral pope Pinay and had survived centuries of suppression by Spaniards and Cebuanos. From this perspective, the history of Eskayan cannot be disentangled from the biography of its presumed creator, of which the language itself is his sole legacy and a primary source of historical data.

I have argued that the Eskayan writing system was clearly influenced by the Roman alphabet and appeared to have been partially engineered for the transliteration of Spanish words, a fact that would place Pinay in the Spanish colonial period or after. Eskayan phonotactics are consistent with the syllable structures found in Visayan and especially in English and Spanish borrowings into Visayan, and the phonemicization and frequency of /ʤ/ point to a palpable east Bohol influence. The syntax and morphology of Eskayan are patterned on Visayan but with widespread verbal suppletion. As Visayan is largely non-suppletive, the most likely models for irregularity are the colonial languages Spanish and English, especially since glosses for these languages are included in the earliest surviving Eskayan wordlists. The lexicon, meanwhile, exhibits evidence of wholesale innovation across semantic domains, with slight but unambiguous inspiration from Spanish, Visayan, and English (Chapter 6). In effect, Pinay used Visayan as a grammatical matrix through which a complete lexicon of Eskayan coinages was expressed, and no Eskayan glosses were allowed to exceed the semantic mold of their designated Visayan counterparts. Moreover, the presence of a Spanish and English influence in core vocabulary, and its conspicuous absence in acculturation terminology, would place the bulk of the purported relexification in the posthispanic era. In this analysis, Eskayan is clearly a post-contact artifact, and the English influence, meager as it may be, would place its likely genesis sometime after the occupation of Bohol by English speakers in 1900. Such an interpretation is consistent with the traditional understanding that Pinay's sole mediator and spokesman was the Boholano–American War veteran Mariano Datahan (ca. 1875–1949).

As a language-engineering experiment, Datahan's revelation of Eskayan was guided by his understandings about the nature and potential of language. Its design features reflect an ideology that languages are grammatically "equal," even if they display minor but conspicuous irregularities in their verbal systems. For Datahan, the formal properties of languages exist in a hierarchy. What characterizes a language as truly *distinctive* is primarily its written form, followed closely by its vocabulary, then morphology and syntax. In his understanding, words have inherent meanings that are bound almost onomatopoeically to their phonetic shape and that are independent of context or morphology. Further, words refer to discrete universal referents that have definitive counterparts across languages. Datahan also appeared to recognize that languages exhibit lexical variability as dialects, are influenced by contact, and evolve over time even if ancestral forms are understood as more pure.

Arguably, Datahan's creation of a literary corpus was an act of relexification at a higher level. Literature would become not only the privileged vessel for the expression of language but a means of demonstrating its cultural value. Such an ideology was incidentally shared by the National Language Institute. A significant justification for the selection of Tagalog as a national language in 1937 was the ready availability of a corpus of Tagalog literature. Indeed, within Eskaya literature language was intimately associated with nationhood and independence.

A unique "native knowledge" was compared to a national flag with the implication that such symbols were functionally substitutable. To pursue the same analogy, the relexification of Visayan appeared to involve a symbolic reinscription whereby Eskayan lexemes were planted like flags on the natural and unchanging terrain of Visayan morphosyntax.

In Datahan's literature, language was characterized as a material "thing" that could be created and destroyed, lost and found, stored and retrieved, and fractured and reconstituted. But far from being a lifeless artifact, the Eskayan language was construed as an anthropomorphic entity created by humans in a human image. After all, Pinay did not receive divine inspiration but was *instructed* to create, leaving linguistic agency in human hands. Even the name 'Bisayan Declarado' suggests the performative act of declaration, an utterance invested with the power to change reality. Nevertheless, this creative act was by no means an entirely artificial intervention. In fact, to some extent the text entitled 'Declared Visayan' underplays creativity, emphasizing that naturalness of Eskayan writing and its associated language: "Not all Philippine letters were created," said Anoy, "because they are just there in the body of a Filipino person" (*Dili' tanan ang pagmugna sa litrang pilipina kay anaa ra man sa lawas sa tawu nga Pilipinhun*). Being "just there," Eskayan was depicted as a revealed human presence, rather than an artificial system.

On the other hand, a spark of supernatural or divine power lurked within the human. Eskayan words are the deus ex machina of the story "The White Bell"; the shaman's incantation reclaims the prized artifact, which is itself symbolic of a submerged pre-colonial culture. Simply uttering Bohol's true language was enough to conjure a once-glorious past into the present. A conception of language that is simultaneously anthropomorphic and divine—the **bidaryu ya Ara** ('language of God')—reflects biblical characterizations of "the Word" possessing its own miraculous power.

Though couched in miraculous terms, Eskaya people nonetheless regard language as a fundamentally material object. For Eskaya users today, writing is not merely substantive evidence for language: it *is* language. Just as language and script are understood as one and the same, no meaningful distinction is drawn between linguistic competence and literacy. Thus, the acquisition of language amounts to a process of formalized transfer with the aid of written pedagogical materials, a notion reinforced in Baja's etymology of **Eskaya'** as 'the people's teachings' (Chapter 7). The protocol that written Eskayan words must not be crossed out or stepped upon is perhaps reflective of an ideology that the graphic representation of language is an animate but fragile embodiment of meaning.

The conflation of language and writing system reinforces the presence of Eskayan as an exteriorized visible reality, indexical of a cultural whole. As Roger Keesing has argued with regard to Melanesian history, the experience of colonial invasion encourages communities to take stock of their powerlessness, prompting a more self-conscious perspective on their way of life. This gives way to a reassessment of culture as a reified object, a "thing" that can be proclaimed, accepted, or rejected (Keesing 1982). Among the Biabas community the intangible markers of identity—language, literature, and tradition—were made overt through the reifying act of writing, even if writing was also vulnerable to suppression at the hands of enemies, and with it the fragile indigenous identity it encapsulated. But the objectifying perspective of Eskayan is then turned back against colonial writing systems that are judged as inferior, along with the cultures they were held to index. Eskayan texts explain that Spanish is linguistically deficient because its writing system is based on frivolous domestic objects. By contrast, the anatomically derived Eskayan language is animate and anthropomorphic, and thus ultimately *less* alienable than its detached rivals.

Datahan's complex of language and literacy ideologies is clearly not confined to the Eskaya community. His projected split between a "universal" grammatical system and an arbitrary lexicon is a common folk characterization of language. Silverstein (2001) has pointed out that, cross-culturally, speakers tend to regard words as representing the core of language since it is this feature of language that is most psychologically prominent, and Joseph (1995, 2000) has traced a tradition in Western scholarship of assuming grammar to be "natural" while lexicons are "conventional" (see also McElvenny 2018).

The belief that writing confers political and empirical authority is witnessed in literate and nonliterate communities the world over, and this attitude is certainly in evidence in Bohol. To take one salient example, dissertations with an oral history component that are submitted to Bohol's two universities are typically accompanied by signed affidavits from the oral sources themselves. Likewise, the primacy given to discrete words, as opposed to structures, in popular ideas about what constitutes language, is in evidence in Visayan lexicographic practice where dictionary headwords are often morphologically dense. Calquing, or the literal word-for-word translation of foreign phrases, has any number of precedents in commonplace Visayan expressions, particularly greetings, phrases for telling the time, and quantifying formulas.[2] Thus, the Eskayan phrase **Griyalu aga** ('good morning') is a literal translation of the Visayan *Maayung buntag* ('good morning'), which is itself a calque of the Spanish *Buenos días* ('good morning', 'good day').

Likewise, the notion that language, particularly foreign or unintelligible language, has innate power was exemplified in the use of archaic ritual speech among

Boholano shamans, as well as Latin as a language of spiritual authority among Bohol's priests. Spanish, too, was the exclusive preserve of foreign authorities and educated *ilustrados*. Like Eskayan, these languages required mediation by elite practitioners, a fact that increased their prestige in the eyes of the uninitiated.

## Imagining indigeneity from below: The view from the village

Bohol's history has been marked by recurring conflicts between the original inhabitants of the island and those who would seek to dominate them. Past antagonisms have typically been historicized in military terms, from the quashed rebellions of Tamblot and Dagohoy, to the eventual downfall of Bohol's republican government. Yet Boholano resistance has also been expressed in a desire to revisit the precolonial past and to ponder what it might mean to be truly free, not only from military domination but also from the interpretive gaze of foreign overseers. When an outside agency wields enough power to cast its subjects in a new mold, there can be no question more subversive than "What if . . . ?"

The utopian impulse to validate pre-contact culture was rarely, if ever, expressed as an all-or-nothing proposition. In Bohol, both Tamblot and Dagohoy sought to reanimate indigenous political agency and spirituality, but they did so by experimenting with the symbols of Spanish authority, such as Christianity and civil government. Similarly, Tapar of Panay and the early-twentieth-century pulahanes throughout the Visayas created indigenous institutions of power by inhabiting Spanish ecclesiastic ranks that were accommodated and reformulated, rather than overthrown. Visayan syncretism was, on these terms, an act of counter-colonization in which Europe's popes and liturgies were compelled to serve the ends of an indigenous spirituality, rather than the other way around. Likewise, Mariano Datahan and his fellow *ladrones fanaticos* were able to recuperate a model of "pure" Philippine indigeneity that nonetheless checked off all the criteria for national legitimacy: a flag, a language and script, a religion, a system of laws, a History.

Datahan's special dialectic of "accommodation and resistance" (Tsing 1993, 71) was thoroughly embodied in the language he revealed. Even at the level of phonology, Eskayan is made to sound "foreign" as if a Visayan speaker were imitating or even mocking colonial languages. For Boholanos of the early twentieth century, Spanish and English were the primary models of linguistic otherness, and their phonological influence on Eskayan may symbolize the value of linguistic distinctiveness more than colonization per se. In other words, Eskaya people were able to project a sense of their own privileged alterity simply by using their language. Even the preponderance of /ʤ/ was a statement of otherness since the vast majority of the Eskaya settlers hailed from a part of Bohol where this feature was not used.

At the level of vocabulary, the calquing of Visayan words with Eskayan counterparts mirrored the conspicuous calquing of colonial categories in Eskaya literature. Thus, Datahan's "word-for-word" lexicography prefigured a commensurate literary strategy of matching "papacy-for-papacy," "language-for-language," "flag-for-flag," and "nation-for-nation." In each case, a unit of perceived equivalence was reproduced and amplified. Even today, in its contemporary use, Eskayan occupies precisely the same domains that the English language came to colonize in twentieth-century Bohol, namely, school, church, singing, speech-making, and writing.

The strategy of "symmetrical schismogenesis" or "mimicry and rejection" has reflexes beyond the Eskaya community. José Rizal pondered the possibility of a complex political order in the Philippines that reflected yet predated Spanish systems of power.[3] Likewise, the eccentric *ilustrado* Pedro Paterno described an ancient Tagalog civilization that matched, predated, and exceeded the religious and political institutions introduced under Spanish rule (Mojares 2006a). Paterno's hypothesis that an early form of Christianity existed in the Philippines was an explanation for why Spanish evangelization had been so swift (Schumacher 1979), an argument taken up a century later by Jes Tirol in relation to the Eskaya (see J.B. Tirol 1991). And arguably, the characterization of the Eskaya as a lost tribe of Israel on the part of local historians was a way of arguing that the Eskaya were not only an indigenous Filipino tribe; they were also a global archetype of preeminent tribehood. The faked Code of Kalantiaw, a hoax promulgated by José E. Marco in 1914, was a codified system of laws purportedly dating from 1433 (Scott 1992; Justiniano 2011). Marco would produce many historical forgeries in his lifetime, and his six-hundred-page work *Las Antiguas Leyendes de la Isla de Negros* and his purported letters of a pre-contact Philippine script directly mapped onto the Spanish alphabet. Like the **abidiha** it even included characters for distinctly Spanish letters such as 'ñ.' Datu Kalantiaw and other historical fantasies would later enter the revised history volumes commissioned by President Ferdinand Marcos as handbooks for the "New Society" (Marcos 1976–1980).

A material manifestation of mimicry-and-rejection in the postcolonial Visayas is on display on nearby Mactan island (Map 3), where Ferdinand Magellan was killed in battle by Datu Lapu Lapu in 1521, a story retold in "Daylinda." A shrine was built there in 1866 in honor of Magellan, bearing the proud inscription "*Glorias Españolas.*" In about 1970, during the administration of Ferdinand Marcos, a victorious bronze statue honoring Lapu Lapu was erected a short distance away, to tower in front of the monument to the

European adventurer (Fig. 10.2). Within the new narrative of an independent Philippines Lapu Lapu was not only the monumental equivalent of Magellan but also his rightful victor.

It is worth remembering that Datahan never tried to depict his community as a cultural curiosity on the margins of Visayan society deserving of sympathy or token recognition. On the contrary, Pinay's Bisayan Declarado language, which one teacher has translated into English as '*True* Visayan,' occupied a central role in his revised narrative of Visayan history, while 'Cebuano'-speakers were represented as migrants with no rightful territorial claim in Bohol. Even though Datahan is unlikely ever to have used words such as *tribu* or *indigena* to describe his community, the later emergence of an indigenous political discourse was perfectly compatible with the aspirations of his successors.

An important advantage of symmetrical schismogenesis, as practiced by Datahan, was that it produced cultural forms that were recognizable to the institutions of power and thus provided ready-made terms of negotiation. Datahan's unique talent for accommodation as well as resistance may explain why Eskaya culture managed to survive and thrive while every other post-revolutionary nativist movement disappeared into obscurity. Long after his death, Datahan's replicated categories would be easily enmeshed with the emerging international

FIGURE 10.2. A calquing of shrines. The Lapu Lapu shrine in Mactan, Cebu, with the Magellan shrine in the background (photograph: Carl Frances Morano Diaman, 2008).

development narrative of the 1980s and 1990s; as outlined in Chapter 3, the Eskaya communities acceded to their new role of state-sanctioned Other in the Indigenous Peoples Rights Act (IPRA) through the appointment of "Tribal Chieftains" and a "Tribal Council." Just as the Biabas "night classes" (Chapter 2) were notionally recognizable to American educators (Chapter 9), Datahan's grandnephew Col. Roberto Datahan would later rebrand these as SIKAT Schools, or Schools of Indigenous Knowledge and Tradition, a term inspired by a Luzon-based NGO of the same name that had no direct association with the Eskaya. The introduction of an Eskayan-language component into the publicly funded elementary school in Taytay is, perhaps, the ultimate endorsement of Mariano Datahan's program. Ignored by President Quezon in 1937, Eskaya pedagogy has now been successfully integrated into the institutional structures it sought to replicate and oppose.

Be that as it may, Eskaya mimicry-and-rejection would also expose a vulnerability. Outsiders would take replicated Eskaya categories at their word and judge them to be deficient in comparison with the models on which they were based. In her funding application Brenda Abregana described Eskaya society in terms of perceived lack. The "old library" in Taytay needed to be updated with the latest information technology, and methods of food and cotton production were to be introduced or reformed according to the "latest science advances." Even artistic expression was wanting, as the Eskaya required training in painting and sculpture (Ramos 1980, 1, 6). For Aida Hinlo, meanwhile, Eskaya schools failed to follow "correct" teaching methodologies, resulting in poor outcomes (Hinlo 1992, 82). Widespread literacy in Eskayan merely highlighted what she assumed to be a diminished literacy in Visayan. In effect, the Eskaya calquing of categories made the disparities overt, giving assimilationists the impetus to "repair" the differences.

## Regional parallels

In the 1980s and 1990s, amateur researchers assumed that the unusual language of Biabas was a regional anomaly and resorted to far-reaching theories that Eskayan was historically displaced from beyond Austronesia, or that it represented a pristine remnant of pre-contact Filipino society. The possibility that its striking idiosyncrasies might be explicable with reference to Eskaya creation mythology was never seriously entertained. Adopting the privileged role of the educated observer, visitors insisted that the Eskaya were "outmoded," "rustic" (Orcullo 2004, 66), "backward" (Hinlo 1992, 62), lacking in "courage," "initiative," "education," and "civilization" (Office for Southern Cultural Communities ca. 1996, 23, 73), and needing urgent introduction to the "latest science advances" (Ramos

1980, 6). A highland community of untutored subsistence farmers could not possibly have been capable of the feats of linguistic and literary ingenuity demonstrated by Pinay or Mariano Datahan without appeal to more civilized influences from abroad or from antiquity. Equally, those who argued that the Eskaya were perpetrating a fraud in order to attract patronage presented the language as a contemporary fabrication of little linguistic or cultural consequence. But in fact, other locally devised languages, registers, and scripts are found across island Southeast Asia, not to mention on Bohol itself. A linguistically gifted spiritual leader who goes by the name of Princesa Analiza has lived on the peak of Mt. Ilihan (Map 3) not far from where Mariano Datahan once owned land. Since 1991, Princesa Analiza has communicated in an artificial language, which her daughter Mervie Batong Orange interprets for her (personal communication, Mervie Batong Orange). A former teacher of Lundag, Orsing Perocho, holds that an old language known as Abakano is still used in his village of Abachanan (Map 3). Perocho is now documenting Abakano using a revived "ancient" script.[4] In my perfunctory analysis, Perocho's Abakano terms are all Visayan nouns, though some are apparently archaic or obsolete while others emphasize the East-Boholano feature [dʒ] in their Roman orthography. Appropriately for the contemporary era, Abakano has alphabetic letters that stand for "foreign" letters found in the English system, like 'x' and 'z,' but not those that are exclusive to Spanish orthographies, like 'ñ,' as the Eskayan **abidiha** does. When I interviewed him, Perocho related an origin story in which the Abakano people were the true indigenous inhabitants of Bohol; the Eskaya had come later to intermarry with them and to introduce their "Sumatran" language to the island. Perocho did not, however, see the Eskaya and Abakano people as rivals but as firm allies in the fight against colonial invaders. Familiar themes of a lowlander–highlander split, the resented dominance of Cebuanos, cultural crisis, and the inspired recuperation of lost documents enter into his account.[5] If Perocho manages to transmit his Abakano alphabet and vocabulary to a community that goes on to use it in stable domains, we may well be witnessing the unfolding of another Pinay story in Bohol.

When it comes to linguistic ingenuity, southeast Bohol is clearly a remarkable case. Nonetheless, recognizable aspects of this creativity can be found elsewhere in the Philippines and Southeast Asia at large. Comparable to the sophisticated language games endemic to Bohol (discussed in Chapter 4), a highly complex speech disguise register for Tagalog has been described by Harold Conklin (1956) involving convoluted combinations of infixation with phoneme and syllable reversals. Such Tagalog games may go back as far as the eighteenth century or earlier. Slang words in Cebuano-Visayan, created through phoneme and syllable reversal, are recorded by John Wolff (1972a, 1972b),[6] and Swardspeak, a back slang used by Cebu's gay community, has been reported by Hart and Hart (1990). Further south, various back slangs are documented in Malaysia (Evans 1923, cited in Blust 2013), and Indonesia (Fox 2005). In Indonesia and Papua New Guinea, special registers are used for hunting or fishing or when entering particular territories. For these situations, using ordinary words is believed to bring about danger or poor luck in finding food. In a particular area of Buru, for example, a language known as Li Garan is spoken exclusively in order to avoid "sudden and violent storms, wind, rain, thunder, lightning, branches breaking and trees falling over, or other disturbing consequences that may extend to future generations" (Maryott and Grimes 1994, 281). Li Garan is taught to children and has the phonology and syntax of Buruese, but like Eskayan its entire lexicon has been substituted for new forms. In Papua New Guinea, a relexified form of the Kalam language is used when cooking or eating cassowary, or during expeditions to collect pandanus nuts in the forest (Pawley 1992), and the Kewa, Huli, and Awiakay people use an avoidance vocabulary when traveling in certain areas (Franklin 1972; Hoenigman 2012). Meanwhile, the Damin language once spoken by male initiates on Mornington Island is a full relexification of the local Lardil language but with a reduction of semantic categories (see Prologue). On mainland Australia, the various mother-in-law registers involve wide lexical substitution as a means of indexing social distance (McGregor 1989).

What these auxiliary languages have in common is that they derive a disguised register from a natural language, either through basic lexical substitution or phonemic and syllabic rearrangement. In effect, there can be no speakers of Eskayan, Li Garan, or Damin who are not already native speakers of Visayan, Buruese, Lardil, etc. Further, in each case the new register is used to mark out a sphere of action and interaction with associated norms of group identity or behavior.

Eskayan arguably fits the criteria of an 'anti-language,' a term coined by M.A.K. Halliday to describe the complex argot developed by an 'anti-society,' defined as "a society that is set up within another society as a conscious alternative to it" (Halliday 1976). To illustrate his definition, Halliday discussed the special registers developed by such outsider groups as Elizabethan vagabond thieves, Polish prisoners, and Calcutta criminals. For Halliday, it is the registers themselves that project oppositional communities, or, as he put it, "[a]n anti-language is not only parallel to an anti-society; it is in fact generated by it" (570). But although relexification is a feature of these rare varieties, none involve total relexification in all word classes as Eskayan does.

The essential split in Eskayan between a mostly Visayan grammar and a mostly innovated lexicon (with inspiration from local and colonial languages) is suggestive of a bilingual mixed language. According to Sarah Thomason's typology, such varieties are created abruptly by bilinguals, are not genetically connected to their parent languages, have linguistic material that can be easily separated according to language of origin, and serve as "a symbol of a new ethnic (sub) group" (Thomason 1997). Thomason's appeal for a historical perspective in classifying contact languages is equally relevant to unusual cases like Eskayan where the motivating circumstances of creation have a direct bearing on the form of the finished artifact. Indeed, Thomason later foregrounded sociohistorical factors— such as a desire for prestige, the promotion of distinct political identities, the need to keep outsiders at a distance, or expressing play and creativity—in her theoretical account of deliberate language change (2007). Of course, Eskayan differs in at least one respect from other documented mixed languages in the fact that its grammar is partially simplified (Kelly 2012).

Comparisons with other registers and lects are instructive to an extent, but what ultimately distinguishes Eskayan from anti-languages, bilingual mixed languages, or lects such as Li Garan is that its speakers regard it as a fully formed, natural, and reclaimed language rather than an alternative code or new hybrid. Moreover, the reclaimed group identity that is generated in the use of Eskayan is of a pre-colonial nationhood, as distinct from, say, the subcultural identity indexed through Swardspeak or the restricted group status displayed by initiated men in their use of Damin. In short, without a firm understanding of speakers' motivations and their particular historical circumstances, efforts to capture typologies of languages like Eskayan will continue to prove elusive.

Another distinguishing characteristic of Eskayan is its representation in a complex writing system that is as elaborate and obtuse as its lexicon. The story of Datahan's ancestral or otherworldly revelation of language-and-script has telling parallels with the almost contemporary emergence of messianic scripts in other neighboring communities engaged in conflict with the state. Inspired rebels have created at least nine new writing systems across the upland region of mainland Southeast Asia (Kelly 2018a), and further examples are known across island Southeast Asia and the Pacific. The most recent instance that I am aware of is that of the Naasioi Otomaung script, revealed during the Bougainville Civil War of the 1990s, to Naasioi speakers on the Siaang river in Kieta district. Though isolated from one another, these cases exhibit conspicuous similarities: speakers of a minority language experience violent conflict resulting in a community crisis, a prophet emerges with a new cultural and spiritual program presented in terms of both a return to traditional ways of life and the building of a modern nation, and a supernatural entity reveals an authentic indigenous script to the prophet who teaches it to his followers. The prophet maintains that the new script will bring a corrective influence on a suffering society, the perceived degeneration of which is viewed a driving cause of political marginalization and ill fortune.

In none of these cases, however, was a whole new *language* created to accompany the script. From this perspective, the closest parallels to the Eskayan phenomenon that I am aware of are from West Africa, another zone of extraordinary scribal creativity (Kelly 2018b). Among the twenty-seven new writing systems invented across the region since the 1830s is the Bamum (ꚶꚳ ꚲ ꚸ) language and script, developed over the years between circa 1896 and 1910 by an illiterate noble of Cameroon. Its lexicon was generated, in large part, by reassigning meanings to French, German, and English words. Later, in Nigeria, the Medefaidrin (ꚰꚳꞃꚱꚮꞃꚯꚱ) language and script was created in about 1928 (Adams 1947; Hau 1961), and one of its grammatical models appears to be English, although in-depth analyses of it are still lacking.

Viewed in a broader regional and historical context, the "restitution" of the Eskayan language and script is by no means an exceptional or fraudulent occurrence. Indeed, the inspired recuperation of scripts across the region appears to co-occur with political upheavals among ethnolinguistic minorities. As Smalley, Vang, and Yang have argued with reference to Pahawh Hmong, nativist movements are responses to cultural stress and spring up "where values are threatened by changes taking place in part of the culture, or where people feel that they are losing their roots and can no longer cope" (Smalley, Vang, and Yang 1990, 11).

Of course, when marginalized communities seek cultural renewal it is not solely words and their written form that may become a focus of reinvention but the utopian visions encapsulated by those words. A revised historiography was central to Datahan's revivalism, as it has been for other popular movements. In the 1970s, to take a final regional example, a charismatic female Meratus Dayak leader of Borneo by the name of Uma Adang heard voices from the ancient Indonesian kingdom of Majapahit instructing her in the true history, traditions, and laws of her people (Tsing 1993). Adang delivered improvised recitations of the Koran, barely intelligible patriotic speeches, and miraculous prophecies. Just like Mariano Datahan, she was reputed to speak every language in the world.

## The (re)invention of linguistic tradition

Language, writing, and native historiography become, in these scenarios, subaltern tools of popular cultural revisionism, not dissimilar from their counterpart discourses in nationalist imaginaries. Anthony Wallace, who made revitalization movements an object of study in the 1950s and 1960s, worried that "avowedly revival movements are never entirely what they claim to be, for the image of the ancient culture to be revived is distorted by historical ignorance and by the presence of imported and innovative elements" (Wallace 1956, 276). Others such as Babadzan (1988, cited in Jolly 1992) contend that recent political claims to indigenous authenticity in the Pacific are the direct product of a postcolonial modernity, or in Jolly's critical summation of his argument: "Pacific peoples have adopted the Western pursuit of alterity, becoming 'other' to their own selves" (Jolly 1992, 53). It would be tempting to view the history of Eskayan in similarly reductive terms, as an instance of strategic essentialism in the face of a dominant and dominating culture. In her concluding remarks, about the Eskaya situation Martinez attempted to reclaim for the Eskaya a greater purpose than a "Western pursuit of alterity" distorted by "imported and innovative elements": "The Eskayas know, and are in a sense telling us," wrote Martinez, "that if a people do not construct, someone else will construct for them" (1993, 237).

However, there is little need to appeal to the construction of European nation-building histories, or the fixing of indigenous colonial subjects in ill-fitting grids and hierarchies, to explain the imaginative uses of historiography in the hands of colonized and uncolonized peoples alike. As Keesing pointed out, long before European contact Pacific communities were already in the habit of reinventing their pasts in order to validate conquests or institutionalize the powers of a warrior leader (Keesing 1989, 24). Today, scholars have moved well beyond the populist opposition between "authenticity" and "invention" by recognizing inventiveness as a foundational element in the production of cultural meanings.[7] For Linnekin, there is no paradox to resolve. Ethnographers, she argues, have no obligation to agree with any traditionalized reformulations of historical events, but they do have a duty to avoid assessing them as invalid or inauthentic (1991, 448).

As popular embodiments of cultural or national identity, languages can be said to occupy a pivotal position in the contestation of authenticity. Although proponents of sociolinguistic naturalism may disavow the constructedness of linguistic identities, well-established categories such as 'Tagalog,' 'Ilocano,' and 'Visayan' were the inventions of Spanish writers, a fact that does not undermine the social density of these concepts today (Rafael 1988, 16). Elsewhere, such a self-identification with constructed tribehood has been described as 'entification,' the process by which a social-political entity comes into being (Ernst 1999). In this context it is crucial to emphasize that the category 'Eskaya' is just as entified as 'Tagalog,' 'Filipino,' or 'American,' and just as socially meaningful too.

For Benedict Anderson, mythic constructions of nationhood rely in part on appeals to historical continuity. Languages, "for which no dated origins can ever be given" (Anderson [1983] 2003, 196), are symbolic of a connection to a deep past. Indeed, "lost" or dead languages were ideal mediums for the propagation of imagined communities, since they appeared to lend everyone access to "a pure world of signs" (13). Nations, it would seem, are rarely obliged to defend their own inherent artificiality. The burden of authenticity always appears to lie with those who seek protections and concessions from them.

Yet Anderson's account of the importance of languages and their written traditions for the imaginative projection of "communities" requires some re-evaluation if it is to be applied to the Eskaya context. Datahan's utopian micro-republic of Biabas was, in effect, a nation-building exercise carried out in reverse. Far from constructing an imaginary community around an existing language, as Anderson might have it, Pinay-through-Datahan assembled a language in order to traditionalize and elevate an existing community. On these terms, Datahan cannot fairly be understood as a subaltern deconstructionist or a postcolonial radical as much as this might appeal to our critical sensibilities. Rather, he embraced essentialist ideologies of nationhood and linguistic prestige without question and harnessed them for his own ends. Exploiting the very same colonial binaries that pushed Boholanos to the margins, Datahan foregrounded his own agenda as the dominant term. As I have shown, in Eskaya historiography there is no attempt to oppose creativity with authenticity. Instead, "creative" events are celebrated in terms of inspired revelation, and the motif of "discovery" recurs in both insider and outsider accounts of Eskayan history: Dangko's discovery of Bohol, Pinay's discovery of language in the body, Magellan's discovery of Panglao, Datahan's discovery of the *yutang natawhan* ('motherland') and thence of Pinay's buried writing, Abregana's discovery of Taytay, and Tirol's discovery of cave inscriptions.

That language, for the Eskaya, is revealed, created, or animate is perhaps not so distinct from Western scholarly characterizations of language as "a process of free creation" (Chomsky [1970] 2003, interpreting Humboldt), or "a supreme achievement of a uniquely human collective genius, as divine and endless a mystery as a living organism" (Hale et al. 1992). Linguists certainly recognize that there is a continuum between "natural" and "artificial" languages, as language-engineering experiments on a national scale have brought about tangible changes to the written and spoken forms of Indonesian, Turkish, and Hebrew, not to mention Tagalog. Indeed, the mandated development of a national language in the Philippines went through discrete stages of engineering (Chapter 2). Even so, programmatic language engineering is not exclusive to nation-building projects. For example, Murray Garde has described a formalized system of contrasting 'patrilects' developed by speakers of Bininj Kun-wok dialects in Western Arnhem Land, Australia (Garde 2008). Innovated without any top-down state intervention, these varieties are distinguished by small sets of lexical features yet are named and recognized as independent languages. Moreover, they are motivated by political concerns that are surprisingly similar to those of modern nation-states, namely, the maintenance and expression of group identities and territorial rights.

Human interventions into language, from the development of in-group registers to large-scale language-planning projects, are but one aspect of the complex and inexorable process of language change. Whether or not the interventions are desired is a political question more than it is a linguistic one. Indeed, it is quite possible that a necessary political precondition of language engineering is the assumption that language is already a bounded construction subject to manipulation—like a human body, an alphabet, or a nation-state—even if we concede that "a well-bounded, homogeneous language is as much an 'imagined' entity as is 'community'" (Rumsey 2010, 163). That Eskayan is characterized as a creation or fabrication, an accommodation or a subversion, is ultimately a reflection of our own attitude to language and the degree to which we apprehend it as a marker of belonging and exclusion.

## The future of Eskayan

The immediate future for Eskayan as a viable language is reasonably assured. Competent speakers have status within the communities; in Biabas and Taytay the language is being actively learned by children, and plans are well under way to construct an Eskaya school in Cadapdapan. Recent government recognition, through the Indigenous Peoples Rights Act, provides additional legitimacy to an already valued language. Nonetheless, speaker numbers and class attendance have clearly declined since the high-water mark of the 1980s when the Taytay school was filled with 150 students. Today, a class of thirty or fewer is the norm. If Eskayan does manage to be viable for another five generations, it will no doubt continue to evolve as rapidly as it has always done, with possible dialects emerging between the main Eskaya villages. The script and its system will inevitably undergo further changes in the process of being recopied by new scribes. If the development of other scripts, such as Pahawh Hmong, Bamum, and Vai, is any indication, the most florid Eskayan symbols will undergo reduction, and the system itself may be simplified, either naturally or through deliberate processes of reform (Kelly et al. forthcoming). Decline in speaker numbers may be reversed through language planning or the emergence of other charismatic spiritual leaders in the stamp of Mariano Datahan or Fabian Baja. Of course, the potential exists for a schism to develop between those Eskaya who see accommodation with national governing structures as the way forward and those who attach their aspirations to spiritual renewal premised on a rejection of outsider discourses. Leaning too far toward accommodation would be to risk permitting someone else to "construct for them"; too far toward resistance and another Aser movement, as witnessed in the Lundag disturbance of 1975, could lead to confrontation and collapse. The impressive survival of the community since at least 1902 can be attributed to the fact that the Eskaya have always known how to strike the right balance between mimicry and rejection, and to recognize that communities, like languages, are porous and expandable. Utopian visions reach toward a future in which the drive to individuate one's community and reject all that is foreign eventually overwhelms and resolves a contrary desire for inclusion in a universal community that elides such boundaries.

"The time will come," announced a Boholano fisherman with polyglottic gifts "when Declared Visayan will be spoken by everyone in the world." In the end it is the idealistic creators, and not their subjugators, who lay claim to the last word.

## Notes

1. These minimally include Jesus Peralta, who did fieldwork in both communities, Ernesto Constantino, who gave an impressionistic assessment of Eskayan to Margarita Logarta (see Chapter 3) and who later analyzed the transcription of the spoken language provided by a Tasaday witness (Salazar 1992), and Laurence A. Reid, who was formally approached to comment on Eskayan but declined (personal communication).

2. Other Visayan calques include *Ginuu ku!* from Spanish *¡Dios mio!*; *Matag karun ug unya* from English 'Every now and then' (but in Visayan this means 'frequently' as opposed to 'sporadically'); *Mas . . .* [adj] *sa . . .* [adj] from Spanish *Más . . . que* ('More . . . than . . .'); *Daghang salamat* from Spanish *Muchas gracias*; and *Kumusta ka?* from Spanish *¿Como estás?* or *¿Cómo está Usted?*

3. In a section discussing native laws in Antonio Morga's *Sucesos de las Islas Filipinas* (Morga [1690] 1890), Rizal added the annotation, "Perhaps there once existed a confederation, since we know from the earliest Spaniards that the Prince of Manila was generalissimo of the Sultan of Borneo. There are also documents from the twelfth century that attest to this" (297). ("Acaso existiera una confederación, pues sabemos por los primeros Españoles que el príncipe de Manila era generalisimo del sultán de Borneo. Existen ademas otros documentos del siglo XII que testifican esto.")

4. See a sample of his documentation at http://catalog.paradisec.org.au/repository/PK2/10/PK2-10-MISC17.pdf.

5. For the full interview see the video recording at http://catalog.paradisec.org.au/collections/PK2/items/48.

6. These include *wanggu* and *wangtigu*, derived from *tiguwang* ('old man') with the same meaning; *yadba* from *bayad* ('pay'); *ul-ul*, from *lu'lu'* ('masturbate'); *yusig* from *sigarilyu* ('cigarette'); *takwar* from *kwarta* ('money'). Words such as *bayad*, *sigarilyu*, and *kwarta* are also available in Tagalog, and a few back slang terms in Wolff's dictionary are identified as Tagalog borrowings, including *wangkata* from Tagalog *kawatan* ('body') and *dihin guli* from Tagalog *hindi' ligu'* ('not bathing,' i.e., 'needing a bath') (Wolff 1972b). Arguably, then, Visayan back slang was imported from Tagalog and adapted to Visayan.

7. See, for example, the various commentaries on this theme by Wagner (1975), Anderson ([1983] 2003), Hanson (1989), Linnekin (1991), Jolly (1992), Wittersheim (1999), and Clifford (2001).

# REFERENCES

Abregana, Brenda. 1981. Abregana to Buenaventura, September 7. Tagbilaran: Bohol Provincial Library archives.

Abregana, Brenda. 1984. "Eskaya: The living fossil language in Bohol." *Focus Philippines*, July 28, 1984, 13–14.

Acocella, Joan. 2012. "One upon a time: The lure of the fairy tale." *The New Yorker*, July 23. http://www.newyorker.com/arts/critics/books/2012/07/23/120723crbo_books_acocella.

Adams, R.F.G. 1947. "Obɛri Ɔkaimɛ: A new African language and script." *Africa: Journal of the International Africa Institute* 17 (1):24–34.

Adelaar, Alexander. 2005. "The Austronesian languages of Asia and Madagascar: A historical perspective." In *The Austronesian languages of Asia and Madagascar*, edited by Nikolaus P Himmelmann and Alexander Adelaar, 1–42. London and New York: Routledge.

Agbayani, Pacita R. 1990. *Duero: Yesterday, today, tomorrow*. Tagbilaran: Department of Education, Culture and Sports.

Aglípay y Labáyan, Gregorio. 1912. *Catequesis de la Iglesia Filipina Independiente*. Manila: Isabelo de los Reyes.

Aguilar, Celedonio G. 1994. *Readings in Filipino literature*. Quezon City: Rex Book Store.

Aguinaldo y Famy, Emiliano. 1898. "Decreto del 23 de junio de 1898, estableciendo el Gobierno Revolucionario." accessed May 31, 2012. http://1898.mforos.com/1035040/6609814-decretos-y-mensajes-de-emilio-aguinaldo/.

Alburo, Erlinda Kintanar. 1980. "A study of two Cebuano legends: The lost lender and Maria Cacao." *Philippine Quarterly of Culture and Society* 8 (1):44–59.

Alcina, Ignacio Francisco. [1668] 2005. *History of the Bisayan people in the Philippine Islands: Evangelization and culture at the contact period: Historia de las Islas e indios de Bisayas*. Part One, Book 3, Volume III. Manila: UST Publishing House.

Amparado, Felicisimo B. 1981. "'Iniskaya': Karaang pinulongan sa Bohol." *Bisaya*, April 15, 12, 55.

Añasco, Carliloso. 2000. *Bohol: The capsulized history*.[Tagbilaran?] Self-pub.

Anderson, Benedict. [1983] 2003. *Imagined communities: Reflections on the origins and spread of nationalism*. Pasig City: Anvil Publishing.

Apalisok, Simplicio M. 1992a. *Bohol without tears: Bohol's wartime years 1937–1947*. Quezon City: Surigao BB Press.

Apalisok, Simplicio M. 1992b. *Bohol without tears. Vol III: Bohol's prehispanic past to the present*. Quezon City: Surigao BB Press.

Apalisok, Simplicio M. 1999. *Bohol without tears: Land of the country's most battered people*. Book 3. Quezon City: Multigraphics and Copy Systems.

Aparece, Ulysses B. 2003. *Sukdan curing practices in Anonang, Inabanga, Bohol: An ethnography of performance*. Cebu City: University of San Carlos, Ph.D. dissertation.

Arens, Richard. 1959. "The early Pulahan movement in Samar and Leyte." *The Journal of History* 7 (4):303–371.

Babadzan, Alain. 1988. "*Kastom* and nation building in the South Pacific." In *Ethnicities and nations: Processes of interethnic relations in Latin America, Southeast Asia, and the Pacific*, edited by R. Guideri, F. Pellizi, and S. Tambiah, 199–228. Houston: Rothko Chapel and University of Texas Press.

Baranera, Francisco X. 1884. *Compendio de la Historia de Filipinas*. Manila: M. Perez.

Bartlett, Lesley, Dina Lopéz, Lalitha Vasudevan, and Doris Warriner. 2016. "The anthropology of literacy." In *A companion to the anthropology of education*, edited by Bradley A. Levinson and Mica Pollock, 154–176. John Wiley & Sons.

Bateson, Gregory. 1936. *Naven*. Cambridge: Cambridge University Press.

Bedford, Zoë. 2004. *Maintaining cultural difference: An insight into the Visaya-Eskaya of Bohol*. Tagbilaran: Australian Youth Ambassadors for Development Program.

Behrens, Dietlinde. 2007. *Yakan texts*. Manila: Linguistic Society of the Philippines.

Bennett, J. Fraser. 1993. *Kayah Li script: A brief description*. Urbana-Champaign: University of Illinois.

Bernido, Esteban, Col. 1981. *Wartime recollections*. Quezon City: Allied Printing.

Beyer, H. Otley. 1979. "The Philippines before Magellan." In *Readings in Philippine prehistory*, edited by Mauro Garcia, 8–34. Manila: The Filipiniana Book Guild.

Blake, Frank R. 1920. "A bibliography of the Philippine languages. Part I." *Journal of the American Oriental Society* 40:25–70.

Blaskett, Beverley A. 1983. *The development policy for Aborigines with particular reference to the education policy of the Roman Catholic missions*. Melbourne: La Trobe University, Ph.D. dissertation.

Blunt, Mason, Cpt. 1912. *An army officer's Philippine studies*. Manila: University Press.

Blust, Robert. 2013. *The Austronesian languages*. 2nd ed. Canberra: Asia-Pacific Linguistics Open Access Monographs.

Borja, Tiburcio. 2001. "Our early ABC's in Bohol." In *Bearers of benevolence: The Thomasites and public education in the Philippines*, edited by Mary Racelis and Judy Celine Ick, 194–198. Pasig City: Anvil Publishing.

Borrinaga, George Emmanuel. 2009. "The Pulahan movement in Samar (1904–1911): Origins and causes." *The Journal of History* 55:226–270.

Borrinaga, Rolando O. 2010. "Disaster in Iti's land: The tragic social history of the datû class in Leyte (1521–1622)." *The Journal of History* 56:58–91.

Brewer, Carolyn. 2004. *Shamanism, Catholicism and gender relations in colonial Philippines: 1521–1685*. Aldershot: Ashgate.

Buzeta, Manuel, and Felipe Bravo. 1851. *Diccionario geográfico, estadístico, histórico de las Islas Filipinas*. Vol. 1. Madrid: D. José C. de la Peña.

Buzeta, Manuel, and Felipe Bravo. 1851. *Diccionario geográfico, estadístico, histórico de las Islas Filipinas*. Vol. 2. Madrid: D. José C. de la Peña.

Campbell, Lyle, and Martha C. Muntzel. 1989. "The structural consequences of language death." In *Investigating obsolescence*, edited by Nancy Dorian, 181–196. Cambridge: Cambridge University Press.

Campos, Zosimo C. 1993. Zosimo Campos to Lorenzo S. Dinlayan, June 23. Tagbilaran: Bohol Provincial Library archives.

Cannell, Fenella. 2006. "Reading as gift and writing as theft." In *The Anthropology of Christianity*, edited by Fenella Cannell, 134–162. Durham and London: Duke University Press.

Carter, E.C. 1905. "Report of the commissioner of public health." In *Annual report of the commissioner of public health: Covering the period from September 1, 1903, to August 31, 1904*. Manila: Bureau of Public Printing.

Chatterjee, Partha. 1993. *The nation and its fragments: Colonial and postcolonial histories*. New Jersey: Princeton University Press.

Chirino, Pedro. [1604] 1969. *Relacion de las Islas filipinas*. Translated by Ramón Echevarria. Manila: Historical Conservation Society.

Chomsky, Noam. [1970] 2003. *For reasons of state*. New York: Penguin.

Clifford, James. 2001. "Indigenous articulations." *The Contemporary Pacific* 13 (2):468–490.

Coben, Herminia Meñez. 2010. *Verbal arts in Philippine indigenous communities: Poetics, society, and history*. Manila: Ateneo de Manila University Press.

Colin, Francisco. [1660] 1904. *Labor Evangélica de los Obreros de la Compañia de Jesús en las Islas Filipinas*. Barcelona: Heinrich y Compañía.

Conklin, Harold C. 1956. "Tagalog speech disguise." *Language* 32 (1):136–139.

Constantino, Ernesto. 1971. "Tagalog and other major languages of the Philippines." In *Current trends in linguistics*, edited by Thomas A. Sebeok, 112–154. The Hague and Paris: Mouton.

Consul, Stella Marie de los Santos. 2005. *Iniskaya: A linear linguistic description*. Cebu City: Cebu Normal University, Ph.D. dissertation.

Coulmas, Florian. 1996. *The Blackwell encyclopedia of writing systems*. Cambridge, MA: Blackwell.

Cruz, Marinel. 2009. "Cesar Montano hot on going global." *Philippine Daily Inquirer*, April 29, 2009.Republished at https://aliwanavenue.wordpress.com/2009/04/29/cesar-montano-hot-on-going-global/, accessed 8 July 2021.

Cullinane, Michael. 2000. "The master and Juan de la Cruz: Hilario C. Moncado, politiko and man of mystery." In *Lives at the margin: Biography of Filipinos, obscure, ordinary, and heroic*, edited by Alfred W. McCoy, 62–147. Madison, WI: Ateneo de Manila University Press.

Dauncey, Campbell, Mrs. 1906. *An Englishwoman in the Philippines*. London: John Murray.

David, E.J.R. 2014. *Brown skin, white minds: Filipino / American postcolonial psychology*. Charlotte: Information Age Publishing.

Dawson, David. 1992. *Allegorical readers and cultural revision in ancient Alexandria*. Berkeley and Los Angeles: University of California Press.

de Achútegui, Pedro S., and Miguel A. Bernad. 1961. *Religious revolution in the Philippines: The life and Church of Gregorio Aglipay: 1860–1960*. Vol. 1. Manila: Ateneo de Manila.

de la Cavada Mendez de Vigo, Agustín. 1877. *Historia geografica, geologica y estadistica de Filipinas*. Vol. 2. Manila: Ramirez y Giraudier.

de la Concepcion, Juan. 1792. *Historia general de Philipinas: Conquistas espiritvales, y temporales de estos Españoles Dominios, establecimientos, progresos, y decadencias*. Vol. 14. Manila: En el Conv. de Nra. Sra de Loreto del pueblo de Sampaloc.

Deguit, Sonieta B. 1991. "Eskaya: A touch with Bohol's past." *Bohol's Pride*, March 18, 1991.

de los Reyes y Florentino, Isabelo. 1889. *El folk-lore filipino*. Vol. 1. Manila: De Chofré.

de los Reyes y Florentino, Isabelo. 1889. *Las Islas Visayas en la epoca de la Conquista*. Manila: De Chofré.

del Pilar, Marcelo Hilario. [1898] 1987. "La soberanía monacal." In *The life and writings of Marcelo Hilario del Pilar*, edited by Magno Gatmaitan, 131–171. Quezon City: R.P. Publishing Co.

Demetrio, Francisco. 1969. "Towards a classification of Bisayan folk beliefs and customs." *Asian Folklore Studies* 28 (2):95–132.

de Noceda, Juan, and Pedro de Sanlucar. [1754] 1860. *Vocabulario de la lengua Tagala*. Manila: Ramírez y Giraudier.

de Tavera, Pardo. 1884. *Contribución para el estudio de los antiguos alfabetos filipinos*. Losana: Juanin Hermanos.

de Viana, Francisco Leandro. [1765] 1907. "Viana's memorial of 1765: Part I." In *The Philippine Islands 1493–1898: Vol. 48*, 197–338. Cleveland: The Arthur H. Clark Company.

Diringer, David. [1948] 1968. *The alphabet: A key to the history of mankind.* London: Hutchinson of London.

Dumont, Jean-Paul. 1988. "The Tasaday, which and whose? Toward the political economy of an ethnographic sign." *Cultural Anthropology* 3 (3):261–275.

Endriga, Divine Angeli P. 2010. *The dialectology of Cebuano: Bohol, Cebu and Davao.* Manila: University of the Philippines. Unpublished MS.

Ernst, Thomas M. 1999. "Land, stories, and resources: Discourse and entification in Onabasulu modernity." *American Anthropologist* 101 (1):88–97.

Estorba, Regina. 2004. "Scribbling the voice of a tende: An ethnography of the women of Eskaya." Unpublished manuscript.

Estorba, Regina. 2006. "Scribbling the voice of a tende." *Kinaadman* 17 (1):1–25.

Evans, Ivor Hugh Norman. 1923. *Studies in religion, folk-lore and custom in British North Borneo and the Malay peninsula.* Cambridge: Cambridge University Press.

Ferandos, Pio B. 1981. *The Bohol guerillas in action.* Cebu City: Our Press Inc.

Ferrándiz, José. 1912. "Prólogo." In *Catequesis de la Iglesia Filipina Independiente,* edited by Gregorio Aglípay y Labáyan, v–xxvi. Manila: Isabelo de los Reyes.

Fox, James J. 2005. "Ritual languages, special registers and speech decorum in Austronesian languages." In *The Austronesian languages of Asia and Madagascar,* edited by Alexander Adelaar and Nikolaus P. Himmelmann, 87–109. London and New York: Routledge.

Francisco, Juan R. 1973. *Philippine palaeography.* Quezon City: Linguistic Society of the Philippines.

Franklin, Karl J. 1972. "A ritual pandanus language of New Guinea." *Oceania* 43 (1):61–76.

Frei, Ernest J. 1959. *The historical development of the Philippine National Language.* Manila: Institute of National Language.

Gal, Susan. 1998. "Multiplicity and contention among language ideologies: A commentary." In *Language ideologies: Practice and theory,* edited by Bambi B. Schieffelin, Kathryn A. Woolard, and Paul V. Kroskrity, 317–331. New York and Oxford: Oxford University Press.

Gal, Susan, and Judith T. Irvine. 1995. "The boundaries of languages and disciplines: How ideologies construct difference." *Social Research* 62 (4):967–1001.

Garde, Murray. 2008. "*Kun-dangwok*: 'clan lects' and *Ausbau* in western Arnhem Land." *International Journal of the Sociology of Language* 191 (2008):141–169.

Gardner, Fletcher. 1906. "Philippine (Tagalog) superstitions." *The Journal of American Folklore* 19 (74):191–204.

Gonzalez, Andrew B. 1980. *Language and nationalism: The Philippine experience thus far.* Quezon City: Ateneo de Manila Press.

Granada, Oriculo. 2010. *Socio-economic profile of Guindulman.* Guindulman: Municipality of Guindulman.

Greenhill, Simon J., Alexei J. Drummond, and Russell D. Gray. 2010. "How accurate and robust are the phylogenetic estimates of Austronesian language relationships?" *PLOS One* 5 (3):e9573.

"Group Claims Territory in the Name of Eskayas." 2005. *The Bohol Standard*, September 25, 3.

Guillaume-Pey, Cécile. 2014. "From blood to scripture: Religious conversions and the making of identity among the Sora." In *The politics of ethnicity in India, Nepal and China*, edited by Marin Carrin, Gérard Toffen, and Pralay Kanungo, 223–239. New Delhi: Primus.

Guillaume-Pey, Cécile. 2021. "A script 'good to drink': The invention of writing systems among the Sora and other tribes of India." In *The social and sultural contexts of historic writing practices,* edited by Philip J Boyes, Philippa M Steele and Natalia Elvira Astoreca, 159–184. Oxford: Oxbow.

Guillén, Félix. 1898. *Gramatica Bisaya par facilitar el estudio del dialecto Bisaya Cebuano.* Malabon: Estab. Tipo-Lit. del Asilo de Huerfanos.

Guingguing, C.B. 1975a. "Final talks set; to yield arms: Massive civic action work on as followers plege faith in gov't (sic)." *The Bohol Chronicle*, October 19, 1975, 1–8.

Guingguing, C.B. 1975b. Gov't presses peace overtures: Emissaries contact rebel group; peaceful confrontation seen." *The Bohol Chronicle*, October 5, 1975, 1–8.

Guingguing, C.B. 1975c. "1 dies, 6 captured in PC encounter." *The Bohol Chronicle*, September 21, 1975, 1–8.

Guingguing, C.B. 1975d. "Pacification, Civil in Pilar: Road-building through embattled area to link inland barrios." *The Bohol Chronicle*, September 28, 1975, 1–8.

Guingguing, C.B. 1975e. "Rebels surrender unconditionally with arms, ammo, papers." *The Bohol Chronicle*, October 26, 1975, 1, 8.

Guingguing, C.B. 1975f. "Rizalians deny rebel affiliation: Head pledges support to government during peace talks." *The Bohol Chronicle*, October 12, 1975, 1–8.

Hale, Kenneth. 1971. "A note on a Walbiri tradition of antonymy." In *Semantics: An interdisciplinary reader in philosophy, linguistics and psychology*, edited by Danny D. Steinberg and Leon A. Jakobovits, 472–482. Cambridge: Cambridge University Press.

Hale, Ken, Michael Krauss, Lucille J. Watahomigie, Akira Y. Yamamoto, Colette Craig, LaVerne Masayesva Jeanne, and Nora C. England. 1992. "Endangered languages." *Language* 68 (1):1–42.

Halliday, M.A.K. 1976. "Anti-languages." *American Anthropologist* 78 (3):570–584.

Hanson, Allan. 1989. "The making of the Maori: Culture invention and its logic." *American Anthropologist* 91 (4):890–902.

Hart, Donn, and Harriett Hart. 1990. "Visayan Swardspeak: The language of a gay community in the Philippines." *Crossroads: An Interdisciplinary Journal of Southeast Asian Studies* 5 (2):27–49.

Hau, Caroline S., and Victoria L. Tinto. 2003. "Language policy and ethnic relations in the Philippines." In *Fighting words: Language, policy and ethnic relations in Asia*, edited by Michael E. Brown and Šumit Ganguly, 319–349. Cambridge, MA: The MIT Press.

Hau, K. 1961. "Oberi Ɔkaimε script, texts, and counting system." *Bulletin de l'I.F.A.N.* 23 (1–2):291–308.

Haugen, Einar. 1950. "The analysis of linguistic borrowing." *Language* 26 (2):210–231.

Hayami, Yujiro, Agnes R. Quisumbing, and Lourdes S. Adriano. 1990. *Toward an alternative land reform paradigm: A Philippine perspective*. Quezon City: Ateneo de Manila Press.

Heath, Shirley B. 1977. "Social history." In *Bilingual education: Current perspectives*, edited by Joshua Fishman, 53–72. Arlington, VA: Center for Applied Linguistics.

Hemley, Robin. 2004. *Invented Eden: The elusive, disputed history of the Tasaday*. Pasig City: Anvil Publishing.

Heyd, Uriel. 1954. *Language reform in modern Turkey*. Jerusalem: Israel Oriental Society.

Hill, Jane H. 1985. "The grammar of consciousness and the consciousness of grammar." *American Ethnologist* 12 (4):725–737.

Hinlo, Aida. 1992. *Proposed nonformal education program for the Eskayas of Bohol*. Manila: Philippine Women's University, Ph.D. dissertation.

Hoenigman, Darja. 2012. "From mountain talk to hidden talk: Continuity and change in Awiakay registers." In *Melanesian languages on the edge of Asia: Challenges for the 21st century*, edited by Nicholas Evans and Marian Klamer, 191–218. Honolulu: Language Documentation & Conservation, Special Publication No. 5.

Hokari, Minoru. 2011. *Gurindji journey: A Japanese historian in the outback*. Sydney: UNSW Press.

Holm, Tom. 2007. *Code talkers and warriors: Native Americans and World War II*. New York: Chelsea House.

Hurley, Vic. 1938. *Jungle Patrol: The story of the Philippine Constabulary (1901–1936)*. New York: Dutton.

Ileto, Reynaldo C. 1979a. *Pasyon and revolution: Popular movements in the Philippines, 1840–1910*. Quezon City, Metro Manila: Ateneo de Manila University Press.

Ileto, Reynaldo C. 1979b. "Tagalog poetry and image of the past during the war against Spain." In *Perceptions of the past in Southeast Asia*, edited by Anthony Reid and David Marr, 379–400. Singapore: Heinmann Educational Books.

Ileto, Reynaldo C. 1982. "Rizal and the underside of Philippine history." In *Moral order and the question of change: Essays on Southeast Asian thought*, edited by David K. Wyatt and Alexander Woodside, 274–337. New Haven: Yale University Southeast Asia Studies.

Ileto, Reynaldo C. 1995. "Cholera and the origins of the American sanitary order in the Philippines." In *Discrepant histories: Translocal essays on Filipino cultures*, edited by Vicente L. Rafael, 125–148. Anvil Publishing: Manila.

Irvine, Judith T. 1989. "When talk isn't cheap: Language and political economy." *American Ethnologist* 16 (2):248–267.

Irvine, Judith T., and Susan Gal. 2000. "Language ideology and linguistic differentiation." In *Regimes of language: Ideologies, polities, and identities*, edited by Paul V. Kroskrity, 35–84. Santa Fe: School of American Research Press.

Jacquet, Eugène. 1831. *Considerations sur les alphabets des Philippines*. Paris: Imprimerie Royale.

Jernudd, Björn H. 1989. "The texture of language purism: An introduction." In *The politics of language purism*, edited by Björn H. Jernudd and Michael J. Shapiro, 1–19. Berlin and New York: Mouton de Gruyter.

Jolly, Margaret. 1992. "Specters of inauthenticity." *The Contemporary Pacific* 4 (1):49–72.

Jose, Regalado Trota. 2008. *Curas de almas: A preliminary listing of parishes and parish priests in the 19th century Philippines based on the Guias de Forasteros, 1834–1898*. Manila: UST Publishing House.

Joseph, John E. 1995. "Natural grammar, arbitrary lexicon: An enduring parallel in the history of linguistic thought." *Language and Communication* 15 (3):213–225.

Joseph, John E. 2000. *Limiting the arbitrary: Linguistic naturalism and its opposites in Plato's Cratylus and modern theories of language*. Amsterdam: John Benjamins.

Juan, V.S. 1922. "Colorums." In *Bisaya Paper No. 195. Data on the "Colorum" movement in Bohol, Leyte, and Surigao. Ethnography of the Bisaya peoples. Vol. 9*, edited by H. Otley Beyer, p3/167. Surigao, Leyte, Manila. Manuscript collection held in the National Library of Australia.

Justiniano, Maureen. 2011. "Jose E. Marco's Kalantiaw Code: Implications for Philippine historiography and Filipinos' historical consciousness." *Explorations: A graduate Student Journal of Southeast Asian Studies* 11 (12):19–30.

Katz, Leonard, and Laurie B. Feldman. 1983. "Relation between pronunciation and recognition of printed words in deep and shallow orthographies." *Journal of Experimental Psychology: Learning, Memory, and Cognition* 9 (1):157–166.

Katz, Leonard, and Ram Frost. 1992. "The reading process is different for different orthograhies: The orthographic depth hypothesis." In *Haskins Laboratories status report on speech research*, edited by Carol A. Fowler, 147–160. New Haven: Haskins Laboratories.

Keats, John. 1963. *They fought alone*. Philadelphia and New York: J.B. Lippincott Company.

Keesing, Roger. 1982. "Kastom in Melanesia: An overview." *Mankind* 13 (4):297–301.

Keesing, Roger. 1989. "Creating the past: Custom and identity in the contemporary Pacific." *The Contemporary Pacific* 1 (1–2):19–42.

Kelly, Piers. 2006. The classification of the Eskayan language of Bohol. Tagbilaran, Bohol: National Commission on Indigenous Peoples.

Kelly, Piers. 2012. "The morphosyntax of a created language of the Philippines: Folk linguistic effects and the limits of relexification." In *Proceedings of the 42nd Australian Linguistic Society Conference - 2011, Australian National University, Canberra ACT, 2–4 December 2011*, edited by Maïa Ponsonnet, Loan Dao, and Margit Bowler, 179–223. Canberra: ANU Research Repository, https://openresearch-repository. anu.edu.au/handle/1885/9404.

Kelly, Piers. 2015. "A comparative analysis of Eskayan and Boholano-Visayan (Cebuano) phonotactics: Implications for the origins of Eskayan lexemes." *Journal of the Southeast Asian Linguistic Society* 8:iii-xiv.

Kelly, Piers. 2016a. "Excavating a hidden bell story from the Philippines: A revised narrative of cultural-linguistic loss and recuperation." *Journal of Folklore Research* 53 (2):86–113.

Kelly, Piers. 2016b. "Introducing the Eskaya writing system: A complex messianic script from the southern Philippines." *The Australian Journal of Linguistics* 36 (1):131–163. doi: 10.1080/07268602.2016.1109433.

Kelly, Piers. 2016c. "The origins of invented vocabulary in a utopian Philippine language." *Asia-Pacific Language Variation* 2 (1):83–121.

Kelly, Piers. 2018a. "The art of not being legible: Invented writing systems as technologies of resistance in mainland Southeast Asia." *Terrain* 70:1–24. doi: 10.4000/ terrain.17103.

Kelly, Piers. 2018b. "The invention, transmission and evolution of writing: Insights from the new scripts of West Africa." In *Paths into script formation in the ancient Mediterranean*, edited by Silvia Ferrara and Miguel Valério, 189–209. Rome: Studi Micenei ed Egeo Anatolici.

Kelly, Piers, James Winters, Helena Miton, and Olivier Morin. Forthcoming. "The predictable evolution of letter shapes: An emergent script of West Africa recapitulates historical change in writing systems." *Current Anthropology*.

Kroskrity, Paul V. 1992. "Arizona Tewa Kiva speech as a manifestation of linguistic ideology." *Pragmatics* 2 (3):297–309.

Labov, William. [1966] 2006. *The social stratification of English in New York City.* Cambridge: Cambridge University Press.

Laktaw, Pedro Serrano. 1910. "Los dialectos secretos en filipinas." *Cultura Filipina* 1 (1):551–553.

Laubach, Frank Charles. 1925. *The people of the Philippines: Their religious progress and preparation for spiritual leadership in the Far East.* New York: George H. Doran Company.

Leach, E.R. 1954. *Political systems of highland Burma: A study of Kachin social structure.* London: The London School of Economics and Political Science.

Lewis, Geoffrey. 1999. *The Turkish language reform: A catastrophic success*. Oxford & New York: Oxford University Press.

Lewis, M. Paul, Gary F. Simons, and Charles D. Fennig, eds. 2021. *Ethnologue: Languages of the World*. 24 ed. Dallas: SIL International.

Linnekin, Jocelyn. 1991. "Cultural invention and the dilemma of authenticity." *American Anthropologist* 93 (2):446–448.

Logarta, Margarita T. 1981. "The Eskaya cult: Children of a lost language." *Who*, September 5, 1981, 22–27.

Luengo, Josemaria Salutan. 1991. *A history of the Philippines: A focus on the Christianization of Bohol (1521–1991)*. Tubigon, Bohol: Mater Dei Publications.

Luspo, Marianito. 2005. *Bohol and the Boholanos*. Tagbilaran. Unpublished MS.

MacLeish, Kenneth. 1972. "Stone Age cavemen of Mindanao." *National Geographic* 142 (2):218–249.

Mannheim, Karl. [1936] 1979. *Ideology and utopia: An introduction to the sociology of knowledge*. Translated by Louise Wirth and Edward Shils. London & Henley: Routledge & Kegan Paul.

Mapes, Victor L. 2000. *The butchers, the baker: The World War II memoir of a United States Army Air Corps soldier captured by the Japanese in the Philippines*. Jefferson, NC: McFarland & Company.

Marcos, Ferdinand E. 1976–1980. *Tadhana: The history of the Filipino people*. Volumes 1–2. Manila: Ferdinand Marcos Foundation.

Martín, Julián. 1842a. "Diccionario hispano-bisaya." In *Diccionario de la lengua bisaya, hiligueina y haraya de la isla de Panay*, 461–827. Manila: D. Manuel y Félix Dayat.

Martín, Julián. 1842b. *Diccionario de la lengua bisaya, hiligueina y haraya de la isla de Panay*. Manila: D. Manuel y Félix Dayat.

Martinez, Cristina J. 1993. *Gahum ug gubat: A study of Eskayan texts, symbolic subversion and cultural constructivity*. Manila: University of the Philippines, Ph.D. thesis.

Maryott, Kenneth R., and Charles E. Grimes. 1994. "Named speech registers in Austronesian languages." In *Language contact and change in the Austronesian-speaking world*, edited by Tom Dutton and Darrell Tryon, 275–319. Berlin: Mouton de Gruyter.

McElvenny, James. 2018. *Language and meaning in the age of modernism: C. K. Ogden and his contemporaries*. Edinburgh: Edinburgh University Press.

McGregor, William B. 1989. "Gooniyandi mother-in-law 'language': Dialect, register and/or code?" In *Status and function of languages and language varieties*, edited by Ulrich Ammon, 630–656. Berlin: Walter de Gruyter.

Miller, Christopher. 2014. "Devanagari's descendants in North and South India, Indonesia and the Philippines." *Writing Systems Research* 6 (1):10–24.

Misa, Sotero Nuñez. 1970. *The life and struggle of Francisco Dagohoy: A historical and cultural heritage to the Filipino people*. Tagbilaran: University of Bohol, Ph.D. dissertation.

Mojares, Resil B. 1976. "The Pulahanes of Cebu." *Philippine Quarterly of Culture and Society* 4:233–242.

Mojares, Resil B. 2006a. *Brains of the nation: Pedro Paterno, TH Pardo de Tavera, Isabelo de los Reyes and the production of modern knowledge*. Quezon City: Ateneo de Manila.

Mojares, Resil B. 2006b. "The formation of Filipino nationality under U.S. colonial rule." *Philippine Quarterly of Culture and Society* 34:11–32.

Moliner, María. 2007. *Diccionario de uso del español*. 3rd ed. Vol. I. Madrid: Gredos.

Moreno, Msg. Robespierre Tan. 2005. *IFI centennial celebration 1905–2005: Ika-100 ka tuig nga panglungtad parokya ni San Pedro, Biabas, Guindulman, Bohol*. Biabas: Parokya ni San Pedro.

Morey, Stephen. 2015. "Metadata and endangered archives: Lessons from the Ahom Manuscripts Project." In *From dust to digital: Ten years of the Endangered Archives Programme*, edited by Maja Kominko, 31–65. Cambridge: Open Book Publishers.

Morga, Antonio de. [1609] 1890. *Sucesos de las Islas Filipinas: por el Doctor Antonio de Morgan, obra publicada en Méjico el año de 1609, nuevamente sacada a luz y anotada por José Rizal y precedida de un prólogo del Prof. Fernando Blumentritt*. Paris: Garnier Hermanos.

Nabayra, Emmanuel S., and Amelia Rogel-Rara. 1992. "The genealogical evidence." In *The Tasaday controversy: Assessing the evidence*, edited by Thomas N. Headland, 89–106. Washington, DC: Special publication of the American Anthropological Association.

Nance, John. 1975. *The gentle Tasaday: A Stone Age people in the Philippine rain forest*. New York: Harcourt Brace Jovanovich.

Nazareno, Clovis L. 1999. "Transcribing the Lost Language of the Eskaya." In *A habit of ahores: Filipino poetry and verse from English, 60's to the 90's*, edited by Gemino H. Abad, 392–393. Quezon City: University of the Philippines Press.

Office for Southern Cultural Communities. ca. 1996. Ancestral Domain Management Plan.

Ongsotto, Rebecca Ramilo, and Reena R. Ongsotto. 2002. *Philippine history: Module-based learning*. Quezon City: Rex Book Store.

Orcullo, Proceso L. 2004. *The Eskaya communities of Taytay, Duero Bohol: A study of change and continuity*. Davao: Ateneo De Davao University, Ph.D. dissertation.

Osorio, Amando. 1913. *Daylinda: Ang Walay Palad: ang Sugbu sa Kanhing Panahon*. Cebu: Falek.

Padley, George Arthur. 1976. *Grammatical theory in Western Europe, 1500–1700: The Latin tradition*. Cambridge and New York: Cambridge University Press.

Padley, George Arthur. 1988. *Grammatical theory in Western Europe 1500–1700: Trends in vernacular grammar II*. Cambridge: Cambridge University Press.

Pajo, Maria Caseñas. 1954. *Bohol folklore*. Cebu City: University of San Carlos, master's thesis.

Panganiban, José Villa. 1965. "Introduction." In *English–Tagalog dictionary*, edited by Leo James English. Manila: Department of Education, Republic of the Philippines.

Paredes, Oona. 2019. "Preserving 'tradition': The business of indigeneity in the modern Philippine context." *Journal of Southeast Asian Studies* 50 (1):86–106.

Paterno, Pedro Alejandro. [1887] 1915. *La antigua civilización tagálog*. Manila: Colegio de Sto. Tomás.

Paterno, Pedro Alejandro. 1890. *Los Itas*. Madrid: Imprenta de los Sucesores de Cuesta.

Pavón, José María [Marco, Jose E]. 1957. *The Robertson translations of the Pavón manuscripts of 1838–1839*. Chicago: Philippine Studies Program, Department of Anthropology, University of Chicago.

Pawley, Andrew. 1992. "Kalam Pandanus language: An Old New Guinea experiment in language engineering." In *The language game: Papers in memory of Don C. Laycock*, edited by Tom Dutton, Malcolm Ross, and Darrell Tryon, 313–334. Canberra: Pacific Linguistics.

Payot, Alberto A. 1981. "Bisayan Eskaya: Karaang pinulongan sa Bohol?" *Bisaya*, June 3, 1981, 11, 55–57.

Peralta, Jesus T. 2005. Jesus T. Peralta to Alfonso B. Catolin, February 23, 2005. NCIP Bohol archives. Manila: Pambansang Komisyon Para sa Kultura at mga Sining.

Philip, Bromeley. 2007. *A seminal study of Iban alphabet*. Unpublished MS.

Philippine Commission. 1900–1907. *Reports of the Philippine Commission*. Washington: Government Printing Office.

Pigafetta, Antonio. [1525] 1903. "Primo viaggio intorno al mondo." In *The Philippine Islands*, edited by Emma Helen Blair and James Alexander Robertson, 37–180. Cleveland: A.H. Clark.

Policarpio, Cherry. 1991. "The Eskaya tribe: The living legacy of a forgotten language." *Mabuhay*, September 1991, 24–27.

Racelis, Mary. 2001. "Introduction: Bearing benevolence in the classroom and community." In *Bearers of benevolence: The Thomasites and public education in the Philippines*, edited by Mary Racelis and Judy Celine Ick, 61–69. Pasig City: Anvil Publishing.

Rafael, Vicente L. 1988. *Contracting colonialism: Translation and Christian conversion in Tagalog society under early Spanish rule*. Ithaca and London: Cornell University Press.

Ramos, Maximo D. 1971. *The aswang syncrasy in Philippine folklore*. Manila: Philippine Folklore Society.

Ramos, Salome. 1980. *National Book Week Project Proposal addressed to Mrs. Corazon M. Nera, FAPE Library, Legaspi Village, Makati, Metro Manila*. Tagbilaran City: Bohol Provincial Library.

Rao, Rahul. 2010. *Third world protest: Between home and the world*. Oxford: Oxford University Press.

Ratcliff, Lucetta K. 1951. "Some folklore from Bicol Province, Philippine Islands." *Western Folklore* 10 (3):231–236.

Real Academia Española. 2004. *Diccionario de la lengua española.* Vol. I. Madrid: Editorial Espasa Calpe.

Reid, Lawrence A. 1992. "The Tasaday language: A key to Tasaday prehistory." In *The Tasaday controversy: Assessing the evidence*, edited by Thomas N. Headland, 180–193. Washington, DC: Special publication of the American Anthropological Association.

Reid, Lawrence A. 1996. "The Tasaday tapes." Pan-Asiatic linguistics: Fourth International Symposium on Languages and Linguistics, Salaya, Thailand.

Reith, Timothy M., and Ethan E. Cochrane. 2018. "The chronology of colonization in remote Oceania." In *The Oxford Handbook of Prehistoric Oceania*, edited by Ethan E. Cochrane and Terry L. Hunt, 133–161. New York: Oxford University Press.

Riesenberg, Saul H., and Shigeru Kaneshiro. 1960. "A Caroline Islands script." In *Bureau of American Ethnology Bulletin 173*, 269–333. Washington DC: Smithsonian Institution.

Rizal, José. [1886] 1997. *Noli me tangere.* Translated by Soledad Lacson-Locsin. Honolulu: University of Hawaii Press.

Robbeets, Martine, and Lars Johanson, eds. 2012. *Copies versus cognates in bound morphology.* Leiden: Brill.

Romanillos, Emmanuel Luis A. 1997. *The Dagohoy rebellion revisited.* Quezon City: University of the Philippines-Diliman.

Ruiz, Licinio. 1925. *Sinopsis histórica de la provincia de San Nicolás de Tolentino de las Islas Filipinas de la Orden de Agustinos Descalzos.* Vol. I. Manila: Tip. Pont. de la Univ. de Sto. Tomás.

Rumsey, Alan. 2010. "Lingual and cultural wholes and fields." In *Experiments in holism: Theory and practice in contemporary anthropology*, edited by Ton Otton and Nils Bubandt, 145–171. Oxford: Blackwell.

Sahlins, Marshall. 2012. "Alterity and autochthony: Austronesian cosmographies of the marvelous." *Hau: Journal of Ethnographic Theory* 2 (1):131–160.

Salazar, Zeus. 1992. "Third and final footnote on the Tasaday." In *The Tasaday controversy: Assessing the evidence*, edited by Thomas N. Headland, 76–85. Washington, DC: Special publication of the American Anthropological Association.

Sanchez de la Rosa, Antonio. 1887. *Gramatica hispano-visaya, con algunas lecciones prácticas, intercaladas en el texto, que facilitan á los niños indigenas de las provincias de Leyte y Samar la verdadera y genuina expresión de la lengua castellana.* Manila: Amigos del Pais.

Santiago, Rey A. 2003. "Archeological overview of Bohol Island prehistory." In *Tubod: The heart of Bohol*, edited by Ramon N. Villegas, 20–27. Manila: National Commission for Culture and the Arts.

Sawyer, Frederic H. 1900. *The Inhabitants of the Philippines*. London: Sampson Low, Marston and Company.

Schleicher, August. 1869. *Darwinism tested by the science of language*. Translated by Alex V. W. Bikkers. London: John Camden Hotten.

Schumacher, John. 1979. "The 'Propagandists'' reconstruction of the Philippine past." In *Perceptions of the past in Southeast Asia*, edited by Anthony Reid and David Marr, 264–280. Singapore: Heinmann Educational Books.

Scott, James C. 1985. *Weapons of the weak: Everyday forms of peasant resistance*. New Haven and London: Yale University Press.

Scott, James C. 2009. *The art of not being governed: An anarchist history of Upland Southeast Asia*. New Haven and London: Yale University Press.

Scott, William Henry. 1974. *The discovery of the Igorots: Spanish contacts with the pagans of northern Luzon*. Quezon City: New Day Publishers.

Scott, William Henry. 1992. *Looking for the prehispanic Filipino and other essays in Philippine history*. Quezon City: New Day Publishers.

Scott, William Henry. 1994. *Barangay: Sixteenth-century Philippine culture and society*. Quezon City: Ateneo De Manila University Press.

Scriven, George Percival. 1900. An American in Bohol, The Philippines, 1899–1901, diary, http://library.duke.edu/rubenstein/scriptorium/scriven/, accessed December 21, 2011.

Semper, Carl. 1869. *Die Philippinen und ihre Bewohner*. Würzburg: A. Stuber.

Seuren, Pieter A.M. 1998. *Western linguistics: An historical introduction*. Oxford, UK, and Malden, MA: Blackwell Publishers.

Siegert, Folker. 1996. "Early Jewish interpretation in a Hellenistic style." In *Hebrew Bible Old Testament: The history of its interpretation I/1: Antiquity*, edited by Christianus Brekelmans and Menahem Iaran, 154–162. Göttingen: Vandenhoeck & Ruprecht.

Silverstein, Michael. 2000. "Whorfianism and the linguistic imagination of nationality." In *Regimes of language: Ideology, polities, identities*, edited by Paul V. Kroskrity. Santa Fe and Oxford: School of American Research Press & James Currey.

Silverstein, Michael. 2001. "The limits of awareness." In *Linguistic Anthropology, a reader*, edited by Alessandro Duranti, 382–401. Oxford: Blackwell.

Smalley, William A., Chia Koua Vang, and Gnia Yee Yang. 1990. *Mother of writing: The origin and development of a Hmong messianic script*. Chicago: University of Chicago Press.

Snyder-Frey, Alicia. 2013. "He kuleana kō kākou: Hawaiian-language learners and the construction of (alter) native identities." *Current Issues in Language Planning* 14 (2):231–243.

Stasch, Rupert. 2012. "Afterword: On relationality of codes and the indexical iconicity of linguistic otherness within wider value formations." *The Australian Journal of Anthropology* 23 (3):398–405.

Street, Brian. 1984. *Literacy in theory and practice*. Cambridge: Cambridge University Press.

Street, Brian, ed. 1993. *Cross-cultural approaches to literacy*. Cambridge and New York: Cambridge University Press.

Stuntz, Homer C. 1904. *The Philippines and the Far East*. Cincinnati: Jennings & Pye.

Sturtevant, David R. 1976. *Popular uprisings in the Philippines, 1840–1940*. New York: Cornell University Press.

Taft, Helen Herron. 1914. *Recollections of full years*. New York: Dodd, Mead & Company.

Thieberger, Nicholas. 1988. *Aboriginal language maintenance: Some issues and strategies*. Melbourne: La Trobe University, Ph.D. dissertation.

Thomas, Megan C. 2012. *Orientalists, propagandists and ilustrados: Filipino scholarship and the end of Spanish colonialism*. Minneapolis and London: University of Minnesota Press.

Thomason, Sarah. 1997. "A typology of contact languages." In *The structure and status of pidgins and creoles*, edited by Arthur K. Spears, 71–88. Amsterdam and Philadelphia: John Benjamins.

Thomason, Sarah. 2007. "Language contact and deliberate change." *Journal of Language Contact, Thema I* 1 (1):41–62.

Tinampay, Miriam Rocha. 1977. *Dialectology of Bohol Cebuano and its implications to teaching English phonology*. Manila: Ateneo de Manila, Ph.D. dissertation.

Tirol, Jes B. 1989. "Bohol: A new Jerusalem?" *The Bohol Chronicle*, March 19, 1989, 1, 3.

Tirol, Jes B. 1990a. "Bohol and its system of writing. *UB Update*, July–September 1990, 4, 7.

Tirol, Jes B. 1990b. "Butuan paleograph deciphered using the Eskaya script." *UB Update*, October–December, 6, 14.

Tirol, Jes B. 1991. "Eskaya of Bohol: Traces of Hebrew influence paving the way for easy Christianization of Bohol." *Bohol's Pride*, July 1991, 50–51, 53.

Tirol, Jes B. 1993a. "Eskaya of Bohol: Is it a tribe?" *The Bohol Chronicle*, June 20, 1993, n.d.

Tirol, Jes B. 1993b. "Eskaya of Bohol: Its numerals and symbols." *The Bohol Chronicle*, July 18, 1993, 42, 45.

Tirol, Jes B. 1993c. "Eskaya of Bohol: Its revered leaders." *The Bohol Chronicle*, June 27, 1993, n.d.

Tirol, Jes B. 1998. *Bohol: From Spanish yoke to American harness*. Tagbilaran City: Universal Press.

Tirol, Jes B. 2000. "Biography of Mariano Datahan Sumatra." Part 5. *The Bohol Chronicle*, June 25, 2000, n.d.

Tirol, Lumin B. 1975. *History of Bohol: Pre-hispanic up to 1972*. Manila: University of Santo Tomas, Ph.D. dissertation.

Tirol, Victoriano B. 1968. *A study of Bohol literature (hero-tale, drama, poetry and short story)*. Manila: University of Santo Tomas, Ph.D. dissertation.

Tomlinson, Matt, and Miki Makihara. 2009. "New paths in the linguistic anthropology of Oceania." *Annual Review of Anthropology* 38:17–31.

Torralba, Milan Ted. 1991a. *Description of preliminary and future data elicitation for linguistic analysis of the Eskaya language of Bohol: A term paper submitted in partial fulfilment of the requirements for the subject of Linguistics 703 (Field Methods in Linguistics)*. M.A. Linguistics. Manila: The Pontifical University of Santo Tomas.

Torralba, Milan Ted. 1991b. *The morphology of the Eskaya language: A term paper submitted in partial fulfilment of the requirements in LNG 704 (Morphology & Syntax)*. Manila: The Pontifical and Royal University of Santo Tomas.

Torralba, Milan Ted. 1993. *A linguistic investigation into the origin and structure of the Eskaya-Bisayan ethnolanguage: A thesis proposal presented to the Graduate School*. Manila: The Pontifical University of Santo Tomas.

Torralba, Sergio. 1916. "Uac-uac." In *Ethnography of the Bisaya peoples*. Volume 3, paper no. 86. Box no. 103, edited by H. Otley Beyer. Manuscript collection held in the National Library of Australia.

Torres, J. 1903. "The United States vs. Estaquio Daligdig G.R. No. 1079." Chan Robles Virtual Law Library: Philippine Supreme Court Decisions, accessed August 2011, http://www.chanrobles.com/cralaw19037.htm.

Totanes, Sebastián de. 1745. *Arte de la lengua tagala, y manual tagalog para la administración de los Santos Sacramentos*. Manila: Convento del Nuestra Señora de Loreto.

Trosdal, Mimi B. 1990. *Formal-functional Cebuano–English dictionary*. Cebu City: Societatis Verbi Divini Roma.

Trudgill, Peter. 1986. *Dialects in contact*. New York: Basil Blackwell.

Tsing, Anna. 1993. *In the realm of the diamond queen: Marginality in an out-of-the-way place*. Princeton: Princeton University Press.

Verzosa, Paul Rodriguez. 1939. *Pangbansang titik nang Pilipinas*. Manila: Institute of National Language.

Villacorte, Francisco. 1833. *Administración espiritual de los Padres Agustinos Calzados de la Provincia del Dulce Nombre de Jesus de las Islas Filipinas*. Valladolid: Roldan.

Villamor, Ignacio. 1922. *La antigua escritura filipina*. Manila: Pontificia del Colegio de Sto. Tomás.

Vitug, Marites Danguilan. 1995. "Faith, hope and politics." In *Boss: 5 case studies of local politics in the Philippines*, edited by Jose F. Lacaba. Pasig, Metro Manila: Philippine Center for Investigative Journalism.

Wagner, Roy. 1975. *The invention of culture*. Englewood Cliffs, NJ: Prentice-Hall.

Wallace, Anthony F.C. 1956. "Revitalization movements." *American Anthropologist* 58 (2):264–281.

Ward, Jack H. 1971. *A bibliography of Philippine linguistics and minor languages*. Ithaca: Cornell University Southeast Asia Program.

Willis, Henry Parker. 1905. *Our Philippine problem: A study of American colonial policy*. New York: Henry Holt and Company.

Wittersheim, Éric. 1999. "Les chemins de l'authenticité: Les anthropologues et la Renaissance mélanésienne." *L'Homme* 151:181–205.

Wolff, John U. 1972a. *A dictionary of Cebuano Visayan*. Vol. I. Ithaca, New York: Cornell University.

Wolff, John U. 1972b. *A dictionary of Cebuano Visayan*. Vol. II. Ithaca, New York: Cornell University.

Woolard, Kathryn A. 1998. "Introduction: Language ideology as a field of inquiry." In *Language ideologies: Practice and theory*, edited by Bambi B. Schieffelin, Kathryn A. Woolard, and Paul V. Kroskrity, 3–47. New York and Oxford: Oxford University Press.

Woolard, Kathryn A. 2016. *Singular and plural: Ideologies of linguistic authority in 21st century Catalonia*. New York: Oxford University Press.

Zaide, Gregorio F. 1959. *History of the Filipino people*. Manila: Villanueva Book Store.

Zincke, Herbert, with Scott A. Mills. 2003. *Mitsui madhouse: Memoir of a U.S. Army Air Corps POW in World War II*. Jefferson, NC, & London: McFarland & Company.

Zorc, David Paul. 1977. The Bisayan dialects of the Philippines: Subgrouping and reconstruction. Canberra: Pacific Linguistics.

Zuckermann, Ghil'ad. 2003. *Language contact and lexical enrichment in Israeli Hebrew*. Houndmills: Palgrave Macmillan.

Zuckermann, Ghil'ad. 2006. "'Etymythological othering' and the power of 'lexical engineering' in Judaism, Islam and Christianity. A socio-philo(sopho)logical perspective." In *Explorations in the sociology of language and religion*, 237–258. Amsterdam: John Benjamins.

# GLOSSARY OF ESKAYAN TERMS USED IN THIS VOLUME

| | | |
|---|---|---|
| **aga** | *buntag* | 'morning' |
| **agad** | *adtu* | 'over there' |
| **agahun; kayra** | *urasan* | 'clock,' 'watch' |
| **agura** | *istasyun* | 'Station of the Cross' |
| **alaba** | *urasiyun* | 'prayer' |
| **alak** | *arak* | 'wine or liquor' |
| **aminahadu** | *bilin* | 'remain' |
| **amirsim** | *ritratu* | 'photograph' |
| **anchdiyaasu** | *kaaway* | 'enemy' |
| **apuysigaru** | *tabaku* | 'tobacco' |
| **ararara** | *diyusdiyus* | 'dios-dios,' false god |
| **argas** | *milyas* | 'mile' |
| **arhitika** | *kita* | 'we' INCL |
| **aripirna** | *sundalu* | 'soldier' |
| **asi** | *arun* | 'in order to' |
| **astru** | *adlaw* | 'day,' 'sun' |
| **aswang** | *wakwak* | 'k.o. bird whose call signifies the presence of a vampire'; 'a vampire' |
| **atsil** | *siya* | 'she,' 'he' |
| **aya** | *asa* | 'where?' |
| **aymahan** | *gimahayan* | 'was subjected to feelings of hurt by' |
| **babaylan** | *babaylan* | 'shaman,' 'priest' |
| **baganhunda** | *huwis* | 'judge' |
| **bagani hibir** | *hiniral* | 'general' |

| | | |
|---|---|---|
| **baganibagani** | *diktadur* | 'dictator' |
| **baganiring** | *kumandanti hiniral* | 'major general' |
| **bahiw** | *gigaid* | 'was tied' |
| **bak** | *suba* | 'river' |
| **balsa** | *sakayan* | 'wooden boat' |
| **bandi** | *bandira* | 'flag' |
| **bandi, panubandi** | *bandira* | 'flag' |
| **bansithi** | *gubirnadur* | 'governor' |
| **baruta** | *asukar* | 'refined sugar' |
| **baruun** | *pas-ana* | 'carry s.t. over the shoulders' |
| **basak** | *sugigi* | 'large basket for grain' |
| **basiku** | *baul, kaban* | 'trunk,' 'chest' |
| **bawik** | *biyulita* | 'violet' |
| **bidaryu** | *pinulungan* | 'language' |
| **biki** | *kardinal* | 'cardinal' |
| **bilik** | *anindut* | 'beautiful' |
| **binil** | *didtu, ngadtu* | 'that there' |
| **bintaal** | *gigamit, migamit* | 'used s.t.,' 'used' |
| **biriil** | *mitrus* | 'meter' |
| **birsirdas** | *mga maistra* | 'female teachers' |
| **bisa** | *simbahan* | 'church' |
| **biyabi** | *bisita* | 'visitor' |
| **biyarga** | *rayna* | 'queen' |
| **bril, dudu** | *kabayu* | 'horse' |
| **bulbing** | *bulbul* ('pubic hair'), *bubuk* ('hair of the head') | 'hair,' 'pubic hair' |
| **bultu** | *tawu* | 'person' |
| **bultulis** | *katawhan* | 'people' |
| **busdi** | *sapa* | 'creek' |
| **chdagwit** | *talinis* | 'sharp-pointed' |
| **chdan** | *sila* | 'they' |
| **chdiktu** | *kamu* | 'you' |
| **chdil** | *iyang* | 'his' |
| **chdin** | *ning* | 'this' |
| **chdiyami** | *mansanas* | 'apple' |
| **chdiyukir** | *timawa* | 'poor,' 'destitute' |
| **damulag** | *baka* | 'cow' |
| **damuti** | *kutsara* | 'spoon' |

| | | |
|---|---|---|
| di'al | *barutu* | 'small boat without a sail' |
| Dibi | *Disimbri* | 'December' |
| digu | *gidakup* | 'was caught,' 'was arrested' |
| dil | *dinhi, nganhi* | 'this over here' |
| dilbi | *ginapus [gapus]* | 'was continuously bound or tied down' |
| dildawusdami | *gilingkusan* | 'was curled up or knotted by' |
| dililu | *gidamag* | 'caused to become sick by ghosts' |
| dilur | *urins* | 'orange' |
| dilyaki | *niana' (ana')* | 'that there' |
| dilyun | *sinsilyu* | 'small change' |
| dirisil | *sinyas* | 'sign made by the body,' 'gesture' |
| ditsu | *kay* | 'because' |
| drinkir, drikis | *sikwati* | 'drink' |
| dutal | *lapis* | 'pencil' |
| gadyus | *sinadur* | 'senator' |
| gal | *higala* | 'friend' |
| gamyu | *giilu* | 'lost a parent,' 'became deprived' |
| giring | *trin* | 'railway train' |
| giyu | *dayun* | 'immediately' |
| grimsi | *dalag* | 'light yellow' |
| griski | *brawun* | 'brown' |
| griyalu | *kamaayu* | 'greatness' |
| gruwirtiri | *giluiban* | 'was betrayed by' |
| gulada | *sapatus, sinilas* | 'shoe,' 'slipper' |
| guldami | *gihay* | 'petal' |
| guwagu | *daku* | 'large' |
| hibinu | *Pibriru* | 'February' |
| hibir | *hiniral* | 'general' (military) |
| hubis | *huwibis* | 'Thursday' |
| huntun | *kampanaryu* | 'bell tower' |
| huntun | *ubus* | 'under' |
| hup | *upisina* | 'office' |
| hus | *kabaw* | 'water buffalo' |
| i | *ug* | 'and,' 'if,' NSPC 'some' |
| idiyumut | *itum* | 'black' |
| idlak | *white* | 'white' |
| idlak | *puti, ugis* | 'white' |
| iklabultu | *pagkatawu* | 'birth,' 'giving birth' |
| ilgatu | *gunting* | 'scissors' |

| | | |
|---|---|---|
| **ilkabultu** | *natawu* | 'born,' 'newly born' |
| **imprus** | *gipuslan* | 'was taken on' |
| **imur** | *daygun [dalayig]* | 'Christmas carols' |
| **inmunsiktur** | *Papa* | 'pope' |
| **inpintir** | *isklibinti* | 'clerk' |
| **insiktur** | *ubispu* | 'bishop' |
| **insil** | *maung* | 'be' |
| **iriyukisim** | *giila* | 'was identified, recognized' |
| **isirdas** | *maistra* | 'female teacher' |
| **iskrit** | *iskwilahan* | 'school' |
| **ispitdu** | *ispirituhanun* | 'spiritual' |
| **istalyi** | *ania (nia)* | 'here' |
| **istalyi (istal)** | *anaa (naa)* | 'there' |
| **istu** | *ang* | 'the' |
| **istuwal** | *istudiyanti* | 'student' |
| **kabrum** | *kabaw* | 'water buffalo' |
| **kandi** | *kandidatu/a* (M/F) | 'leader of a group,' 'political leader' |
| **kanis** | *abiyun* | 'airplane' |
| **karku** | *kana' (na')* | 'that there' |
| **katsila'** | *katsila'* | 'Spaniard' |
| **kayra** | *uras* | 'hour,' 'time of day' |
| **kibir** | *tinidur* | 'fork' |
| **kim** | *kami* | 'we' EXCL |
| **kinya** | *kinsa* | 'who?' |
| **klir** | *makalugas* | 'clear' |
| **kriyusisu** | *ang pulung ni Jesus* | 'the word of Jesus' |
| **kulpanu** | *batasan* | 'proper behavior,' 'code of behavior' |
| **kulyar** | *tubig* | 'water' |
| **kumpanitu** | *kumpari* | 'father, godfather, or father-in-law' |
| **kun** | *ni* | 'of a person' |
| **kunyus** | *apiki* | 'narrow,' 'inadequate in space' |
| **kutik** | *guma* | 'rubber' |
| **kuy** | *tulu* | 'three' |
| **kuyba** | *buhu* | 'hole' |
| **laban** | *laba ('wash clothing')* | 'wash' |
| **labila** | *daku* | 'large' |
| **labu** | *arinula* | 'chamber pot' |
| **lad** | *anak* | 'child' |

| | | |
|---|---|---|
| lakiri | *gidulngan [dulung]* | 'was approaching' |
| lam | *pista, pyista* | 'fiesta' |
| langam | *langaw* | 'fly' [insect] |
| langis | *ngalan* | 'name' |
| lasiku | *lamisa* | 'table' |
| latin | *latin* | 'Latin' |
| libirsim | *libirtad* | 'freedom' |
| librit | *libru* | 'book' |
| ligar | *libut* | 'surround,' 'go around' |
| ligarti | *gilibutan* | 'was surrounded by' |
| liksun | *butilya* | 'bottle' |
| limanus | *yawi* | 'key' |
| limur | *away* | 'quarrel' |
| limurdil | *awaya* | 'this specific fight' |
| limursidi | *awayun* | 'will fight' |
| lindil | *liyun* | 'lion' |
| lini | *lunis* | 'Monday' |
| liyir | *tinta', tintiru* | 'ink' |
| lumad | *tribu* | 'tribe' |
| lundu | *munisipyu* | 'town hall' |
| lup | *sagsag* | 'lip,' 'lips' |
| lurim | *apilyidu* | 'surname' |
| luris | *dautan* | 'bad in character or effect'; 'sorcery' |
| lurisima | *himaya* | 'glory,' 'spiritual joy' |
| luriski | *kadautan* | 'wickedness,' 'evil' |
| lyunggu | *duminggu* | 'Sunday' |
| masu | *Marsu* | 'March' |
| maw | *Mayu* | 'May' |
| mibul | *mirkulis* | 'Wednesday' |
| midikil | *duktur* | 'doctor' |
| midyu | *upisyalis* | 'person holding an office' |
| milagral | *milagru* | 'miracle' |
| mimati | *martis* | 'Tuesday' |
| mininus | *niya* | 'of her/him' |
| miridu | *bana* | 'husband' |
| mirikilyu | *duktur* | 'doctor' |
| miyur | *kumpisal* | 'go to confession' |
| muldisiyun | *gubat* | 'war' |
| muruki | *gilukdu* | 'was carried on the head' |

| | | |
|---|---|---|
| muybanal | *gilungguan [lunggu]* | 'was beheaded by' |
| muyistawitis | *gibuhat* | 'did work,' 'made,' 'created' |
| muyluris | *mangilad* | 'cheat,' 'swindle' |
| muynunung | *pagmanihu* | 'drive a vehicle' |
| muytuyu | *gidistinu* | 'was assigned for employment' |
| muyyupin | *gibabagan [balabag]* | 'laid across a path' |
| nani | *nanay* | 'mother' |
| narin | *aku* | 'I' |
| ngiyus | *ngitngit* | 'darkness' |
| nintiyasas | *kaawayan* | 'group of enemies' |
| ninus | *kaniya* | 'for her/him' |
| nistru | *nimu* | 'of you,' 'for you' |
| nuku | *kagaw* | 'itch-mite' |
| num | *unum* | 'six' |
| num | *unum* | 'six' |
| pakan | *anghil* | 'angel' |
| pan | *upat* | 'four' |
| pan | *upat* | 'four' |
| pansi | *kwarinta* | 'forty' |
| paypaypling | *alibangbang* | 'butterfly' |
| pil, piyil | *panit* | 'skin' |
| pilipayin | *Pilipinhun* | 'Filipino' |
| pim | *pitsa* | 'date' (of year) |
| pin | *pitu* | 'seven' |
| pinal | *sinugdan, primiru* | 'first,' 'firstly' |
| pirsiyan | *nila* | 'of them,' 'for them' |
| planu | *bandira* | 'flag' |
| prin | *dinamita* | 'dynamite' |
| pruk | *bariyu* | 'district' |
| pulpul | *pabrika* | 'factory' |
| pun | *pulu* | 'ten' |
| punlas | *sabun* | 'soap' |
| purchdidi | *sakramintu* | 'sacrament' |
| purgampi | *nga tagi* | 'hail from' |
| purmu | *abug* | 'ashes,' 'dust' |
| puwim | *pula* | 'red' |
| puy, sam | *kang* | 'for a person' |
| ribus | *insinsu* | 'incense' |
| ridil'ayis | *ipahinungud [tungud]* | 'dedicate s.t to s.o' |

| | | |
|---|---|---|
| ridilyan | *kaninyu* | 'for you' |
| rigani | *gihapun* | 'still,' 'as before' |
| riihada | *gihandum* | 'was recalled and thought of fondly' |
| rikas | *abat* | 'support' |
| riklus | *gilungkat* | 'was pried open' |
| rimuy | *mga* | PL |
| rinarilya | *gihimu* | 'was done,' 'was made' |
| risinglun | *giingun* | 'was like,' 'was similar to' |
| ritilda | *kilumitru* | 'kilometer' |
| riyablansu | *gibasulan* | 'was blamed for' |
| salay | *bintana* | 'window' |
| sampris | *papil* | 'paper' |
| samu | *ikaw* | 'you' |
| sandiya | *gihukman [hukum]* | 'was judged by' |
| sapaw | *midyas* | 'socks' |
| sapitu | *bagtak* | 'calf of leg' |
| sawardit | *iksaminisyun* | 'examination' |
| sikadu | *iliksiyun, piliay* | 'election' |
| sikrit | *bilyiti* | 'note,' 'short letter,' 'love letter' |
| silmunsi | *balakburd* | 'blackboard' |
| silyis | *tirmus* | 'thermos bottle' |
| sim | *siyam* | 'nine' |
| sim | *siyam* | 'nine' |
| simri | *kini, kani, (ni)* | 'this over here' |
| sing | *singku, lima* | 'five' |
| sirdas | *mungha* | 'nun' |
| sirdas | *mungha* | 'nun' |
| Sitibi | *Siptimbri* | 'September' |
| sul | *alimuut* | 'warm' |
| sutbagani | *hari* | 'king' |
| tadlang | *niadtu (adtu)* | 'that there' |
| tap, uwis | *pisu* | 'peso' |
| tarbu | *kalis* | 'chalice' |
| tindas | *salapi* | 'money' |
| tingbuk | *buktun* | 'arms' |
| tiyunmiridu | *magtiayun* | 'romantic couple' |
| tri | *duha* | 'two' |
| tugarira | *atua (tua)* | 'over there' |

| | | |
|---|---|---|
| **tuispitduing, ispitduing** | *ispiritu* | 'spirit' |
| **tumpuy** | *naku* | 'of me,' 'for me' |
| **turbati** | *takuri* | 'kettle' |
| **tutulan** | *magtutudlo* | 'teacher' |
| **tuylup** | *kadtu (tu)* | 'that there' |
| **unyada** | *sibuyas* | 'onion' |
| **urinitril** | *urihinal* | 'original' |
| **Utkubi** | *Uktubri* | 'October' |
| **uwan** | *uwak* | 'crow' |
| **uy** | *usa* | 'one' |
| **wal** | *walu* | 'eight' |
| **wintiskis** | *iditur* | 'editor' |
| **wirdu** | *asul* | 'blue' |
| **wirhang** | *bitay* | 'hang' |
| **witsiktur** | *arsubispu* | 'archbishop' |
| **wuntu** | *birdi* | 'green' |
| **ya** | *sa* | 'to,' 'of' |
| **yadinal** | *giilung [lilung]* | 'was concealed'; 'was made dizzy' |
| **yaduwal** | *giihaw* | 'slaughtered (of an animal)' |
| **yardi** | *anha'* | 'there' |
| **yi** | *si* | SPEC for a person |
| **yitalim** | *gibati* | 'felt effects in the body' |
| **yu** | *ku* | 'of me' |
| **yupir** | *giluwatan* | 'was accidentally let go' |

# INDEX

The letter *f* following a page locator indicates a figure, *m* indicates a map, and *t* indicates a table.

Abakano, 242
Abidiha (alphabet). *See* alphabet
    (Abidiha)
Ablem, Faustino, 190
Aboriginal language acquisition, 35n13
Abregana, , Brenda, 39–41, 44, 46, 48–49,
    54–55, 57, 75, 159, 194, 228–229,
    231, 241, 247
accommodation and resistance
    dialectic, 9
Acocella, Joan, 140
Acquaviva, Claudius, 20
Adam, the biblical, xxxi
Adam and Eve narrative, 149, 189
Adam and Idam, 189
Adang, Uma, 245
Agastya, xxx
Aglipay, Gregorio, 25, 32, 173, 186–187,
    189, 192, 198
Aglipayanism, 194, 228
Aglipayan missionization period,
    186–189
Aglipayans, 36n16, 192
Aguinaldo, Emilio, 23–25, 178
Alburang, 160
Alcala, Francisco, 182
Alcina, Ignacio, 20–21

alphabet (Abidiha)
    example of, 96t
    expansion of the, 218
    first uses of, 212
    forgeries, 239
    importance of, 141
    learning the, 79, 93f, 102
    lettershapes, anthropomorphism of, 8,
        88, 92, 101–102, 136, 146, 159–161,
        163–164, 175
    models for the, 103–104
    overview, 92–95
    personified as plants, 161–163
    retrieval of, 215–218
    revealed, 229
alphabet (Abidiha), literature of the
    "Atikisis," 161–163
    "The Spanish and Eskayan
        Alphabets," 159–161, 163, 167,
        216–217
American era
    Aglipay's threat, 25
    annexation of the Philippines, 24
    colonial narrative, 22
    education during the, 114, 199, 211,
        213–214
    ladrones fanaticos, 190, 196, 228, 238

American era (*cont.*)
 lowlands, domination of, 3
 nation building, 26
 Philippines, attempts at understanding
  the, 26, 32–33
American era, conflicts
 Boholano-American war, 200, 214
 Kabantian Pass, Battle of, 178–179, 182
 Philippine-American war, 24, 32, 178,
  181, 184–185, 199, 213
American flag, 153, 155
Amgay, 160
Amoy, 205n4
Analiza, Princesa, 242
Ancestral Domain Claim, 55, 59n11, 72
Ancestral Domain Claim area, xvm
Anderson, Benedict, 166, 246–247
*Ang tocsaon sa pangadyeon nga cristianos*
 (*'The catechism for Christian prayer*
 (Astete), 220–222f
Anoy, 147, 153–154, 161, 164–167, 189,
  212, 218–220, 228
anti-language, 67, 243–244
Anugar, 190
Apalisok, Simplicio, 176, 180, 200
Aparece, Alma E., 68
Apodaca, Juan Ruiz de, 24
Arcamo, Pablo, 201
Arens, Richard, 190
Astete, Gaspar, 220, 221f
"Atikisis," 139, 161–163, 216
avoidance vocabulary, 243

Babadzan, Alain, 245
back slangs, 242–243
Baja, Fabian, 42, 46, 49, 51, 104, 112, 117,
  135, 137–138, 147, 168, 175, 201,
  203–204, 212, 248
Balaba, Zenon, 202
Balili, Antonio, 182
balinsiya, story of, 134, 149

Bamum language and script, 245
Bando, Roman T. del, 201
Baranera, Francisco, 22
Bas, 160
Bateson, Gregory, 9, 167
Bedford, Zoë, 189
Ben-Yehuda, Eliezer, 204
Bernales, Catalina, 193, 196
Bernales, Felix (Lantayug), 196
Bernido, Esteban, 176, 200
Beronilla, Juan, 200
Beronilla, Juan Pilimon ('Philemon'),
  181
Beyer, H. Otley, 22, 151
Biabas
 church service, language of, 81
 Dagohoy rebellion, 31–32
 Datahan in, 199
 discovery of, xxx
 education in Eskayan, 216
 Eskayan, reawakening in, 175
 history of, research project
  overview, 4–5
 landscape, 72–73, 74f
 linguistic landscape of, 83
 literature, analysis of, 142–143
 literature transcription in, 141
 migration from, 203
 migration to, 183–186, 184m, 233
 population, 184, 185
 religion in, 188–189, 202
 settlement of, 3–4
 strategic military position,
  186, 199
 true texts in, 142
Biabas encampment, origins of the,
  176–179
Biabas Force, 200
Bininj Kun-wok dialects, 247
Bisaya', xxi–xxii, xxx, 64–65
Bisaya'-Eskaya, xxii

Bisayan Declarado, xxx, 51, 146, 220, 236, 240
Bisayan Diklaradu, xxi–xxii
Bohol
   Aglipayan missionization period, 186–189
   agriculture, 65–66, 72–73, 75
   American invasion, 185
   Datahan in, 176
   earliest inhabitants, 65
   economy, 66
   education in, 31, 69, 213–214
   history of, 238
   housing construction, 75
   illness, 185, 214
   indigenous outlaws in, 29–31
   Japanese occupation, 177
   land reforms, 198
   landscape, 65, 72–75, 73–74f
   location of places mentioned in the text, xivm
   migration from, 194, 196
   millenarianism, 196–197
   population, 66
   pre-contact, 154–155
   prophecies surrounding, 29–30
   religion, 66
   research on, 46–47
   roads, 65, 75, 186
   shamanic rebellion, 29–31
   Spanish colonial period, 10, 185
   in the Visayas, 64–66
Bohol, language use in
   documentation, 29
   English as a catalyst for Eskayan, 212–214
   intra-island linguistic variation, 66–67, 85n6
   languages in their domains, 68f, 69–70
   ritual, 70–72, 71f
   as speech disguised, 70–72, 71f
   spoken, xxii, 64

Boholano, xxvi–xxviif, xxvif, xxvii
Boholano-American war, 200, 214
Boholano identity, 67
Boholanos
   Dagohoy, association with, 152
   Dagohoy rebellion, importance to, 30–32
   language spoken by, xxii, 29, 155
   Lonoy ambush deaths, 182
   resistance movements, 32–34, 192
   voice of the, 64
Boholano-Visayan, xxi, 64–67, 154–155
*Bohol: From Spanish Yoke to American Harness* (Tirol), 47
Bonifacio, Andres, 23
Booy, 160
Borja, Salustiano, 192
Bucas Grande, Laureano Solamo's colorum in, 194, 196
Butalid, Rolando, 40–41, 46

Cadapdan, xxii–xxiii, 72, 73f, 141, 142, 144
Cagas, Victorio, 138
Calderon, Diego Landa de, 19
Campos, Zosimo, 51–52
Canta-ub, 72
Carias, Patricio, 138
Carlos I, 23
Carmen, 192, 197
Castañares, Domingo, 112, 138, 223
Castañares, Eleuterio, 138
Castañares, Olimpio, 183
Castañares manuscript, 113f, 114, 220, 221–222f, 226
Castrodes, Maximo, 200
Catolin, Alfonso, 52–53, 55
Ceblish, 70
Cebu, 19, 146, 161, 164, 194
Cebuano, xxi, 29, 65–66, 85n7, 146, 164, 215
Cebuano-Visayan, 16–18, 17f, 163–164, 214

Certificate of Ancestral Domain Claim (CADC), 51, 55, 72
Chatterjee, Partha, 167
Cherokee writing system, 100
Chirino, Pedro, 19–20
Chocolate Hills, xxiii
churches
    Eskayan domain of, 80–81, 203–204
    language of services, 81
    native Filipino, 25–26, 31
Cirunay, Fausto, 201
Cisneros, Julian, 180
Coben, Herminia Meñez, 197
Code of Kalantiaw, 239
Colin, Francisco, 21, 22
Commonwealth of the Philippines, 27–29
Conklin, Harold, 242
Constantino, Ernesto, 16, 43
Coulmas, Florian, 91
Cuadra, Isteven, 183
cult communities, 189–191, 194, 196

Dagohoy, Francisco, xxiii, 41, 56, 117, 146, 151–152, 159–160, 180
Dagohoy rebellion, xvi*m*, xxiii, 30–33, 151–152, 197, 238
Daligdig, Eustaquio, 181
Damin, xxx, 243, 244
Dangko, 141–142, 146, 150–151, 160, 227–228, 247
Darwin, Charles, 189
Datag, 160
Datahan, Bonifacio, 206n12
Datahan, Clotilde, 198
Datahan, Francisco, 180, 198
Datahan, José, 144
Datahan, Juan, 49, 73, 137–138, 142, 181, 184, 195*f*, 198, 201–203
Datahan, Marcos, 137
Datahan, Mariano

Abregana research, 46
accommodation and resistance dialectic, 238–239, 240–241
Americans, promised protection from, 184
background, 168
Biabas encampment origins and, 176–179
characteristics, 147
death date celebrated, 81
identity of, 87, 138, 147, 175, 212
learning and teaching English, position on, 104
mentioned, 63, 103
nation-building, 247
photograph of, 177*f*
politics, 6
prophecies of, 28, 143–144, 237
scribes, 138, 225
supernatural talents, 143, 168, 176, 178, 186, 193
Vargas correspondence, xxv–xxvi*f*, 28, 83–84
words of, errors in recording, 140–141
Datahan, Mariano 'Anoy,' xxx
Datahan, Mariano, Eskayan and foundation myth, 177
    innovation in reconstruction of, 211–212
    inspirations, 146
    lexicography, 239
    purpose of, 6–7
    reanimating, xxx, 5–6, 135, 136, 146, 159
    relexification method, 235
    revealed to, 211, 235
    scriptures discovered, copies of, 137
Datahan, Mariano, ideology
    Aglipayan missionization period, 186–189
    crypto-utopian agenda, 187

essentialist of nationhood and
    linguistic prestige, 247
longevity, 197
militant cults, 189–191
nationalism, 155
nativism, 189
Pamatasan ('proper behavior')
    code, 187
Datahan, Mariano, legacy
    education, 201, 216–218
    linguistic and literary, 199
    religion, 206n13
    threats to, 202–203
Datahan, Mariano, life story
    autobiography, 177–178
    Biabas, arrival to, 185–186
    contradictions in, 178–180
    death date, 179
    documentation, 182–183
    early years, 161, 179–182
    eastward migration, 182–186
    education and literacy, 178, 180–181,
        212–214, 245
    exploits, oral stories of, 143
    land ownership, 5, 178, 181, 198–199
    name change, 151, 181–182
    near-death experiences, 178, 180
    religion, 5, 32, 178, 179–180, 213
    U.S., accomodation and resistance,
        192, 197–199
    wives and children, 5, 193, 196,
        198–199
Datahan, Mariano, military service
    battle with Americans in Bohol, 182
    claims to, 177, 194
    court martial, 182
    Japanese occupation, 200–201
    Katipunan, involvement with the, 194
    Philippine-American war, 201
    Philippine Revolution, 180
    sedition, arrest and trial for, 201

Spanish army, conscription into the, 5,
    180–181
U.S. army, 178–179, 201
Datahan, Mariano, movement
    Laureano Solamo's colorum, parallels
        with, 194, 196
    millenarianism, persistence of,
        196–197
    Visayan pulahans and, 191–194
Datahan, Panfilo, 184
Datahan, Pascual, 181
Datahan, Pedro, 198
Datahan, Riche, 137
Datahan, Roberto, 55, 82f, 199, 241
Datahan, Sisinia, 198
Datahan, Teodulo, 201
Dayak, Meratus, 245
"Daylinda," 137, 141, 165, 228, 239
Daylinda (Osorio), 215, 228
"Declared Visayan," 146, 161–164, 236
Degracia, Espredion, 138
Deliman, Eusebio, 182
"Desarollo y no Creación"
    ("Development, not Creation")
    (Datahan), 189
Dimabasa, Bernadino, 18
Dinlayan, Lorenzo, 51
Diringer, David, 100
Doctrina Christiana en lengua española y
    tagala, 19
Doctrina Christiana en letra y lengua
    china, 19
Drake, Dennis, 47
Dumont, Jean-Paul, 233
Duya, 160
dyusdus movements, 190, 192

East Boholano-Visayan, xxi
Ecleo, Ruben, 202
education
    American era, 114, 199, 211, 213–214

education (*cont.*)
  in Bohol, 31, 69, 213–214
  Datahan, Mariano, 178, 180–181,
    212–214, 245
  in Eskayan, 42–44, 203–204,
    216–218, 217*f*, 241
  Philippines, 79–80
  Spanish colonial period, 23, 24, 213
  in Taytay, 80, 104
  in Visayan, 69
education in Eskayan
  in Biabas, 216
  in Taytay, 203–204, 218, 241
English
  as a catalyst for Eskayan, 212–214
  use in Bohol, 69
entertainment, languages of, 69–70
Escalera, Terry "Aser," 202
Eskaya
  alterity, 238–239, 241, 246
  authenticity, 43, 234, 242
  becoming, 80
  categorizing the, 52–53, 56
  characterizations of, 241–242
  described, xxviii, xxx, 48
  discovery of, xxiii–xxv, 33, 39–41, 204,
    233–234
  dress, 42*f*, 48, 51, 78, 194, 195*f*, 203
  economic status, 75
  government partnership, 51–54
  government recognition, xxv, xxviii,
    48, 78
  historical consciousness, 54–55
  homes, 48, 49*f*
  hostilities toward, 188
  identity, 136, 237, 244
  indigeneity, xxv, xxviii, 43–51, 55–56,
    182, 241
  languages spoken by, 75–76
  local knowledge of and beliefs
    about, 38
  meaning of, 135–136

  media attention, 41–48, 55
  migrations, 183–186, 184*m*, 194, 196,
    203, 233
  origin stories, 13, 134, 135
  population, 72
  religion, 188–189, 193
  scholarship on the, xxviii–xxix
  self-identified as, numbers of, 78
Eskaya, researching the
  Abregana investigation, 39–41, 46
  Logarta report, 42–44
  National Museum report, 39, 52–53
  OSCC report, 48, 51, 52
  present-day, 56–57, 59n13
  purposes of, 40–41
  support for, 41
Eskaya (term), xxi, 54
Eskayan. *See also* Datahan, Mariano,
    Eskayan and; Pinay, Eskayan of
  Abregana investigation, 39–40, 57
  altering, prohibitions of, 63, 84, 91,
    103, 226, 236
  authenticity, xxix–xxx, 43–45, 44*f*, 53,
    109, 136, 167, 245
  Baja's promotion of, 203–204
  Boholano dialect, relation to, xxvii
  characteristics, 244
  characterizations of, historically,
    xxvii–xxix
  complexity of, 5
  conflation of systems, 236–237
  Datahan's prophecies, 144
  discovery of, 10, 33
  diversification and expansion, 230
  documentary materials, 16
  education in, 42–44, 216–218, 217*f*, 241
  English as a catalyst for, 212–214
  example of, xxvii–xxvii*f*, 40*f*
  first encoding of, 227–229, 235
  future of, 247–248
  history of, Eskayan beliefs about,
    54–55

history of, research project overview,
1–6
identity through, 237
Inambacan cave writings, 47–48
influences on, 211
inspiration for, 215–218
language-and-literacy ideologies, 6–8
language becoming, 91
learning, 64, 102, 103
linguistic validation, 52–53, 56
media attention, 41–48
origin stories, xxiv, xxx, 7, 53, 87,
136, 149
outsider's use of, 91
present-day, xxvii, 63–64
prophecies of, 10–11
pseudo-diacritics, 102–104, 216
replacement and diversification, 84,
148, 225
romanized, xxvii*f*
script only, terms denoting, 91
script-phonology relation, 90–91
simplification, 103
Simplit (syllabary), 79, 92, 95–98, 101,
141, 216, 218
Spanish influence, 10
superiority of, 163–164, 167
symbols, xxix
term usage, xxi
transmission of, 101–103
Visayan, relationship to, xxvii, 107–
108, 168, 215, 218, 220, 221–222*f*,
223–226, 234–236
vocabulary, xxix
writing, ideologies of, 83–85
Eskayan, speakers of
ancestral, 146
on Bohol, 196
mother-tongue, 76
numbers of, 78
script-speech relation, 7
Spanish suppression of, 146

Eskayan, spoken and sung domains of
church, 80–81, 203–204
education in, 203–204
excluding outsiders, 76, 78
schools, 76, 76*f*, 77*f*, 78–80, 203–204
song, 79, 81, 203
speech-making, 81–82, 203
Eskayan lexicon, xxix, 111–114, 218–220,
219*f*, 223–226, 239
"Eskaya of Bohol: Is It a Tribe?" (Tirol), 55
*Eskaya: The Quick Brown Fox* (film), 54
Esperanto, 2
evolution, Darwinian, 148–149, 189

Ferandos, Pio, 200, 201
Ferrándiz, José, 188
Fertig, Wendell, 201
Filipino nationalism, 23–27
"The First People in the Land of Bohol,"
140, 142, 150–154, 186, 224, 228
Franco, Dionicio, 180

Gal, Susan, 8
Galambao, Alberta, 112, 139*f*
Galambao, Hilario, 55, 137
Gallares, Felix, 180
Gallares, Vicente, 180
Garde, Murray, 247
Gibbens, Lt., 185
Gobierno Republicano de Bohol, 185
*Gramática Bisaya para facilitar el
estudio del dialecto Bisaya Cebuano
(Visayan Grammar for Assisting in
the Study of the Cebuano-Visayan
Dialect)* (Guillén), 181, 213
grammar, Eskayan, 107–111
*The Great Raid* (film), 54
Green Revolution, xxiii, 39
Grimm, Jacob, 140
Grimm, Wilhelm, 140
Guillén, Felix, 180–181, 213
Halliday, M.A.K., 243

Handug, 151
Hantud, 151
Hart, Donn, 243
Hart, Harriett, 243
Hawaiian language-revitalization
    initiatives, 80
Hemley, Robin, 233
Hildegard of Bingen, 1–2
Hill, Jane, 78
Hindu script, 102
Hinlo, Aida, 241
Hokari, 136
Homestead Act, 198
Hughes, Robert P., 185
Humanos, Alonso de, 86n13
"Hurayhaber's Dream," 141
hyperdialectism, 67

Idam and Hidam, 134, 148–149
Idam and Iba, 148
Iglesia Filipina Independiente (IFI), 178,
    186–188, 192, 203
ilustrados, 23–24, 101–102
Inambacan cave writings, 47–48, 159
Indigenous Cultural Communities
    (ICCs), 49, 51, 58n9
Indigenous Peoples Rights Act (IPRA),
    xxviii, 51–52, 54–55, 241
Indigenous Person (IP), 58n9, 182
Irvine, Judith T., 8
Isio, 190
"The Itch-mite Tumaw" (**Nuku Tumaw**),
    137, 141, 145, 145f, 147–150, 165–166,
    189

Jagannath, 102
Japanese occupation, 191, 199–201, 228
Jaradic, Lt., 201
Jesus Christ, 142, 153, 155, 202
Jolly, Margaret, 246
José Maria, 157

Joseph, John E., 237
Jumawan, Maura Galambao, 80
Junta Provincial de Bohol, 185

Kabantian Pass, Battle of, 178–179, 182
Kachin people, 165
Kalam, 243
Kangkay, 160
Kariyapa, 29
Katipunan, 23–24, 25, 178, 191, 194,
    201–202
Katuna, 18, 29
Keesing, Roger, 237, 246
Kelly, Piers, 90
Kroskrity, Paul, 117
Kubalan of Samar, 191
Kurang, 160
Kurarang, 160

Labastilla, Marcelina, 183
ladrones fanaticos, 190, 196, 228, 238
land reforms, 198
language
    authenticity, contestation of, 246–247
    auxiliary, 243
    constructed, 2
    minoritized, xxix–xxx
    new, 242–245
    power conferred with, 237–238
    true ancestry of a, xxx–xxxi
language-and-literacy ideologies, 6–7
language-as-body, 8, 88, 92, 101–102,
    136, 146, 159–161, 163–164, 175
language change, deliberate, 244
language diversication, process of, 22
language without writing, 83, 136
Lapiang Malaya movement, 196–197
Lapu Lapu, Datu, 16, 239–240, 240f
Lardil, 243
*Las Antiguas Leyendes de la Isla de Negros*
    (Marco), 239

Leach, Edmund, 166
Legaspi, Miguel Lopez de, 29
Legazpi, Miguel de, 18, 146
letters (**litri**), anatomic iconicity of, 8,
    88, 92, 101–102, 136, 146, 159–161,
    163–164
Li Garan, 242–243, 244
Lindbergh, Charles, 231
Lingua Ignota, 1–2
linguistic tradition, (re)invention of,
    245–248
Linnekin, Jocelyn, 246
literacy
    Datahan, Mariano, 178, 180–181,
        212–214, 245
    Pinay, 7, 108, 220
    pre-contact, 16–19
    Visayan, 16–19
literature
    Anoy's narration and transcribers of,
        227–229
    authenticity, 167
    balinsiya, story of, 134
    categorization, 168n1
    facing-page documents, 138, 139*f*
    the individual's relationship to the,
        142–143
    intertextuality, 145
    language-as-object in, 80
    language history in, 146–147
    mimicry and rejection in, 150
    Old Books, 40*f*, 137, 229
    revelation and prophecy, 226–228
    traditional, audience for, 136
    traditional documents of, 135
    Visayan, translation from
        the, 138–139, 139*f*
literature, analysis of
    "Atikisis," 161–163
    "Declared Visayan," 163–164
    discussion, 165–168

"The First People in the Land of
    Bohol," 150–153
introduction, 135
"The Itch-mite Tumaw" (**Nuku
    Tumaw**), 147–150, 189
language history, 146–147
"Pinay," 153–156
"The Spanish and Eskayan Alphabets,"
    159–161
"The White Bell," 156–159, 157*f*, 192
literature, origins and scope
    authoritative texts, 83
    differences across texts, 140–142
    hermeneutics, 142–143
    historiography, 142–143
    introduction, 137–139
    oral interpretations of, 143, 145–146
    performance, 145–146
    primary source of all, 216–217
    prophecies, 143–144
    recuperation narratives, 156–159
    texts, primary, 141–142
    time depth, 228–229
    true versions, 140–142
    variation and intelligibility, 139–141
literature, primary stories in the
    "Atikisis," 139, 161–163, 216
    "Daylinda," 228, 239
    "Declared Visayan," 162, 163–164
    'Declared Visayan,' 236
    "The First People in the Land of
        Bohol," 140, 142, 150–154, 186,
        224, 228
    "The Itch-mite Tumaw" (**Nuku
        Tumaw**), 141, 147–150, 189, 228
    "Pinay," 139, 141, 153–156
    "The Spanish and Eskayan
        Alphabets," 159–161, 162, 167,
        216–217
    "The White Bell," 141, 152, 156–159,
        157*f*, 164, 188, 192, 236

Loarca, Miguel de, 18
Logarta, Margarita, 42–44, 55
Lollobrigida, Gina, 231
Lonoy ambush, 182
Loon, 183–184, 185–186, 233
lost bell story, 47, 158
Luengo, Josemaria Salutan, 51
Lumud, 158
Lundag, 72
Luneta, 150–151, 152, 154
Luspo, Marianito, 48, 182

Madalandag, Regina Estorba, 68
Magellan, Ferdinand, 16, 117, 120, 153–
    156, 228, 239–240, 240f, 247
magic, 190, 191
Malta, 160
Mangyan, 17–18
Manuero, Nemesia, 183
Maranao, 69–70
Marco, José E., 27, 239
Marcos, Ferdinand, xxiii, 42, 231, 239
Marcos, Imelda, xxiii
Martín, Julián, 147
Martinez, Cristina, 56, 84, 134, 138, 189,
    194, 203, 228, 246
McClish, Colonel, 201
Medefaidrin (language-script), 2, 245
Meratus, 167
Mexicano (Nahuatl), 78
Miano, Ederick, 53
millenarianism, 196–197
mimicry and rejection
    on display, 239–241, 240f
    Eskayan, 9, 101, 105–106, 220,
        248–249
    in literature, 150
    post-colonial theorizations, 167, 220
Misa, Sotero Nuñez, 31
Mojares, Resil, 27
Moncadistas, 202

Montano, Cesar, 54
Monteclaro, 27
Morga, Antonio, 151
Mornington Island, 243
Moro forces, 177
mother-in-law registers, 243
Mutia, Maria, 18
mysticism, Pulahan, 191, 193

Naasioi Otomaung script, 244
Najarro, Terencio, 186
National Commission on Indigenous
    Peoples (NCIP), 51, 78, 182
nationalism, 36n16
National Museum, 52–53
nation-building, 247
nativism, 189, 190, 196–197, 245
Nazareno, Clovis L., 13
neo-Katipunan warriors, 191, 194
New People's Army (NPA), 43
Nilugao, Calexta, 183
Njoya, Ibrahim Mbouombouo, 2
Noli me tangere (Rizal), 62
Norch [Knortz], Capitan, 200–201
numbers, 98–101, 99f, 100f, 104

Office for Southern Cultural
    Communities (OSCC), 48,
    51–52
Old Books, 40f, 137, 229
Orange, Mervie Batong, 242
origin myths in literature, 228
Osorio, Amando, 215, 228

Pahawh Hmong script, 99–100,
    103, 245
Pajo, Maria Caseñas, 176, 181
Pakpak, Datu, 178, 180
Palaca, Elpidio, 49, 55–56, 144, 193
Palma, Gemina, 141
Patentes, Luciana, 196

Paterno, Pedro Alejandro, 18, 27,
101–102, 239
Paulit, 160
Pavón manuscripts, 18
Peligro, Sisinia, 112, 116
Peligro wordlist, 225
Peralta, Jesus, 48, 52–53, 55–56, 231
Perocho, Orsing, 242
Phelan, John Leddy, 197
Philippine-American war, 24, 32,
178, 181, 184–185, 199,
201, 213
Philippine Benevolent Missionaries
Association (PBMA), 202
Philippine Ecumenical Christian
Church, 202
Philippine independence, 24
Philippine Independent Church (PIC),
73, 80–81
Philippine Insurrection, 24
Philippine Revolution, 24, 101, 177,
180, 181
Philippines
American era, 24–27
Chocolate Hills, xxiii
education system, 79–80
ethnolinguistic diversity, 19–29
Green Revolution, xxiii, 39
highlander-lowlander dualism, 22
indigineous/non-indigenous
binary, 15
land reforms, 198
linguistic diversity, problem of, 19–29
Martial Law period, 234
minority languages, historical status
of, 16–19
national language, 27–29
National Language Problem, 28
national linguistic consciousness,
26–29
native churches, 25–26, 31

New Society of the, xxiii
pre-colonial culture, preservation of
the, 30–32
unique new scripts and textual
traditions invented, 9
writing, legitimate, 90
Philippine Script, 18, 101–102
Pigafetta, Antonio, 16–18
Pilar, Marcelo H. del, 24–25
Pinay
abisi of, 163
authenticity, 87–88
Bisaya,' creation of, xxx
Bisayan Declarado language, 240
characteristics, 108
depiction of, 88f
divine instruction, 146
identity of, 130, 147, 154, 161, 175, 212,
234–238
language and literacy, 7, 108, 220
mentioned, 103, 143
nicknames, 154
papacy conferred, 155, 188
substitution policy, 4–5
"Pinay," 137, 139, 141, 153–156, 165
Pinay, Eskayan of
colonial forms, imitated and
extended, 110
creation of, 80, 87, 108, 146, 152–154,
175
inspiration for, 5
irregularity in, 111
language in the body, discovery of,
136, 175, 247
lexical agenda, 109, 129–132
materiality, property of, 8
mimicry and rejection strategy, 101,
105–106, 220
non-systematicity, 105
number system, innovation and
inspiration, 98–99, 101

Pinay, Eskayan of (*cont.*)
  post-contact-related terms, 124,
    125–127*t*
  relexification, 111–112
  relexification method, 116, 118, 131
  revealed, 146, 214–218
  social and political regimes,
    reshaping, 8
  sound and script materialized, 175
  sound-sense complementarityy, 120
  suppression and recuperation of, 47
  wordlists used, 112–113
  writing system, 8
Pizaña, Gaudencia, 82
prayer, 80–81, 145
Presentes, Dominga, 177
pulahanism, 36n16
pulahan movements, 32, 190–194, 196,
  199, 201–202, 238
Purana, 102

Quezon, Manuel L., 28–29, 33, 199, 241

Ramos, Fidel, 51
Rao, Rahul, 9, 167
recuperation narratives, 47, 156–159, 165
Reid, Lawrence A., 231
relexification
  Datahan's use of, 235
  litterae ignotae, Hildegard of
    Bingen, 2
  Mornington Island, 243
  Pinay's use of, 111–112, 116, 118, 131
  of Visayan, 223–225, 235–236
religion
  in Biabas, 188–189, 202
  Bohol, 66
  Datahan's, 5, 32, 178, 179–180,
    206n13, 213
  Eskaya, 188–189, 193
  languages of, 69–70
  Visayan religious movements, 202

"Resurrection" (Aglipay), 173
Reyes, Isabelo de los, 22, 25, 190
Reyes, Marla, 68
ritual objects, potency of, 86n13
Rizal, José, 23, 27, 62, 143, 151–152, 191,
  196, 202, 205n4, 239
Ruiz, Licinio, 187

Sahlins, Marshall, 9, 166–167
Sajol, Julio, 49
Sajulga, Galu, 201
Salbadur Sunu, 157–158, 192
Salingay, Nida, 144
Salvador, Felipe, 191
Salvadur Sunu, 158
sameness and otherness in tension, 167
Samson, Pedro, 185, 198
Sanchez, Gabriel, 29
Santiago, Anapulco, 164
Santos, Valentin de los, 196
Sanz, Manuel, 30
Schleicher, August, 7
Schools of Indigenous Knowledition and
  Tradition (SIKAT), 241
Scott, James C., 3, 8–9, 22, 49–50, 197
Scott, William Henry, 18, 22, 121
Sendrijas, Francisco "Dagohoy," 30–31
Sequoyah, 100
shamans, languages of, 70
Shan script of Burma, 104
Shiva, xxx
SIKAT schools, 241
Sikatuna, 146, 160, 180
Silverstein, Michael, 237
Simplit (syllabary). *See* syllabary (Simplit)
*Sinopsis histórica* (Ruiz), 187
Sirol, 160
slang words, 242–243
Smalley, William A., 245
sociolinguistic naturalism, 7–8
Solamo, Laureano, 194
song, 79, 81, 145, 203–204

Sora script, 102
Southeast Asia
  incursions, strategic adaptation to, 22
  linguistic diversity, 8–9
  lowland-highland interactions, 9
  unique new scripts and textual
    traditions invented, 9
Spain in Bohol's past, 10
Spanish, influence on Eskayan vocabulary
  direct inspirations, 121, 122– 123*t*, 123
  hispanic phonotactics, 118–119
  semantic domains and time depth,
    123–124, 127–128
  via Visayan, 119–120*t*, 119–121, 216,
    223–225
"The Spanish and Eskayan Alphabets,"
  159–161, 163, 165, 168, 216
Spanish colonial period
  Bohol during the, 29–31
  Christianization during the, 29–31
  church-state relation, 25
  Dagohoy rebellion, xvi*m*, xxiii, 30–33,
    151–152, 197, 238
  education system, 23, 24, 213
  end of the, 185
  ethnolinguistic diversity,
    understanding, 29–33
  "The First People in the Land of
    Bohol," 228
  friar class rule, 24–25
  linguistic diversity, problem of, 19–29
  nationalist movement, 23–24
  native records, destruction of, 19, 33,
    136–137
  opposition, xxiii
  ritual objects, destruction of, 86n13
  Spanish, diffusion of, 23–25
speech-making, 81–82, 145, 203
Stasch, Rupert, 109
Street, Brian, 7
Stuntz, Homer C., 187
Sturtevant, David, 1, 196

*Succesos de las islas Filipinas* (Morga), 151
Sumatra, Juan, 177
Sumatra, Julia, 183
Sumatra, Mariano, 151, 178
Sumatra, Mariano Datahan, 151, 181
Sumatra, Santiago, 183
Sunu (Santo Niño), 146
Swardspeak, 243, 244
syllabary (Simplit), 79, 92, 95–98, 101,
  141, 216, 218
symmetrical schismogenesis, 9, 239

Taft, William, 25, 36n18, 198
Tagalog, 16–17, 19–21, 24, 27–29, 69, 90,
  123, 235
Tagalog language games, 242–243
Tamblot, 29, 32, 56, 117, 196–197, 228
Tamblot (Lumud), 158
Tamblot rebellion, 197, 238
Tamil (language), xxx
Tapar of Panay, 30, 32, 238
Taytay
  Abregana investigation, 39–40
  agriculture, 204
  church service, language of, 81
  Datahan's prophecies remembered, 144
  described, 73, 75
  discovery of, 204, 231–234, 232*f*, 247
  education in, 80, 104
  education in Eskayan, 203–204, 218, 241
  Eskaya culture, center of, 204
  Eskayan history in, 203–204
  establishment of, xxiv
  first encounters, xxiii–xxiv
  landscape, 72–73, 74*f*
  linguistic landscape of, 83
  literature, discussions of, 142–143
  literature, transcription of, 141
  OSCC report, 48
  religion in, 203–204
  settlement of, 203
  written characters, 91

Thomason, Sarah, 243–244
Tikopians, 9, 166–167
Timuri, 70, 71*f,* 72
Timuri-Binali, 70
Tirol, Jes, 46–48, 51, 54–55, 83, 144,
    159, 192–193, 239, 247
Tirol, Lumin, 46
Tirol, Victoriano B., 85n6
Tirol, Victoriano D., 46
Tirol, Victoriano Jr., 46, 193
Torralba, Milan Ted, 56
Torres, Juan de, 29
Totanes, Sebastian de, 21
"Transcribing the Lost Language of the
    Eskaya" (Nazareno), 13
Tsing, Anna, 9, 167
Tugpa, 132, 151–152, 160
Tugpa (cave), 152
Tumud the Shaman, 157–159, 164, 228
Turkish, reformation of, 104

Vang, Chia Koua, 245
Vargas, Jorge B., xxv–xxvi fig, 28, 83–84,
    229
Villamor, Ignacio, 18
"The Virtues and Experiences of Mariano
    Datahan Sumatra" (Datahan),
    177–179
Visayan
    Boholano dialect, relation to, xxvii
    in church services, 81
    colonizers perception of, 19–20
    Datahan-Vargas correspondence
        in, xxvi*f*
    dialects of, xvi*m,* 64–65
    education in, 69
    Eskayan, relation to, xxvii, 88–90,
        107–109, 168, 215, 218, 220,
        221–222*f,* 223–226, 234–236
    Eskayan vocabulary, influence
        on, 115–121, 115*f,* 119–120*t*

linguistic classification, 64–65
literacy, pre-contact, 16–19
number of speakers of, 64
phonology, Eskayan vs., 88–90
pre-contact, 64
regions where spoken, xvi*m*
relexification of, 235–236
relexification process, 223–225, 235
roots-affixes, 110
term usage, xxi, 64–65
use in Bohol, 69
varietal differences, xxi
Visayan archipelago, 16–17, 64
Visayan religious movements, 202
Visayan-Tagalog, 69
"Visayan Teachings," 139
Visayas, Bohol in the, 64–66
Viscayda, Eleuteria, 138, 141, 203–204,
    228–229
Volapük, 2

Wallace, Anthony, 245
"The White Bell," 141, 152, 156–159,
    157*f,* 164, 165, 188, 192, 236
Williams, Stephen, 47
Wolff, John, 243
Woolard, Kathryn A., 67, 90
wordlists, 112–114, 112*f,* 113*f,* 132n1, 219*f,*
    223–226, 229, 269–276
words (vocabulary)
    acculturation terms without
        Spanish or English cognates,
        125–127*t*
    avoidance, 243
    borrowings, 107–108, 111–112
    influences on, 128–129, 128*t*
    inspiration, sources of, 114–115
    non-borrowed terms, 168
    pre-contact, 168
    roots-affixes, 110
    syllable structures, 110

Visayan inspirations, 115–118, 115*f*
words (vocabulary), Spanish
   inspirations
   direct, 121, 122– 123*t*, 123
   hispanic phonotactics, 118–119
   semantic domains and time depth,
     123–124, 127–128
   via Visayan, 119–120*t*, 119–121
writing, language without, 83, 136
writing system
   consonant-vowel (CV-) sequences, 89
   future of, 105–106
   iconicity, 89
   logographic symbols, 89
   numbers, 98–101, 99*f*, 100*f*, 104
   origin and development, 103–106

orthographic choices, 89
phonology, Visayan vs., 88, 89–90
production of, 89
sounds, writing, 89–92
spacing and punctuation, 91–92
supplementary signs encoding syllable
   shapes, 89
systematicity, lack of, 104–105
writing systems, new, 243–245

Yang, Gnia Yee, 245
Yang, Shong Lue, 99–100
Yuki, xxx

Zomia/Zomians, 8–9, 13
Zuckermann, Ghil'ad, 220

Printed in the USA/Agawam, MA
January 15, 2024

859406.066